writing on the body

Female

Embodiment

and

Feminist

Theory

Edited by Katie Conboy,

Nadia Medina,

and Sarah Stanbury

COLUMBIA UNIVERSITY PRESS **NEW YORK**

Columbia University Press

Publishers Since 1893

New York   Chichester, West Sussex

Copyright © 1997 Columbia University Press

Library of Congress Cataloging-in-Publication Data

Writing on the body : female embodiment and feminist

theory / edited by Katie Conboy, Nadia Medina, and

Sarah Stanbury.

     p.   cm. — (A Gender and culture reader)

     Includes bibliographical references.

     ISBN 0–231–10544–4 (cloth) (alk. paper).

     —ISBN 0–231–10545–2 (pbk. : alk. paper)

    1. Feminist literary criticism.   2. Body, Human,

in literature.   3. Women in literature.   4. Sex in

literature.   5. Feminism and the arts.   I. Conboy,

Katie.   II. Medina, Nadia.   III. Stanbury, Sarah.

IV. Series.

PN98.W64W687   1997

305.4—dc21   96–48177

                             CIP

For our daughters

Tania

Lydia

Mairéad

Caitríona

Siobhán

contents

*Woman as a sign of
difference is monstrous.*
—Rosi Braidotti

PART **2** *Bodies in Production*

*The body of woman is
the site where culture
manufactures the
blockade of woman.*
—Valerie Export

PART 3   *The Body Speaks*

Your body must be heard.

   —Hélène Cixous

PART **4**   *Body on Stage*

The opposite sex—
is neither!
—Kate Bornstein

Acknowledgments

The editors gratefully acknowledge the generous support of the Committee on Fellowships, Research, and Publication at The College of the Holy Cross, as well as the offices of the academic dean and the president at Stonehill College.

Acknowledgments

The editors gratefully acknowledge the generous support of the Committee on Fellowships, Research, and Publication at The College of the Holy Cross, as well as the offices of the academic dean and the president at Stonehill College.

PART **4**   *Body on Stage*

The opposite sex—
is neither!
—Kate Bornstein

Contents

writing on the body

introduction

*If . . . we admit,
provisionally, that women do
exist, then we must face the
question: what is a woman?*

—Simone de Beauvoir

Ain't I a woman?

—Sojourner Truth

*It is compatible to suggest
that 'women' don't exist—
while maintaining a politics
of 'as if they existed.'*

—Denise Riley

At first glance, the answer to Simone de Beauvoir's question—"What is a woman?"—appears simple, for is the female body not the marker of womanhood? The body has, however, been at the center of feminist theory precisely because it offers no such "natural" foundation for our pervasive cultural assumptions about femininity. Indeed, there is a tension between women's lived bodily experiences and the cultural meanings inscribed on the female body that always mediate those experiences. Historically, women have been determined by their bodies: their individual awakenings and actions, their pleasure and their pain compete with representations of the female body in larger social frameworks. When we ask, "What is a woman," we are really asking questions about ideology: about how discourse has contoured the category of "woman" and about what is at stake—politically, economically, and socially—in maintaining or dismissing that category.

That Simone de Beauvoir articulates this question in 1949 is especially important, for her work anticipates the lengthy debates within the feminist movement about whether women have some "essential" shared characteristics or whether the whole idea of woman is a social construct. *The Second Sex* clearly lays the groundwork for our understanding of the "cultural construction" of woman: as de Beauvoir argues, woman is not born, but made.

In fact, de Beauvoir's crucial contribution to feminist theory emerges from her application of the philosophical categories of Self and Other to the divisions of gender—an application that reveals the sexual politics at work in a system that fashions man as Self/Subject and woman as Other/Object. As de Beauvoir explains, men "profit . . . from the otherness, the alterity of woman."[1] Specifically, she recognizes that the Self has been imagined as transcendent (associated with mind, it is an entity that floats free of a body or appears superior to bodily functions), while the Other is trapped in immanence, defined and evaluated by its bodily shape, size, and functions. De Beauvoir ultimately demonstrates that the self/other, man/woman, mind/body division provides the basis for all the binary oppositions so familiar to Western culture.

For woman, this entrapment is particularly centered in the biological processes of childbirth that have delineated her productivity and circumscribed her movements. While woman, de Beauvoir argues, is fenced in by the details of her biology, man remains free of such limitations only because he "superbly ignores the fact that his anatomy also includes glands, such as the testicles, and that they also secrete hormones. He thinks of his body as a direct and normal connection with the world, which he believes he apprehends objectively."[2] Men have created a concept of woman's "nature," but in doing so, they project their own ambivalent relationship to external "Nature" onto the female body.

Just as man's civilizing impetus transforms wildlife, land, and vegetation into territories to tame and control, so too does it render woman a form of nature to apprehend, dominate, and defeat. In fact, culture has, variously, valued supposedly "natural" feminine bodily characteristics (narrow waists, small feet, long hair, for example), which have required the most unnatural maintenance (corsets, foot-binding, products for straightening or de-tangling). De Beauvoir masterfully demonstrates that "In woman dressed and adorned, nature is present but under restraint. . . . A woman is rendered more desirable to the extent that nature is more highly developed in her and more rigorously confined."[3] Judith Williamson clarifies how insidious this construction can be in the advertising field, where women of color often function visually as nature waiting to be colonized (dressed in leopard skins, surrounded by exotic trees and animals, linked with verdant islands). Yet the models' bodies are always already enculturated, displaying the lightest of dark skin and the most European of features.

To make the transition from nature to culture woman must deny her potentially "dangerous" appetites and continuously shape what Foucault calls a non-threatening "docile" body.[4] Women are encouraged to internalize and embody all the values of domesticity. In Williamson's words, "Women, the guardians of 'personal life,' become a dumping ground for all the values society wants off its back but must be perceived to cherish: a function rather like a zoo, or nature reserve, whereby a culture can proudly proclaim its inclusion of precisely what it has excluded."[5] To guarantee our man-made place in culture, we are still exhorted to "become" women through increasingly complex regulatory practices of ornamentation such as weight control, skin and hair care, attention to fashion, and, above all, resistance to aging. But we continue to ask, "What is a woman?"

Perhaps the question itself is problematic, for it seems to imply an answer. De Beauvoir names the problem: she exposes the constructedness of femininity and substantiates both how women are oppressed and how men reap benefits from that arrangement. She establishes a foundation on which contemporary feminists have built an architecture of difference by mapping the ways oppression varies for women in different racial, ethnic, and social groups and for women who are ambiguously gendered. Partly in an attempt to achieve political consensus, feminists have often assumed a universal female body, an assumption that has usually left some women silenced, inhabiting the borderlands. Clearly, any definition of the category woman necessarily produces exclusions and leads to divisions among women.

This is the point emphasized by Sojourner Truth in her well-known question, "Ain't I a woman?" In fact, Truth's impromptu speech at the Akron women's suffrage convention in 1851 can, in retrospect, be seen to prefigure the very issues of bodily construction that pervade late twentieth-century feminism. An emancipated slave and field hand, Truth invited her listeners to interrogate monolithic male constructions of femininity that divide women against one another and against themselves. Truth recognizes that men have produced and enforced a representation of the female body as passive, helpless, or in danger of violation. (Ironically, she does not acknowledge that slave women, not white women, were at greatest risk for such abuse.) She insists that her audience turn its gaze on a black female body it has deliberately disregarded. "Look at me," she says. "Look at my arm" (p. 231). Challenging popular stereotypes surrounding the female body, Truth openly displayed what a contemporary called her "tremendous muscular power" and her "almost Amazon form, which stood nearly six feet high."

Sojourner Truth's question is ultimately more aggressive than de Beauvoir's, for she demonstrates the fragility of the very category woman by inviting public scrutiny of her particular female body, thus showing how issues of race and class permeate the supposedly "natural" grouping of women. The simple facts of Truth's physique—black, robust, substantial—contradict the pale, weak, dainty image of "true womanhood" popular in the mid-nineteenth century. Her physical presence invites questions about the similarities between women who are so differently embodied. Truth's speech exposes how the chivalric promises of protections and privileges men offer white heterosexual women in lieu of rights are unequally distributed; in fact, these privileges have, historically, depended on the labor of culture's un-women—slaves, prostitutes, lesbians. The elevated place man claims to reserve for woman is closed to some who are embodied female. As Truth puts it, "Nobody ever helps me into carriages, or over mud-puddles, or gives me any best place! And ain't I a woman?" (231).

This position is elaborated through Truth's examples of how the traditional division of labor—so often justified by the biblical injunctions offered to Adam and Eve in Genesis—was never employed to determine the work of women like herself, who were forced to compete with and indeed to outperform men in plowing, planting, and gathering. And even childbirth, that preeminently celebrated function of the female body, has been treated differently for black women. Truth claims to have "borne thirteen children, and seen them most all sold off to slavery" (231); maternity could not have been seen as her proper sphere, for both she and her children were considered, in Patricia Williams's phrase, "objects of property" (155).

Truth's examples express what feminist theorists still argue today: that the category woman is entirely constructed, but it is not constructed evenly. As Jane Flax suggests, "Unlike women of color, white women have the 'privilege' of 'forgetting' or not noticing the operations of race and many socially sanctioned opportunities for doing so."[6] Asking "Ain't I a woman?" Truth queries the roles of race and class in gender arrangements, but her question opens possibilities for other differences among women to deconstruct the category of woman.

Certainly, we can see how social discomfort with female sexuality is projected onto the bodies of women of color, as Sander Gilman convincingly demonstrates. He argues that "by the eighteenth century, the sexuality of the black, both male and female, becomes an icon for deviant sexuality" in artistic representation, but by the nineteenth century, he contends, the black female represents all black sexuality as "primitive" and appetitive.[7] Further-more, as bell hooks points out, such representations of black women's sex-uality commodify the black body through a form of "racialized fascination" (115). Nor are African-American women the only ones framed as sexual-ized "others": reports of Asian "brides for sale" and of state-supported pros-titution in Thailand underscore that there are multiple constructions of female sexuality.

Like race, social class affects our ways of understanding the differences among women. In medical constructions of womanhood, for example, ideas about "feminine needs" were based on the experiences of upper-class wo-men. Working-class women made it possible for upper-class white women to enjoy certain advantages, such as lying down when they menstruated or rest-ing for long periods after childbirth. Of course, such "advantages," once accepted, have paradoxically had the effect of excluding some women from equal participation in work. In some institutions, even worker compensation rules still categorize maternity leave as a "temporary disability."

Moreover, sexual orientation has raised further questions for our as-sumptions about femininity. Even today, if we come out as lesbian, we can be dismissed as unnatural—as a threat to social order so great that we must anticipate, if we have children, that they may be taken from us. If we refuse to have children, we are likewise categorized as aberrant. And as Nancy Mairs so powerfully indicates in an essay (included in this volume) about her battle with multiple sclerosis, disability also destroys established "standards of feminine grace" (305). In all these cases, external factors clearly have a role in determining who the culture sees as a "real" woman. One can hear so many voices emerging from bodies of color, from unclassed bodies, from lesbian bodies, from disabled bodies, from the bodies of transsexuals: a ver-itable chorus of "Ain't I a woman?"

Thus while it is clear that women have been oppressed as a class—in vari-ous cultures they have been denied the right to vote, to own property, to speak in public, to live out their own sexual orientation—every culture also subdivides this class when it elevates as "natural" only certain feminine char-acteristics. In other words, when men deny women rights, the category woman applies to all who are clearly embodied female, but when men offer privileges, the very entitlements that appear to be rooted in female anatomy can be shown to emerge from the grounds of race and class, heterosexual ori-entation and physical ability. Such prerogatives serve only to separate women from one another, which is why Monique Wittig argues that we must destroy the category woman: "For what makes a woman is a specific social relation to a man, a relation that we have previously called servitude, a relationship which implies personal and physical obligation as well as economic obligation (316)."

We can see then that the advantages offered to white, upper-class, heterosexual women, for example, are purchased through the subjugation of women who are defined as outside the category. All women may be oppressed, but they are not equally oppressed. Truth's speech reminds us, in ways valuable to contemporary feminist theory, that membership in the cult of true womanhood, reserved for the few, is procured through the exclusion of the many. But contemporary theorists point out that some women themselves refuse to participate in traditional gender binaries. Judith Butler, for example, argues that the body is a site for play with categories. Gender, she argues, "is not passively scripted on the body" but rather "put on, invariably, under constraint, daily and incessantly, with anxiety and pleasure" (415). And Kathleen Woodward, in her work on aging, corroborates that even conventional femininity has always been a performative act as she illustrates woman's burden to embody eternal youth. Youthfulness, she points out, is itself a masquerade that many older women are grateful to be free of, whatever other ambivalence they may have about the aging process.[8]

These theorists expand our understanding of the cultural construction of woman. Yet we are left with a question: how can women recognize and respect the differences that problematize the category woman but also employ the category to unite for political action?

De Beauvoir recognizes this difficulty when she argues that women have had problems organizing because "they have no past, no history, no religion of their own"; nor do they have the "solidarity of work," or the "community feeling" that comes from being part of a racial or class group. The fact that "they live dispersed among the males" compromises, she suggests, their relationship to other women.[9] Sojourner Truth, too, implies that if women could unite, they would have great force; celebrating Mother Eve, she claims, "if the first woman God ever made was strong enough to turn the world upside down all alone, these women together ought to be able to turn it back and get it right side up again"(232). Contemporary theory has asked whether such unity is even desirable. Once the category has been called into question, how can any group of women assume that the issues they want to organize around are even shared by others? Denise Riley suggests that we maintain "a politics of 'as if . . . [women] existed.' "[10] As we work to discover such possibilities, though, we must, in Butler's words, "do so in a way that does not distort and reify the very collectivity the theory is supposed to emancipate" (414).

The issues raised in the work of de Beauvoir and Truth correspond in manifold ways to the debates in contemporary discourse about the female body. De Beauvoir defines the problem: women have been made the Other and the other is inferior—the "second sex," always defined by a "lack" of masculine qualities that men assume results from natural defectiveness. Truth focuses on political struggle, both the externalized struggle (against men) for women's rights and the internalized struggle (the inability of some women to organize because they don't fit even the category as it has been defined). Current debates about the female body articulate a similar tension between defining and challenging the category of woman: more specifically, these debates inquire about the physical features that mark a body as female and about the attributes and practices that make that body "feminine." Suggesting that gender itself may be performative act, these theorists demonstrate that bodies and genders are not necessarily coterminous. They amplify the recognition that "one is not born a woman" to explore specific ways in which individuals act out gender possibilities—for example, by literally altering their bodies in an attempt to repair what they perceive as an incompatible relationship between the body and the self or by playing with the boundaries of gender as it is commonly understood. As Butler argues, we can treat gender "as a *corporeal style*, an 'act,' as it were, which is both intentional and performative, where 'performative' itself carries the double meaning of 'dramatic' and 'non-referential' " (404). These essays challenge not only the assumed fixedness of gender identification but also the preservation of heterosexist presumptions.

This combination of exploration and challenge characterizes our volume. We have organized twenty-four essays around the idea of the female body, even as assumptions about that body are radically destabilized in many of the represented texts. Through a range of theoretical essays, we attempt to illustrate inclusively ways of thinking through female embodiment. All the essays have in common an understanding of the female body as a contested site—a battleground for competing ideologies.

Teaching, reading, and writing in a variety of fields, we became aware of the need for such a volume during the last few years when each of us—independently designing courses in feminist theory—decided to use "the female body" as the organizing principle for our courses. In many academic fields the body is the topic generating the most exciting new research and the most interdisciplinary theoretical inquiry. Such diverse areas as gender and queer studies, cultural and literary studies, fine arts, and film are now exploring how our understanding of the body—particularly the female body—is constructed through ideologies, discourses, and practices. A focus on the body offers a creative alternative to a historical overview of feminist and gender theories because the body, that space where gender difference seems materially inscribed, has always been central to feminist investigations of representation. While recognizing that the volume might be organized in many ways for teaching purposes, we chose a structure that creates a dialogue among some of the major issues in contemporary gender theory: language, commodification, sexuality, and performance.

hmmm

The essays in part 1, Reading the Body, articulate the relationship of the body to language. Several articles examine the terms in which the female body is a text to be read—as inferior, sick, or even monstrous—by law, medicine, and technology. Essays by Catharine MacKinnon and Emily Martin scrutinize the differences between accounts of the female body in legal and medical texts and women's actual experiences of rape or menstruation or menopause. Rosi Braidotti explores the association of femininity, especially maternity, with monstrosity. Moira Gatens argues that the model of the body politic is actually that of a masculine body parading as a human body, an image that derives from the liberal notion that humans speak with "one voice, one reason" (86). Such a construction displaces the female body as an other and makes that body's speech inarticulate. Expressions of female desire can thus be misread as inhuman: "the language of an hysteric, the wails of a hyena, the jabbering of a savage" (86).

Susan Bordo also translates the language of the body, showing how, in certain pathologies, the female becomes a performance artist, acting out and giving voice to dramas of social oppression. In anorexia, agoraphobia, and hysteria, for example, bodily "conditions that are objectively (and on one level, experientially) constraining, enslaving, and even murderous, come to be experienced as liberating, transforming, and life-giving" (93). The body, as she reads it, is "a text of culture" (90) but also a site of social control. Thus the essays in this section both reveal the cultural metaphors that have been imposed on the body and decipher women's internalization of those signs.

The essays included in part 2, Bodies in Production, chart the pervasive commodification of women in Western culture in marketplaces from slavery to body-building, from fine art to music videos. So material are women's bodies to the reproduction of capitalism that they can be sold—or used to sell other commodities or products. Demonstrating the materiality of the female body, bell hooks examines representations of black women in film and advertising to show how perceptions of black female sexuality today derive directly from the apparatus of racism. Whereas hooks explores culture's selling of the female body, Sandra Lee Bartky identifies the ways women come to participate in their own commodification by adopting systems of self-surveillance in which they constantly measure their individual attributes against valued cultural norms. As she argues, "Modern technologies of behavior are thus oriented toward the production of isolated and self-policing subjects" (147–48). Patricia J. Williams powerfully demonstrates the conflicts that occur when a single body incorporates the contradictions between the dominant white culture and the colonized "other" culture in a kind of split subjectivity.

Our selections on women in film represent what might be called the visibility politics of the female body by investigating the ways in which film versions of that body reinforce social codes about looking—often forcing the female viewer to position herself against herself. In an essay informed by the ongoing dialogue in psychoanalytic feminist film theory, Mary Ann Doane considers the space carved out for the female spectator of Hollywood film. This spectator is caught in a system of production in which the female body is a fetish for male hegemonic desire. How that body can be shaped, and shaped to resist systems of desire, however, is addressed, albeit differently, by Annette Kuhn. Her essay interrogates differences in female bodies—specifically among women body-builders—to widen questions of representation. She frames her questions in this way: "What is a woman's body? Is there a point at which a woman's body becomes something else? What is the relationship between a certain type of body and 'femininity'?" (199). Returning to issues of race with similar questions, Tania Modleski, in a kind of dialogue with bell hooks, examines the mechanisms through which, in Hollywood film and in feminist theory, the black woman has come to signify embodiment, both sexual and maternal.

From the sites of resistance represented in Bodies in Production, we move, in part 3, The Body Speaks, to essays that attempt to reinterpret the struggle or even to discover powerful new forms of speech and writing. One such form is articulated by Gloria Anzaldúa, who argues that the bilingual, bicultural body is a battleground—a "borderland" both for the culture to appropriate and name, and for the individual to "read" and understand. This struggle, however, can produce a new consciousness, what Anzaldúa calls the consciousness of the "mestiza" (233).

One might say that many of these essays grow out of the same revisionist attitude Mary Ann Doane playfully expresses when she names woman "A Lass But Not A Lack" (180). Indeed, the work of Luce Irigaray rewrites the Freudian and Lacanian paradigm, suggesting that rather than a lack, woman's sexuality is, "always at least double, goes even further: it is plural. . . . [W]oman has sex organs more or less everywhere. She finds pleasure almost anywhere" (252). Irigaray urges us to understand how woman's sexuality can be translated into a language which might seem to operate in a nonlinear, antilogical way.

A language of the body is not always easily understood, as Dianne Hunter makes clear in her analysis of Freud's treatment of Anna O. Like the expression of the anorexic body interpreted by Susan Bordo, the hysteric finds her way of literalizing through her body her felt psychic condition. But several writers in this section are optimistic that women can effect change—on the personal level by taking back their own eroticism (Lorde) and on a cultural level by influencing change even in scientific writing. Science, Donna Haraway suggests, needs to drop the pretense of objective vision, what she calls "the god trick," and instead join "partial views and halting voices in a collective subject position that promises a vision of the means of ongoing, finite embodiments" (292). Nancy Mairs demonstrates how her own body has resisted external misconception. Her "story," which uses Irigaray for a model, maps the way from passive acceptance of the rules of femininity to an active reconstruction of the relationship between body and voice: "The voice is the creature of the body that produces it. I speak as a crippled woman. At the same time, in the utterance I redeem both 'cripple' and 'woman' from the shameful silences by which I have often felt surrounded, contained, set apart" (305).

In part 4, Body on Stage, we include essays that explode the boundaries of traditionally gendered bodies. If "woman is a dark continent," these essays explore newly discovered countries—map huge continental drifts. Evolving out of Monique Wittig's deconstruction of the "myth" of woman, several essays trace the world of gender play—a world in which the unruly woman erupts from the docile body in which culture has imprisoned her. Mary Russo, drawing on the work of Bakhtin and Mary Douglas, offers versions of such bodies, "grotesque" bodies that challenge the rules of feminine containment; she hopes this "category" of the grotesque "might be used affirmatively to destabilize the idealizations of female beauty, or to realign the mechanism of desire" (327). In challenging bodily boundaries, transsexuals might be understood as embracing—albeit in very different ways—terms similar to those explored by Russo, who sees the possibilities inherent in a "grotesque body . . . [,] the body of becoming, process, and change" (325). Feeling wrongfully embodied as male, transsexuals have challenged gender assignations and, through surgical alterations, claimed *no acknowledgement of feminist resistence to this idea* ↺

membership under the category of woman. But, as Sandy Stone argues in her manifesto, "The Empire Strikes Back," transsexuals "must take responsibility for all of their history" (354) and claim a cyborg space for a new configuration of gender identity.

In the act of redefining gender, some of these essays deconstruct categories and celebrate fluidity. Refusing the role of object scripted for women by pornography, Annie Sprinkle, performance artist and the subject of Linda Williams's essay, seizes the spotlight and displaces male pleasure, taking it for herself. Thus, Williams proposes, even pornography—the arena in which women have been most graphically commodified—can be reclaimed. Sue-Ellen Case explores queer desire by recuperating the vampire as trope for "the queer in its lesbian mode" (388). This reclamation, she suggests, "punctures the life/death and generation/destructive bipolarities that enclose the heterosexist notion of being" (384).

Judith Butler's essay is broadly theoretical in accounting for the dramatic consequences of gender acts. Arguing that the gender identities we take to be natural are merely reifications of particular bodily performances, she demonstrates that buying into traditional gender binaries guarantees the reproduction of a culture in which "there are strict punishments for contesting the script by performing out of turn or through unwarranted improvisation" (415). Indeed, such performances break social codes that, even if unwritten, are thoroughly inscribed and make of the performers what Kate Bornstein might call "gender outlaws."[11] Mary Russo suggests, however, that women have nothing to lose in such transgressions, especially since it is clear that "certain bodies, in certain public framings, in certain public spaces, are always already transgressive, dangerous and in danger" (323). Thus, in spite of the threat of punishment, every dramatic experiment illuminates a woman unafraid to make a spectacle of herself.

Couldn't this be seen as elitist? where is class in this anthology?

NOTES

The epigraph from Simone de Beauvoir comes from *The Second Sex*, trans. H. M. Parshley (New York: Vintage Books, 1974), p. xvii.

The epigraph from Sojourner Truth is the title commonly given to her impromptu speech from the Akron Women's Suffrage Convention in 1851. We have reprinted Miriam Schneier's modernized version from *Feminism: The Essential Historical Writings* (1972).

The epigraph quoted from Denise Riley appears in *"Am I That Name?"Feminism and the Category of "Women" in History* (Minneapolis: University of Minnesota Press, 1988), p.105.

Notes in this introduction refer to books and essays not published in this volume. Parenthetical page references indicate quotations from essays included in the text.

1. de Beauvoir, *The Second Sex*, p. xxix.

2. Ibid., p. xviii.

3. Ibid., p. 179.

4. Michel Foucault, *Discipline and Punish: The Birth of the Prison* (New York: Penguin, 1979), pp. 135–69.

5. Judith Williamson, "Woman Is an Island," in *Studies in Entertainment: Critical Approaches to Mass Culture*, ed. Tania Modleski (Bloomington: Indiana University Press), p. 106.

6. Jane Flax, *Thinking Fragments: Psychoanalysis, Feminism, and Postmodernism in the Contemporary West* (Berkeley: University of California Press, 1990), p. 175.

7. Sander Gilman, "Black Bodies, White Bodies: Toward an Iconography of Female Sexuality in Late Nineteenth-Century Art, Medicine, and Literature," in *"Race," Writing, and Difference*, ed. Henry Louis Gates (Chicago: University of Chicago Press, 1985), pp. 228–31.

8. Kathleen Woodward, "Youthfulness as Masquerade," *Discourse* 11, no.2 (1988–89): 119–42.

9. de Beauvoir, p. xxii.

10. Riley, *"Am I That Name?,"* p. 105.

11. Kate Bornstein, *Gender Outlaw: On Men, Women, and the Rest of Us* (New York: Routledge, 1994).

part 1

Reading the Body

*Woman as a sign of
difference is monstrous.*
—Rosi Braidotti

1

Medical Metaphors of Women's Bodies

MENSTRUATION AND MENOPAUSE

Emily Martin

Lavoisier makes experiments with substances in his laboratory and now he concluded that this and that takes place when there is burning. He does not say that it might happen otherwise another time. He has got hold of a definite world-picture—not of course one that he invented: he learned it as a child. I say world-picture and not hypothesis, because it is the matter-of-course foundation for his research and as such also goes unmentioned.

—Ludwig Wittgenstein,

On Certainty

It is difficult to see how our current scientific ideas are infused by cultural assumptions; it is easier to see how scientific ideas from the past, ideas that now seem wrong or too simple, might have been affected by cultural ideas of an earlier time. To lay the groundwork for a look at contemporary scientific views of menstruation and menopause, I begin with the past.

It was an accepted notion in medical literature from the ancient Greeks until the late eighteenth century that male and female bodies were structurally similar. As Nemesius, bishop of Emesa, Syria, in the fourth century, put it, "women have the same genitals as men, except that theirs are inside the body and not outside it." Although increasingly detailed anatomical understanding (such as the discovery of the nature of the ovaries in the last half of the seventeenth century) changed the details, medical

scholars from Galen in second-century Greece to Harvey in seventeenth-
century Britain all assumed that women's internal organs were structurally
analogous to men's external ones.[1]

Although the genders were structurally similar, they were not equal. For
one thing, what could be seen of men's bodies was assumed as the pattern for
what could not be seen of women's. For another, just as humans as a species
possessed more "heat" than other animals, and hence were considered more
perfect, so men possessed more "heat" than women and hence were considered
more perfect. The relative coolness of the female prevented her reproductive
organs from extruding outside the body but, happily for the species, kept them
inside where they provided a protected place for conception and gestation.[2]

During the centuries when male and female bodies were seen as composed of analogous structures, a connected set of metaphors was used to
convey how the parts of male and female bodies functioned. These
metaphors were dominant in classical medicine and continued to operate
through the nineteenth century:

> The body was seen, metaphorically, as a system of dynamic interactions
> with its environment. Health or disease resulted from a cumulative inter-
> action between constitutional endowment and environmental circum-
> stance. One could not well live without food and air and water; one had
> to live in a particular climate, subject one's body to a particular style of life
> and work. Each of these factors implied a necessary and continuing phys-
> iological adjustment. The body was always in a state of becoming—and
> thus always in jeopardy.[3]

Two subsidiary assumptions governed this interaction: first, that "every part of
the body was related inevitably and inextricably with every other" and, second,
that "the body was seen as a system of intake and outgo—a system which had,
necessarily, to remain in balance if the individual were to remain healthy."[4]

Given these assumptions, changes in the relationship of body functions
occurred constantly throughout life, though more acutely at some times than
at others. In Edward Tilt's influential mid-nineteenth-century account, for
example, after the menopause blood that once flowed out of the body as
menstruation was then turned into fat:

> Fat accumulates in women after the change of life, as it accumulates in ani-
> mals from whom the ovaries have been removed. The withdrawal of the

sexual stimulus from the ganglionic nervous system, enables it to turn into fat and self-aggrandisement that blood which might otherwise have perpetuated the race.[5]

During the transition to menopause, or the "dodging time," the blood could not be turned into fat, so it was either discharged as hemorrhage or through other compensating mechanisms, the most important of which was "the flush":

> As for thirty-two years it had been habitual for women to lose about 3 oz. of blood every month, so it would have been indeed singular, if there did not exist some well-continued compensating discharges acting as wastegates to protect the system, until/health could be permanently re-established by striking new balances in the allotment of blood to the various parts . . . The flushes determine the perspirations. Both evidence a strong effect of conservative power, and as they constitute the most important and habitual safety-valve of the system at the change of life, it is worth while studying them.[6]

In this account, compensating mechanisms like the "flush" are seen as having the positive function of keeping intake and outgo in balance.

These balancing acts had exact analogues in men. In Hippocrates' view of purification, one that was still current in the seventeenth century,

> women were of colder and less active disposition than men, so that while men could sweat in order to remove the impurities from their blood, the colder dispositions of women did not allow them to be purified in that way. Females menstruated to rid their bodies of impurities.[7]

Or in another view, expounded by Galen in the second century and still accepted into the eighteenth century, menstruation was the shedding of an excess of blood, a plethora.[8] But what women did through menstruation men could do in other ways, such as by having blood let.[9] In either view of the mechanism of menstruation, the process itself not only had analogues in men, it was seen as inherently health-maintaining. Menstrual blood, to be sure, was often seen as foul and unclean,[10] but the process of excreting it was not intrinsically pathological. In fact, failure to excrete was taken as a sign of disease, and a great variety of remedies existed even into the nineteenth century specifically to reestablish menstrual flow if it stopped.[11]

By 1800, according to Laqueur's important recent study, this long-estab-
lished tradition that saw male and female bodies as similar both in structure
and in function began to come "under devastating attack. Writers of all sorts
were determined to base what they insisted were fundamental differences
between male and female sexuality, and thus between man and woman, on
discoverable biological distinctions."[12] Laqueur argues that this attempt to
ground differences between the genders in biology grew out of the crum-
bling of old ideas about the existing order of politics and society as laid down
by the order of nature. In the old ideas, men dominated the public world and
the world of morality and order by virtue of their greater perfection, a result
of their excess heat. Men and women were arranged in a hierarchy in which
they differed by degree of heat. They were not different in kind.[13]

The new liberal claims of Hobbes and Locke in the seventeenth century
and the French Revolution were factors that led to a loss of certainty that the
social order could be grounded in the natural order. If the social order were
merely convention, it could not provide a secure enough basis to hold
women and men in their places. But after 1800 the social and biological sciences were brought to the rescue of male superiority. "Scientists in areas as
diverse as zoology, embryology, physiology, heredity, anthropology, and psychology had little difficulty in proving that the pattern of male-female relations that characterized the English middle classes was natural, inevitable,
and progressive."[14]

The assertion was that men's and women's social roles themselves were
grounded in nature, by virtue of the dictates of their bodies. In the words of
one nineteenth-century theorist, "the attempt to alter the present relations
of the sexes is not a rebellion against some arbitrary law instituted by a
despot or a majority—not an attempt to break the yoke of a mere convention; it is a struggle against Nature; a war undertaken to reverse the very conditions under which not man alone, but all mammalian species have reached
their present development."[15] The doctrine of the two spheres—men as
workers in the public, wage-earning sphere outside the home and women
(except for the lower classes) as wives and mothers in the private, domestic
sphere of kinship and morality inside the home—replaced the old hierarchy
based on body heat.

During the latter part of the nineteenth century, new metaphors that
posited fundamental differences between the sexes began to appear. One
nineteenth-century biologist, Patrick Geddes, perceived two opposite kinds
of processes at the level of the cell: "upbuilding, constructive, synthetic
processes," summed up as anabolism, and a "disruptive, descending series of

chemical changes," summed up as katabolism.[16] The relationship between the two processes was described in frankly economic terms:

> The processes of income and expenditure must balance, but only to the usual extent, that expenditure must not altogether outrun income, else the cell's capital of living matter will be lost,—a fate which is often not successfully avoided . . . Just as our expenditure and income should balance at the year's end, but may vastly outstrip each other at particular times, so it is with the cell of the body. Income too may continuously preponderate, and we increase in wealth, or similarly, in weight, or in anabolism. Conversely, expenditure may predominate, but business may be prosecuted at a loss; and similarly, we may live on for a while with loss of weight, or in katabolism. This losing game of life is what we call a katabolic habit.[17]

Geddes saw these processes not only at the level of the cell, but also at the level of entire organisms. In the human species, as well as in almost all higher animals, females were predominantly anabolic, males katabolic. Although in the terms of his saving-spending metaphor it is not at all clear whether katabolism would be an asset, when Geddes presents male-female differences, there is no doubt which he thought preferable:

> It is generally true that the males are more active, energetic, eager, passionate, and variable; the females more passive, conservative, sluggish, and stable . . . The more active males, with a consequently wider range of experience, may have bigger brains and more intelligence; but the females, especially as mothers, have indubitably a larger and more habitual share of the altruistic emotions. The males being usually stronger, have greater independence and courage; the females excel in constancy of affection and in sympathy.[18]

In Geddes, the doctrine of separate spheres was laid on a foundation of separate and fundamentally different biology in men and women, at the level of the cell. One of the striking contradictions in his account is that he did not carry over the implications of his economic metaphors to his discussion of male-female differences. If he had, females might have come off as wisely conserving their energy and never spending beyond their means, males as in the "losing game of life," letting expenditures outrun income.

Geddes may have failed to draw the logical conclusions from his metaphor, but we have to acknowledge that metaphors were never meant to be logical. Other nineteenth-century writers developed metaphors in exactly opposite directions: women spent and men saved. The Rev. John Todd saw women as voracious spenders in the marketplace, and so consumers of all that a man could earn. If unchecked, a woman would ruin a man, by her own extravagant spending, by her demands on him to spend, or, in another realm, by her excessive demands on him for sex. Losing too much sperm meant losing that which sperm was believed to manufacture: a man's lifeblood.[19]

Todd and Geddes were not alone in the nineteenth century in using images of business loss and gain to describe physiological processes. Susan Sontag has suggested that nineteenth-century fantasies about disease, especially tuberculosis, "echo the attitudes of early capitalist accumulation. One has a limited amount of energy, which must be properly spent . . . Energy, like savings, can be depleted, can run out or be used up, through reckless expenditure. The body will start 'consuming' itself, the patient will 'waste away.' "[20]

Despite the variety of ways that spending-saving metaphors could be related to gender, the radical difference between these metaphors and the earlier intake-outgo metaphor is key. Whereas in the earlier model, male and female ways of secreting were not only analogous but desirable, now the way became open to denigrate, as Geddes overtly did, functions that for the first time were seen as uniquely female, without analogue in males. For our purposes, what happened to accounts of menstruation is most interesting: by the nineteenth century, the process itself was seen as soundly pathological. In Geddes's terms,

> it yet evidently lies on the borders of pathological change, as is evidenced not only by the pain which so frequently accompanies it, and the local and constitutional disorders which so frequently arise in this connection, but by the general systemic disturbance and local histological changes of which the discharge is merely the outward expression and result.[21]

Whereas in earlier accounts the blood itself may have been considered impure, now the process itself is seen as a disorder.

Nineteenth-century writers were extremely prone to stress the debilitating nature of menstruation and its adverse impact on the lives and activities of women.[22] Medical images of menstruation as pathological were remarkably vivid by the end of the century. For Walter Heape, the militant antisuffragist and Cambridge zoologist, in menstruation the entire epithelium was torn away, leaving behind a ragged wreck of tissue, torn glands, ruptured vessels, jagged edges of stroma, and masses of blood corpuscles, which it would seem hardly possible to heal satisfactorily without the aid of surgical treatment.[23]

A few years later, Havelock Ellis could see women as being "periodically wounded" in their most sensitive spot and "emphasize the fact that even in the healthiest woman, a worm however harmless and unperceived, gnaws periodically at the roots of life."[24]

If menstruation was consistently seen as pathological, menopause, another function which by this time was regarded as without analogue in men, often was too: many nineteenth-century medical accounts of menopause saw it as a crisis likely to bring on an increase of disease.[25] Sometimes the metaphor of the body as a small business that is either winning or losing was applied to menopause too. A late-nineteenth-century account specifically argued against Tilt's earlier adjustment model: "When the period of fruitfulness is ended the activity of the tissues has reached its culmination, the secreting power of the glandular organs begins to diminish, the epithelium becomes less sensitive and less susceptible to infectious influences, and atrophy and degeneration take the place of the active up-building processes."[26] But there were other sides to the picture. Most practitioners felt the "climacteric disease," a more general disease of old age, was far worse for men than for women.[27] And some regarded the period after menopause far more positively than it is being seen medically in our century, as the "Indian summer' of a woman's life—a period of increased vigor, optimism, and even of physical beauty."'[28]

Perhaps the nineteenth century's concern with conserving energy and limiting expenditure can help account for the seeming anomaly of at least some positive medical views of menopause and the climacteric. As an early-twentieth-century popular health account put it,

> [Menopause] is merely a conservative process of nature to provide for a higher and more stable phase of existence, an economic lopping off of a function no longer needed, preparing the individual for different forms of activity, but is in no sense pathologic. It is not sexual or physical decrepitude, but belongs to the age of invigoration, marking the fullness of the bodily and mental powers.[29]

Those few writers who saw menopause as an "economic" physiological function might have drawn very positive conclusions from Geddes's description of females as anabolic, stressing their "thriftiness" instead of their passivity, their "growing bank accounts" instead of their sluggishness.

If the shift from the body as an intake-outgo system to the body as a small business trying to spend, save, or balance its accounts is a radical one, with deep importance for medical models of female bodies, so too is another shift that began in the twentieth century with the development of scientific medicine. One of the early-twentieth-century engineers of our system of scientific medicine, Frederick T. Gates, who advised John D. Rockefeller on how to use his philanthropies to aid scientific medicine, developed a series of interrelated metaphors to explain the scientific view of how the body works:

It is interesting to note the striking comparisons between the human body and the safety and hygienic appliances of a great city. Just as in the streets of a great city we have "white angels" posted everywhere to gather up poisonous materials from the streets, so in the great streets and avenues of the body, namely the arteries and the blood vessels, there are brigades of corpuscles, white in color like the "white angels," whose function it is to gather up into sacks, formed by their own bodies, and disinfect or eliminate all poisonous substances found in the blood. The body has a network of insulated nerves, like telephone wires, which transmit instantaneous alarms at every point of danger. The body is furnished with the most elaborate police system, with hundreds of police stations to which the criminal elements are carried by the police and jailed. I refer to the great numbers of sanitary glands, skilfully placed at points where vicious germs find entrance, especially about the mouth and throat. The body has a most complete and elaborate sewer system. There are wonderful laboratories placed at convenient points for a subtle brewing of skillful medicines . . . The fact is that the human body is made up of an infinite number of microscopic cells. Each one of these cells is a small chemical laboratory, into which its own appropriate raw material is constantly being introduced, the processes of chemical separation and combination are constantly taking place automatically, and its own appropriate finished product being necessary for the life and health of the body. Not only is this so, but the great organs of the body like the liver, stomach, pancreas, kidneys, gall bladder are great local manufacturing centers, formed of groups of cells in infinite numbers, manufacturing the same sorts of products, just as industries of the same kind are often grouped in specific districts.[30]

Although such a full-blown description of the body as a model of an industrial society is not often found in contemporary accounts of physiology, elements of the images that occurred to Gates are commonplace. In recent
years, the "imagery of the biochemistry of the cell [has] been that of the factory, where functions [are] specialized for the conversion of energy into particular products and which [has] its own part to play in the economy of the
organism as a whole."[31] There is no doubt that the basic image of cells as factories is carried into popular imagination, and not only through college textbooks: an illustration from the April 30, 1984, copy of *Time* magazine depicts
cells explicitly as factories (and AIDS virus cells as manufacturing armored
tanks! [p. 67]).

Still more recently, economic functions of greater complexity have been
added: ATP is seen as the body's "energy currency": "Produced in particular
cellular regions, it [is] placed in an 'energy bank' in which it [is] maintained
in two forms, those of 'current account' and 'deposit account.' Ultimately,
the cell's and the body's energy books must balance by an appropriate mix of
monetary and fiscal policies."[32] Here we have not just the simpler nineteenth-century saving and spending, but two distinct forms of money in the
bank, presumably invested at different levels of profit.

Development of the new molecular biology brought additional metaphors
based on information science, management, and control. In this model, flow
of information between DNA and RNA leads to the production of protein.[33]
Molecular biologists conceive of the cell as "an assembly line factory in which
the DNA blueprints are interpreted and raw materials fabricated to produce
the protein end products in response to a series of regulated requirements."[34]
The cell is still seen as a factory, but, compared to Gates's description, there
is enormous elaboration of the flow of information from one "department" of
the body to another and exaggeration of the amount of control exerted by the
center. For example, from a college physiology text:

> All the systems of the body, if they are to function effectively, must be sub-
> jected to some form of control . . . The precise control of body function is
> brought about by means of the operation of the nervous system and of the
> hormonal or endocrine system . . . The most important thing to note about
> any control system is that before it can control anything it must be supplied
> with information . . . Therefore the first essential in any control system is an
> adequate system of collecting information about the state of the body . . .
> Once the CNS [central nervous system] knows what is happening, it must

then have a means for rectifying the situation if something is going wrong. There are two available methods for doing this, by using nerve fibres and by using hormones. The motor nerve fibres . . . carry instructions from the CNS to the muscles and glands throughout the body . . . As far as hormones are concerned the brain acts via the pituitary gland . . . the pituitary secretes a large number of hormones . . . the rate of secretion of each one of these is under the direct control of the brain.[35]

Although there is increasing attention to describing physiological processes as positive and negative feedback loops so that like a thermostat system no single element has preeminent control over any other, most descriptions of specific processes give preeminent control to the brain, as we will see below.

Metaphors in Descriptions of Female Reproduction

In overall descriptions of female reproduction, the dominant image is that of a signaling system. Lein, in a textbook designed for junior colleges, spells it out in detail:

Hormones are chemical signals to which distant tissues or organs are able to respond. Whereas the nervous system has characteristics in common with a telephone network, the endocrine glands perform in a manner somewhat analogous to radio transmission. A radio transmitter may blanket an entire region with its signal, but a response occurs only if a radio receiver is turned on and tuned to the proper frequency . . . the radio receiver in biological systems is a tissue whose cells possess active receptor sites for a particular hormone or hormones.[36]

The signal-response metaphor is found almost universally in current texts for premedical and medical students (emphasis in the following quotes is added):

The hypothalamus *receives signals* from almost all possible sources in the nervous system.[37]

    The endometrium *responds directly* to stimulation or withdrawal of estrogen and progesterone. In turn, regulation of the secretion of these steroids involves a well-integrated, highly structured series of activities by the hypothalamus and the anterior lobe of the pituitary. Although the ovaries do not function autonomously, they *influence*, through *feedback* mechanisms, the level of performance *programmed* by the hypothalamic-pituitary axis.[38]

As a result of strong stimulation of FSH, a number of follicles *respond* with growth.[39]

And the same idea is found, more obviously, in popular health books:

Each month from menarche on, [the hypothalamus] acts as elegant inter-preter of the body's rhythms, *transmitting messages* to the pituitary gland that set the menstrual cycle in motion.[40]

Each month, *in response to a message* from the pituitary gland, one of the unripe egg cells develops inside a tiny microscopic ring of cells, which gradually increases to form a little balloon or cyst called the Graafian follicle.[41]

Although most accounts stress signals or stimuli traveling in a "loop" from hypothalamus to pituitary to ovary and back again, carrying positive or neg-ative feedback, one element in the loop, the hypothalamus, a part of the brain, is often seen as predominant. The female brain-hormone-ovary system is usually described not as a feedback loop like a thermostat system but as a hierarchy, in which the "directions" or "orders" of one element dominate (emphasis in the following quotes from medical texts is added):

Both positive and negative feedback control must be invoked, together with *superimposition* of control by the CNS through neurotransmitters released into the hypophyseal portal circulation.[42]

Almost all secretion by the pituitary is *controlled* by either hormonal or nervous signals from the hypothalamus.[43]

The hypothalamus is a collecting center for information concerned with the internal well-being of the body, and in turn much of this infor-mation is used *to control* secretions of the many globally important pitu-itary hormones.[44]

As Lein puts it into ordinary language, "The cerebrum, that part of the brain that provides awareness and mood, can play a significant role in the control of the menstrual cycle. As explained before, it seems evident that these higher regions of the brain exert their influence by modifying the actions of the hypothalamus. So even though the hypothalamus is a kind of master gland dominating the anterior pituitary, and through it the ovaries also, it does not act with complete independence or without influence from outside itself . . . there are also pathways of control from the higher centers of the brain."[45]

So this is a communication system organized hierarchically, not a committee reaching decisions by mutual influence.[46] The hierarchical nature of the organization is reflected in some popular literature meant to explain the nature of menstruation simply: "From first menstrual cycle to menopause, the hypothalamus acts as the conductor of a highly trained orchestra. Once its baton signals the downbeat to the pituitary, the hypothalamus-pituitary-ovarian axis is united in purpose and begins to play its symphonic message, preparing a woman's body for conception and child-bearing." Carrying the metaphor further, the follicles vie with each other for the role of producing the egg like violinists trying for the position of concertmaster; a burst of estrogen is emitted from the follicle like a "clap of tympani."[47]

The basic images chosen here—an information-transmitting system with a hierarchical structure—have an obvious relation to the dominant form of organization in our society.[48] What I want to show is how this set of metaphors, once chosen as the basis for the description of physiological events, has profound implications for the way in which a change in the basic organization of the system will be perceived. In terms of female reproduction, this basic change is of course menopause. Many criticisms have been made of the medical propensity to see menopause as a pathological state.[49] I would like to suggest that the tenacity of this view comes not only from the negative stereotypes associated with aging women in our society, but as a logical outgrowth of seeing the body as a hierarchical information-processing system in the first place. (Another part of the reason menopause is seen so negatively is related to metaphors of production, which I discuss later in this essay.)

What is the language in which menopause is described? In menopause, according to a college text, the ovaries become "unresponsive" to stimulation from the gonadotropins, to which they used to respond. As a result the ovaries "regress." On the other end of the cycle, the hypothalamus has gotten estrogen "addiction" from all those years of menstruating. As a result of the "withdrawal" of estrogen at menopause, the hypothalamus begins to give "inappropriate orders."[50] In a more popular account, "the pituitary gland during the change of life becomes disturbed when the ovaries fail to respond to its secretions, which tends to affect its control over other glands. This results in a temporary imbalance existing among all the endocrine glands of the body, which could very well lead to disturbances that may involve a person's nervous system."[51]

In both medical texts and popular books, what is being described is the breakdown of a system of authority. The cause of ovarian "decline" is the "decreasing ability of the aging ovaries to respond to pituitary gonadotropins."[52] At every point in this system, functions "fail" and falter. Follicles "fail to muster the strength" to reach ovulation.[53] As functions fail, so do the members of the system decline: "breasts and genital organs gradually atrophy,"[54] "wither,"[55] and become "senile."[56] Diminished, atrophied relics of their former vigorous, functioning selves, the "senile ovaries" are an example of the vivid imagery brought to this process. A text whose detailed illustrations make it a primary resource for medical students despite its early date describes the ovaries this way:

> the *senile ovary* is a shrunken and puckered organ, containing few if any follicles, and made up for the most part of old corpora albincantia and corpora atretica, the bleached and functionless remainders of corpora lutia and follicles embedded in a dense connective tissue stroma.[57]

Ovaries cease to respond and fail to produce. Everywhere else there is regression, decline, atrophy, shrinkage, and disturbance.

The key to the problem connoted by these descriptions is functionlessness. Susan Sontag has written of our obsessive fear of cancer, a disease that we see as entailing a nightmare of excessive growth and rampant production. These images frighten us in part because in our stage of advanced capitalism, they are close to a reality we find difficult to see clearly: broken-down hierarchy and organization members who no longer play their designated parts represent nightmare images for us. One woman I have talked to said her doctor gave her two choices for treatment of her menopause: she could take estrogen and get cancer or she could not take it and have her bones dissolve. Like this woman, our imagery of the body as a hierarchical organization gives us no good choice when the basis of the organization seems to us to have changed drastically. We are left with breakdown, decay, and atrophy. Bad as they are, these might be preferable to continued activity, which because it is not properly hierarchically controlled, leads to chaos, unmanaged growth, and disaster.

But let us return to the metaphor of the factory producing substances, which dominates the imagery used to describe cells. At the cellular level DNA communicates with RNA, all for the purpose of the cell's production of pro-

teins. In a similar way, the system of communication involving female reproduction is thought to be geared toward production of various things. My discussion in this essay is confined to the normal process of the menstrual cycle.
It is clear that the system is thought to produce many good things: the ovaries
produce estrogen, the pituitary produces FSH and LH, and so on. Follicles also
produce eggs in a sense, although this is usually described as "maturing" them
since the entire set of eggs a woman has for her lifetime is known to be present at birth. Beyond all this the system is seen as organized for a single preeminent purpose: "transport" of the egg along its journey from the ovary to
the uterus[58] and preparation of an appropriate place for the egg to grow if it
is fertilized. In a chapter titled "Prepregnancy Reproductive Functions of the
Female, and the Female Hormones," Guyton puts it all together: "Female
reproductive functions can be divided into two major phases: first, preparation of the female body for conception and gestation, and second, the period
of gestation itself."[59] This view may seem commonsensical and entirely justified by the evolutionary development of the species, with its need for reproduction to ensure survival.

Yet I suggest that assuming this view of the purpose for the process slants
our description and understanding of the female cycle unnecessarily. Let us
look at how medical textbooks describe menstruation. They see the action of
progesterone and estrogen on the lining of the uterus as "ideally suited to
provide a hospitable environment for implantation and survival of the
embryo"[60] or as intended to lead to "the monthly renewal of the tissue that
will cradle [the ovum]."[61] As Guyton summarizes, "The whole purpose of all
these endometrial changes is to produce a highly secretory endometrium
containing large amounts of stored nutrients that can provide appropriate
conditions for implantation of a fertilized ovum during the latter half of the
monthly cycle."[62] Given this teleological interpretation of the purpose of the
increased amount of endometrial tissue, it should be no surprise that when a
fertilized egg does not implant, these texts describe the next event in very
negative terms. The fall in blood progesterone and estrogen "deprives" the
"highly developed endometrial lining of its hormonal support," "constriction" of blood vessels leads to a "diminished" supply of oxygen and nutrients,
and finally "disintegration starts, the entire lining begins to slough, and the
menstrual flow begins." Blood vessels in the endometrium "hemorrhage" and
the menstrual flow "consists of this blood mixed with endometrial debris."[63]
The "loss" of hormonal stimulation causes "necrosis" (death of tissue).[64]

The construction of these events in terms of a purpose that has failed is
beautifully captured in a standard text for medical students (a text otherwise

noteworthy for its extremely objective, factual descriptions) in which a discussion of the events covered in the last paragraph (sloughing, hemorrhaging) ends with the statement "When fertilization fails to occur, the endometrium is shed, and a new cycle starts. This is why it used to be taught that 'menstruation is the uterus crying for lack of a baby.' "[65]

I am arguing that just as seeing menopause as a kind of failure of the authority structure in the body contributes to our negative view of it, so does seeing menstruation as failed production contribute to our negative view of it. We have seen how Sontag describes our horror of production gone out of control. But another kind of horror for us is *lack* of production: the disused factory, the failed business, the idle machine. In his analysis of industrial civilization, Winner terms the stopping and breakdown of technological systems in modern society "apraxia" and describes it as "the ultimate horror, a condition to be avoided at all costs."[66] This horror of idle workers or machines seems to have been present even at earlier stages of industrialization. A nineteenth-century inventor, Thomas Ewbank, elaborated his view that the whole world "was designed for a Factory."[67] "It is only as a Factory, a *General Factory,* that the whole materials and influences of the earth are to be brought into play."[68] In this great workshop, humans' role is to produce: "God employs no idlers—creates none."[69]

Like artificial motors, we are created for the work we can do—for the useful and productive ideas we can stamp upon matter. Engines running daily without doing any work resemble men who live without labor; both are spendthrifts dissipating means that would be productive if given to others.[70]

Menstruation not only carries with it the connotation of a productive system that has failed to produce, it also carries the idea of production gone awry, making products of no use, not to specification, unsalable, wasted, scrap. However disgusting it may be, menstrual blood will come out. Production gone awry is also an image that fills us with dismay and horror. Amid the glorification of machinery common in the nineteenth century were also fears of what machines could do if they went out of control. Capturing this fear, one satirist wrote of a steam-operated shaving machine that "sliced the noses off too many customers."[71] This image is close to the one Melville created in "The Bell-Tower," in which an inventor, who can be seen as an allegory of America, is killed by his mechanical slave,[72] as well as to Mumford's sorcerer's apprentice applied to modern machinery:[73]

> Our civilization has cleverly found a magic formula for setting both industrial and academic brooms and pails of water to work by themselves, in

ever-increasing quantities at an ever-increasing speed. But we have lost the Master Magician's spell for altering the tempo of this process, or halting it when it ceases to serve human functions and purposes.[74]

Of course, how much one is gripped by the need to produce goods effi-ciently and properly depends on one's relationship to those goods. While packing pickles on an assembly line, I remember the foreman often holding up improperly packed bottles to us workers and trying to elicit shame at the bad job we were doing. But his job depended on efficient production, which meant many bottles filled right the first time. This factory did not yet have any effective method of quality control, and as soon as our supervisor was out of sight, our efforts went toward filling as few bottles as we could while still concealing who had filled which bottle. In other factories, workers seem to express a certain grim pleasure when they can register objections to com-pany policy by enacting imagery of machinery out of control. Noble reports an incident in which workers resented a supervisor's order to "shut down their machines, pick up brooms, and get to work cleaning the area. But he forgot to tell them to stop. So, like the sorcerer's apprentice, diligently and obediently working to rule, they continued sweeping up all day long."[75]

Perhaps one reason the negative image of failed production is attached to menstruation is precisely that women are in some sinister sense out of con-trol when they menstruate. They are not reproducing, not continuing the species, not preparing to stay at home with the baby, not providing a safe, warm womb to nurture a man's sperm. I think it is plain that the negative power behind the image of failure to produce can be considerable when applied metaphorically to women's bodies. Vern Bullough comments opti-mistically that "no reputable scientist today would regard menstruation as pathological,"[76] but this paragraph from a recent college text belies his hope:

> If fertilization and pregnancy do not occur, the corpus luteum degenerates and the levels of estrogens and progesterone decline. As the levels of these hormones decrease and their stimulatory effects are withdrawn, blood vessels of the endometrium undergo prolonged spasms (contractions) that reduce the bloodflow to the area of the endometrium supplied by the ves-sels. The resulting lack of blood causes the tissues of the affected region to degenerate. After some time, the vessels relax, which allows blood to flow through them again. However, capillaries in the area have become so weakened that blood leaks through them. This blood and the deteriorating endometrial tissue are discharged from the uterus as the menstrual flow.

As a new ovarian cycle begins and the level of estrogens rises, the functional layer of the endometrium undergoes repair and once again begins to proliferate.[77]

In rapid succession the reader is confronted with "degenerate," "decline," "withdrawn," "spasms," "lack," "degenerate," "weakened," "leak," "deteriorate," "discharge," and, after all that, "repair."

In another standard text, we read:

The sudden lack of these two hormones [estrogen and progesterone] causes the blood vessels of the endometrium to become spastic so that blood flow to the surface layers of the endometrium almost ceases. As a result, much of the endometrial tissue dies and sloughs into the uterine cavity. Then, small amounts of blood ooze from the denuded endometrial wall, causing a blood loss of about 50 ml during the next few days. The sloughed endometrial tissue plus the blood and much serous exudate from the denuded uterine surface, all together called the *menstrum*, is gradually expelled by intermittent contractions of the uterine muscle for about 3 to 5 days. This process is called *menstruation*.[78]

The illustration that accompanies this text captures very well the imagery of catastrophic disintegration: "ceasing," "dying," "losing," "denuding," and "expelling."

These are not neutral terms; rather, they convey failure and dissolution. Of course, not all texts contain such a plethora of negative terms in their descriptions of menstruation. But unacknowledged cultural attitudes can seep into scientific writing through evaluative words. Coming at this point from a slightly different angle, consider this extract from a text that describes male reproductive physiology. "The mechanisms which guide the *remarkable* cellular transformation from spermatid to mature sperm remain uncertain . . . Perhaps the most *amazing* characteristic of spermatogenesis is its *sheer magnitude*: the normal human male may manufacture several hundred million sperm per day (emphasis added)."[79] As we will see, this text has no parallel appreciation of female processes such as menstruation or ovulation, and it is surely no accident that this "remarkable" process involves precisely what menstruation does not in the medical view: production of something deemed valuable. Although this text sees such massive sperm production as unabashedly positive, in fact, only about one out of every 100 billion sperm ever makes it to fertilize an egg: from the very same point of view that sees menstruation as a waste product, surely here is something really worth crying about!

When this text turns to female reproduction, it describes menstruation in the same terms of failed production we saw earlier.

> The fall in blood progesterone and estrogen, which results from *regression* of the corpus luteum, *deprives* the highly developed endometrial lining of its hormonal support; the immediate result is *profound constriction* of the uterine blood vessels due to production of vasoconstrictor prostaglandins, which leads to *diminished* supply of oxygen and nutrients. *Disintegration* starts, and the entire lining (except for a thin, deep layer which will regenerate the endometrium in the next cycle) begins to slough . . . The endometrial arterioles dilate, resulting in *hemorrhage* through the weakened capillary walls; the menstrual flow consists of this blood mixed with endometrial *debris* . . . The menstrual flow ceases as the endometrium *repairs* itself and then grows under the influence of rising blood estrogen concentration. [Emphasis added.][80]

And ovulation fares no better. In fact part of the reason ovulation does not merit the enthusiasm that spermatogenesis does may be that all the ovarian follicles containing ova are already present at birth. Far from being *produced* as sperm is, they seem to merely sit on the shelf, as it were, slowly degenerating and aging like overstocked inventory.

> At birth, normal human ovaries contain an estimated one million follicles, and no new ones appear after birth. Thus, in marked contrast to the male, the newborn female already has all the germ cells she will ever have. Only a few, perhaps four hundred, are destined to reach full maturity during her active productive life. All the others degenerate at some point in their development so that few, if any, remain by the time she reaches menopause at approximately fifty years of age. One result of this is that the ova which are released (ovulated) near menopause are thirty to thirty-five years older than those ovulated just after puberty; it has been suggested that certain congenital defects, much commoner among children of older women, are the result of aging changes in the ovum.[81]

How different it would sound if texts like this one stressed the vast excess of follicles produced in a female fetus, compared to the number she will actually need. In addition, males are also born with a complement of germ cells (spermatogonia) that divide from time to time, and most of which will eventually differentiate into sperm. This text could easily discuss the fact that these male germ cells and their progeny are also subject to aging, much as female germ cells are. Although we would still be operating within the terms of the production metaphor, at least it would be applied in an evenhanded way to both males and females.

One response to my argument would be that menstruation just *is* in some objective sense a process of breakdown and deterioration. The particular words are chosen to describe it because they best fit the reality of what is happening. My counterargument is to look at other processes in the body that are fundamentally analogous to menstruation in that they involve the shedding of a lining to see whether they also are described in terms of breakdown and deterioration. The lining of the stomach, for example, is shed and replaced regularly, and seminal fluid picks up shedded cellular material as it goes through the various male ducts.

The lining of the stomach must protect itself against being digested by the hydrochloric acid produced in digestion. In the several texts quoted above, emphasis is on the *secretion* of mucus,[82] the *barrier* that mucous cells present to stomach acid,[83] and—in a phrase that gives the story away—the periodic *renewal* of the lining of the stomach.[84] There is no reference to degenerating, weakening, deteriorating, or repair, or even the more neutral shedding, sloughing, or replacement.

> The primary function of the gastric secretions is to begin the digestion of proteins. Unfortunately, though, the wall of the stomach is itself constructed mainly of smooth muscle, which itself is mainly protein. Therefore, the surface of the stomach must be exceptionally well protected at all times against its own digestion. This function is performed mainly by mucus that is secreted in great abundance in all parts of the stomach. The entire surface of the stomach is covered by a layer of very small *mucous cells*, which themselves are composed almost entirely of mucus; this mucus prevents gastric secretions from ever touching the deeper layers of the stomach wall.[85]

In this account from an introductory physiology text, the emphasis is on production of mucus and protection of the stomach wall. It is not even mentioned, although it is analogous to menstruation, that the mucous cell layers must be continually sloughed off (and digested). Although all the general physiology texts I consulted describe menstruation as a process of disintegration needing repair, only specialized texts for medical students describe the stomach lining in the more neutral terms of "sloughing" and "renewal."[86] One can choose to look at what happens to the lining of stomachs and uteruses negatively as breakdown and decay needing repair or positively as continual production and replenishment. Of these two sides of the same coin, stomachs, which women *and* men have, fall on the positive side; uteruses, which only women have, fall on the negative.

One other analogous process is not handled negatively in the general physiology texts. Although it is well known to those researchers who work with male ejaculates that a very large proportion of the ejaculate is composed of shedded cellular material, the texts make no mention of a shedding process let alone processes of deterioration and repair in the male reproductive tract.[87]

What applies to menstruation once a month applies to menopause once in every lifetime. As we have seen, part of the current imagery attached to menopause is that of a breakdown of central control. Inextricably connected to this imagery is another aspect of failed production. Recall the metaphors of balanced intake and outgo that were applied to menopause up to the mid-nineteenth century, later to be replaced by metaphors of degeneration. In the early 1960s new research on the role of estrogens in heart disease led to arguments that failure of female reproductive organs to produce much estrogen after menopause was debilitating to health.

This change is marked unmistakably in successive editions of a major gynecology text. In the 1940s and 1950s menopause was described as usually not entailing "any very profound alteration in the woman's life current."[88] By the 1965 edition dramatic changes had occurred: "In the past few years there has been a radical change in viewpoint and some would regard the menopause as a possible pathological state rather than a physiological one and discuss therapeutic prevention rather than the amelioration of symptoms."[89]

In many current accounts menopause is described as a state in which ovaries fail to produce estrogen.[90] The 1981 World Health Organization report defines menopause as an estrogen-deficiency disease.[91] Failure to produce estrogen is the leitmotif of another current text: "This period during which the cycles cease and the female sex hormones diminish rapidly to almost none at all is called the *menopause*. The cause of the menopause is the 'burning out' of the ovaries . . . Estrogens are produced in subcritical quantities for a short time after the menopause, but over a few years, as the final remaining primordial follicles become atretic, the production of estrogens by the ovaries falls almost to zero." Loss of ability to produce estrogen is seen as central to a woman's life: "At the time of the menopause a woman must readjust her life from one that has been physiologically stimulated by estrogen and progesterone production to one devoid of those hormones."[92]

Of course, I am not implying that the ovaries do not indeed produce much less estrogen than before. I am pointing to the choice of these textbook authors to emphasize above all else the negative aspects of ovaries failing to produce female hormones. By contrast, one current text shows us a positive view of the decline in estrogen production: "It would seem that although menopausal women do have an estrogen milieu which is lower than that necessary for *reproductive* function, it is not negligible or absent but is perhaps satisfactory for *maintenance* of *support tissues*. The menopause could then be regarded as a physiologic phenomenon which is protective in nature—protective from undesirable reproduction and the associated growth stimuli."[93]

I have presented the underlying metaphors contained in medical descriptions of menopause and menstruation to show that these ways of describing events are but one method of fitting an interpretation to the facts. Yet seeing that female organs are imagined to function within a hierarchical order whose members signal each other to produce various substances, all for the purpose of transporting eggs to a place where they can be fertilized and then grown, may not provide us with enough of a jolt to begin to see the contingent nature of these descriptions. Even seeing that the metaphors we choose fit very well with traditional roles assigned to women may still not be enough to make us question whether there might be another way to represent the same biological phenomena. In my other writings I examine women's ordinary experience of menstruation and menopause looking for alternative visions.[94] Here I suggest some other ways that these physiological events could be described.

First, consider the teleological nature of the system, its assumed goal of implanting a fertilized egg. What if a woman has done everything in her power to avoid having an egg implant in her uterus, such as birth control or abstinence from heterosexual sex. Is it still appropriate to speak of the single purpose of her menstrual cycle as dedicated to implantation? From the woman's vantage point, it might capture the sense of events better to say the purpose of the cycle is the production of menstrual flow. Think for a moment how that might change the description in medical texts: "A drop in the formerly high levels of progesterone and estrogen creates the appropriate environment for reducing the excess layers of endometrial tissue. Constriction of capillary blood vessels causes a lower level of oxygen and nutrients and paves the way for a vigorous production of menstrual fluids. As a part of the renewal of the remaining endometrium, the capillaries begin to reopen, contributing some blood and serous fluid to the volume of endometrial material already beginning to flow." I can see no reason why the menstrual blood itself could not be seen as the desired "product" of the female cycle, except when the woman intends to become pregnant.

Would it be similarly possible to change the nature of the relationships assumed among the members of the organization—the hypothalamus, pituitary, ovaries, and so on? Why not, instead of an organization with a controller, a team playing a game? When a woman wants to get pregnant, it would be appropriate to describe her pituitary, ovaries, and so on as combining together, communicating with each other, to get the ball, so to speak, into the basket. The image of hierarchical control could give way to specialized function, the way a basketball team needs a center as well as a defense. When she did not want to become pregnant, the purpose of this activity could be considered the production of menstrual flow.

Eliminating the hierarchical organization and the idea of a single purpose to the menstrual cycle also greatly enlarges the ways we could think of menopause. A team which in its youth played vigorous soccer might, in advancing years, decide to enjoy a quieter "new game" where players still interact with each other in satisfying ways but where gentle interaction *itself* is the point of the game, not getting the ball into the basket—or the flow into the vagina.

NOTES

1. Thomas Laqueur, " Female Orgasm, Generation, and the Politics of Reproductive Biology." *Representations* 14 (Spring 1986): 1–82.

2. Ibid., p. 10.

3. Charles E. Rosenberg, "The Therapeutic Revolution: Medicine, Meaning, and Social Change in Nineteenth-Century America." In Morris J. Vogel and Charles E. Rosenberg, ed., *The Therapeutic Revolution: Essays in the Social History of American Medicine*, p. 5 (Philadelphia: University of Pennsylvania Press, 1979).

4. Ibid., pp. 5–6.

5. Edward John Tilt, *The Change of Life in Health and Disease* (London: John Churchill, 1857), p. 54.

6. Ibid., pp. 54, 57.

7. Patricia Crawford, "Attitudes to Menstruation in Seventeenth-Century England." *Past and Present* 91 (1981): 50.

8. Ibid., p. 50.

9. William G. Rothstein, *American Physicians in the Nineteenth Century: From Sects to Science* (Baltimore: John Hopkins University Press, 1972), pp. 45–49.

10. Crawford, *Attitudes to Menstruation*, p. 63.

11. See Kristen Luker, *Abortion and the Politics of Motherhood* (Berkeley: University of California Press, 1984), p. 18; Crawford, *Attitudes to Menstruation*, pp. 53–54; and Vieda Skultans, "The Symbolic Significance of Menstruation and the Menopause," *Man* 5, no. 4 (1970): 639—51.

12. Laqueur, "Female Orgasm," p. 4.

13. Ibid., p. 8.

14. Elizabeth Fee, "Science and the Woman Problem: Historical Perspectives. In Michael S. Teitelbaum, ed., *Sex Difference: Social and Biological Perspectives*, (New York: Doubleday, 1976), p. 190.

15. Walter Bagehot, quoted in Fee, *Science*, p. 190.

16. Patrick Geddes and J. Arthur Thompson, *The Evolution of Sex* (New York: Scribner and Wilford, 1890). p. 122.

17. Ibid., p. 123.

18. Ibid., pp. 270–71.

19. G. J. Barker-Benfield, *The Horrors of the Half-Known Life: Male Attitudes Toward Women and Sexuality in Nineteenth-Century America* (New York: Harper and Row, 1976), pp. 195–96.

20. Susan Sontag, *Illness as Metaphor* (New York: Vintage, 1979), pp. 61–62.

21. Geddes and Thompson, *Evolution of Sex*, p. 244; see also Carroll Smith-Rosenberg, "Puberty to Menopause: The Cycle of Femininity in Nineteenth-Century America." In Mary Hartman and Lois W. Bonner, ed., *Clio's Consciousness Raised* (New York: Harper and Row, 1974), pp. 28–29.

22. Smith-Rosenberg, "Puberty to Menopause," pp. 25–27.

23. Quoted in Laqueur, "Female Orgasm," p. 32.

24. Havelock Ellis, *Men and Women* (London: Walter Scott, 1904), pp. 284, 293, quoted in Laqueur, "Female Orgasm," p. 32.

25. Smith-Rosenberg, "Puberty to Menopause," pp. 30–31; Joel Wilbush, "What's in a Name? Some Linguistic Aspects of the Climacteric." *Maturitas* 3 (1981): 5.

26. Andrew F. Currier, *The Menopause* (New York: Appleton, 1897), pp. 25–26.

27. Carole Haber, *Beyond Sixty-Five: The Dilemma of Old Age in America's Past* (Cambridge: Cambridge University Press, 1983), p. 69. See John Mason Good, *The Study of Medicine*, vol. 2 (New York: Harper and Row, 1843), pp. 23–25 for an explanation of why the climacteric affects men more severely than women.

28. Smith-Rosenberg, "Puberty to Menopause," p. 30.

29. J. Madison Taylor, "The Conservation of Energy in Those of Advancing Years," *Popular Science Monthly* 64 (1904), p. 413.

30. Quoted in Howard Berliner, "Medical Modes of Production." In Peter Wright and Andrew Treacher, ed., *The Problem of Medical Knowledge: Examining the*

Social Construction of Medicine, pp. 170–71 (Edinburgh: Edinburgh University Press, 1982).

31. R. C. Lewontin, Steven Rose, and Leon J. Kamin, *Not in Our Genes: Biology, Ideology, and Human Nature*, p. 58 (New York: Pantheon, 1984).

32. Lewontin et al., *Not in Our Genes*, p. 59; see also Arthur C. Guyton, *Textbook of Medical Physiology*, 7th. ed. (Philadelphia: Saunders, 1986), pp. 23–24.

33. In an extremely important series of papers, Donna Haraway has traced the replacement of organic functional views in biology by cybernetic systems views and shown the permeation of genetics and population biology by metaphors of investment, quality control, and maximization of profit. See Haraway, "Animal Sociology and a Natural Economy of the Body Politic," *Signs* 4 (1978): 21–36, and "The Biological Enterprise: Sex, Mind, and Profit from Human Engineering to Sociobiology," *Radical History Review* 20 (1979): 206–37.

34. Lewontin et al., *Not in Our Genes*, p. 59.

35. David F. Horrobin, *Introduction to Human Physiology* (Philadelphia: Davis, 1973), pp. 7–8. See also Guyton, *Physiology of the Human Body*, 6th. ed. (Philadelphia: Saunders, 1984), p. 7. In general, more sophisticated advanced texts such as Guyton, *Textbook*, p. 879 give more attention to feedback loops.

36. Allen Lein, *The Cycling Female: Her Menstrual Rhythm* (San Francisco: Freeman, 1979), p. 14.

37. Guyton, *Textbook*, p. 885.

38. Ralph C. Benson, *Current Obstetric and Gynecologic Diagnosis and Treatment* (Los Altos, Calif.: Lange, 1982), p. 129.

39. Frank H. Netter, *A Compilation of Paintings on the Normal and Pathologic Anatomy of the Reproductive System* (The CIBA Collection of Medical Illustrations, vol. 2) (Summit, N.J.: CIBA, 1965), p. 115.

40. Ronald V. Norris, *PMS: Premenstrual Syndrome* (New York: Berkeley, 1984), p. 6.

41. Katharina Dalton and Raymond Greene, "The Premenstrual Syndrome,"*British Medical Journal* (May 1983): 6.

42. Vernon B. Mountcastle, *Medical Physiology*, 14th. ed, vol. 2 (St. Louis, Mo.: Mosby, 1980), p. 1615.

43. Guyton, *Textbook*, p. 885.

44. Ibid.

45. Lein, *The Cycling Female*, p. 84.

46. Evelyn Fox Keller documents the pervasiveness of hierarchical models at the cellular level in *Reflections on Gender and Science* (New Haven: Yale University Press, 1985), pp. 154–56.

47. Norris, *PMS*, p. 6.

48. Anthony Giddens, *The Class Structure of the Advanced Societies* (New York: Harper and Row, 1975), p. 185.

49. Frances B. McCrea, "The Politics of Menopause: The 'Discovery' of a Deficiency Disease," *Social Problems* 31 (1983): 111–23.

50. Lein, *The Cycling Female*, pp. 79, 97.

51. Daniel J. O'Neill 1982:11.

52. Arthur J. Vander, James H. Sherman, and Dorothy S. Luciano, *Human Physiology:The Mechanisms of Body Functions*, 4th. ed. (New York: McGraw Hill, 1985), p. 597.

53. Norris, *PMS*, p. 181.

54. Vander et al., *Human Physiology*, p. 598.

55. Norris, *PMS*, p. 181.

56. Netter, *A Compilation*, p. 121.

57. Ibid., p. 116.

58. Vander et al., *Human Physiology*, p. 580.

59. Guyton, *Textbook*, p.968.

60. Vander et al., *Human Physiology*, p. 576.

61. Lein, *The Cycling Female*, p. 43.

62. Guyton, *Textbook*, p. 976.

63. Vander et al., *Human Physiology*, p. 577.

64. Guyton, *Textbook*, p. 976; see very similar accounts in Lein, *The Cycling Female*, p. 69; Mountcastle, *Medical Physiology*, p. 1612; Elliot B. Mason, *Human Physiology* (Menlo Park, Calif.: 1983), p. 518; Benson, *Current Obstetric*, pp. 128–29.

65. William F. Ganong, *Review of Medical Physiology*, 11th. ed. (Los Altos, Calif.: Lange, 1985), p. 63.

66. Langdon Winner, *Autonomous Technology: Technics-out-of-Control as a Theme in Political Thought* (Cambridge: MIT Press, 1977), pp. 185, 187.

67. Thomas Ewbank, *The World as a Workshop, or: The Physical Relationship of Man to the Earth* (New York: Appleton, 1855), pp. 21–22.

68. Ibid., p. 23.

69. Ibid., p. 27.

70. Ibid., p. 141; on Ewbank, see John F. Kasson, *Civilizing the Machine: Technology and Republican Values in America, 1796–1900* (New York: Penguin, 1976), pp. 148–51.

71. Marvin Fisher, *Workshops in the Wilderness: The European Response to American Industrialization, 1830–1860* (New York: Oxford University Press, 1967), p. 153.

72. Ibid., p. 153; see also Fisher, "Melville's 'Bell-Tower': A Double Thrust." *American Quarterly* 18 (1966): 200–7.

73. Lewis Mumford, *The Myth of the Machine: Technics and Human Development*, vol. 1 (New York: Harcourt, Brace, and World, 1967), p. 282.

74. Mumford, *The Myth of the Machine: The Pentagon of Power*, vol. 2 (New York: Harcourt, Brace, and World, 1970), p. 180.

75. David Noble, *The Forces of Production* (New York: Knopf, 1984), p. 312.

76. Vern Bullough, "Sex and the Medical Model," *The Journal of Sex Research* 11, no. 4 (1975): 298.

77. Mason, *Human Physiology*, p. 525.

78. Guyton, *Physiology*, p. 624.

79. Arthur J. Vander et al., *Human Physiology*, 3d. ed. (1980), pp. 483–84. The latest (4th.) edition of this text has removed the first of these sentences but kept the second (see 4th. ed. [1985], p. 557).

80. Vander et al., *Human Physiology*, 4th. ed., p. 577.

81. Ibid., pp. 567, 568.

82. Mason, *Human Physiology*, p. 419; Vander et al. *Human Physiology*, 4th. ed., p. 483.

83. Ganong, *Review*, p. 776.

84. Mason, *Human Physiology*, p. 423.

85. Guyton, *Physiology*, pp. 498–99.

86. Thomas Sernka and Eugene Jacobson, *Gastrointestinal Physiology: The Essentials* (Baltimore: Williams and Wilkins, 1983), p. 7.

87. Vander et al., *Human Physiology*, 4th. ed., pp. 557–58; Ganong, *Review*, p. 356.

88. Emil Novak, *Textbook of Gynecology*, 2d. ed. (Baltimore: Williams and Wilkins 1944), p.536; Novak and Edmund Novak, *Textbook of Gynecology* (Baltimore: Williams and Wilkins, 1952), p. 600.

89. Edmund Novak, Georgeanna Seegar Jones, and Howard W. Jones, *Textbook of Gynecology*, 7th. ed. (Baltimore: Williams and Wilkins, 1965), p. 642.

90. See Frances B. McCrea and Gerald E. Markle, "The Estrogen Replacement Controversy in the USA and UK: Different Answers to the Same Question?," *Social Studies of Science* 14 (1984): 1–26, for the very different clinical treatment for this lack in the United States and the United Kingdom.

91. Patricia A. Kaufert and Penny Gilbert, "Women, Menopause, and Medicalization," *Culture, Medicine, and Psychiatry* 10, no. 1 (1986): 7–21; World Health Organization Scientific Group, *Research on the Menopause*, World Health Organization Technical Report Series 670 (Geneva: World Health Organization, 1981): 74.

92. Guyton, *Textbook*, p. 979.

93. Howard Jones and Georgeanna Seegar Jones, *Novak's Textbook of Gynecoloy*, 10th. ed. (Baltimore: Williams and Wilkins, 1981), p. 799.

94. Sadly enough, even the women's health movement literature contains the same negative view of menstruation—failed production—as does scientific medicine. See Boston Women's Health Book Collective. *The New Our Bodies Ourselves* (New York: Simon and Schuster, 1984), p. 217 and Federation of Feminist Women's Health Centers, *A New View of a Woman's Body* (New York: Simon and Schuster, 1981), p. 74. As in the case of prepared childbirth literature, this is evidence of the invisible power of the ideology of the dominant culture.

2

Rape:
On Coercion and Consent

Catharine A. MacKinnon

Negotiations for sex are not carried on like those for the rent of a house. There is often no definite state on which it can be said that the two have agreed to sexual intercourse. They proceed by touching, feeling, fumbling, by signs and words which are not generally in the form of a Roman stipulation.

—Honoré,

twentieth-century British legal scholar and philosopher

If you're living with a man, what are you doing running around the streets getting raped?

—Edward Harrington, defense attorney in New Bedford gang rape case

If sexuality is central to women's definition and forced sex is central to sexuality, rape is indigenous, not exceptional, to women's social condition. In feminist analysis, a rape is not an isolated event or moral transgression or individual interchange gone wrong but an act of terrorism and torture within a systemic context of group subjection, like lynching. The fact that the state calls rape a crime opens an inquiry into the state's treatment of rape as an index to its stance on the status of the sexes.

Under law, rape is a sex crime that is not regarded as a crime when it looks like sex. The law, speaking generally, defines rape as intercourse with force or coercion and without consent.[1] Like sexuality under male supremacy, this definition assumes the sadomasochistic definition of sex: intercourse with force or coercion

Catharine A. MacKinnon, "Rape: On Coercion and Consent." From *Toward a Feminist Theory of the State* by Catharine A. MacKinnon. Copyright © 1989 by Catharine MacKinnon. Reprinted by permission of Harvard University Press.

Rape is an extension of sexism in some ways, and that's an extension of dealing with a woman as an object . . . Stinky [her rapist] seemed to me as though he were only a step further away, a step away from the guys who sought me on the streets, who insist, my mother could have died, I could be walking down the street and if I don't answer their rap, they got to go get angry and get all hostile and stuff as though I walk down the street as a . . . that my whole being is there to please men in the streets. But Stinky only seemed like someone who had taken it a step further . . . he felt like an extension, he felt so common, he felt so ordinary, he felt so familiar, and it was maybe that what frightened me the most was that how similar to other men he seemed. They don't come from Mars, folks.

—Carolyn Craven, reporter

can be or become consensual. It assumes pornography's positive-outcome-rape scenario: dominance plus submission is force plus consent. This equals sex, not rape. Under male supremacy, this is too often the reality. In a critique of male supremacy, the elements "with force and without consent" appear redundant. Force is present because consent is absent.

Like heterosexuality, male supremacy's paradigm of sex, the crime of rape centers on penetration.[2] The law to protect women's sexuality from forcible violation and expropriation defines that protection in male genital terms. Women do resent forced penetration. But penile invasion of the vagina may be less pivotal to women's sexuality, pleasure, or violation, than it is to male sexuality. This definitive element of rape centers upon a male-defined loss. It also centers upon one way men define loss of exclusive access. In this light, rape, as legally defined, appears more a crime against female monogamy (exclusive access by one man) than against women's sexual dignity or intimate integrity. Analysis of rape in terms of concepts of property, often invoked in Marxian analysis to criticize this disparity, fail to encompass the realities of rape.[3] Women's sexuality is, socially, a thing to be stolen, sold, bought, bartered, or exchanged by others. But women never own or possess it, and men never treat it, in law or in life, with the solicitude with which they treat property. To be property would be an improvement. The moment women "have" it—"have sex" in the dual gender/sexuality sense—it is lost as theirs. To have it is to have it taken away. This may explain the male incomprehension that, once a woman has had sex, she loses anything when subsequently raped.

To them women have nothing to lose. It is true that dignitary harms, because nonmaterial, are ephemeral to the legal mind. But women's loss through rape is not only less tangible; it is seen as unreal. It is difficult to avoid the conclusion that penetration itself is considered a violation from the male point of view, which is both why it is the centerpiece of sex and why women's sexuality, women's gender definition, is stigmatic. The question for social explanation becomes not why some women tolerate rape but how any women manage to resent it.

Rape cases finding insufficient evidence of force reveal that acceptable sex, in the legal perspective, can entail a lot of force. This is both a result of the way specific facts are perceived and interpreted within the legal system and the way the injury is defined by law. The level of acceptable force is adjudicated starting just above the level set by what is seen as normal male sexual behavior, including the normal level of force, rather than at the victim's, or women's, point of violation.[4] In this context, to seek to define rape as violent not sexual is as understandable as it is futile. Some feminists have reinterpreted rape as an act of violence, not sexuality, the threat of which intimidates all women.[5] Others see rape, including its violence, as an expression of male sexuality, the social imperatives of which define as well as threaten all women.[6] The first, epistemologically in the liberal tradition, comprehends rape as a displacement of power based on physical force onto sexuality, a preexisting natural sphere to which domination is alien. Susan Brownmiller, for example, examines rape in riots, wars, pogroms, and revolutions; rape by police, parents, prison guards; and rape motivated by racism. Rape in normal circumstances, in everyday life, in ordinary relationships, by men as men, is barely mentioned.[7] Women are raped by guns, age, white supremacy, the state—only derivatively by the penis. The view that derives most directly from victims' experiences, rather than from their denial, construes sexuality as a social sphere of male power to which forced sex is paradigmatic. Rape is not less sexual for being violent. To the extent that coercion has become integral to male sexuality, rape may even be sexual to the degree that, and because, it is violent.

The point of defining rape as "violence not sex" has been to claim an ungendered and nonsexual ground for affirming sex (heterosexuality) while rejecting violence (rape). The problem remains what it has always been: telling the difference. The convergence of sexuality with violence, long used at law to deny the reality of women's violation, is recognized by rape survivors with a difference: where the legal system has seen the intercourse in rape, victims see the rape in intercourse. The uncoerced context for sexual expression becomes as elusive as the physical acts come to feel indistinguishable. Instead of asking what is the violation of rape, their experience suggests that the more relevant question is, what is the nonviolation of intercourse? To know what is wrong with rape, know what is right about sex. If this, in turn, proves difficult, the difficulty is as instructive as the difficulty men have in telling the difference when women see one. Perhaps the wrong of rape has proved so difficult to define because the unquestionable starting point has been that rape is defined as distinct from intercourse,[8] while for women it is difficult to distinguish the two under conditions of male dominance.

In the name of the distinction between sex and violence, reform of rape statutes has sought to redefine rape as sexual assault.[9] Usually, assault is not consented to in law; either it cannot be consented to, or consensual assault remains assault.[10] Yet sexual assault consented to is intercourse, no matter how much force was used. The substantive reference point implicit in existing legal standards is the sexually normative level of force. Until this norm is confronted as such, no distinction between violence and sexuality will prohibit more instances of women's experienced violation than does the existing definition. Conviction rates have not increased under the reform statutes.[11] The question remains what is seen as force, hence as violence, in the sexual arena.[12] Most rapes, as women live them, will not be seen to violate women until sex and violence are confronted as mutually definitive rather than as mutually exclusive. It is not only men convicted of rape who believe that the only thing they did that was different from what men do all the time is get caught.

Consent is supposed to be women's form of control over intercourse, different from but equal to the custom of male initiative. Man proposes, woman disposes. Even the ideal in it is not mutual. Apart from the disparate consequences of refusal, this model does not envision a situation the woman controls being placed in, or choices she frames. Yet the consequences are attributed to her as if the sexes began at arm's length, on equal terrain, as in the contract fiction. Ambiguous cases of consent in law are archetypically referred to as "half won arguments in parked cars."[13] Why not half lost? Why isn't half enough? Why is it an argument? Why do men still want "it," feel entitled to "it," when women do not want them? The law of rape presents consent as free exercise of sexual choice under conditions of equality of power without exposing the underlying structure of constraint and disparity. Fundamentally, desirability to men is supposed a woman's form of power because she can both arouse it and deny its fulfillment. To woman is attributed both the cause of man's initiative and the denial of his satisfaction.

This rationalizes force. Consent in this model becomes more a metaphysical quality of a woman's being than a choice she makes and communicates. Exercise of women's so-called power presupposes more fundamental social powerlessness.[14]

The law of rape divides women into spheres of consent according to indices of relationship to men. Which category of presumed consent a woman is in depends upon who she is relative to a man who wants her, not what she says or does. These categories tell men whom they can legally fuck, who is open season, and who is off limits, not how to listen to women. The paradigm categories are the virginal daughter and other young girls, with whom all sex is proscribed, and the whorelike wives and prostitutes, with whom no sex is proscribed. Daughters may not consent; wives and prostitutes are assumed to, and cannot but.[15] Actual consent or nonconsent, far less actual desire, is comparatively irrelevant. If rape laws existed to enforce women's control over access to their sexuality, as the consent defense implies, no would mean no, marital rape would not be a widespread exception,[16] and it would not be effectively legal to rape a prostitute.

All women are divided into parallel provinces, their actual consent counting to the degree that they diverge from the paradigm case in their category. Virtuous women, like young girls, are unconsenting, virginal, rapable. Unvirtuous women, like wives and prostitutes, are consenting, whores, unrapable. The age line under which girls are presumed disabled from consenting to sex, whatever they say, rationalizes a condition of sexual coercion which women never outgrow. One day they cannot say yes, and the next day they cannot say no. The law takes the most aggravated case for female powerlessness based on gender and age combined and, by formally prohibiting all sex as rape, makes consent irrelevant on the basis of an assumption of powerlessness. This defines those above the age line as powerful, whether they actually have power to consent or not. The vulnerability girls share with boys—age—dissipates with time. The vulnerability girls share with women—gender—does not. As with protective labor laws for women only, dividing and protecting the most vulnerable becomes a device for not protecting everyone who needs it, and also may function to target those singled out for special protection for special abuse. Such protection has not prevented high rates of sexual abuse of children and may contribute to eroticizing young girls as forbidden.

As to adult women, to the extent an accused knows a woman and they have sex, her consent is inferred. The exemption for rape in marriage is consistent with the assumption underlying most adjudications of forcible rape:

to the extent the parties relate, it was not really rape, it was personal.[17] As marital exemptions erode, preclusions for cohabitants and voluntary social companions may expand. As a matter of fact, for this purpose one can be acquainted with an accused by friendship or by meeting him for the first time at a bar or a party or by hitchhiking. In this light, the partial erosion of the marital rape exemption looks less like a change in the equation between women's experience of sexual violation and men's experience of intimacy, and more like a legal adjustment to the social fact that acceptable heterosexual sex is increasingly not limited to the legal family. So although the rape law may not now always assume that the woman consented simply because the parties are legally one, indices of closeness, of relationship ranging from nodding acquaintance to living together, still contraindicate rape. In marital rape cases, courts look for even greater atrocities than usual to undermine their assumption that if sex happened, she wanted it.[18]

This approach reflects men's experience that women they know do meaningfully consent to sex with them. *That* cannot be rape; rape must be by someone else, someone unknown. They do not rape women they know. Men and women are unequally socially situated with regard to the experience of rape. Men are a good deal more likely to rape than to be raped. This forms their experience, the material conditions of their epistemological position. Almost half of all women, by contrast, are raped or victims of attempted rape at least once in their lives. Almost 40 percent are victims of sexual abuse in childhood.[19] Women are more likely to be raped than to rape and are most often raped by men whom they know.[20]

Men often say that it is less awful for a woman to be raped by someone she is close to: "The emotional trauma suffered by a person victimized by an individual with whom sexual intimacy is shared as a normal part of an ongoing marital relationship is not nearly as severe as that suffered by a person who is victimized by one with whom that intimacy is not shared."[21] Women often feel as or more traumatized from being raped by someone known or trusted, someone with whom at least an illusion of mutuality has been shared, than by some stranger. In whose interest is it to believe that it is not so bad to be raped by someone who has fucked you before as by someone who has not? Disallowing charges of rape in marriage may, depending upon one's view of normalcy, "remove a substantial obstacle to the resumption of normal marital relationships."[22] Note that the obstacle is not the rape but the law against it. Apparently someone besides feminists finds sexual victimization and sexual intimacy not all that contradictory under current conditions. Sometimes it seems as though women and men live in different cultures.

Having defined rape in male sexual terms, the law's problem, which becomes the victim's problem, is distinguishing rape from sex in specific cases. The adjudicated line between rape and intercourse commonly centers on some assessment of the woman's "will." But how should the law or the accused know a woman's will? The answer combines aspects of force with aspects of nonconsent with elements of resistance, still effective in some states.[23] Even when nonconsent is not a legal element of the offense, juries tend to infer rape from evidence of force or resistance. In Michigan, under its reform rape law, consent was judicially held to be a defense even though it was not included in the statute.[24]

The deeper problem is that women are socialized to passive receptivity; may have or perceive no alternative to acquiescence; may prefer it to the escalated risk of injury and the humiliation of a lost fight; submit to survive. Also, force and desire are not mutually exclusive under male supremacy. So long as dominance is eroticized, they never will be. Some women eroticize dominance and submission; it beats feeling forced. Sexual intercourse may be deeply unwanted, the woman would never have initiated it, yet no force may be present. So much force may have been used that the woman never risked saying no. Force may be used, yet the woman may prefer the sex—to avoid more force or because she, too, eroticizes dominance. Women and men know this. Considering rape as violence not sex evades, at the moment it most seems to confront, the issue of who controls women's sexuality and the dominance/submission dynamic that has defined it. When sex is violent, women may have lost control over what is done to them, but absence of force does not ensure the presence of that control. Nor, under conditions of male dominance, does the presence of force make an interaction nonsexual. If sex is normally something men do to women, the issue is less whether there was force than whether consent is a meaningful concept.[25]

To explain women's gender status on a rape theory, Susan Brownmiller argues that the threat of rape benefits all men.[26] How is unspecified. Perhaps it benefits them sexually, hence as a gender: male initiatives toward women carry the fear of rape as support for persuading compliance, the resulting appearance of which has been considered seduction and termed consent. Here the victims' perspective grasps what liberalism applied to women denies: that forced sex as sexuality is not exceptional in relations between the sexes but constitutes the social meaning of gender. "Rape is a man's act, whether it is a male or a female man and whether it is a man relatively permanently or relatively temporarily; and being raped is a woman's experience, whether it is a female or a male woman and whether it is a woman relatively permanently or relatively temporarily."[27] To be rapable, a position that is social not biological, defines what a woman is.

Marital rape and battery of wives have been separated by law. A feminist analysis suggests that assault by a man's fist is not so different from assault by a penis, not because both are violent but because both are sexual. Battery is often precipitated by women's noncompliance with gender requirements.[28] Nearly all incidents occur in the home, most in the kitchen or bedroom. Most murdered women are killed by their husbands or boyfriends, usually in the bedroom. The battery cycle accords with the rhythms of heterosexual sex.[29] The rhythm of lesbian sadomasochism is the same.[30] Perhaps violent interchanges, especially between genders, make sense in sexual terms.

The larger issue raised by sexual aggression for the interpretation of the relation between sexuality and gender is: what is heterosexuality? If it is the erotization of dominance and submission, altering the participants' gender does not eliminate the sexual, or even gendered, content of aggression. If heterosexuality is males over females, gender matters independently. Arguably, heterosexuality is a fusion of the two, with gender a social outcome, such that the acted upon is feminized, is the "girl" regardless of sex, the actor correspondingly masculinized. Whenever women are victimized, regardless of the biology of the perpetrator, this system is at work. But it is equally true that whenever powerlessness and ascribed inferiority are sexually exploited or enjoyed—based on age, race, physical stature or appearance or ability, or socially reviled or stigmatized status—the system is at work.

Battery thus appears sexual on a deeper level. Stated in boldest terms, sexuality is violent, so perhaps violence is sexual. Violence against women is sexual on both counts, doubly sexy. If this is so, wives are beaten, as well as raped, as women—as the acted upon, as gender, meaning sexual, objects. It further follows that acts by anyone which treat a woman according to her object label, woman, are in a sense sexual acts. The extent to which sexual acts are acts of objectification remains a question of one's account of women's freedom to live their own meanings as other than illusions, of individuals' ability to resist or escape, even momentarily, prescribed social meanings short of political change. Clearly, centering sexuality upon genitality distinguishes battery from rape at exactly the juncture that both existing law, and seeing rape as violence not sex, do.

Most women get the message that the law against rape is virtually unenforceable as applied to them. Women's experience is more often delegitimated by this than the law is. Women, as realists, distinguish between rape and experiences of sexual violation by concluding that they have not "really" been raped if they have ever seen or dated or slept with or been married to the man, if they were fashionably dressed or not provably virgin, if they are prostitutes, if they put up with it or tried to get it over with, if they were force-fucked for years. The implicit social standard becomes: if a woman probably could not prove it in court, it was not rape.

The distance between most intimate violations of women and the legally perfect rape measures the imposition of an alien definition. From women's point of view, rape is not prohibited; it is regulated. Even women who know they have been raped do not believe that the legal system will see it the way they do. Often they are not wrong. Rather than deterring or avenging rape, the state, in many victims' experiences, perpetuates it. Women who charge rape say they were raped twice, the second time in court. Under a male state, the boundary violation, humiliation, and indignity of being a public sexual spectacle makes this more than a figure of speech.[31]

Rape, like many other crimes, requires that the accused possess a criminal mind (*mens rea*) for his acts to be criminal. The man's mental state refers to what he actually understood at the time or to what a reasonable man should have understood under the circumstances. The problem is that the injury of rape lies in the meaning of the act to its victim, but the standard for its criminality lies in he meaning of the act to the assailant. Rape is only an injury from women's point of view. It is only a crime from the male point of view, explicitly including that of the accused.

The crime of rape is defined and adjudicated from the male standpoint, presuming that forced sex is sex and that consent to a man is freely given by a woman. Under male supremacist standards, of course, they are. Doctrinally, this means that the man's perceptions of the woman's desires determine whether she is deemed violated. This might be like other crimes of subjective intent if rape were like other crimes. With rape, because sexuality defines gender norms, the only difference between assault and what is socially defined as a noninjury is the meaning of the encounter to the woman. Interpreted this way, the legal problem has been to determine whose view of that meaning constitutes what really happened, as if what happened objectively exists to be objectively determined. This task has been assumed to be separable from the gender of the participants and the gendered nature of their exchange, when the objective norms and the assailant's perspective are identical.

As a result, although the rape law oscillates between subjective tests and objective standards invoking social reasonableness, it uniformly presumes a single underlying reality, rather than a reality split by the divergent meanings inequality produces. Many women are raped by men who know the meaning of their acts to their victims perfectly well and proceed anyway.[32] But women are also violated every day by men who have no idea of the meaning of their acts to the women. To them it is sex. Therefore, to the law it is sex. That becomes the single reality of what happened. When a rape prosecution is lost because a woman fails to prove that she did not consent, she is not considered to have been injured at all. It is as if a robbery victim, finding himself unable to prove he was not engaged in philanthropy, is told he still has his money. Hermeneutically unpacked, the law assumes that, because the rapist did not perceive that the woman did not want him, she was not violated. She had sex. Sex itself cannot be an injury. Women have sex every day. Sex makes a woman a woman. Sex is what women are for.

Men set sexual mores ideologically and behaviorally, define rape as they imagine women to be sexually violated through distinguishing that from their image of what they normally do, and sit in judgment in most accusations of sex crimes. So rape comes to mean a strange (read Black) man who does not know his victim but does know she does not want sex with him, going ahead anyway. But men are systematically conditioned not even to notice what women want. Especially if they consume pornography, they may have not a glimmer of women's indifference or revulsion, including when women say no explicitly. Rapists typically believe the woman loved it. "Probably the single most used cry of rapist to victim is 'You bitch . . . slut . . . you know you want it. You all want it' and afterward, 'there now, you really enjoyed it, didn't you?' "[33] Women, as a survival strategy, must ignore or devalue or mute desires, particularly lack of them, to convey the impression that the man will get what he wants regardless of what they want. In this context, to measure the genuineness of consent from the individual assailant's point of view is to adopt as law the point of view which creates the problem. Measuring consent from the socially reasonable, meaning objective man's, point of view reproduces the same problem under a more elevated label.[34]

Men's pervasive belief that women fabricate rape charges after consenting to sex makes sense in this light. To them, the accusations are false because, to them, the facts describe sex. To interpret such events as rapes distorts their experience. Since they seldom consider that their experience of the real is anything other than reality, they can only explain the woman's version as maliciously invented. Similarly, the male anxiety that rape is easy to charge and difficult to disprove, also widely believed in the face of overwhelming evidence to the contrary, arises because rape accusations express one thing men cannot seem to control: the meaning to women of sexual encounters.

Thus do legal doctrines, incoherent or puzzling as syllogistic logic, become coherent as ideology. For example, when an accused wrongly but sincerely believes that a woman he sexually forced consented, he may have a defense of mistaken belief in consent or fail to satisfy the mental requirement of knowingly proceeding against her will.[35] Sometimes his knowing disregard is measured by what a reasonable man would disregard. This is considered an objective test. Sometimes the disregard need not be reasonable so long as it is sincere. This is considered a subjective test. A feminist inquiry into the distinction between rape and intercourse, by contrast, would inquire into the meaning of the act from women's point of view, which is neither. What is wrong with rape in this view is that it is an act of subordination of women to men. It expresses and reinforces women's inequality to men. Rape with legal impunity makes women second-class citizens.

This analysis reveals the way the social conception of rape is shaped to interpret particular encounters and the way the legal conception of rape authoritatively shapes that social conception. When perspective is bound up with situation, and situation is unequal, whether or not a contested interaction is authoritatively considered rape comes down to whose meaning wins. If sexuality is relational, specifically if it is a power relation of gender, consent is a communication under conditions of inequality. It transpires somewhere between what the woman actually wanted, what she was able to express about what she wanted, and what the man comprehended she wanted.

Discussing the conceptually similar issue of revocation of prior consent, on the issue of the conditions under which women are allowed to control access to their sexuality from one penetration to the next, one commentator notes: "Even where a woman revokes prior consent, such is the male ego that, seized of an exaggerated assessment of his sexual prowess, a man might genuinely believe her still to be consenting; resistance may be misinterpreted as enthusiastic cooperation; protestations of pain or disinclination, a spur to more sophisticated or more ardent love-making; a clear statement to stop, taken as referring to a particular intimacy rather than the entire performance."[36] This vividly captures common male readings of women's indications of disinclination under many circumstances[37] and the perceptions that determine whether a rape occurred. The specific defense of mistaken belief in consent merely carries this to its logical apex. From whose standpoint, and in whose interest, is a law that allows one person's conditioned unconsciousness to contraindicate another's violation? In conceiving a cognizable injury from the viewpoint of the reasonable rapist, the rape law affirmatively rewards men with acquittals for not comprehending women's point of view on sexual encounters.

Whether the law calls this coerced consent or defense of mistaken belief in consent, the more the sexual violation of women is routine, the more pornography exists in the world the more legitimately, the more beliefs equating sexuality with violation become reasonable, and the more honestly women can be defined in terms of their fuckability. It would be comparatively simple if the legal problem were limited to avoiding retroactive falsification of the accused's state of mind. Surely there are incentives to lie. The deeper problem is the rape law's assumption that a single, objective state of affairs existed, one that merely needs to be determined by evidence, when so many rapes involve honest men and violated women. When the reality is split, is the woman raped but not by a rapist? Under these conditions, the law is designed to conclude that a rape did not occur. To attempt to solve this problem by adopting reasonable belief as a standard without asking, on a substantive social basis, to whom the belief is reasonable and why—meaning, what conditions make it reasonable—is onesided: male-sided.[38] What is it reasonable for a man to believe concerning a woman's desire for sex when heterosexuality is compulsory? What is it reasonable for a man (accused or juror) to believe concerning a woman's consent when he has been viewing positive-outcome-rape pornography?[39] The one whose subjectivity becomes the objectivity of "what happened" is a matter of social meaning, that is, a matter of sexual politics. One-sidedly erasing women's violation or dissolving presumptions into the subjectivity of either side are the alternatives dictated by the terms of the object/subject split, respectively. These alternatives will only retrace that split to women's detriment until its terms are confronted as gendered to the ground.

NOTES

1. W. LaFave and A. Scott, *Substantive Criminal Law* (St. Paul: West, 1986), sec. 5.11 (pp. 688–9); R. M. Perkins and R. N. Boyce, *Criminal Law* (Mineola, N.Y.: Foundation Press, 1980), p. 210.

2. One component of Sec. 213.0 of the Model Penal Code (Philadelphia: American Law Institute, 1980) defines rape as sexual intercourse with a female not the wife of the perpetrator, "with some penetration however slight." Most states follow. New York requires penetration (sec. 130.00 [I]). Michigan's gender-neutral sexual assault statute includes penetration by objects (sec. 750.520 a[h];

720.520[b]). The 1980 Annotation to Model Penal Code (Official Draft and Revised Comments, sec. 213.1[d]) questions and discusses the penetration requirement at 346–48. For illustrative case law, see Liptroth v. State, 335 So.2d 683 (Ala. Crim. App. 1976), *cert. denied* 429 U.S. 963 (1976); State v. Kidwell, 556 P.2d 20, 27 Ariz. App. 466 (Ariz. Ct. App. 1976); People v. O'Neal, 50 III. App. 3d 900, 365 N.E. 2d 1333 (III. App. Ct. 1977); Commonwealth v. Usher, 371 A.2d 995 (Pa. Super. Ct. 1977); Commonwealth v. Grassmyer, 237 Pa. Super. 394, 352 A.2d 178 (Pa. Super. Ct. 1975) (statutory rape conviction reversed because defendant's claim that five-year-old child's vaginal wound was inflicted with a broomstick could not be disproved and commonwealth could therefore not prove requisite penetration; indecent assault conviction sustained). Impotence is sometimes a defense and can support laws that prevent charging underage boys with rape or attempted rape; Foster v. Commonwealth, 31 S.E. 503, 96 Va. 306 (1896) (boy under fourteen cannot be guilty of attempt to commit offense that he is legally assumed physically impotent to perpetrate).

3. In the manner of many socialist-feminist adaptations of marxian categories to women's situation, to analyze sexuality as property short-circuits analysis of rape as male sexuality and presumes rather than develops links between sex and class. Concepts of property need to be rethought in light of sexuality as a form of objectification. In some ways, for women legally to be considered property would be an improvement, although it is not recommended.

4. For contrast between the perspectives of the victims and the courts, see Rusk v. State, 43 Md. App. 476, 406 A.2d 624 (Md. Ct. Spec. App. 1979) (*en banc banc*), *rev'd*, 289 Md. 230, 424 A.2d 720 (1981); Gonzales v. State, 516 P.2d 592 (1973).

5. Susan Brownmiller, *Against Our Will: Men, Women, and Rape* (New York: Simon and Schuster, 1975), p. 15.

6. Diana E. H. Russell, *The Politics of Rape: The Victim's Perspective* (New York: Stein and Day, 1977); Andrea Medea and Kathleen Thompson, *Against Rape* (New York: Farrar, Straus and Giroux, 1974); Lorenne M. G. Clark and Debra Lewis, *Rape: The Price of Coercive Sexuality* (Toronto: Women's Press, 1977); Susan Griffin, "Rape: The All-American Crime," *Ramparts* (September 1971), pp. 26–35. Ti-Grace Atkinson connects rape with "the institution of sexual intercourse," *Amazon Odyssey: The First Collection of Writings by the Political Pioneer of the Women's Movement* (New York: Links Books, 1974), pp. 13–23. Kalamu ya Salaam, "Rape: A Radical Analysis from the African-American Perspective," in *Our Women Keep Our Skies from Falling* (New Orleans: Nkombo, 1980), pp. 25–40.

7. Racism is clearly everyday life. Racism in the United States, by singling out Black men for allegations of rape of white women, has helped obscure the fact that it is men who rape women, disproportionately women of color.

8. Pamela Foa, "What's Wrong with Rape?" in *Feminism and Philosophy*, ed. Mary Vetterling-Braggin, Frederick A. Elliston, and Jane English (Totowa, N.J.: Littlefield, Adams, 1977), pp. 347–59; Michael Davis, "What's So Bad about Rape?" (Paper presented at the annual meeting of the Academy of Criminal Justice Sciences, Louisville, Ky., March 1982). "Since we would not want to say that there is anything morally wrong with sexual intercourse per se, we conclude that the wrongness of rape rests with the matter of the woman's consent"; Carolyn M. Shafer and Marilyn Frye, "Rape and Respect," in Vetterling-Braggin, Elliston, and English, *Feminism and Philosophy*, p. 334. "Sexual contact is not inherently harmful, insulting or provoking. Indeed, ordinarily it is something of which we are quite fond. The difference is [that] ordinary sexual intercourse is more or less consented to while rape is not"; Davis, "What's So Bad?" p. 12.

9. Liegh Bienen, "Rape III—National Developments in Rape Reform Legislation," 6 *Women's Rights Law Reporter* 170 (1980). See also Camille LeGrande, "Rape and Rape Laws: Sexism in Society and Law," 61 *California Law Review* 919 (May 1973).

10 People v. Samuels, 58 Cal. Rptr. 439, 447 (1967).

11. Julia R. Schwendinger and Herman Schewendinger, *Rape and Inequality* (Berkeley: Sage Library of Social Research, 1983), p. 44; K. Polk, "Rape Reform and Criminal Justice Processing," *Crime and Delinquency* 31 (April 1985): 191–05. "What can be concluded about the achievement of the underlying goals of the rape reform movement? . . . If a major goal is to increase the probability of convictions, then the results are slight at best . . . or even negligible" (p. 199) (California data). See also P. Bart and P. O'Brien. *Stopping Rape: Successful Survival Strategies* (Elmsford, N.Y.: Pergamon, 1985). pp. 129–31.

12. See State v. Alston, 310 N.C. 399, 312 S.E. 2d 470 (1984) and discussion in Susan Estrich, *Real Rape* (Cambridge: Harvard University Press, 1987), pp. 60–62.

13. Note, "Forcible and Statutory Rape: An Exploration of the Operation and Objectives of the Consent Standard," 62 *Yale Law Journal* 55 (1952).

14. A similar analysis of sexual harassment suggests that women have such "power" only so long as they behave according to male definitions of female desirability, that is, only so long as they accede to the definition of their sexuality (hence, themselves, as gender female) on male terms. Women have this power, in other words, only so long as they remain powerless.

15. See Comment, "Rape and Battery between Husband and Wife," 6 *Stanford Law Review* 719 (1954). On rape of prostitutes, see, e.g., People v. McClure, 42 Ill. App. 952, 356 N.E. 2d 899 (1st Dist. 3d Div. 1976) (on indictment for rape and armed robbery of prostitute where sex was admitted to have occurred, defendant acquitted of rape but "guilty of robbing her while armed with a knife"); Magnum

v. State, I Tenn. Crim. App. 155, 432 S.W. 2d 497 (Tenn. Crim. App. 1968) (no conviction for rape; conviction for sexual violation of age of consent overturned on ground that failure to instruct jury to determine if complainant was "a bawd, lewd or kept female" was reversible error; "A bawd female is a female who keeps a house of prostitution, and conducts illicit intercourse. A lewd female is one given to unlawful indulgence of lust, either for sexual indulgence or profit . . . A kept female is one who is supported and kept by a man for his own illicit intercourse"; complainant "frequented the Blue Moon Tavern; she had been there the night before . . . she kept company with . . . a married man separated from his wife . . . There is some proof of her bad reputation for truth and veracity"). Johnson v. State, 598 S.W. 2d 803 (Tenn. Crim. App. 1979) (unsuccessful defense to charge of rape that "even [if] technically a prostitute can be raped . . . the act of the rape itself was no trauma whatever to this type of unchaste woman"); People v. Gonzales, 96 Misc. 2d 639, 409 N.Y.S. 2d 497 (Crm. Crt. N.Y. City 1978) (prostitute can be raped if "it can be proven beyond a reasonable doubt that she revoked her consent prior to sexual intercourse because the defendant . . . used the coercive force of a pistol).

16. People v. Liberta, 64 N.Y. 2d 152, 474 N.E. 2d 567, 485 N.Y.S. 2d 207 (1984) (marital rape recognized, contrary precedents discussed). For a summary of the current state of the marital exemption, see Joanne Schulman, "State-by-State Information on Marital Rape Exemption Laws," in Diana E. H. Russell, *Rape in Marriage* (New York: Macmillan, 1982), pp. 375–81; Patricia Searles and Ronald Berger, "The Current Status of Rape Reform Legislation: An Examination of State Statutes," 10 *Women's Rights Law Reporter* 25 (1987).

17. On "social interaction as an element of consent" in a voluntary social companion context, see Model Penal Code, sec. 213.1. "The prior social interaction is an indicator of consent in addition to actor's and victim's behavioral interaction during the commission of the offense"; Wallace Loh, "Q: What Has Reform of Rape Legislation Wrought? A: Truth in Criminal Labeling," *Journal of Social Issues* 37, no. 4 (1981): 47.

18. E.g., People v. Burnham, 176 Cal. App. 3d 1134, 222 Cal. Rptr. 630 (Cal. App. 1986).

19. Diana E. H. Russell and Nancy Howell, "The Prevalence of Rape in the United States Revisited," *Signs: Journal of Women in Culture and Society* 8 (Summer 1983): 668–95; and D. Russell, *The Secret Trauma: Incestuous Abuse of Women and Girls* (New York: Basic Books, 1986).

20. Pauline Bart found that women were more likely to be raped—that is, less able to stop a rape in progress—when they knew their assailant, particularly when they had a prior or current sexual relationship; "A Study of Women Who Both Were

Raped and Avoided Rape," *Journal of Social Issues* 37 (1981): 132. See also Linda Belden, "Why Women Do Not Report Sexual Assault" (Portland, Ore.: City of Portland Public Service Employment Program, Portland Women's Crisis Line, March 1979); Menachem Amir, *Patterns in Forcible Rape* (Chicago: University of Chicago Press, 1971), pp. 229–52.

21. Answer Brief for Plaintiff-Appellee, People v. Brown, Sup. Ct. Colo., Case No. 81SA102 (1981): 10.

22. Note, "Forcible and Statutory Rape," p. 55.

23. La. Rev. Stat. 14.42. Delaware law requires that the victim resist, but "only to the extent that it is reasonably necessary to make the victim's refusal to consent known to the defendant"; II Del. Code 761(g). See also Sue Bessmer, *The Laws of Rape* (New York: Praeger, 1984).

24. See People v. Thompson, 117 Mich. App. 522, 524, 324 N.W. 2d 22, 24 (Mich. App. 1982); People v. Hearn, 100 Mich. App. 749, 300 N.W. 2d 396 (Mich. App. 1980).

25. See Carol Pateman, "Women and Consent," *Political Theory* 8 (May 1980): 149–68: "Consent as ideology cannot be distinguished from habitual acquiescence, assent, silent dissent, submission, or even enforced submission. Unless refusal of consent or withdrawal of consent are real possibilities, we can no longer speak of 'consent' in any genuine sense . . . Women exemplify the individuals whom consent theorists declared are incapable of consenting. Yet, simultaneously, women have been presented as always consenting, and their explicit non-consent has been treated as irrelevant or has been reinterpreted as 'consent'" (p. 150).

26. Brownmiller, *Against Our Will*, p. 5.

27. Shafer and Frye, "Rape and Respect," p. 334.

28. See R. Emerson Dobash and Russell Dobash, *Violence against Wives: A Case against the Patriarchy* (New York: Free Press, 1979), pp. 14–21.

29. On the cycle of battering, see Lenore Walker, *The Battered Woman* (New York: Harper and Row, 1979).

30. Samois, *Coming to Power* (Palo Alto, Calif.: Alyson Publications, 1983).

31. If accounts of sexual violation are a form of sex, as argued in Chapter 11, victim testimony in rape cases is a form of live oral pornography.

32. This is apparently true of undetected as well as convicted rapists. Samuel David Smithyman's sample, composed largely of the former, contained self-selected respondents to his ad, which read: "Are you a rapist? Researchers Interviewing Anonymously by Phone to Protect Your Identity. Call . . ." Presumably those who chose to call defined their acts as rapes, at least at the time of responding; "The Undetected Rapist" (Ph.D. diss., Claremont Graduate School, 1978), pp. 54–60, 63–76, 80–90, 97–107.

33. Nancy Gager and Cathleen Schurr, *Sexual Assault: Confronting Rape in America* (New York: Grosset and Dunlap, 1976), p. 244.

34. Susan Estrich proposes this; *Real Rape*, pp. 102–103. Her lack of inquiry into social determinants of perspective (such as pornography) may explain her faith in reasonableness as a legally workable standard for raped women.

35. See Director of Public Prosecutions v. Morgan, 2 All E.R.H.L. 347 (1975) [England]; Pappajohn v. The Queen, III D.L.R. 3d 1 (1980) [Canada]; People v. Mayberry, 542 P. 2d 1337 (Cal. 1975).

36. Richard H. S. Tur, "Rape: Reasonableness and Time," 3 *Oxford Journal of Legal Studies* 432, 441 (Winter 1981). Tur, in the context of the *Morgan* and *Pappajohn* cases, says the "law ought not to be astute to equate wickedness and wishful, albeit mistaken, thinking" (p. 437). Rape victims are typically less concerned with wickedness than with injury.

37. See Silke Vogelmann-Sine, Ellen D. Ervin, Reenie Christensen, Carolyn H. Warmsun, and Leonard P. Ullmann, "Sex Differences in Feelings Attributed to a Woman in Situations Involving Coercion and Sexual Advances," *Journal of Personality* 47 (September 1979): 429–30.

38. Estrich has this problem in *Real Rape*.

39. E. Donnerstein, "Pornography: Its Effect on Violence against Women," in *Pornography and Sexual Aggression*, ed. N. Malamuth and E. Donnerstein (Orlando, Fla.: Academic Press, 1984), pp. 65–70. Readers who worry that this could become an argument for defending accused rapists should understand that the reality to which it points already provides a basis for defending accused rapists. The solution is to attack the pornography directly, not to be silent about its exonerating effects, legal or social, potential or actual.

3

Mothers, Monsters, and Machines

Rosi Braidotti

Figuring Out

I would like to approach the sequence "mothers, monsters, and machines" both thematically and methodologically, so as to work out possible connections between these terms. Because women, the biological sciences, and technology are conceptually interrelated, there can not be only one correct connection but, rather, many, heterogeneous and potentially contradictory ones.

The quest for multiple connections—or conjunctions—can also be rendered methodologically in terms of Donna Haraway's "figurations."[1] The term refers to ways of expressing feminist forms of knowledge that are not caught in a mimetic relationship to dominant scientific discourse. This is a way of marking my own difference: as an intellectual woman who has acquired and earned the right to speak publicly in an academic context, I have also inherited a tradition of female silence. Centuries of exclusion of women from the exercise of discursive power are ringing through my words. In speaking the language of man, I also intend to let the silence of woman echo gently but firmly; I shall not conform to the phallogocentric mode.[2] I want to question the status of feminist theory in terms not only of the conceptual tools and the gender-specific perceptions that govern the production of feminist research but also of the form our perceptions take.

The "nomadic" style is the best suited to the quest for feminist figurations, in the sense of adequate representations of female experience as that which cannot easily be fitted within the parameters of phallogocentric language.

The configuration of ideas I am trying to set up: mothers, monsters, machines, is therefore a case study— not only in terms of its propositional content but also in defining my place of enunciation and, therefore, my relationship to the readers who are my partners in this discursive game. It is a new figuration of feminist subjectivity.

Quoting Deleuze,[3] I would like to define this relationship as "rhizomatic"; that is to say not only cerebral, but related to experience, which implies a strengthened connection between thought and life, a renewed proximity of the thinking process to existential reality.[4] In my thinking, "rhizomatic" thinking leads to what I call a "nomadic" style.

Moreover, a "nomadic" connection is not a dualistic or oppositional way of thinking[5] but rather one that views discourse as a positive, multilayered network of power relations.[6]

Let me develop the terms of my nomadic network by reference to Foucauldian critiques of the power of discourse: he argues that the production of scientific knowledge works as a complex, interrelated network of truth, power, and desire, centered on the subject as a bodily entity. In a double movement that I find most politically useful, Foucault highlights both the normative foundations of theoretical reason and also the rational model of power. "Power" thus becomes the name for a complex set of interconnections, between the spaces where truth and knowledge are produced and the systems of control and domination. I shall unwrap my three interrelated notions in the light of this definition of power.

Last, but not least, this style implies the simultaneous dislocation not only of my place of enunciation as a feminist intellectual but also accordingly of the position of my readers. As my interlocutors I am constructing those readers to be "not just" traditional intellectuals and academics but also active, interested, and concerned participants in a project of research and experimentation for new ways of thinking about human subjectivity in general and female subjectivity in particular. I mean to appeal therefore not only to a requirement for passionless truth but also to a passionate engagement in the recognition of the theoretical and discursive implications of sexual difference. In this choice of a theoretical style that leaves ample room for the exploration of subjectivity, I am following the lead of Donna Haraway, whose plea for "passionate detachment" in theory making I fully share.[7]

Let us now turn to the thematic or propositional content of my constellation of ideas: mothers, monsters and machines.

For the sake of clarity, let me define them: "mothers" refers to the maternal function of women. By *WOMEN* I mean not only the biocultural entities thus represented, as the empirical subjects of sociopolitical realities, but also a discursive field: feminist theory. The kind of feminism I want to defend rests on the presence and the experience of real-life women whose political consciousness is bent on changing the institution of power in our society.

Feminist theory is a two-layered project involving the critique of existing definitions, representations as well as the elaboration of alternative theories about women. Feminism is the movement that brings into practice the dimension of sexual difference through the critique of gender as a power institution. Feminism is the question; the affirmation of sexual difference is the answer.

This point is particularly important in the light of modernity's imperative to think differently about our historical condition. The central question seems to be here: how can we *affirm* the positivity of female subjectivity at a time in history when our acquired perceptions of "the subject" are being radically questioned? How can we reconcile the recognition of the problematic nature of the notion and the construction of the subject with the political necessity to posit female subjectivity?

By *MACHINES* I mean the scientific, political, and discursive field of technology in the broadest sense of the term. Ever since Heidegger the philosophy of modernity has been trying to come to terms with technological reason. The Frankfurt School refers to it as "instrumental reason": one that places the end of its endeavors well above the means and suspends all judgment on its inner logic. In my work, as I mentioned in the previous chapter, I approach the technology issue from within the French tradition, following the materialism of Bachelard, Canguilhem, and Foucault.

By *MONSTERS* I mean a third kind of discourse: the history and philosophy of the biological sciences, and their relation to difference and to different bodies. Monsters are human beings who are born with congenital mal-

but is this historical or her pronouncement?

formations of their bodily organism. They also represent the in between, the mixed, the ambivalent as implied in the ancient Greek root of the word "monsters," *teras*, which means both horrible and wonderful, object of aberration and adoration. Since the nineteenth century, following the classification system of monstrosity by Geoffroy Saint-Hilaire, bodily malformations have been defined in terms of "excess," "lack," or "displacement of organs."[8] Before any such scientific classification was reached, however, natural philosophy had struggled to come to terms with these objects of abjection. The constitution of teratology as a science offers a paradigmatic example of the ways in which scientific rationality dealt with differences of the bodily kind.

The discourse on monsters as a case study highlights a question that seems to me very important for feminist theory: the status of difference within rational thought. Following the analysis of the philosophical ratio suggested by Derrida[9] and other contemporary French philosophers, it can be argued that Western thought has a logic of binary oppositions that treats difference as that which is other-than the accepted norm. The question then becomes: can we free difference from these normative connotations? Can we learn to think differently about difference?[10]

The monster is the bodily incarnation of difference from the basic human norm; it is a deviant, an a-nomaly; it is abnormal. As Georges Canguilhem points out, the very notion of the human body rests upon an image that is intrinsically prescriptive: a normally formed human being is the zero-degree of monstrosity. Given the special status of the monster, what light does he throw on the structures of scientific discourse? How was the difference of/in the monster perceived within this discourse?

When set alongside each other, mothers/monsters/machines may seem puzzling. There is no apparent connection among these three terms and yet the link soon becomes obvious if I add that recent developments in the field of biotechnology, particularly artificial procreation, have extended the power of science over the maternal body of women. The possibility of mechanizing the maternal function is by now well within our reach; the manipulation of life through different combinations of genetic engineering has allowed for the creation of new artificial monsters in the high-tech labs of our biochemists. There is therefore a political urgency about the future of women in the new reproductive technology debate, which gives a polemical force to my constellation of ideas—mothers, monsters, and machines.

The legal, economic, and political repercussions of the new reproductive technologies are far-reaching. The recent stand taken by the Roman Catholic church and by innumerable "bioethics committees" all across Western

Europe against experimentation and genetic manipulations may appear fair enough. They all invariably shift the debate, however, far from the power of science over the women's body in favor of placing increasing emphasis on the rights of the fetus or of embryos. This emphasis is played against the rights of the mother—and therefore of the woman—and we have been witnessing systematic slippages between the discourse against genetic manipulations and the rhetoric of the antiabortion campaigners. No area of contemporary technological development is more crucial to the construction of gender than the new reproductive technologies. The central thematic link I want to explore between mothers, monsters, and machines is therefore my argument that contemporary biotechnology displaces women by making procreation a high-tech affair.

Conjunction 1: Woman / Mother as Monster

As part of the discursive game of nomadic networking I am attempting here, let us start by associating two of these terms: let us superimpose the image of the woman/mother onto that of the monstrous body. In other words, let us take the case study of monsters, deviants, or anomalous entities as being paradigmatic of how differences are dealt with within scientific rationality. Why this association of femininity with monstrosity?

The association of women with monsters goes as far back as Aristotle who, in *The Generation of Animals*, posits the human norm in terms of bodily organization based on a male model. Thus, in reproduction, when everything goes according to the norm a boy is produced; the female only happens when something goes wrong or fails to occur in the reproductive process. The female is therefore an anomaly, a variation on the main theme of man-kind. The emphasis Aristotle places on the masculinity of the human norm is also reflected in his theory of conception: he argues that the principle of life is carried exclusively by the sperm, the female genital apparatus providing only the passive receptacle for human life. The sperm-centered nature of this early theory of procreation is thus connected to a massive masculine bias in the general Aristotelian theory of subjectivity. For Aristotle, not surprisingly, women are not endowed with a rational soul.[11]

The *topos* of women as a sign of abnormality, and therefore of difference as a mark of inferiority, remained a constant in Western scientific discourse. This association has produced, among other things, a style of misogynist literature with which anyone who has read *Gulliver's Travels* must be familiar: the

topos-horror of the female body. The interconnection of women as monsters with the literary text is particularly significant and rich in the genre of satire. In a sense, the satirical text is implicitly monstrous, it is a deviant, an aberration in itself. Eminently transgressive, it can afford to express a degree of misogyny that might shock in other literary genres.

Outside the literary tradition, however, the association of femininity with monstrosity points to a system of pejoration that is implicit in the binary logic of oppositions that characterizes the phallogocentric discursive order. The monstrous as the negative pole, the pole of pejoration, is structurally analogous to the feminine as that which is other-than the established norm, whatever the norm may be. The actual propositional content of the terms of opposition is less significant for me than its logic. Within this dualistic system, monsters are, just like bodily female subjects, a figure of devalued difference; as such, it provides the fuel for the production of normative discourse. If the position of women and monsters as logical operators in discursive production is comparable within the dualistic logic, it follows that the misogyny of discourse is not an irrational exception but rather a tightly constructed system that requires difference as pejoration in order to erect the positivity of the norm. In this respect, misogyny is not a hazard but rather the structural necessity of a system that can only represent "otherness" as negativity.

The theme of woman as devalued difference remained a constant in Western thought; in philosophy especially, "she" is forever associated to, unholy, disorderly, subhuman, and unsightly phenomena. It is as if "she" carried within herself something that makes her prone to being an enemy of mankind, an outsider in her civilization, an "other." It is important to stress the light that psychoanalytic theory has cast upon this hatred for the feminine and the traditional patriarchal association of women with monstrosity.

The woman's body can change shape in pregnancy and childbearing; it is therefore capable of defeating the notion of fixed *bodily form*, of visible, recognizable, clear, and distinct shapes as that which marks the contour of the body. She is morphologically dubious. The fact that the female body can change shape so drastically is troublesome in the eyes of the logocentric economy within which to see is the primary act of knowledge and *the gaze* the basis of all epistemic awareness.[12] The fact that the male sexual organ does, of course, change shape in the limited time span of the erection and that this operation—however precarious—is not exactly unrelated to the changes of shape undergone by the female body during pregnancy constitutes, in psychoanalytic theory, one of the fundamental axes of fantasy about sexual difference.

The appearance of symmetry in the way the two sexes work in reproduction merely brings out, however, the separateness and the specificity of each sexual organization. What looks to the naked eye like a comparable pattern: erection/pregnancy, betrays the ineluctable difference. As psychoanalysis successfully demonstrates, reproduction does not encompass the whole of human sexuality and for this reason alone anatomy is *not* destiny. Moreover, this partial analogy also leads to a sense of (false) anatomical complementarity between the sexes that contrasts with the complexity of the psychic representations of sexual difference. This double recognition of both proximity and separation is the breeding ground for the rich and varied network of misunderstandings, identifications, interconnections, and mutual demands that is what sexual human relationships are all about.

Precisely this paradoxical mixture of "the same and yet other" between the sexes generates a drive to denigrate woman in so far as she is "other-than" the male norm. In this respect hatred for the feminine constitutes the phallogocentric economy by inducing in both sexes the desire to achieve order, by means of a one-way pattern for both. As long as the law of the One is operative, so will be the denigration of the feminine, and of women with it.[13]

Woman as a sign of difference is monstrous. If we define the monster as a bodily entity that is anomalous and deviant vis-à-vis the norm, then we can argue that the female body shares with the monster the privilege of bringing out a unique blend of *fascination and horror*. This logic of attraction and repulsion is extremely significant; psychoanalytic theory takes it as the fundamental structure of the mechanism of desire and, as such, of the constitution of the neurotic symptom: the spasm of the hysteric turns to nausea, displacing itself from its object.

Julia Kristeva, drawing extensively on the research of Mary Douglas, connects this mixture[14] to the maternal body as the site of the origin of life and consequently also of the insertion into mortality and death. We are all of woman born, and the mother's body as the threshold of existence is both sacred and soiled, holy and hellish; it is attractive and repulsive, all-powerful and therefore impossible to live with. Kristeva speaks of it in terms of "abjection"; the abject arises in that gray, in between area of the mixed, the ambiguous. The monstrous or deviant is a figure of abjection in so far as it trespasses and transgresses the barriers between recognizable norms or definitions.

Significantly, the abject approximates the sacred because it appears to contain within itself a constitutive ambivalence where life and death are reconciled. Kristeva emphasizes the dual function of the maternal site as both life- and death-giver, as object of worship and of terror. The notion of the sacred is generated precisely by this blend of fascination and horror, which prompts an intense play of the imaginary, of fantasies and often nightmares about the ever-shifting boundaries between life and death, night and day, masculine and feminine, active and passive, and so forth.

In a remarkable essay about the head of the Medusa, Freud connected this logic of attraction and repulsion to the sight of female genitalia; because there is *nothing to see* in that dark and mysterious region, the imagination goes haywire. Short of losing his head, the male gazer is certainly struck by castration anxiety. For fear of losing the thread of his thought, Freud then turns his distress into the most overdetermined of all questions: "what does woman want?"

A post-Freudian reading of this text permits us to see how the question about female desire emerges out of male anxiety about the representation of sexual difference. In a more Lacanian vein, Kristeva adds an important insight: the female sex as the site of origin also inspires awe because of the psychic and cultural imperative to separate from the mother and accept the Law of the Father. The incest taboo, the fundamental law of our social system, builds on the mixture of fascination and horror that characterizes the feminine/maternal object of abjection. As the site of primary repression, and therefore that which escapes from representation, the mother's body becomes a turbulent area of psychic life.

Obviously, this analysis merely describes the mechanisms at work in our cultural system; no absolute necessity surrounds the symbolic absence of Woman. On the contrary, feminists have been working precisely to put into images that which escapes phallogocentric modes of representation. Thus, in her critique of psychoanalysis, Luce Irigaray points out that the dark continent of all dark continents is the mother-daughter relationship. She also suggests that, instead of this logic of attraction and repulsion, sexual difference may be thought out in terms of recognition and wonder. The latter is one of the fundamental passions in Descartes' treatise about human affectivity: he values it as the foremost of human passions, that which makes everything else possible. Why Western culture did not adopt this way of conceptualizing and experiencing difference and opted instead for difference as a sign of negativity remains a critical question for me.

It is because of this phallogocentric perversion that femininity and monstrosity can be seen as isomorphic. Woman/mother is monstrous by excess; she transcends established norms and transgresses boundaries. She is monstrous by lack: woman/mother does not possess the substantive unity of the masculine subject. Most important, through her identification with the feminine she is monstrous by displacement: as sign of the in between areas, of the indefinite, the ambiguous, the mixed, woman/mother is subjected to a constant process of metaphorization as "other-than."

In the binary structure of the logocentric system, "woman," as the eternal pole of opposition, the "other," can be assigned to the most varied and often contradictory terms. The only constant remains her "becoming-metaphor," whether of the sacred or the profane, of heaven or hell, of life or death. "Woman" is that which is assigned and has no power of self-definition. "Woman" is the anomaly that confirms the positivity of the norm.

Conjunction 2: Teratology and the Feminine

The history of teratology, or the science of monsters, demonstrates clearly the ways in which the body in general and the female body in particular have been conceptualized in Western scientific discourse, progressing from the fantastic dimension of the bodily organism to a more rationalistic construction of the body-machine. The monster as a human being born with congenital malformations undergoes a series of successive representations historically, before it gives rise, in the latter part of the eighteenth century, to an acceptable, scientific discourse.

The work of French epistemologist and philosopher of science Georges Canguilhem and of his disciple Michel Foucault is extremely useful in studying the modes of interaction of the normal and the pathological, the normative and the transgressive in Western philosophy. For Canguilhem, the stakes in theory of monstrosity are the questions of reproduction, of origins: "how can such monstrous creatures be conceived?" The conception of monsters is what really haunts the scientific imagination. Whereas psychoanalysts like Lacan and Irigaray argue that the epistem(ophil)ic question of the origin lies at the heart of *all* scientific investigation, Canguilhem is interested in providing the historical perspective on how the scientific discourse about monsters emerged. He argues that teratology became constituted as a discipline when it required the conceptual and technological means of mastering the pro/reproduction of monsters. In other words, the scientific and technological know-how necessary for the artificial reproduction of human anomalies is the precondition for the establishment of a scientific discipline concerned with abnormal beings.

This means that on the discursive level, the monster points out the major epistemological function played by anomalies, abnormalities, and pathology in the constitution of biological sciences. Historically, biologists have privileged phenomena that deviate from the norm, in order to exemplify the normal structure of development. In this respect the study of monstrous births is a forerunner of modern embryology. Biologists have set up abnormal cases in order to elucidate normal behavior; psychoanalysis will follow exactly the same logic for mental disorders. The proximity of the normal and the pathological demonstrates the point Foucault made in relation to madness and reason: scientific rationality is implicitly normative, it functions by exclusion and disqualification according to a dualistic logic.

The history of discourse about monsters conventionally falls into three chronological periods. In the first, the Greeks and Romans maintained a notion of a "race" of monsters, an ethnic entity possessing specific characteristics. They also relied on the notion of "abjection," seeing the monster not only as the sign of marvel but also of disorder and divine wrath. The practice of exposing monstrous children as unnatural creatures was inaugurated by the Greeks. Thus Oedipus himself—"swollen foot"—was not "normal," and his destruction should have been in the order of things.

More generally, classical mythology represents no founding hero, no main divine creature or demigod as being of woman born. In fact, one of the constant themes in the making of a god is his "unnatural" birth: his ability, through subterfuges such as immaculate conceptions and other tricks, to short-circuit the orifice through which most humans beings pop into the spatio-temporal realm of existence. The fantastic dimension of classical mythological discourse about monsters illustrates the paradox of aberration and adoration that I mentioned earlier, and it therefore inscribes an antimaternal dimension at the very heart of the matter.

We can make a further distinction between the baroque and enlightened or "scientific" discourses on monsters. In the sixteenth and seventeenth centuries, the monster still possesses the classical sense of something wonderful, fantastic, rare, and precious. Just like the madman, the dwarf and other marvels, it participates in the life of his/her town and enjoys certain privileges. For instance, dwarves as court jesters and fools can transgress social conventions, can say and do things that "normal" human beings cannot afford to say or do.

The imagination of the times runs wild as to the origins of monsters as objects of horror and fascination, as something both exceptional and ominous. The question of the origins of monsters accompanies the development of the medical sciences in the prescientific imagination; it conveys an interesting mixture of traditional superstitions and elements of reflection that will lead to a more scientific method of enquiry. Out of the mass of documentary evidence on this point, I will concentrate on one aspect that throws light on my question about the connection between monstrosity and the feminine. Ambroise Paré's treatise[15] on wondrous beings lists among the causes for their conception various forms of unnatural copulation ranging from bestiality to everyday forms of immorality, such as having sexual intercourse too often, or on a Sunday night (sic), or on the night of any major religious holiday. As a matter of fact, all sexual practices other than those leading to healthy reproduction are suspected to be conducive to monstrous events. Food can also play a major role; the regulation of diet is extremely important and implicitly connected to religious regulations concerning time, season and cycles of life.[16]

Bad weather can adversely affect procreation, as can an excess or a lack of semen; the devil also plays an important role, and he definitely interferes with normal human reproduction. Well may we laugh at such beliefs; many still circulate in rural areas of Western Europe. Besides, the whole fantastic discourse about the origins of monsters becomes considerably less amusing when we consider that women paid a heavy price for these wild notions. The history of women's relationship to "the devil" in Western Europe is a history too full of horrors for us to take these notions lightly.

It is not surprising, therefore, that the baroque mind gave a major role to the maternal imagination in procreation generally and in the conception of monsters particularly.[17] The mother was said to have the actual power of producing a monstrous baby simply by: (a) *thinking* about awful things during intercourse (it's the close-your-eyes-and-think-of-England principle); (b) *dreaming* very intensely about something or somebody; or (c) *looking* at animals or evil-looking creatures (this is the Xerox-machine complex: if a woman looked at a dog, for instance, with a certain look in her eyes, then she would have the power of transmitting that image to the fetus and reproducing it exactly, thus creating a dog-faced baby).

I let you imagine the intense emotion that struck a village in Northern France in the seventeenth century when a baby was born who looked remarkably like the local bishop. The woman defended herself by claiming gazing rights: she argued that she had stared at the male character in church with such intense devotion that … she xeroxed him away! She saved her life and proved the feminist theory that female gaze as the expression of female desire is always perceived as a dangerous, if not deadly, thing.

In other words, the mother's imagination is as strong as the force of nature; in order to assess this, one needs to appreciate the special role that the *imagination* plays in the seventeenth century theories of knowledge. It is a fundamental element in the classical worldview, and yet it is caught in great ambivalence: the imagination is the capacity to draw connections and consequently to construct ideas and yet it is potentially antirational.

The Cartesian *Meditations* are the clearest example of this ambivalence, which we find projected massively onto the power of the mother. She can direct the fetus to normal development or she can de-form it, un-do it, dehumanize it.

It is as if the mother, as a desiring agent, has the power to undo the work of legitimate procreation through the sheer force of her imagination. By deforming the product of the father, she cancels what psychoanalytic theory calls "the Name-of-the-Father." The female "signature" of the reproductive pact is unholy, inhuman, illegitimate, and it remains the mere pre-text to horrors to come. Isn't the product of woman's creativity always so?

This belief is astonishing however, when it is contextualized historically: consider that the debate between the Aristotelian theory of conception, with its sperm-centered view of things, and mother-centered notions of procreation, has a long history. The seventeenth century seems to have reached a paroxysm of hatred for the feminine; it inaugurated a flight from the female body in a desire to master the woman's generative powers.

Very often feminist scholars have taken this point as a criticism of classical rationalism, especially in the Cartesian[18] form, far too provocatively. The feminist line has been "I think therefore *he* is," thus emphasizing the male-centered view of human nature that is at work in this discourse. Whatever Descartes' responsibility for the flight from womanhood may be—and I maintain that it should be carefully assessed—for the purpose of my research what matters is the particular form that this flight took in the seventeenth century.

Conjunction 3: The Fantasy of Male-Born Children

The flight from and rejection of the feminine can also be analyzed from a different angle: the history of the biological sciences in the prescientific era, especially the sixteenth and seventeenth centuries. I argue that the flight from the feminine, and particularly from the monstrous power of the maternal imagination and desire, lies at the heart of the recurring fantasy of a child born from man alone.

We find, for instance, alchemists busy at work to try to produce the philosopher's son—the homunculus, a man-made tiny man popping out of the alchemists' laboratories, fully formed and endowed with language. The alchemists' imagination pushes the premises of the Aristotelian view of procreation to an extreme, stressing the male role in reproduction and minimizing the female function to the role of a mere carrier. Alchemy is a *reductio ad absurdum* of the male fantasy of self-reproduction.

How can a child be of man born? In a recent article, S. G. Allen and J. Hubbs[19] argue that alchemical symbolism rests on a simple process—the appropriation of the womb by male "art," that is to say the artifact of male techniques. Paracelsus, the master theoretician of alchemy, is certain that a man should and could be born outside a woman's body. Womb envy, alias the envy for the matrix or the uterus, reaches paradoxical dimensions in these texts—art being more powerful than nature itself.

The recipe is quite simple, as any reader of *Tristram Shandy* will know. It consists of a mixture of sperm and something to replace the uterus, such as the alchemist's jars and other containers so efficiently described in Mary Shelley's *Frankenstein*. At other times the matrix is replaced by an ox-hide, or by a mere heap of compost or manure. The basic assumption is that the alchemists can not only imitate the work of woman, they can also do it much better because the artifact, the artificial process of science and technique, perfects the imperfection of the natural course of events and thus avoids mistakes. Once reproduction becomes the pure result of mental efforts, the appropriation of the feminine is complete.

On the imaginary level, therefore, the test-tube babies of today mark the long-term triumph of the alchemists' dream of dominating nature through their self-inseminating, masturbatory practices. What is happening with the new reproductive technologies today is the final chapter in a long history of fantasy of self-generation by and for the men themselves—men of science, but men of the male kind, capable of producing new monsters and fascinated by their power.

Ever since the mid nineteenth century, the abnormal monstrous beings, which had been objects of wonder, have fallen prey to the massive medicalization of scientific discourse. The marvelous, imaginary dimension of the monster is forgotten in the light of the new technologies of the body. Michel Foucault's analysis of modern rationality describes the fundamental shift that has taken place in scientific discourse of the modern era.

By the late eighteenth century, the monster has been transferred to hospital or rather, to the newly established institution of the anatomy clinic, where it could be analyzed in the context of the newly evolved practice of comparative anatomy and experimental biomedicine. Thus is born the science of teratology. Founded by G. Saint-Hilaire, by the end of the century it had become an experimental science. Its aim was to study malformations of the embryo so as to understand in the light of evolutionary theory the genesis of monstrous beings. Notice that the initial curiosity as to the origin of such horrendous creatures remains, but it is expressed differently.

The experimental study of the conditions that would lead to the production of anomalous or monstrous beings provides the basic epistemological structure of modern embryology. Foucault's analysis of modernity emphasizes the epistemological shifts between the normal and the pathological, reason and madness, in terms of the understanding of the body, the bodily roots of human subjectivity. The biomedical sciences occupy a very significant place in the discursive context of modernity.

Two institutions of learning appear in the modern era—the clinic and the hospital. The appearance of these structures is in turn related to a major theoretical breakthrough—the medical practice of anatomy. In Foucault's archaeological mode, for comparative clinical anatomy to come into being as a scientific discourse, a century-old taboo had to be lifted, the one that forbade the dissection of corpses for the purpose of scientific investigation.

Western culture had respected a fundamental taboo of the body up until then—the medical gaze could not explore the inside of the human body because the bodily container was considered as a metaphysical entity, marked by the secrets of life and death that pertain to the divine being. The anatomical study of the body was therefore forbidden until the fifteenth century and after then was strictly controlled. The nineteenth century sprang open the doors of bodily perception; clinical anatomy thus implies a radical transformation in the epistemological status of the body. It is a practice that consists in deciphering the body, transforming the organism into a text to be read and interpreted by a knowledgeable medical gaze.

Anatomy as a theoretical representation of the body implies that the latter is a clear and distinct configuration, a visible and intelligible structure. The dead body, the corpse, becomes the measure of the living being, and death thus becomes one of the factors epistemologically integrated into scientific knowledge.

Today, the right to scrutinize the inside of the body for scientific purposes is taken for granted, although dissections and the transferal of organs as a practice are strictly regulated by law. As a matter of fact, contemporary molecular biology is making visible the most intimate and minute fires of life.

Where has the Cartesian passion of wonder gone? When compared to the earlier tradition, the medicalization of the body in the age of modernity and its corollary, the perfectibility of the living organism and the gradual abolition of anomalies, can also be seen—though not exclusively—as a form of denial of the sense of wonder, of the fantastic, of that mixture of fascination and horror I have already mentioned. It marks the loss of fascination about the living organism, its mysteries and functions.

Psychoanalytic theory has explained this loss of fascination as the necessary toll that rational theory takes on human understanding. In the psychoanalytic perspective, of Freudian and Lacanian inspiration, the initial curiosity that prompts the drive and the will to know is first and foremost *desire*, which takes knowledge as its object.

The desire to know is, like all desires, related to the problem of representing one's origin, of answering the most childish and consequently fundamental of questions: "where did I come from?" This curiosity, as I stated in the previous chapter, is the matrix for all forms of thinking and conceptualization. Knowledge is always the desire to know about desire, that is to say about things of the body as a sexual entity.

Scientific knowledge becomes, in this perspective, an extremely perverted version of that original question. The desire to go and see how things work is related to primitive sadistic drives, so that, somewhere along the line, the scientist is like the anxious little child who pulls apart his favorite toy to see how it's made inside. Knowing in this mode is the result of the scopophilic drive—to go and see, and the sadistic one—to rip it apart physically so as to master it intellectually. All this is related to the incestuous drive, to the web of curiosity and taboos surrounding the one site of certain origin—the mother's body.

From a psychoanalytic perspective the establishment of clinical comparative anatomy in the modern era is very significant because it points out the rationalistic obsession with visibility, which I have analyzed earlier. Seeing is the prototype of knowing. By elaborating a scientific technique for analyzing the bodily organs, Western sciences put forward the assumption that a body is precisely that which can be seen and looked at, no more than the sum of its parts. Modern scientific rationality slipped from the emphasis on visibility to the mirage of absolute transparence of the living organism, as I have argued previously.

Contemporary biological sciences, particularly molecular biology, have pushed to the extreme these assumptions that were implicit in the discourse of Western sciences. When compared to the clinical anatomy of the nineteenth century, contemporary biomedical sciences have acquired the right and the know-how necessary to act on the very structure of the living matter, on an infinitely small scale.

Foucault defined the modern era as that of biopower; power over life and death in a worldwide extension of man's control of outer space, of the bottom of the oceans as well as of the depths of the maternal body. There are no limits today for what can be shown, photographed, reproduced—even a technique such as echography perpetuates this pornographic re-presentation of bodily parts, externalizing the interior of the womb and its content.

The proliferation of images is such that the very notion of the body, of its boundaries and its inner structure is being split open in an everregressing vision. We seem to be hell bent on xeroxing even the invisible particles of matter.

Philosophers of science, such as Kuhn and Fayarabend, have stressed the modern predicament in scientific discourse. Kuhn points out the paradoxical coincidence of extreme rationalism of the scientific and technological kind, with a persisting subtext of wild fantastic concoctions. In the discourse of monstrosity, rational enquiries about their origin and structure continue to coexist with superstitious beliefs and fictional representations of "creeps." The two registers of the rational and the totally nonrational seem to run alongside each other, never quite joined together.

The question nevertheless remains—where has the wonder gone? What has happened to the fantastic dimension, to the horror and the fascination of difference? What images were created of the bodily marks of difference, after they became locked up in the electronic laboratories of the modern alchemists?

Was there another way, other than the phallogocentric incompetence with, and antipathy to, differences—its willful reduction of otherness, to negativity? Is there another way out, still?

Conjunction 4: The Age of Freaks

As the Latin etymology of the term *monstrum* points out, malformed human beings have always been the object of display, subjected to the public gaze. In his classic study, *Freaks*, Leslie Fiedler[20] analyses the exploitation of monsters for purposes of entertainment. From the county fairs, right across rural Europe to the Coney Island sideshows, freaks have always been entertaining.

Both Fiedler and Bogdan[21] stress two interrelated aspects of the display of freaks since the turn of the century. The first is that their exhibition displays racist and orientalist undertones: abnormally formed people were exhibited alongside tribal people of normal stature and bodily configuration, as well as exotic animals.

Second, the medical profession benefited considerably by examining these human exhibits. Although the freak is presented as belonging to the realm of zoology or anthropology, doctors and physicians examined them regularly and wrote scientific reports about them.

Significantly, totalitarian regimes such as Hitler's Germany or the Stalinist Soviet Union prohibited the exhibition of freaks as being degenerate specimens of the human species. They also dealt with them in their campaigns for eugenics and race or ethnic hygiene, by preventing them from breeding.

Fiedler sees a connection between the twentieth-century medicalization of monsters, the scientific appropriation of their generative secrets, and an increased commodification of the monster as freak, that is, the object of display.

Contemporary culture deals with anomalies by a fascination for the freaky. The film *Freaks* by Tod Browning (1932) warns us that monsters are an endangered species. Since the sixties a whole youth culture has developed around freaks, with special emphasis on genetic mutation as a sign of nonconformism and social rebellion. Whole popular culture genres such as science fiction, horror, rock'n'roll comics, and cyberpunk are about mutants.

Today, the freaks are science fiction androids, cyborgs, bionic women and men, comparable to the grotesque of former times; the whole rock'n'roll scene is a huge theater of the grotesque, combining freaks, androgynes, satanies, ugliness, and insanity, as well as violence.

In other words, in the early part of our century we watch the simultaneous formalization of a scientific discourse about monsters and their elimination as a problem. This process, which falls under the rationalist aggression of scientific discourse, also operates a shift at the level of representation, and of the cultural imaginary. The dimension of the "fantastic," that mixture of aberration and adoration, loathing and attraction, which for centuries has escorted the existence of strange and difficult bodies, is now displaced. The "becoming freaks" of monsters both deflates the fantastic projections that have surrounded them and expands them to a wider cultural field. The whole of contemporary popular culture is about freaks, just as the last of the physical freaks have disappeared. The last metaphorical shift in the status of monsters—their becoming freaks—coincides with their elimination.

In order not to be too pessimistic about this aspect of the problem, however, I wish to point out that the age of the commodification of freaks is also the period that has resulted in another significant shift: abnormally formed people have organized themselves in the handicapped political movement, thereby claiming not only a renewed sense of dignity but also wider social and political rights.[22]

In Transit; or, for Nomadism

Mothers, monsters, and machines. What is the connection, then? What con/dis-junctions can we make in telling the tale of feminism, science, and technology? How do feminist fabulations or figurations help in figuring out alternative paradigms? To what extent do they speak the language of sexual difference? Where do we situate ourselves in order to create links, construct theories, elaborate hypotheses? Which way do we look to try and see the possible impact modern science will have on the status of women? How do we assess the status of difference as an ontological category at the end of the twentieth century? How do we think about all this?

The term "trandisciplinary" can describe one position taken by feminists. Passing in between different discursive fields, and through diverse spheres of intellectual discourse. The feminist theoretician today can only be "in transit," moving on, passing through, creating connections where things were previously dis-connected or seemed un-related, where there seemed to be "nothing to see." In transit, moving, dis-placing—this is the grain of hysteria without which there is no theorization at all.[23] In a feminist context it also implies the effort to move on to the invention of new ways of relating, of building footbridges between notions. The epistemic nomadism I am advocating can only work, in fact, if it is properly situated, securely anchored in the "in between" zones.

I am assuming here a definition of "rigor" away from the linear Aristotelian logic that dominated it for so long. It seems to me that the rigor feminists are after is of a different kind—it is the rigor of a project that emphasizes the necessary interconnection-connections between the theoretical and the political, which insists on putting real-life experience first and foremost as a criterion for the validation of truth. It is the rigor of passionate investment in a project and in the quest of the discursive means to realize it.

In this respect feminism acts as a reminder that in the postmodern predicament, rationality in its classical mode can no longer be taken as representing the totality of human reason or even of the all-too-human activity of thinking.

By criticizing the single-mindedness and the masculine bias of rationality I do not intend to fall into the opposite and plead for easy ready-made irrationalism. Patriarchal thought has for too long confined women in the irrational for me to claim such a non-quality. What we need instead is a redefinition of what we have learned to recognize as being the structure and the aims of human subjectivity in its relationship to difference, to the "other."

In claiming that feminists are attempting to redefine the very meaning of thought, I am also suggesting that in time the rules of the discursive game will have to change. Academics will have to agree that thinking adequately about our historical condition implies the transcendence of disciplinary boundaries and intellectual categories.

More important, for feminist epistemologists, the task of thinking adequately about the historical conditions that affect the medicalization of the maternal function forces upon us the need to reconsider the inextricable interconnection of the bodily with the technological. The shifts that have taken place in the perception and the representation of the embodied subject, in fact, make it imperative to think the unity of body and machine, flesh and metal. Although many factors point to the danger of commodification of the body that such a mixture makes possible, and although this process of commodification conceals racist and sexist dangers that must not be underestimated, this is not the whole story. There is also a positive side to the new interconnection of mothers, monsters, and machines, and this has to do with the loss of any essentialized definition of womanhood—or indeed even of motherhood. In the age of biotechnological power motherhood is split open into a variety of possible physiological, cultural, and social functions. If this were the best of all possible worlds, one could celebrate the decline of one consensual way of experiencing motherhood as a sign of increased freedom for women. Our world being as male-dominated as it is, however, the best option is to construct a *nomadic* style of feminism that will allow women to rethink their position in a postindustrial, post-metaphysical world, without nostalgia, paranoia, or false sentimentalism. The relevance and political urgency of the configuration "mothers, monsters and machines" makes it all the more urgent for the feminist nomadic thinkers of the world to connect and to negotiate new boundaries for female identity in a world where power over the body has reached an implosive peak.

I fail to see how this nomadicism is demonstrated in 95% of this article

NOTES

I wish to thank Margaret R. Higonnet, of the Center for European Studies at Harvard, and Sissel Lie, of the Women's Research Center at Tronheim, Norway, for their helpful comments on an earlier draft of this paper.

1. Donna Haraway, "'Gender' for a Marxist Dictionary: The Sexual Politics of a Word," in *Simians, Cyborgs, and Women*, pp. 127–48 (London: Free Association Books, 1991).

2. For an enlightening and strategic usage of the notion of "mimesis," see Luce Irigaray, *Ce sexe qui n'en est pas un* (Paris: Minuit, 1977).

3. To refer to the concept elaborated by the French philosopher of difference, see Gilles Deleuze in collaboration with Felix Guattari, *Rhizome* (Paris: Minuit, 1976).

4. The notion of "experience" has been the object of intense debates in feminist theory. See for example, Teresa de Lauretis, *Alice Doesn't* (Bloomington: Indiana University Press, 1984); Sandra Harding, *The Science Question in Feminism* (London: Open University, 1986), and *Feminism and Methodology* (London: Open University, 1987); Joan Scott, "Experience," in Joan Scott and Judith Butler, eds., *Feminists Theorize the Political* (London and New York: Routledge, 1992), pp. 22–40.

5. Genevieve Lloyd, *The Man of Reason* (London: Methuen, 1985).

6. Cf. Michel Foucault, *L'ordre du discours* (Paris: Gallimard, 1971); *Surveiller et punir* (Paris: Gallimard, 1975); "Les intellectuels et le pouvoir," *L'Arc*, no. 49 (1972).

7. This expression, originally coined by Laura Mulvey in film criticism, has been taken up and developed by Donna Haraway in a stunning exploration of this intellectual mode; see "Situated Knowledges: The Science Question in Feminism and the Privilege of Partial Perspective," and "A Cyborg Manifesto: Science, Technology, and Socialist-Feminism in the Late Twentieth Century," in *Simians, Cyborgs, and Women*, pp. 183–202 and 127–48.

8. I explored this notion of monstrosity at some length in a seminar held jointly with Marie-Jo Dhavernas at the College international de Philosophie in Paris in 1984–1985. The report of the sessions was published in *Cahier du College International de Philosophie*, no. 1 (1985): 42–45.

9. See Jacques Derrida, *L'écriture et al différence* (Paris: Seuil, 1967); *Marges de la philosophie* (Paris: Minuit, 1972); *La carte postale* (Paris: Flammarion, 1980).

10. On this point, see Alice Jardine, *Gynesis: Configurations of Woman in Modernity*, (Ithaca: Cornell University Press, 1984).

11. For a feminist critique of Aristotle, see Sandra Harding and Maryl Hintikka, eds., *Discovering Reality* (Boston: Reidel, 1983).

12. The most enlightening philosophical analysis of the scopophilic mode of scientific knowledge is Michel Foucault's *Naissance de la clinique* (Paris: Gallimard, 1963).

13. This is the fundamental starting point for the work of feminist philosopher of sexual difference Luce Irigaray; see, for instance *L'éthique de la différence sexuelle* (Paris: Minuit, 1984).

14. Julia Kristeva, *Pouvoirs de l'horreur* (Paris: Seuil, 1980).

15. Ambroise Paré, *Des monstres et prodiges* (1573; Geneva: Droz, 1971).

16. The second and third volume of Foucault's *History of Sexuality* (New York: Pantheon, 1987–1988) outline quite clearly all these regulations in the art of existence.

17. Pierre Darmon, *Le mythe de la procreation à l'âge baroque,* (Paris: Seuil, 1981).

18. See for instance Susan Bordo, "The Cartesian Masculinization of Thought," *Signs* 11, no. 3 (1986); Evelyn Fox Keller, *Reflections on Gender and Science* (New Haven: Yale University Press, 1985).

19. S. G. Allen and J. Hubbs, "Outrunning Atlanta: Destiny in Alchemical Transmutation," *Signs* 6, no. 2 (Winter 1980): 210–29.

20. Leslie Fiedler, *Freaks* (New York: Simon & Schuster, 1978).

21. Robert Bogdan, *Freak Show* (Chicago and London: University of Chicago Press 1988).

22. David Hevey, ed., *The Creatures Time Forgot: Photography and Disability Imagery* (London and New York: Routledge, 1992).

23. As Monique David-Menard argues in *L'Hystérique entre Freud et Lacan* (Paris: Ed. Universitaire, 1983).

4

Corporeal Representation in/and the Body Politic

Moira Gatens

The rather awkward title of this paper is intended to draw attention to an ambiguity in the term "representation" as it is used in political theory. First, I want to focus on the construction of the *image* of the modern body politic. This involves examining the claim that the body politic is constituted by a creative act, by a work of art or artifice, that uses the human body as its model or metaphor. The background to this claim is provided by certain seventeenth- and eighteenth-century social contract theorists who argued in favor of the conventionality or artificiality of monarchical political authority.[1] If such authority is neither natural nor God-given but rather based on agreement and convention then it is mutable. The way the metaphor of the body functions here is by analogy. Just as man can be understood as a representation of God's creative power, so the political

Moira Gatens, "Corporeal Representation in/and the Body Politic." Originally appeared in *Cartographies: Poststructuralism and the Mapping of Bodies and Spaces*, edited by Rosalyn Disprose and Robyn Ferrel, 1991. Reprinted with permission from Allen and Unwin Press.

body can be understood as a representation of man's creative power, that is, as *art(ifice)*.

The second sense of "representation" surfaces when considering whose body it is that is entitled to be represented by this political corporation. This involves understanding "representation" in the sense where one body or agent is taken to stand for a group of diverse bodies. Here we are considering the metonymical representation of a complex body by a privileged part of that body. The metaphor here slides into metonymy. The relevant background literature to this question is provided by various texts, from the seventeenth century on, concerning the natural authority of men over women and the propriety of taking the male head of households as representative of the concerns of the entire household.[2]

The first use of "representation"—what I have called the metaphorical—concerns the way in which this image effects who is represented by the body politic. To address the first strand—the metaphorical—I will begin with a quotation from a mid-seventeenth-century text that posits, in a manner typical of the period, a detailed correspondence between the parts and functions of the human body and the parts and functions of the political body. The text is the *Leviathan*, the author is Thomas Hobbes. He writes:

> by art is created that great LEVIATHAN called a COMMONWEALTH, or STATE, in Latin CIVITAS, which is but an artificial man; though of greater stature and strength than the natural, for whose protection and defence it was intended; and in which the *sovereignty* is an artificial *soul*, as giving life and motion to the whole body; the *magistrates*, and other *officers* of judicature and execution, artificial *joints*; *reward* and *punishment*, by which fastened to the seat of the sovereignty every joint and member is moved to perform his duty, are the *nerves*, that do the same in the body natural; and *wealth* and *riches* of all the particular members are the *strength*; *salus populi*, the people's safety, its *business*; *counsellors*, by whom all things needful for it to know are suggested unto it, are the *memory*; *equity* and *laws*, an artificial *reason* and *will*; *concord*, *health*; *sedition*, *sickness*; and civil war, death. Lastly the *pacts* and *covenants*, by which the parts of this body politic were at first made, set together, and united, resemble that *fiat*, or the *let us make man*, pronounced by God in the creation.[3]

I want to draw attention to two important aspects of the view Hobbes offers. First, Hobbes claims that the motivation behind the creation of the artificial

man is the "protection" or "defence" of natural man. We may well wonder
from whom or what natural man requires protection. Hobbes's answer is that
he requires protection from other men and from nature. Man, in a state of
nature, he tells us, is in "continual fear" and in "danger of violent death" and
the quality of his life is summed up with the words "solitary, poor, nasty,
brutish, and short."[4] The second thing I want to highlight is the *fiat*, the
Godlike pronouncement, that breathes life into the political body. For
Hobbes this *fiat* refers to the pacts and covenants made by men between
men. These demigods, whose speech has such awesome creative power, do
not go on, in Godlike fashion, to create an artificial Eve. Perhaps the sons can
learn from the father's mistakes, after all.

The artificial man, a creation of "the word" of men united, thus renders itself
free from the necessary but difficult dealings with both women and nature. This
masculine image of unity and independence from women and nature has
strong resonances in psychoanalytic accounts of infantile anxieties and the fantasies created to cope with them.[5] The image of artificial man, the body politic,
perfectly mirrors the infantile wish for independence from the maternal body.
It is a fantasy that can be found in mythology too. Classical Athens, often considered to be the first true body politic, is named after Athena who was born
not "of woman" but "of man": she sprang from the head of Zeus. Athens is
named after Athena as a tribute to her for ridding that city of its "uncivilized"
divinities. When she relegates the feminine Furies to the subterranean regions
of Athens, she confirms the masculinity of the Athenian political body. Like
Hobbes's artificial man, she is the product of man's reason; she has no mother.
Or has she? An often neglected part of this myth is that Zeus "gave birth" to
Athena only after he had swallowed whole the body of his pregnant wife.

In the absence of a female leviathan, natural woman is left unprotected,
undefended, and so is easy prey for the monstrous masculine leviathan. Like
the hapless Jonah, she dwells in the belly of the artificial man, swallowed
whole, made part of the corporation not by pact, nor by covenant, but by
incorporation. The modern body politic has "lived off" its consumption of
women's bodies. Women have serviced the internal organs and needs of this
artificial body, preserving its viability, its unity and integrity, without ever
being seen to do so.

The metaphor of the unified body functions, in political theory, to achieve
two important effects. First, the artificial man incorporates and so controls
and regulates women's bodies in a manner which does not undermine his
claim to autonomy, since her contributions are neither visible nor acknowledged. Second, insofar as he can maintain this apparent unity through incor-

poration, he is not required to acknowledge difference. The metaphor functions to restrict our political vocabulary to one voice only: a voice that can speak of only *one* body, *one* reason, and *one* ethic.

Perhaps the metaphor of the human body is an obvious way of describing political life; so obvious that the metaphor passes into common usage, no longer mindful of its origins. If this is the case then perhaps it seems far-fetched to argue that the conception of the body politic is anthropomorphic. Yet, there is a sense in which the image of the polity is anthropomorphic if we limit this claim to a literal, or etymological, understanding of "anthropos," which means "man." This leads me into the second strand of the use of "representation" in modern political theory—the metonymical.

Here we need to consider *who* is represented by this image of bodily unity. Certainly not any human form, by virtue of its humanity, is entitled to consider itself author of or actor in the body politic. From its classical articulation in Greek philosophy, only a body deemed capable of reason and sacrifice can be admitted into the political body as an active member. Such admission always involves *forfeit*. From the original covenant between God and Abraham— which involved the forfeit of his very flesh, his foreskin—corporeal sacrifice has been a constant feature of the compact. Even the Amazons, the only female body politic that we "know" of, practiced ritual mastectomy. *contested point*

At different times, different kinds of beings have been excluded from the pact, often simply by virtue of their corporeal specificity. Slaves, foreigners, women, the conquered, children, the working classes, have all been excluded from political participation, at one time or another, by their bodily specificity. Could the common denominator of these exclusions be "those incapable of fulfilling the appropriate forfeit"? That is, those whose corporeal specificity marks them as inappropriate analogs to the political body. Constructing women as incapable of performing military service and so incapable of defending the political body from attack could serve as an example here. This incapacity, constructed or not, is sufficient to exclude her from active citizenship. At this level the metonymical aspects of the metaphor of the body function to exclude. Those who are not capable of the appropriate political forfeit are excluded from political and ethical relations. They are defined by *mere* nature, *mere* corporeality and they have no place in the semidivine political body except to serve it at its most basic and material level. To explain how the metonymical aspects of the image of the body politic function to exclude it is necessary to examine this image of bodily unity in greater detail.

Discourses which employ the image of the unified political body assume that the metaphor of the human body is a coherent one, and of course it's not. At least I have never encountered an image of a *human* body. Images of human bodies are images of either men's bodies or women's bodies. A glance at any standard anatomical text offers graphic evidence of the problem with this phrase: "the human body." Representations of the human body are most often of the male body and, perhaps, around the borders, one will find insets of representations of the female reproductive system: a lactating breast, a vagina, ovaries; bits of bodies, body-fragments. They appear there in a way that reminds one of specialized pornographic magazines which show pictures of isolated, fragmented, disjointed bits: breasts, vaginas, behinds. Female-bits, fragments to be consumed, devoured a bit at a time.

This imaging has its correlate in political theory. Recent feminist work has shown that the neutral body, assumed by the liberal state, is implicitly a masculine body.[6] Our legal and political arrangements have man as the model, the centerpiece, with the occasional surrounding legislative insets concerning abortion, rape, maternity allowance, and so on. None of these insets, however, take female embodiment seriously. It is still the exception, the deviation, confined literally to the margins of man's representations. It is still "anthropos" who is taken to be capable of representing the universal type, the universal body. Man is the model and it is his body which is taken for the human body; his reason which is taken for Reason; his morality which is formalized into a system of ethics.

In our relatively recent history, the strategies for silencing those who have dared to speak in another voice, of another reason and another ethic, are instructive. Here I will mention two strategies that seem to be dominant in the history of feminist interventions. The first is to "animalize" the speaker, the second, to reduce her to her "sex." Women who step outside their allotted place in the body politic are frequently abused with terms like: harpy, virago, vixen, bitch, shrew; terms that make it clear that if she attempts to speak from the political body, about the political body, her speech is not recognized as *human* speech. When Mary Wollstonecraft, for example, had the audacity to address the issue of women's political rights,[7] Walpole called her a "hyena in petticoats." The strategy of reducing woman to her "sex" involves treating her speech and her behavior as hysterical. The root of "hysteria" is the Greek "hystera," meaning uterus. Disorder created by women, in the political body, is thus retranslated into a physical disorder thought to be inherent in the female sex.

Both these strategies insist on the difference between the image of the political body and the image of woman's body. However, it is a difference which is interpreted as evidence of woman's inadequacy in the political sphere. But, perhaps this difference no longer exists. After all, women are now admitted to the public sphere, they participate in politics, and sometimes, they even become Prime Ministers. However, to say this would be to miss the point. It is true that if women want to escape from the dreary cycles of repetition in the private sphere, then often they can. If they want to escape from the hysteria and mutism of domestic confinement, then often they can. But at what cost? We can be "cured" of mere animal existence by "becoming men"; "cured" of hysteria by "hysterectomy."

I am willing to concede that the metaphor of the body politic is quite anachronistic and precariously anchored in present political and social practices. This body has been fragmented and weakened by successive invasions from the excluded: the slaves, the foreigners, the women, the working class; but this does not imply that we presently have a polymorphous body politic. Certainly, the last two to three hundred years have witnessed the removal of many formal barriers and formal methods of exclusion, but there is a lot more to be said about methods of exclusion than formalized principles of equity can address. If woman, for example, speaks from this body, she is limited in what she can say. If she lives by this reason and this ethic, she lives still from the body of another: an actress, still a body-bit, a mouthpiece.

It is not clear to me, taking into account the history of the constitution of this body politic, that it can accommodate anything but the same. I have suggested that the modern body politic is based on an image of a *masculine* body which reflects fantasies about the value and capacities of that body. The effects of this image shows its contemporary influence in our social and political behavior, which continues to implicitly accord privilege to particular bodies and their concerns as they are reflected in our ways of speaking and in what we speak about. It refuses to admit anyone who is not capable of miming its reason and its ethics, in its voice. Its political language has no vocabulary and no space for the articulation of certain questions. Our political body continues to assume that its active members are free from the tasks of reproduction, free from domestic work, free from any desires other than those "whispered" to it by one of its Hobbesian "counsellors" or "willed" in it by one of its laws. All this body can address is questions of access to "predefined" positions and "preconstituted" points of power or authority. It cannot address the question of *how* or in what manner one occupies these points or positions. Nor can it address the limiting conditions, dictated by the corporeal specificity of the occupant, on the possible actions open to that occupant. What it cannot address is how different bodies "fill" the same "empty" social or political space. I wonder, in this context, whether the withdrawal of

Pat Schroeder from the U.S. Presidential candidacy was related to this problem. She said, in her speech, that she was withdrawing because she could not "figure out" how to occupy the political sphere without turning over her desires, behavior, and plans to predetermined meanings which were at odds with her own intentions.

I would suggest that this problem is, at least partly, related to the continuing fascination that we have for the image of the one body. It is an image that belongs to a dream of equity, based on corporeal interchangeability, that was developed to the full in nineteenth-century liberalism. And it is a "dream of men." Women, and others, were not copartners in this dream and to attempt to join it at this late stage is as futile as trying to share someone's psychosis. The socially shared psychosis of egalitarianism was constructed to deal with a specific problem: to diffuse the power structure of seventeenth- and eighteenth-century politics. This fantasy of the modern body politic, constituted by "the word" of men united, is not appropriate to women, and others, who were specifically excluded from it. For these "others," who have never experienced the satisfaction of having their image reflected back to themselves "whole" or "complete," the fascination with this dream is not so binding. The cultural ego-ideal was never something that they could live up to without a massive act of bad faith. But what are the alternatives?

If what one is fascinated by is the image of one body, one voice, one reason, any deviation takes the form of gibberish. If woman speaks from her body, with her voice, who can hear? Who can decipher the language of an hysteric, the wails of a hyena, the jabbering of a savage—apart from other hysterics, hyenas, and savages? Our political vocabulary is so limited that it is not possible, within its parameters, to raise the kinds of questions that would allow the articulation of bodily difference: it will not tolerate an embodied speech.

The impotence of our political vocabulary leads me to suggest that the more appropriate sphere for a consideration of these questions may be the ethical. And here I am using "ethical" in a sense perhaps long forgotten, where ethics is crucially concerned with the specificity of one's embodiment. It is certainly a pre-Kantian notion.[8] It is prior to the ever-narrowing *political* organization of ethics and prior to the conceptualization of ethics as reducible to a set of universal principles, dictated by reason (whose reason?). It is opposed to any system of ethics which elevates itself from a contingent form of life to the pretension of being the *one* necessary form of life. The most a universal ethic will permit is the *expansion* of the one body. Under pressure from its own insistence on equity, it may be forced to admit women, slaves, and others. It will not, however, tolerate the positing of a second, or a third, or a fourth body. Prime Minister Hawke's courting of the Aboriginal land rights movement prior to the Australian Bicentennial celebrations in 1988, could provide an example of my point here. He wanted to take the body politic off to the beauty parlor so it would look its best for its big birthday party. An important component of this beauty treatment involved attending to the blemishes on this body caused by the history of its abuse of Aboriginal bodies. It is instructive that Hawke wanted to "make up" by calling for a *compact*, a term that is more at home in seventeenth-century political texts. The term carries connotations of an agreement between equals, between like beings, to join as a single body. Some Aborigines, on the other hand, called for a *treaty*, a term that carries connotations of an agreement between unlike beings to respect each other's differences. It also implies a demand for the recognition of *two* bodies. Hawke resisted a treaty because this would be to recognize another voice, another body, and this raises the deepest fears. To recognize another body is to be open to *dialog*, debate and engagement with the other's law and the other's ethics.

It seems important, if the possibility of dialog and engagement is to be opened up, that feminist politics recognize the futility of continuing to ask to be fully admitted into this fantasy of unity. This would be to stop asking of that body that it be "host," since for women this would be to ask how can I live off myself—how can I engage in self-cannibalism? I would rather want to raise the question: whose body is this? How many metamorphoses has it undergone? and what possible forms could it take? And in responding to these questions it seems crucial to resist the temptation, noticeable in some feminist writing, to replace *one* body with *two*, one ethic with two, one reason with two. For this would be merely to repeat, in dual fashion, the same old narcissistic fascination involved in the contemplation of one's own image. The most this will achieve is that we would succeed in throwing off the persona of Echo, who speaks but is not heard, only to join Narcissus at the pool.

Since this paper opened with a quotation that I take to be typical of a certain kind of male fantasy, I will also close with one. It comes from Italo Calvino's book, *Invisible Cities*, which is constructed as a dialog of sorts between Kublai Khan—the demigod State-builder, and Marco Polo—the inquisitive explorer who entertains Kublai Khan with accounts of the many cities he has seen. It is from a section entitled "Cities and Desire."

From there, after six days and seven nights, you arrive at Zobeide, the White City, well exposed to the moon, with streets wound about themselves as in a skein. They tell this story of its foundation: men of various nations had an identical dream. They saw a woman running at night through an unknown city; she was seen from behind, with long hair and she was naked. They dreamed of pursuing her. As they twisted and turned, each of them lost her. After the dream they set out in search of that city; they never found it, but they found one another; they decided to build a city like the one in the dream. In laying out the streets, each followed the course of his pursuit; at the place where they had lost the fugitive's trail, they arranged spaces and walls differently from the dream, so she would be unable to escape again.

This was the city of Zobeide, where they settled, waiting for that scene to be repeated one night. None of them, asleep or awake, ever saw the woman again. The City's streets were streets where they went to work every day, with no link any more to the dreamed chase. Which, for that matter, had long been forgotten.

The first to arrive could not understand what drew these people to Zobeide, this ugly City, this trap.[9]

I take this dream to be rather atypical, for it tells of the failure of the desire to "capture" and to "contain" difference in a monument to unity. It also speaks of masculine impotence in the face of a loss suffered but not remembered. There is an interesting point of overlap between these dreams and fantasies of cities and states. The women of Zobeide are walled into that city just as surely as the Furies are contained in Athens. The possibility of hearing the speech of women and others is crucially tied to the remembrance and "working through" of this initial dream.

NOTES

I would like to acknowledge the assistance given me by Rosalyn Disprose, Reta Gear, and Paul Patton in preparing this paper for publication. An earlier version was presented to the Politics of the Body Conference, Performance Space, Sydney, 1987, and was published in *Spectator Burns* 2 (1987).

1. For example, John Locke *Two Treatises of Government* (London: Cambridge University Press, 1967); Jean-Jacques Rousseau *The Social Contract,* (Harmondsworth: Penguin, 1968).

2. Both Locke and Rousseau held this view. See Locke, *Two Treatises of Government*, book 2, section 82; and Rousseau, *Emile* (London: Dent and Sons, 1972), pp. 370, 412, 442.

3. Thomas Hobbes *Leviathan* (Harmondsworth: Penguin, 1968), pp. 81–2.

4. Ibid., p. 186.

5. See Jane Flax, "Mother-Daughter Relationships: Psychodynamics, Politics, and Philosophy," in H. Eisenstein and A. Jardine, eds., *The Future of Difference* (Boston: G. K. Hall, 1980), especially p. 29f.

6. See C. Pateman, *The Sexual Contract* (Cambridge: Polity Press, 1988), especially chapter 4.

7. Mary Wollstonecraft *A Vindication of the Rights of Woman*, 1792 (Harmondsworth: Penguin, 1975)

8. The notion of ethics which I have in mind is one that takes the body, its pleasures, powers, and capacities into account. A good example is B. Spinoza's *Ethics*. For an account of what Spinoza's ethical theory can offer us today, see Gilles Deleuze *Spinoza: Practical Philosophy* (San Francisco: City Lights Books, 1988), especially chapters 2 and 6.

9. Italo Calvino *Invisible Cities* (London: Picador, 1979), p. 39.

5

The Body and the
Reproduction of Femininity

Susan Bordo

Reconstructing Feminist Discourse
on the Body

The body—what we eat, how we dress, the daily rituals through which we attend to the body—is a medium of culture. The body, as anthropologist Mary Douglas has argued, is a powerful symbolic form, a surface on which the central rules, hierarchies, and even metaphysical commitments of a culture are inscribed and thus reinforced through the concrete language of the body.[1] The body may also operate as a metaphor for culture. From quarters as diverse as Plato and Hobbes to French feminist Luce Irigaray, an imagination of body morphology has provided a blueprint for diagnosis and/or vision of social and political life.

The body is not only a *text* of culture. It is also, as anthropologist Pierre Bourdieu and

already this is troubled

philosopher Michel Foucault (among others) have argued, a *practical, direct* locus of social control. Banally, through table manners and toilet habits, through seemingly trivial routines, rules, and practices, culture is "*made* body," as Bourdieu puts it—converted into automatic, habitual activity. As such it is put "beyond the grasp of consciousness . . . [untouchable] by voluntary, deliberate transformations."[2] Our conscious politics, social commitments, strivings for change may be undermined and betrayed by the life of our bodies—not the craving, instinctual body imagined by Plato, Augustine, and Freud, but what Foucault calls the "docile body," regulated by the norms of cultural life.[3]

Throughout his later "genealogical" works (*Discipline and Punish*, *The History of Sexuality*), Foucault constantly reminds us of the primacy of practice over belief. Not chiefly through ideology, but through the organization and regulation of the time, space, and movements of our daily lives, our bodies are trained, shaped, and impressed with the stamp of prevailing historical forms of selfhood, desire, masculinity, femininity. Such an emphasis casts a dark and disquieting shadow across the contemporary scene. For women, as study after study shows, are spending more time on the management and discipline of our bodies than we have in a long, long time. In a decade marked by a reopening of the public arena to women, the intensification of such regimens appears diversionary and subverting. Through the pursuit of an ever-changing, homogenizing, elusive ideal of femininity—a pursuit without a terminus, requiring that women constantly attend to minute and often whimsical changes in fashion—female bodies become docile bodies—bodies whose forces and energies are habituated to external regulation, subjection, transformation, "improvement." Through the exacting and normalizing disciplines of diet, makeup, and dress—central organizing principles of time and space in the day of many women—we are rendered less socially oriented and more centripetally focused on self-modification. Through these disciplines, we continue to memorize on our bodies the feel and conviction of lack, of insufficiency, of never being good enough. At the farthest extremes, the practices of femininity may lead us to utter demoralization, debilitation, and death.

Viewed historically, the discipline and normalization of the female body—perhaps the only gender oppression that exercises itself, although to different degrees and in different forms, across age, race, class, and sexual orientation—has to be acknowledged as an amazingly durable and flexible strategy of social control. In our own era, it is difficult to avoid the recognition that the contemporary preoccupation with appearance, which still affects women far more powerfully than men, even in our narcissistic and visually oriented culture, may function as a backlash phenomenon, reasserting existing gender configurations against any attempts to shift or transform power relations.[4] Surely we are in the throes of this backlash today. In newspapers and magazines we daily encounter stories that promote traditional gender relations and prey on anxieties about change: stories about latchkey children, abuse in day-care centers, the "new woman's" troubles with men, her lack of marriageability, and so on. A dominant visual theme in teenage magazines involves women hiding in the shadows of men, seeking solace in their arms, willingly contracting the space they occupy. The last, of course, also describes our contemporary aesthetic ideal for women, an ideal whose obsessive pursuit has become the central torment of many women's lives. In such an era we desperately need an effective political discourse about the female body, a discourse adequate to an analysis of the insidious, and often paradoxical, pathways of modern social control.

Developing such a discourse requires reconstructing the feminist paradigm of the late 1960s and early 1970s, with its political categories of oppressors and oppressed, villains and victims. Here I believe that a feminist appropriation of some of Foucault's later concepts can prove useful. Following Foucault, we must first abandon the idea of power as something possessed by one group and leveled against another; we must instead think of the network of practices, institutions, and technologies that sustain positions of dominance and subordination in a particular domain.

Second, we need an analytics adequate to describe a power whose central mechanisms are not repressive, but *constitutive:* "a power bent on generating forces, making them grow, and ordering them, rather than one dedicated to impeding them, making them submit, or destroying them." Particularly in the realm of femininity, where so much depends on the seemingly willing acceptance of various norms and practices, we need an analysis of power "from below," as Foucault puts it; for example, of the mechanisms that shape and proliferate—rather than repress—desire, generate and focus our energies, construct our conceptions of normalcy and deviance.[5]

And, third, we need a discourse that will enable us to account for the subversion of potential rebellion, a discourse that, while insisting on the necessity of objective analysis of power relations, social hierarchy, political backlash, and so forth, will nonetheless allow us to confront the mechanisms by which the subject at times becomes enmeshed in collusion with forces that sustain her own oppression.

This essay will not attempt to produce a general theory along these lines. Rather, my focus will be the analysis of one particular arena where the interplay of these dynamics is striking and perhaps exemplary. It is a limited and unusual arena, that of a group of gender-related and historically localized disorders: hysteria, agoraphobia, and anorexia nervosa.[6] I recognize that these disorders have also historically been class- and race-biased, largely (although not exclusively) occurring among white middle- and upper-middle-class women. Nonetheless, anorexia, hysteria, and agoraphobia may provide a paradigm of one way in which potential resistance is not merely undercut but *utilized* in the maintenance and reproduction of existing power relations.[7]

The central mechanism I will describe involves a transformation (or, if you wish, duality) of meaning, through which conditions that are objectively (and, on one level, experientially) constraining, enslaving, and even murderous, come to be experienced as liberating, transforming, and life-giving. I offer this analysis, although limited to a specific domain, as an example of how various contemporary critical discourses may be joined to yield an understanding of the subtle and often unwitting role played by our bodies in the symbolization and reproduction of gender.

agency?

The Body as a Text of Femininity

The continuum between female disorder and "normal" feminine practice is sharply revealed through a close reading of those disorders to which women have been particularly vulnerable. These, of course, have varied historically: neurasthenia and hysteria in the second half of the nineteenth century; agoraphobia and, most dramatically, anorexia nervosa and bulimia in the second half of the twentieth century. This is not to say that anorectics did not exist in the nineteenth century—many cases were described, usually in the context of diagnoses of hysteria[8]—or that women no longer suffer from classical hysterical symptoms in the twentieth century. But the taking up of eating disorders on a mass scale is as unique to the culture of the 1980s as the epidemic of hysteria was to the Victorian era.[9]

The symptomatology of these disorders reveals itself as textuality. Loss of mobility, loss of voice, inability to leave the home, feeding others while starving oneself, taking up space, and whittling down the space one's body takes up—all have symbolic meaning, all have *political* meaning under the varying rules governing the historical construction of gender. Working within this framework, we see that whether we look at hysteria, agoraphobia, or anorexia, we find the body of the sufferer deeply inscribed with an ideological construction of femininity emblematic of the period in question. The construction, of course, is always homogenizing and normalizing, erasing racial, class, and other differences and insisting that all women aspire to a coercive, standardized ideal. Strikingly, in these disorders the construction of femininity is written in disturbingly concrete, hyperbolic terms: exaggerated, extremely literal, at times virtually caricatured presentations of the ruling feminine mystique. The bodies of disordered women in this way offer themselves as an aggressively graphic text for the interpreter—a text that insists, actually demands, that it be read as a cultural statement, a statement about gender.

Both nineteenth-century male physicians and twentieth-century feminist critics have seen, in the symptoms of neurasthenia and hysteria (syndromes that became increasingly less differentiated as the century wore on), an exaggeration of stereotypically feminine traits. The nineteenth-century "lady" was idealized in terms of delicacy and dreaminess, sexual passivity, and a charmingly labile and capricious emotionality.[10] Such notions were formalized and scientized in the work of male theorists from Acton and Krafft-Ebing to Freud, who described "normal," mature femininity in such terms.[11] In this context, the dissociations, the drifting and fogging of perception, the nervous tremors and faints, the anesthesias, and the extreme mutability of symptomatology associated with nineteenth-century female disorders can be seen to be concretizations of the feminine mystique of the period, produced according to rules that governed the prevailing construction of femininity. Doctors described what came to be known as the hysterical personality as "impressionable, suggestible, and narcissistic; highly labile, their moods changing suddenly, dramatically, and seemingly for inconsequential reasons . . . egocentric in the extreme . . . essentially asexual and not uncommonly frigid"[12]—all characteristics normative of femininity in this era. As Elaine Showalter points out, the term "hysterical" itself became almost interchangeable with the term "feminine" in the literature of the period.[13]

The hysteric's embodiment of the feminine mystique of her era, however, seems subtle and ineffable compared to the ingenious literalism of agoraphobia and anorexia. In the context of our culture this literalism makes sense. With the advent of movies and television, the rules for femininity have come to be culturally transmitted more and more through standardized visual images. As a result, femininity itself has come to be largely a matter of constructing, in the manner described by Erving Goffman, the appropriate surface presentation of the self.[14] We are no longer given verbal descriptions or exemplars of what a lady is or of what femininity consists. Rather, we learn the rules directly through bodily discourse: through images that tell us what clothes, body shape, facial expression, movements, and behavior are required.

In agoraphobia and, even more dramatically, in anorexia, the disorder presents itself as a virtual, though tragic, parody of twentieth-century constructions of femininity. The 1950s and early 1960s, when agoraphobia first began to escalate among women, was a period of reassertion of domesticity and dependency as the feminine ideal. "Career woman" became a dirty word, much more so than it had been during the war, when the economy depended on women's willingness to do "men's work." The reigning ideology of femininity, so well described by Betty Friedan and perfectly captured in the movies and television shows of the era, was childlike, nonassertive, helpless without a man, "content in a world of bedroom and kitchen, sex, babies and home."[15] The housebound agoraphobic lives this construction of femininity literally. "You want me in this home? You'll have me in this home—with a vengeance!" The point, upon which many therapists have commented, does not need belaboring. Agoraphobia, as I. G. Fodor has put it, seems "the logical—albeit extreme—extension of the cultural sex-role stereotype for women" in this era.[16]

The emaciated body of the anorectic, of course, immediately presents itself as a caricature of the contemporary ideal of hyperslenderness for women, an ideal that, despite the game resistance of racial and ethnic difference, has become the norm for women today. But slenderness is only the tip of the iceberg, for slenderness itself requires interpretation. "C'est le sens qui fait vendre," said Barthes, speaking of clothing styles—it is meaning that makes the sale.[17] So, too, it is meaning that makes the body admirable. To the degree that anorexia may be said to be "about" slenderness, it is about slenderness as a citadel of contemporary and historical meaning, not as an empty fashion ideal. As such, the interpretation of slenderness yields multiple readings, some related to gender, some not. For the purposes of this essay I will offer an abbreviated, gender-focused reading. But I must stress that this reading illuminates only partially, and that many other currents not discussed here—economic, psychosocial, and historical, as well as ethnic and class dimensions—figure prominently.[18]

We begin with the painfully literal inscription, on the anorectic's body, of the rules governing the construction of contemporary femininity. That construction is a double bind that legislates contradictory ideals and directives. On the one hand, our culture still widely advertises domestic conceptions of femininity, the ideological moorings for a rigorously dualistic sexual division of labor that casts woman as chief emotional and physical nurturer. The rules for this construction of femininity (and I speak here in a language both symbolic and literal) require that women learn to feed others, not the self, and to construe any desires for self-nurturance and self-feeding as greedy and excessive.[19] Thus, women must develop a totally other-oriented emotional economy. In this economy, the control of female appetite for food is merely the most concrete expression of the general rule governing the construction of femininity: that female hunger—for public power, for independence, for sexual gratification—be contained, and the public space that women be allowed to take up be circumscribed, limited. Women's magazine fashion spreads dramatically illustrate the degree to which slenderness, set off against the resurgent muscularity and bulk of the current male body-ideal, carries connotations of fragility and lack of power in the face of a decisive male occupation of social space. On the body of the anorexic woman such rules are grimly and deeply etched.

On the other hand, even as young women today continue to be taught traditionally "feminine" virtues, to the degree that the professional arena is open to them they must also learn to embody the "masculine" language and values of that arena—self-control, determination, cool, emotional discipline, mastery, and so on. Female bodies now speak symbolically of this necessity in their slender spare shape and the currently fashionable men's-wear look. Our bodies, too, as we trudge to the gym every day and fiercely resist both our hungers and our desire to soothe ourselves, are becoming more and more practiced at the "male" virtues of control and self-mastery. The anorectic pursues these virtues with single-minded, unswerving dedication. "Energy, discipline, my own power will keep me going," says ex-anorectic Aimee Liu, recreating her anorexic days. "I need nothing and no one else. . . . I will be master of my own body, if nothing else, I vow."[20]

The ideal of slenderness, then, and the diet and exercise regimens that have become inseparable from it offer the illusion of meeting, through the body, the contradictory demands of the contemporary ideology of femininity. Popular images reflect this dual demand. In a single issue of *Complete Woman* magazine, two articles appear, one on "Feminine Intuition," the other asking, "Are you the New Macho Woman?" In *Vision Quest*, the young male hero falls in love with the heroine, as he says, because "she has all the best things I like in girls and all the best things I like in guys," that is, she's tough and cool, but warm and alluring. In the enormously popular *Aliens*, the heroine's personality has been deliberately constructed, with near-comic book explicitness, to embody traditional nurturant femininity alongside breathtaking macho prowess and control; Sigourney Weaver, the actress who portrays her, has called the character "Rambolina."

In the pursuit of slenderness and the denial of appetite the traditional construction of femininity intersects with the new requirement for women to embody the "masculine" values of the public arena. The anorectic, as I have argued, embodies this intersection, this double bind, in a particularly painful and graphic way.[21] I mean "double bind" quite literally here. "Masculinity" and "femininity," at least since the nineteenth century and arguably before, have been constructed through a process of mutual exclusion. One cannot simply add the historically feminine virtues to the historically masculine ones to yield a New Woman, a New Man, a new ethics, or a new culture. Even on the screen or on television, embodied in created characters like the *Aliens* heroine, the result is a parody. Unfortunately, in this image-bedazzled culture, we find it increasingly difficult to discriminate between parodies and possibilities for the self. Explored as a possibility for the self, the "androgynous" ideal ultimately exposes its internal contradiction and becomes a war that tears the subject in two—a war explicitly thematized, by many anorectics, as a battle between male and female sides of the self.[22]

Protest and Retreat in the Same Gesture

In hysteria, agoraphobia, and anorexia, then, the woman's body may be viewed as a surface on which conventional constructions of femininity are exposed starkly to view, through their inscription in extreme or hyperliteral form. They are written, of course, in languages of horrible suffering. It is as though these bodies are speaking to us of the pathology and violence that lurks just around the corner, waiting at the horizon of "normal" femininity. It is no wonder that a steady motif in the feminist literature on female disorder is that of pathology as embodied *protest*—unconscious, inchoate, and counterproductive protest without an effective language, voice, or politics, but protest nonetheless.

American and French feminists alike have heard the hysteric speaking a language of protest, even or perhaps especially when she was mute. Dianne Hunter interprets Anna O.'s aphasia, which manifested itself in an inability to speak her native German, as a rebellion against the linguistic and cultural rules of the father and a return to the "mother-tongue": the semiotic babble of infancy, the language of the body. For Hunter, and for a number of other feminists working with Lacanian categories, the return to the semiotic level is both regressive and, as Hunter puts it, an "expressive" communication "addressed to patriarchal thought," "a self-repudiating form of feminine discourse in which the body signifies what social conditions make it impossible to state linguistically."[23] "The hysterics are accusing; they are pointing," writes Catherine Clément in *The Newly Born Woman*; they make a "mockery of culture."[24] In the same volume, Hélène Cixous speaks of "those wonderful hysterics, who subjected Freud to so many voluptuous moments too shameful to mention, bombarding his mosaic statute/law of Moses with their carnal, passionate body-words, haunting him with their inaudible thundering denunciations." For Cixous, Dora, who so frustrated Freud, is "the core example of the protesting force in women."[25]

The literature of protest includes functional as well as symbolic approaches. Robert Seidenberg and Karen DeCrow, for example, describe agoraphobia as a "strike" against "the renunciations usually demanded of women" and the expectations of housewifely functions such as shopping, driving the children to school, accompanying their husband to social events.[26] Carroll Smith-Rosenberg presents a similar analysis of hysteria, arguing that by preventing the woman from functioning in the wifely role of caretaker of others, of "ministering angel" to husband and children, hysteria "became one way in which conventional women could express—in most cases unconsciously—dissatisfaction with one or several aspects of their lives."[27] A number of feminist writers, among whom Susie Orbach is the most articulate and forceful, have interpreted anorexia as a species of unconscious feminist protest. The anorectic is engaged in a "hunger strike," as Orbach calls it, stressing that this is a political discourse, in which the action of food refusal and dramatic transformation of body size "expresses with [the] body what [the anorectic] is unable to tell us with words"—her indictment of a culture that disdains and suppresses female hunger, makes women ashamed of their appetites and needs, and demands that women constantly work on the transformation of their body.[28]

The anorectic, of course, is unaware that she is making a political statement. She may, indeed, be hostile to feminism and any other critical perspectives that she views as disputing her own autonomy and control or questioning the cultural ideals around which her life is organized. Through embodied rather than deliberate demonstration she exposes and indicts those ideals, precisely by pursuing them to the point at which their destructive potential is revealed for all to see.

The same gesture that expresses protest, moreover, can also signal retreat; this, indeed, may be part of the symptom's attraction. Kim Chernin, for example, argues that the debilitating anorexic fixation, by halting or mitigating personal development, assuages this generation's guilt and separation anxiety over the prospect of surpassing our mothers, of living less circumscribed, freer lives.[29] Agoraphobia, too, which often develops shortly after marriage, clearly functions in many cases as a way to cement dependency and attachment in the face of unacceptable stirrings of dissatisfaction and restlessness.

Although we may talk meaningfully of protest, then, I want to emphasize the counterproductive, tragically self-defeating (indeed, self-deconstructing) nature of that protest. Functionally, the symptoms of these disorders isolate, weaken, and undermine the sufferers; at the same time they turn the life of the body into an all-absorbing fetish, beside which all other objects of attention pale into unreality. On the symbolic level, too, the protest collapses into its opposite and proclaims the utter capitulation of the subject to the contracted female world. The muteness of hysterics and their return to the level of pure, primary bodily expressivity have been interpreted, as we have seen, as rejecting the symbolic order of the patriarchy and recovering a lost world of semiotic, maternal value. But *at the same time*, of course, muteness is the condition of the silent, uncomplaining woman—an ideal of patriarchal culture. Protesting the stifling of the female voice through one's own voicelessness—that is, employing the language of femininity to protest the conditions of the female world—will always involve ambiguities of this sort. Perhaps this is why symptoms crystallized from the language of femininity are so perfectly suited to express the dilemmas of middle-class and upper-middle-class women living in periods poised on the edge of gender change, women who have the social and material resources to carry the traditional construction of femininity to symbolic excess but who also confront the anxieties of new possibilities. The late nineteenth century, the post-World War II period, and the late twentieth century are all periods in which gender becomes an issue to be discussed and in which discourse proliferates about "the Woman Question," "the New Woman," "What Women Want," "What Femininity Is."

Collusion, Resistance, and the Body

The pathologies of female protest function, paradoxically, as if in collusion with the cultural conditions that produce them, reproducing rather than transforming precisely that which is being protested. In this connection, the fact that hysteria and anorexia have peaked during historical periods of cultural backlash against attempts at reorganization and redefinition of male and female roles is significant. Female pathology reveals itself here as an extremely interesting social formation through which one source of potential for resistance and rebellion is pressed into the service of maintaining the established order.

In our attempt to explain this formation, objective accounts of power relations fail us. For whatever the objective social conditions are that create a pathology, the symptoms themselves must still be produced (however unconsciously or inadvertently) by the subject. That is, the individual must invest the body with meanings of various sorts. Only by examining this productive process on the part of the subject can we, as Mark Poster has put it, "illuminate the mechanisms of domination in the processes through which meaning is produced in everyday life"; that is, only then can we see how the desires and dreams of the subject become implicated in the matrix of power relations.[30]

Here, examining the context in which the anorexic syndrome is produced may be illuminating. Anorexia will erupt, typically, in the course of what begins as a fairly moderate diet regime, undertaken because someone, often the father, has made a casual critical remark. Anorexia *begins in*, emerges out of, what is, in our time, conventional feminine practice. In the course of that practice, for any number of individual reasons, the practice is pushed a little beyond the parameters of moderate dieting. The young woman discovers what it feels like to crave and want and need and yet, through the exercise of her own will, to triumph over that need. In the process, a new realm of meanings is discovered, a range of values and possibilities that Western culture has traditionally coded as "male" and rarely made available to women: an ethic and aesthetic of self-mastery and self-transcendence, expertise, and power over others through the example of superior will and control. The experience is intoxicating, habit-forming.

At school the anorectic discovers that her steadily shrinking body is admired, not so much as an aesthetic or sexual object, but for the strength of will and self-control it projects. At home she discovers, in the inevitable battles her parents fight to get her to eat, that her actions have enormous power over the lives of those around her. As her body begins to lose its traditional feminine curves, its breasts and hips and rounded stomach, begins to feel and look more like a spare, lanky male body, she begins to feel untouchable, out of reach of hurt, "invulnerable, clean and hard as the bones etched into my silhouette," as one student described it in her journal. She despises, in particular, all those parts of her body that continue to mark her as female. "If only I could eliminate [my breasts]," says Liu, "cut them off if need be."[31] For her, as for many anorectics, the breasts represent a bovine, unconscious, vulnerable side of the self. Liu's body symbolism is thoroughly continuous with dominant cultural associations. Brett Silverstein's studies on the "Possible Causes of the Thin Standard of Bodily Attractiveness for Women"[32] testify empirically to what is obvious from every comedy routine involving a dramatically shapely woman: namely, our cultural association of curvaceousness with incompetence. The anorectic is also quite aware, of course, of the social and sexual vulnerability involved in having a female body; many, in fact, were sexually abused as children. *just thrown in for authority sake?*

Through her anorexia, by contrast, she has unexpectedly discovered an entry into the privileged male world, a way to become what is valued in our culture, a way to become safe, to rise above it all—for her, they are the same thing. She has discovered this, paradoxically, by pursuing conventional feminine behavior—in this case, the discipline of perfecting the body as an object—to excess. At this point of excess, the conventionally feminine deconstructs, we might say, into its opposite and opens onto those values our culture has coded as male. No wonder the anorexia is experienced as liberating and that she will fight family, friends, and therapists in an effort to hold onto it—fight them to the death, if need be. The anorectic's experience of power is, of course, deeply and dangerously illusory. To reshape one's body into a male body is *not* to put on male power and privilege. To *feel* autonomous and free while harnessing body and soul to an obsessive body-practice is to serve, not transform, a social order that limits female possibilities. And, of course, for the female to become male is only for her to locate herself on the other side of a disfiguring opposition. The new "power look" of female body-building, which encourages women to develop the same hulklike, triangular shape that has been the norm for male body-builders, is no less determined by a hierarchical, dualistic construction of gender than was the conventionally "feminine" norm that tyrannized female body-builders such as Bev Francis for years. *IMPLANTS! way to have both*

Although the specific cultural practices and meanings are different, similar mechanisms, I suspect, are at work in hysteria and agoraphobia. In these cases too, the language of femininity, when pushed to excess—when shouted and asserted, when disruptive and demanding—deconstructs into its opposite and makes available to the woman an illusory experience of power previously forbidden to her by virtue of her gender. In the case of nineteenth-century femininity, the forbidden experience may have been the bursting of fetters—particularly moral and emotional fetters. John Conolly, the asylum reformer, recommended institutionalization for women who "want that restraint over the passions without which the female character is lost."[33] Hysterics often infuriated male doctors by their lack of precisely this quality.

S. Weir Mitchell described these patients as "the despair of physicians," whose "despotic selfishness wrecks the constitution of nurses and devoted relatives, and in unconscious or half-conscious self-indulgence destroys the comfort of everyone around them."[34] It must have given the Victorian patient some illicit pleasure to be viewed as capable of such disruption of the staid nineteenth-century household. A similar form of power, I believe, is part of the experience of agoraphobia.

This does not mean that the primary reality of these disorders is not one of pain and entrapment. Anorexia, too, clearly contains a dimension of physical addiction to the biochemical effects of starvation. But whatever the physiology involved, the ways in which the subject understands and thematizes her experience cannot be reduced to a mechanical process. The anorectic's ability to live with minimal food intake allows her to feel powerful and worthy of admiration in a "world," as Susie Orbach describes it, "from which at the most profound level [she] feels excluded" and unvalued.[35] The literature on both anorexia and hysteria is strewn with battles of will between the sufferer and those trying to "cure" her; the latter, as Orbach points out, very rarely understand that the psychic values she is fighting for are often more important to the woman than life itself.

Textuality, Praxis, and the Body

The "solutions" offered by anorexia, hysteria, and agoraphobia, I have suggested, develop out of the practice of femininity itself, the pursuit of which is still presented as the chief route to acceptance and success for women in our culture. Too aggressively pursued, that practice leads to its own undoing, in one sense. For if femininity is, as Susan Brownmiller has said, at its core a "tradition of imposed limitations,"[36] then an unwillingness to limit oneself, even in the pursuit of femininity, breaks the rules. But, of course, in another sense the rules remain fully in place. The sufferer becomes wedded to an obsessive practice, unable to make any effective change in her life. She remains, as Toril Moi has put it, "gagged and chained to [the] feminine role," a reproducer of the docile body of femininity.[37]

This tension between the psychological meaning of a disorder, which may enact fantasies of rebellion and embody a language of protest, and the practical life of the disordered body, which may utterly defeat rebellion and subvert protest, may be obscured by too exclusive a focus on the symbolic dimension and insufficient attention to praxis. As we have seen in the case of some Lacanian feminist readings of hysteria, the result of this can be a one-sided interpretation that romanticizes the hysteric's symbolic subversion of the phallocentric order while confined to her bed. This is not to say that confinement in bed has a transparent, univocal meaning—in powerlessness, debilitation, dependency, and so forth. The "practical" body is no brute biological or material entity. It, too, is a culturally mediated form; its activities are subject to interpretation and description. The shift to the practical dimension is not a turn to biology or nature, but to another "register," as Foucault puts it, of the cultural body, the register of the "useful body" rather than the "intelligible body."[38] The distinction can prove useful, I believe, to feminist discourse.

The intelligible body includes our scientific, philosophic, and aesthetic representations of the body—our cultural *conceptions* of the body, norms of beauty, models of health, and so forth. But the same representations may also be seen as forming a set of *practical* rules and regulations through which the living body is "trained, shaped, obeys, responds," becoming, in short, a socially adapted and "useful body."[39] Consider this particularly clear and appropriate example: the nineteenth-century hourglass figure, emphasizing breasts and hips against a wasp waist, was an intelligible *symbolic* form, representing a domestic, sexualized ideal of femininity. The sharp cultural contrast between the female and the male form, made possible by the use of corsets and bustles, reflected, in symbolic terms, the dualistic division of social and economic life into clearly defined male and female spheres. At the same time, to achieve the specified look, a particular feminine *praxis* was required—straitlacing, minimal eating, reduced mobility—rendering the female body unfit to perform activities outside its designated sphere. This, in Foucauldian terms, would be the "useful body" corresponding to the aesthetic norm.

The intelligible body and the useful body are two arenas of the same discourse; they often mirror and support each other, as in the above illustration. Another example can be found in the seventeenth-century philosophic conception of the body as a machine, mirroring an increasingly more automated productive machinery of labor. But the two bodies may also contradict and mock each other. A range of contemporary representations and images, as noted earlier, have coded the transcendence of female appetite and its public display in the slenderness ideal in terms of power, will, mastery, the possibilities of success in the professional arena. These associations are carried visually by the slender superwomen of prime-time television and popular movies and promoted explicitly in advertisements and articles appearing

wonder what Bordo thinks of Ally McBeal?

routinely in women's fashion magazines, diet books, and weight-training publications. Yet the thousands of slender girls and women who strive to embody these images and who in that service suffer from eating disorders, exercise compulsions, and continual self-scrutiny and self-castigation are anything *but* the "masters" of their lives.

Exposure and productive cultural analysis of such contradictory and mystifying relations between image and practice are possible only if the analysis includes attention to and interpretation of the "useful" or, as I prefer to call it, the practical body. Such attention, although often in inchoate and theoretically unsophisticated form, was central to the beginnings of the contemporary feminist movement. In the late 1960s and early 1970s the objectification of the female body was a serious political issue. All the cultural paraphernalia of femininity, of learning to please visually and sexually through the practices of the body—media imagery, beauty pageants, high heels, girdles, makeup, simulated orgasm—were seen as crucial in maintaining gender domination.

Disquietingly, for the feminists of the present decade, such focus on the politics of feminine praxis, although still maintained in the work of individual feminists, is no longer a centerpiece of feminist cultural critique.[40] On the popular front, we find *Ms.* magazine presenting issues on fitness and "style," the rhetoric reconstructed for the 1980s to pitch "self-expression" and "power." Although feminist theory surely has the tools, it has not provided a critical discourse to dismantle and demystify this rhetoric. The work of French feminists has provided a powerful framework for understanding the inscription of phallocentric, dualistic culture on gendered bodies, but it has offered very little in the way of concrete analyses of the female body as a locus of practical cultural control. Among feminist theorists in this country, the study of cultural representations of the female body has flourished, and it has often been brilliantly illuminating and instrumental to a feminist rereading of culture.[41] But the study of cultural representations alone, divorced from consideration of their relation to the practical lives of bodies, can obscure and mislead.

Here, Helena Michie's significantly titled *The Flesh Made Word* offers a striking example. Examining nineteenth-century representations of women, appetite, and eating, Michie draws fascinating and astute metaphorical connections between female eating and female sexuality. Female hunger, she argues, and I agree, "figures unspeakable desires for sexuality and power."[42] The Victorian novel's "representational taboo" against depicting women eating (an activity, apparently, that only "happens offstage," as Michie puts it) thus functions as a "code" for the suppression of female sexuality, as does the general cultural requirement, exhibited in etiquette and sex manuals of the day, that the well-bred woman eat little and delicately. The same coding is drawn on, Michie argues, in contemporary feminist "inversions" of Victorian values, inversions that celebrate female sexuality and power through images exulting in female eating and female hunger, depicting it explicitly, lushly, and joyfully.

Despite the fact that Michie's analysis centers on issues concerning women's hunger, food, and eating practices, she makes no mention of the grave eating disorders that surfaced in the late nineteenth century and that are ravaging the lives of young women today. The practical arena of women dieting, fasting, straitlacing, and so forth is, to a certain extent, implicit in her examination of Victorian gender ideology. But when Michie turns, at the end of her study, to consider contemporary feminist literature celebrating female eating and female hunger, the absence of even a passing glance at how women are *actually* managing their hungers today leaves her analysis adrift, lacking any concrete social moorings. Michie's sole focus is on the inevitable failure of feminist literature to escape "phallic representational codes."[43] But the feminist celebration of the female body did not merely deconstruct on the written page or canvas. Largely located in the feminist counterculture of the 1970s, it has been culturally displaced by a very different contemporary reality. Its celebration of female flesh now presents itself in jarring dissonance with the fact that women, feminists included, are starving themselves to death in our culture.

This is not to deny the benefits of diet, exercise, and other forms of body management. Rather, I view our bodies as a site of struggle, where we must *work* to keep our daily practices in the service of resistance to gender domination, not in the service of docility and gender normalization. This work requires, I believe, a determinedly skeptical attitude toward the routes of seeming liberation and pleasure offered by our culture. It also demands an awareness of the often contradictory relations between image and practice, between rhetoric and reality. Popular representations, as we have seen, may forcefully employ the rhetoric and symbolism of empowerment, personal freedom, "having it all." Yet female bodies, pursuing these ideals, may find themselves as distracted, depressed, and physically ill as female bodies in the nineteenth century were made when pursuing a feminine ideal of dependency, domesticity, and delicacy. The recognition and analysis of such contradictions, and of all the other collusions, subversions, and enticements through which culture enjoins the aid of our bodies in the reproduction of gender, require that we restore a concern for female praxis to its formerly central place in feminist politics.

presupposing gender is a knowable assessible thing common to all women

NOTES

Early versions of this essay, under various titles, were delivered at the philosophy department of the State University of New York at Stony Brook, the University of Massachusetts conference on Histories of Sexuality, and the twenty-first annual conference for the Society of Phenomenology and Existential Philosophy. I thank all those who commented and provided encouragement on those occasions. The essay was revised and originally published in Alison Jaggar and Susan Bordo, eds., *Gender / Body / Knowledge: Feminist Reconstructions of Being and Knowing* (New Brunswick: Rutgers University Press, 1989).

1. Mary Douglas, *Natural Symbols* (New York: Pantheon, 1982), and *Purity and Danger* (London: Routledge and Kegan Paul, 1966).

2. Pierre Bourdieu, *Outline of a Theory of Practice* (Cambridge: Cambridge University Press, 1977), p. 94 (emphasis in original).

3. On docility, see Michel Foucault, *Discipline and Punish* (New York: Vintage, 1979), pp. 135–69. For a Foucauldian analysis of feminine practice, see Sandra Bartky, "Foucault, Femininity, and the Modernization of Patriarchal Power," in her *Femininity and Domination* (New York: Routledge, 1990); see also Susan Brownmiller, *Femininity* (New York: Ballantine, 1984).

4. During the late 1970s and 1980s, male concern over appearance undeniably increased. Study after study confirms, however, that there is still a large gender gap in this area. Research conducted at the University of Pennsylvania in 1985 found men to be generally satisfied with their appearance, often, in fact, "distorting their perceptions [of themselves] in a positive, self-aggrandizing way" ("Dislike of Own Bodies Found Common Among Women," *New York Times*, March 19, 1985, p. C1). Women, however, were found to exhibit extreme negative assessments and distortions of body perception. Other studies have suggested that women are judged more harshly than men when they deviate from dominant social standards of attractiveness. Thomas Cash et al., in "The Great American Shape-Up," *Psychology Today* (April 1986), p. 34, report that although the situation for men has changed, the situation for women has more than proportionally worsened. Citing results from 30,000 responses to a 1985 survey of perceptions of body image and comparing similar responses to a 1972 questionnaire, they report that the 1985 respondents were considerably more dissatisfied with their bodies than the 1972 respondents, and they note a marked intensification of concern among men. Among the 1985 group, the group most dissatisfied of all with their appearance, however, were teenage women. Women today constitute by far the largest number of consumers of diet products,

attenders of spas and diet centers, and subjects of intestinal by-pass and other fat-reduction operations.

5. Michel Foucault, *The History of Sexuality*. Vol. 1: *An Introduction* (New York: Vintage, 1980), pp. 136, 94.

6. On the gendered and historical nature of these disorders: the number of female to male hysterics has been estimated at anywhere from 2:1 to 4:1, and as many as 80 percent of all agoraphobics are female (Annette Brodsky and Rachel Hare-Mustin, *Women and Psychotherapy* [New York: Guilford Press, 1980], pp. 116, 122). Although more cases of male eating disorders have been reported in the late eighties and early nineties, it is estimated that close to 90 percent of all anorectics are female (Paul Garfinkel and David Garner, *Anorexia Nervosa: A Multidimensional Perspective* [New York: Brunner/Mazel, 1982], pp. 112–13). For a sophisticated account of female psychopathology, with particular attention to nineteenth-century disorders but, unfortunately, little mention of agoraphobia or eating disorders, see Elaine Showalter, *The Female Malady:Women, Madness, and English Culture, 1830–1980* (New York: Pantheon, 1985). For a discussion of social and gender issues in agoraphobia, see Robert Seidenberg and Karen DeCrow, *Women Who Marry Houses: Panic and Protest in Agoraphobia* (New York: McGraw-Hill, 1983). On the history of anorexia nervosa, see Joan Jacobs Brumberg, *Fasting Girls:The Emergence of Anorexia Nervosa as a Modern Disease* (Cambridge: Harvard University Press, 1988).

7. In constructing such a paradigm I do not pretend to do justice to any of these disorders in its individual complexity. My aim is to chart some points of intersection, to describe some similar patterns, as they emerge through a particular reading of the phenomenon—a political reading, if you will.

8. Showalter, *The Female Malady,* pp. 128–29.

9. On the epidemic of hysteria and neurasthenia, see Showalter, *The Female Maladay*, Carroll Smith-Rosenberg, "The Hysterical Woman: Sex Roles and Role Conflict in Nineteenth-Century America," in her *Disorderly Conduct:Visions of Gender in Victorian America* (Oxford: Oxford University Press, 1985).

10. Martha Vicinus, "Introduction: The Perfect Victorian Lady," in Martha Vicinus, *Suffer and Be Still:Women in theVictorian Age* (Bloomington: Indiana University Press, 1972), pp. x–xi.

11. See Carol Nadelson and Malkah Notman, *The Female Patient* (New York: Plenum, 1982), p. 5; E. M. Sigsworth and T. J. Wyke, "A Study of Victorian Prostitution and Venereal Disease," in Vicinus, *Suffer and Be Still,* p. 82. For more general discussions, see Peter Gay, *The Bourgeois Experience:Victoria to Freud.* Vol. 1: *Education of the Senses* (New York: Oxford University Press, 1984), esp. pp. 109–68; Showalter, *The Female Malady,* esp. pp. 121–44. The delicate lady, an ideal that had very strong class connotations (as does slenderness today), is not the only concep-

tion of femininity to be found in Victorian cultures. But it was arguably the single most powerful ideological representation of femininity in that era, affecting women of all classes, including those without the material means to realize the ideal fully. See Helena Michie, *The Flesh Made Word* (New York: Oxford, 1987), for discussions of the control of female appetite and Victorian constructions of femininity.

12. Smith-Rosenberg, *Disorderly Conduct*, p. 203.

13. Showalter, *The Female Malady*, p. 129.

14. Erving Goffman, *The Presentation of the Self in Everyday Life* (Garden City, N. J.: Anchor Doubleday, 1959).

15. Betty Friedan, *The Feminine Mystique* (New York: Dell, 1962), p. 36. The theme song of one such show ran, in part, "I married Joan . . . What a girl . . . what a whirl . . . what a life! I married Joan . . . What a mind . . . love is blind . . . what a wife!"

16. See I. G. Fodor, "The Phobic Syndrome in Women," in V. Franks and V. Burtle, eds:, *Women in Therapy* (New York: Brunner/Mazel, 1974), p. 119; see also Kathleen Brehony, "Women and Agoraphobia," in Violet Franks and Esther Rothblum, eds., *The Stereotyping of Women* (New York: Springer, 1983).

17. In Jonathan Culler, *Roland Barthes* (New York: Oxford University Press, 1983), p. 74.

18. For other interpretive perspectives on the slenderness ideal, see Kim Chernin, *The Obsession: Reflections on the Tyranny of Slenderness* (New York: Harper and Row, 1981); Susie Orbach, *Hunger Strike: The Anorectic's Struggle as a Metaphor for Our Age* (New York: W. W. Norton, 1985).

19. See Susan Bordo, "Hunger as Ideology," in Susan Bordo, *Unbearable Weight: Feminism, Western Culture, and the Body* (Berkeley: University of California Press, 1993), pp. 99–134 for a discussion of how this construction of femininity is reproduced in contemporary commercials and advertisements concerning food, eating, and cooking.

20. Aimee Liu, *Solitaire* (New York: Harper and Row, 1979), p. 123.

21. Striking, in connection with this, is Catherine Steiner-Adair's 1984 study of high-school women, which reveals a dramatic association between problems with food and body image and emulation of the cool, professionally "together" and gorgeous superwoman. On the basis of a series of interviews, the high schoolers were classified into two groups: one expressed skepticism over the superwoman ideal, the other thoroughly aspired to it. Later administrations of diagnostic tests revealed that 94 percent of the pro-superwoman group fell into the eating-disordered range of the scale. Of the other group, 100 percent fell into the noneating-disordered range. Media images notwithstanding, young women today appear to sense, either consciously or through their bodies, the impossibility of simultaneously meeting the

demands of two spheres whose values have been historically defined in utter opposition to each other.

22. See Susan Bordo, "Anorexia Nervosa" in Bordo, *Unbearable Weight*, pp. 139–64.

23. Dianne Hunter, "Hysteria, Psychoanalysis, and Feminism," in Shirley Garner, Claire Kahane, and Madelon Sprengnether, eds., *The (M)Other Tongue* (Ithaca: Cornell University Press, 1985), p. 114.

24. Catherine Clément and Hélène Cixous, *The Newly Born Woman*, trans. Betsy Wing (Minneapolis: University of Minnesota Press, 1986), p. 42.

25. Clément and Cixous, *The Newly Born Woman*, p. 95.

26. Seidenberg and DeCrow, *Women Who Marry Houses*, p. 31.

27. Smith-Rosenberg, *Disorderly Conduct*, p. 208.

28. Orbach, *Hunger Strike*, p. 102. When we look into the many autobiographies and case studies of hysterics, anorectics, and agoraphobics, we find that these are indeed the sorts of women one might expect to be frustrated by the constraints of a specified female role. Sigmund Freud and Joseph Breuer, in *Studies on Hysteria* (New York: Avon, 1966), and Freud, in the later *Dora: An Analysis of a Case of Hysteria* (New York: Macmillan, 1963), constantly remark on the ambitiousness, independence, intellectual ability, and creative strivings of their patients. We know, moreover, that many women who later became leading social activists and feminists of the nineteenth century were among those who fell ill with hysteria and neurasthenia. It has become a virtual cliché that the typical anorectic is a perfectionist, driven to excel in all areas of her life. Though less prominently, a similar theme runs throughout the literature on agoraphobia.

   One must keep in mind that in drawing on case studies, one is relying on the perceptions of other acculturated individuals. One suspects, for example, that the popular portrait of the anorectic as a relentless overachiever may be colored by the lingering or perhaps resurgent Victorianism of our culture's attitudes toward ambitious women. One does not escape this hermeneutic problem by turning to autobiography. But in autobiography one is at least dealing with social constructions and attitudes that animate the subject's own psychic reality. In this regard the autobiographical literature on anorexia, drawn on in a variety of places in this volume, is strikingly full of anxiety about the domestic world and other themes that suggest deep rebellion against traditional notions of femininity.

29. Kim Chernin, *The Hungry Self: Women, Eating, and Identity* (New York: Harper and Row, 1985), esp. pp. 41–93.

30. Mark Poster, *Foucault, Marxism, and History* (Cambridge: Polity Press, 1984), p. 28.

31. Liu, *Solitaire*, p. 99.

32. Brett Silverstein, "Possible Causes of the Thin Standard of Bodily Attractiveness for Women," *International Journal of Eating Disorders* 5 (1986): 907–16.

33. Showalter, *The Female Malady*, p. 48.

34. Smith-Rosenberg, *Disorderly Conduct*, p. 207.

35. Orbach, *Hunger Strike*, p. 103.

36. Brownmiller, *Femininity*, p. 14.

37. Toril Moi, "Representations of Patriarchy: Sex and Epistemology in Freud's *Dora*," in Charles Bernheimer and Claire Kahane, eds., *In Dora's Case: Freud— Hysteria—Feminism* (New York: Columbia University Press, 1985), p. 192.

38. Foucault, *Discipline and Punish*, p. 136.

39. Foucault, *Discipline and Punish*, p. 136.

40. A focus on the politics of sexualization and objectification remains central to the antipornography movement (e.g., in the work of Andrea Dworkin, Catherine MacKinnon). Feminists exploring the politics of appearance include Sandra Bartky, Susan Brownmiller, Wendy Chapkis, Kim Chernin, and Susie Orbach. And a developing feminist interest in the work of Michel Foucault has begun to produce a post-structuralist feminism oriented toward practice; see, for example, Irene Diamond and Lee Quinby, *Feminism and Foucault: Reflections on Resistance* (Boston: Northeastern University Press, 1988).

41. See, for example, Susan Suleiman, ed., *The Female Body in Western Culture* (Cambridge: Harvard University Press, 1986).

42. Michie, *The Flesh Made Word*, p. 13.

43. Michie, *The Flesh Made Word*, p. 149.

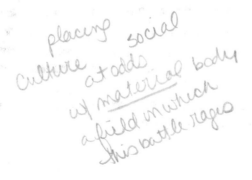

part 2

Bodies in Production

*The body of woman is
the site where culture
manufactures the
blockade of woman.*
—Valerie Export

6

Selling Hot Pussy

REPRESENTATIONS OF BLACK FEMALE SEXUALITY IN THE CULTURAL MARKETPLACE

bell hooks

Friday night in a small midwestern town—I go with a group of artists and professors to a late night dessert place. As we walk past a group of white men standing in the entry way to the place, we overhear them talking about us, saying that my companions, who are all white, must be liberals from the college, not regular "townies," to be hanging out with a "nigger." Everyone in my group acts as though they did not hear a word of this conversation. Even when I call attention to the comments, no one responds. It's like I am not only not talking, but suddenly, to them, I am not there. I am invisible. For my colleagues, racism expressed in everyday encounters—this is our second such experience together—is only an unpleasantness to be avoided, not something to be confronted or challenged. It is just something negative disrupting the good time, better to not notice and pretend it's not there.

bell hooks, "Selling Hot Pussy: Representations of Black Female Sexuality in the Cultural Marketplace." From *Black Looks: Race and Representation*. 1992. Reprinted by permission of South End Press.

As we enter the dessert place they all burst into laughter and point to a row of gigantic chocolate breasts complete with nipples—huge edible tits. They think this is a delicious idea—seeing no connection between this racialized image and the racism expressed in the entry way. Living in a world where white folks are no longer nursed and nurtured primarily by black female caretakers, they do not look at these symbolic breasts and consciously think about "mammies." They do not see this representation of chocolate breasts as a sign of displaced longing for a racist past when the bodies of black women were commodity, available to anyone white who could pay the price. I look at these dark breasts and think about the representation of black female bodies in popular culture. Seeing them, I think about the connection between contemporary representations and the types of images popularized from slavery on. I remember Harriet Jacobs's powerful exposé of the psychosexual dynamics of slavery in *Incidents in the Life of a Slave Girl*. I remember the way she described that "peculiar" institution of domination and the white people who constructed it as "a cage of obscene birds."

Representations of black female bodies in contemporary popular culture rarely subvert or critique images of black female sexuality which were part of the cultural apparatus of nineteenth-century racism and which still shape perceptions today. Sander Gilman's essay "Black Bodies, White Bodies: Toward an Iconography of Female Sexuality in Late Nineteenth-Century Art, Medicine, and Literature" calls attention to the way black presence in early North American society allowed whites to sexualize their world by projecting onto black bodies a narrative of sexualization disassociated from whiteness. Gilman documents the development of this image, commenting that "by the eighteenth century, the sexuality of the black, male and female, becomes an icon for deviant sexuality." He emphasizes that it is the black female body that is forced to serve as "an icon for black sexuality in general."

Most often attention was not focused on the complete black female on display at a fancy ball in the "civilized" heart of European culture, Paris. She is there to entertain guests with the naked image of Otherness. They are not to look at her as a whole human being. They are to notice only certain parts. Objectified in a manner similar to that of black female slaves who stood on auction blocks while owners and overseers described their important, salable parts, the black women whose naked bodies were displayed for whites at social functions had no presence. They were reduced to mere spectacle. Little is known of their lives, their motivations. Their body parts were offered as evidence to support racist notions that black people were more akin to animals than other humans. When Sarah Bartmann's body was exhibited in 1810, she was ironically and perversely dubbed "the Hottentot Venus." Her naked body was displayed on numerous occasions for five years. When she died, the mutilated parts were still subject to scrutiny. Gilman stressed that: "The audience which had paid to see her buttocks and had fantasized about the uniqueness of her genitalia when she was alive could, after her death and dissection, examine both." Much of the racialized fascination with Bartmann's body concentrated attention on her buttocks.

A similar white European fascination with the bodies of black people, particularly black female bodies, was manifest during the career of Josephine Baker. Content to "exploit" white eroticization of black bodies, Baker called attention to the "butt" in her dance routines. Phyllis Rose, though often condescending in her recent biography, *Jazz Cleopatra: Josephine Baker In Her Time*, perceptively explores Baker's concentration on her ass:

> She handled it as though it were an instrument, a rattle, something apart from herself that she could shake. One can hardly overemphasize the importance of the rear end. Baker herself declared that people had been hiding their asses too long. "The rear end exists. I see no reason to be ashamed of it. It's true there are rear ends so stupid, so pretentious, so insignificant that they're good only for sitting on." With Baker's triumph, the erotic gaze of a nation moved downward: she had uncovered a new region for desire.

Many of Baker's dance moves highlighting the "butt" prefigure movements popular in contemporary black dance.

Although contemporary thinking about black female bodies does not attempt to read the body as a sign of "natural" racial inferiority, the fascination with black "butts" continues. In the sexual iconography of the traditional black pornographic imagination, the protruding butt is seen as an indication of a heightened sexuality. Contemporary popular music is one of the primary cultural locations for discussions of black sexuality. In song lyrics, "the butt" is talked about in ways that attempt to challenge racist assumptions that suggest it is an ugly sign of inferiority, even as it remains a sexualized sign. The popular song "Doin' the Butt" fostered the promotion of a hot new dance favoring those who could most protrude their buttocks with pride and glee. A scene in Spike Lee's film *School Daze* depicts an all black party where everyone is attired in swimsuits dancing—doing the butt. It is one of the most compelling moments in the film. The black "butts" on display are unruly and outrageous. They are not the still bodies of the female slave made to appear as mannequin.

They are not a silenced body. Displayed as playful cultural nationalist resistance, they challenge assumptions that the black body, its skin color and shape, is a mark of shame. Undoubtedly the most transgressive and provocative moment in *School Daze*, this celebration of buttocks either initiated or coincided with an emphasis on butts, especially the buttocks of women, in fashion magazines. Its potential to disrupt and challenge notions of black bodies, specifically female bodies, was undercut by the overall sexual humiliation and abuse of black females in the film. Many people did not see the film so it was really the song "Doin' the Butt" that challenged dominant ways of thinking about the body which encourage us to ignore asses because they are associated with undesirable and unclean acts. Unmasked, the "butt" could be once again worshiped as an erotic seat of pleasure and excitement.

When calling attention to the body in a manner inviting the gaze to mutilate black female bodies yet again, to focus solely on the "butt," contemporary celebrations of this part of the anatomy do not successfully subvert sexist/racist representations. Just as nineteenth-century representations of black female bodies were constructed to emphasize that these bodies were expendable, contemporary images (even those created in black cultural production) give a similar message. When Richard Wright's protest novel *Native Son* was made into a film in the 1980s, the film did not show the murder of Bigger's black girlfriend Bessie. This was doubly ironic. She is murdered in the novel and then systematically eliminated in the film. Painters exploring race as artistic subject matter in the nineteenth century often created images contrasting white female bodies with black ones in ways that reinforced the greater value of the white female icon. Gilman's essay colludes in this critical project: he is really most concerned with exploring white female sexuality.

A similar strategy is employed in the Wright novel and in the film version. In the novel, Bessie is expendable because Bigger has already committed the more heinous crime of killing a white woman. The first and more important murder subsumes the second. Everyone cares about the fate of Mary Dalton, the ruling-class white female daughter; no one cares about the fate of Bessie. Ironically, just at the moment when Bigger decides that Bessie's body is expendable, that he will kill her, he continues to demand that she help him, that she "do the right thing." Bigger intends to use her then throw her away, a gesture reinforcing that hers is an expendable body. While he must transgress dangerous boundaries to destroy the body of a white female, he can invade and violate a black female body with no fear of retribution and retaliation.

Black and female, sexual outside the context of marriage, Bessie represents "fallen womanhood." She has no protectors, no legal system will defend her rights. Pleading her cause to Bigger, she asks for recognition and compassion for her specific condition.

> Bigger, please! Don't do this to me! Please! All I do is work, work like a dog! From morning till night. I ain't got no happiness. I ain't never had none. I ain't got nothing and you do this to me . . .

Poignantly describing the lot of working-class poor black women in the 1940s, her words echo those of poet Nikki Giovanni describing the status of black women in the late 1960s. The opening line to "Woman Poem" reads: "You see my whole life is tied up to unhappiness." There is a radical difference, however. In the 1960s, the black female is naming her unhappiness to demand a hearing, an acknowledgment of her reality, and change her status. This poem speaks to the desire of black women to construct a sexuality apart from that imposed upon us by a racist/sexist culture, calling attention to the ways we are trapped by conventional notions of sexuality and desirability:

> It's a sex object if you're pretty and no love or love and no sex if you're fat get back fat black woman be a mother grandmother strong thing but not woman gameswoman romantic woman love needer man seeker dick eater sweat getter fuck needing love seeking woman.

"Woman Poem" is a cry of resistance urging those who exploit and oppress black women, who objectify and dehumanize, to confront the consequences of their actions. Facing herself, the black female realizes all that she must struggle against to achieve self-actualization. She must counter the representation of herself, her body, her being as expendable.

Bombarded with images representing black female bodies as expendable, black women have either passively absorbed this thinking or vehemently resisted it. Popular culture provides countless examples of black female appropriation and exploitation of "negative stereotypes" to either assert control over the representation or at least reap the benefits of it. Since black female sexuality has been represented in racist/sexist iconography as more free and liberated, many black women singers, irrespective of the quality of their voices, have cultivated an image which suggests they are sexually available and licentious. Undesirable in the conventional sense, which defines beauty and sexuality as desirable only to the extent that it is idealized and unattainable, the black female body gains attention only when it is synonymous with accessibility, availability, when it is sexually deviant.

Tina Turner's construction of a public sexual persona most conforms to this idea of black female sexuality. In her recent autobiography, *I, Tina*, she presents a sexualized portrait of herself—providing a narrative that is centrally "sexual confession." Even though she begins by calling attention to the fact that she was raised with puritanical notions of innocence and virtuous womanhood which made her reticent and fearful of sexual experience, all that follows contradicts this portrait. Since the image that has been cultivated and commodified in popular culture is of her as "hot" and highly sexed—the sexually ready and free black woman—a tension exists in the autobiography between the reality she presents and the image she must uphold. Describing her first sexual experience, Turner recalls:

> Naturally, I lost my virginity in the backseat of a car. This was the fifties, right? I think he had planned it, the little devil—he knew by then that he could get into my pants, because there's already been a lot of kissing and touching inside the blouse, and then under the skirt and so forth. The next step was obvious. And me, as brazen as I was, when it came down to finally doing the real thing, it was like: "Uh-oh, it's time." I mean, I was scared. And then it happened.
>
> Well, it hurt so bad—I think my earlobes were hurting. I was just dying, God. And he wanted to do it two or three times! It was like poking an open wound. I could hardly walk afterwards.
>
> But I did it for love. The pain was excruciating; but I loved him and he loved me, and that made the pain less—Everything was right. So it was beautiful.

Only there is nothing beautiful about the scenario Turner describes. A tension exists between the "cool" way she describes this experience, playing it off to suggest she was in control of the situation, and the reality she recounts where she succumbs to male lust and suffers sex. After describing a painful rite of sexual initiation, Turner undermines the confession by telling the reader that she felt good. Through retrospective memory, Turner is able to retell this experience in a manner that suggests she was comfortable with sexual experience at an early age, yet cavalier language does not completely mask the suffering evoked by the details she gives. However, this cavalier attitude accords best with how her fans "see" her. Throughout the biography she will describe situations of extreme sexual victimization and then undermine the impact of her words by evoking the image of herself and other black women as sexually free, suggesting that we assert sexual agency in ways that are never confirmed by the evidence she provides.

Tina Turner's singing career has been based on the construction of an image of black female sexuality that is made synonymous with wild animalistic lust. Raped and exploited by Ike Turner, the man who made this image and imposed it on her, Turner describes the way her public persona as singer was shaped by his pornographic misogynist imagination:

> Ike explained: As a kid back in Clarksdale, he'd become fixated on the white jungle goddess who romped through Saturday matinee movie serials—revealing rag-clad women with long flowing hair and names like Sheena, Queen of the Jungle, and Nyoka—particularly Nyoka. He still remembered *The Perils of Nyoka*, a fifteen-part Republic Picture serial from 1941, starring Kay Alridge in the title role and featuring a villainess named Vultura, an ape named Satan, and Clayton Moore (later to be TV's Lone Ranger) as love interest. Nyoka, Sheena—Tina! Tina Turner—Ike's own personal Wild Woman. He loved it.

Turner makes no comment about her thoughts about this image. How can she? It is part of the representation which makes and maintains her stardom.

Ike's pornographic fantasy of the black female as wild sexual savage emerged from the impact of a white patriarchal controlled media shaping his perceptions of reality. His decision to create the wild black woman was perfectly compatible with prevailing representations of black female sexuality in a white supremacist society. Of course the Tina Turner story reveals that she was anything but a wild woman; she was fearful of sexuality, abused, humiliated, fucked, and fucked over. Turner's friends and colleagues document the myriad ways she suffered about the experience of being brutally physically beaten prior to appearing on stage to perform, yet there is no account of how she coped with the contradiction (this story is told by witnesses in *I, Tina*). She was on one hand in excruciating pain inflicted by a misogynist man who dominated her life and her sexuality, and on the other hand projecting in every performance the image of a wild tough sexually liberated woman. Not unlike the lead character in the novel *Story of O* by Pauline Reage, Turner must act as though she glories in her submission, that she delights in being a slave of love. Leaving Ike, after many years of forced marital rape and physical abuse, because his violence is utterly uncontrollable, Turner takes with her the "image" he created.

Despite her experience of abuse rooted in sexist and racist objectification, Turner appropriated the "wild woman" image, using it for career advancement. Always fascinated with wigs and long hair, she created the blonde lioness mane to appear all the more savage and animalistic. Blondeness links her to jungle imagery even as it serves as an endorsement of a racist aesthetics which sees blonde hair as the epitome of beauty. Without Ike, Turner's career has soared to new heights, particularly as she works harder to exploit the visual representation of woman (and particularly black woman) as sexual savage. No longer caught in the sadomasochistic sexual iconography of black female in erotic war with her mate that was the subtext of the Ike and Tina Turner show, she is now portrayed as the autonomous black woman whose sexuality is solely a way to exert power. Inverting old imagery, she places herself in the role of dominator.

Playing the role of Aunty Entity in the film *Mad Max: Beyond the Thunderdome*, released in 1985, Turner's character evokes two racist/sexist stereotypes, that of the black "mammy" turned power hungry and the sexual savage who uses her body to seduce and conquer men. Portrayed as lusting after the white male hero who will both conquer and reject her, Aunty Entity is the contemporary reenactment of that mythic black female in slavery who supposedly "vamped" and seduced virtuous white male slave owners. Of course the contemporary white male hero of *Mad Max* is stronger than his colonial forefathers. He does not succumb to the dangerous lure of the deadly black seductress who rules over a mini-nation whose power is based on the use of shit. Turner is the bad black woman in this film, an image she will continue to exploit.

Turner's video "What's Love Got to Do with It" also highlights the convergence of sexuality and power. Here, the black woman's body is represented as potential weapon. In the video, she walks down rough city streets, strutting her stuff, in a way that declares desirability, allure, while denying access. It is not that she is no longer represented as available; she is "open" only to those whom she chooses. Assuming the role of hunter, she is the sexualized woman who makes men and women her prey (in the alluring gaze of the video, the body moves in the direction of both sexes). This tough black woman has no time for woman bonding, she is out to "catch." Turner's fictive model of black female sexual agency remains rooted in misogynist notions. Rather than being a pleasure-based eroticism, it is ruthless, violent; it is about women using sexual power to do violence to the male Other.

Appropriating the wild woman pornographic myth of black female sexuality created by men in a white supremacist patriarchy, Turner exploits it for her own ends to achieve economic self-sufficiency. When she left Ike, she was broke and in serious debt. The new Turner image conveys the message that happiness and power come to women who learn to beat men at their own game, to throw off any investment in romance and get down to the real dog-eat-dog thing. "What's Love Got to Do with It" sung by Turner evokes images of the strong bitchified black woman who is on the make. Subordinating the idea of romantic love and praising the use of sex for pleasure as commodity to exchange, the song had great appeal for contemporary postmodern culture. It equates pleasure with materiality, making it an object to be sought after, taken, acquired by any means necessary. When sung by black women singers, "What's Love Got to Do with It" called to mind old stereotypes which make the assertion of black female sexuality and prostitution synonymous. Just as black female prostitutes in the 1940s and 1950s actively sought clients in the streets to make money to survive, thereby publicly linking prostitution with black female sexuality, contemporary black female sexuality is fictively constructed in popular rap and R&B songs solely as commodity—sexual service for money and power, pleasure is secondary.

Contrasted with the representation of wild animalistic sexuality, black female singers like Aretha Franklin and younger contemporaries like Anita Baker fundamentally link romance and sexual pleasure. Aretha, though seen as a victim of no-good men, the classic "woman who loves too much" and leaves the lyrics to prove it, also sang songs of resistance. "Respect" was heard by many black folks, especially black women, as a song challenging black male sexism and female victimization while evoking notions of mutual care and support. In a recent PBS special highlighting individual musicians, Aretha Franklin was featured. Much space was given in the documentary to white male producers who shaped her public image. In the documentary, she describes the fun of adding the words "sock it to me" to "Respect" as a powerful refrain. One of the white male producers, Jerry Wexler, offers his interpretation of its meaning, claiming that it was a call for "sexual attention of the highest order." His sexualized interpretations of the song seemed far removed from the way it was heard and celebrated in black communities. Looking at this documentary, which was supposedly a tribute to Aretha Franklin's power, it was impossible not to have one's attention deflected away from the music by the subtext of the film, which can be seen as a visual narrative documenting her obsessive concern with the body and achieving a look suggesting desirability. To achieve this end, Franklin constantly struggles with her weight, and the images in the film chronicle her various shifts in body size and shape. As though mocking this concern with her body, throughout most of the documentary Aretha appears in what seems to be a household setting, a living room maybe, wearing a strapless evening dress, much too small for her breast size, so her breasts appear like two balloons filled with water about to burst. With no idea who shaped and controlled this image, I can only reiterate that it undermined the insistence in the film that she has overcome sexual victimization and remained a powerful singer; the latter seemed more likely than the former.

Black female singers who project a sexualized persona are as obsessed with hair as they are with body size and body parts. As with nineteenth-century sexual iconography, specific parts of the anatomy are designated more sexual and worthy of attention than others. Today much of the sexualized imagery for black female stars seems to be fixated on hair; it and not buttocks signifies animalistic sexuality. This is quintessentially so for Tina Turner and Diana Ross. It is ironically appropriate that much of this hair is synthetic and man-made, artificially constructed as is the sexualized image it is meant to evoke. Within a patriarchal culture where women over forty are not represented as sexually desirable, it is understandable that singers exploiting sexualized representations who are near the age of fifty place less emphasis on body parts that may reflect aging while focusing on hair.

In a course I teach on "The Politics of Sexuality," where we often examine connections between race and sex, we once critically analyzed a *Vanity Fair* cover depicting Diana Ross. Posed on a white background, apparently naked with the exception of white cloth draped loosely around her body, the most striking element in the portrait was the long mane of jet black hair cascading down. There was so much hair that it seemed to be consuming her body (which looked frail and anorexic), negating the possibility that this naked flesh could represent active female sexual agency. The white diaper-like cloth reinforced the idea that this was a portrait of an adult female who wanted to be seen as childlike and innocent. Symbolically, the hair that is almost a covering hearkens back to early pictorial images of Eve in the garden. It evokes wildness, a sense of the "natural" world, even as it shrouds the body, repressing it, keeping it from the gaze of a culture that does not invite women to be sexual subjects. Concurrently, this cover contrasts whiteness and blackness. Whiteness dominates the page, obscuring and erasing the possibility of any assertion of black power. The longing that is most visible in this cover is that of the black woman to embody and be encircled by whiteness, personified by the possession of long straight hair. Since the hair is produced as commodity and purchased, it affirms contemporary notions of female beauty and desirability as that which can be acquired.

According to postmodern analyses of fashion, this is a time when commodities produce bodies, as this image of Ross suggests. In her essay "Fashion and the Cultural Logic of Postmodernity," Gail Faurshou explains that beauty is no longer seen as a sustained "category of precapitalist culture." Instead, "the colonization and the appropriation of the body as its own production/consumption machine in late capitalism is a fundamental theme of contemporary socialization." This cultural shift enables the bodies of black women to be represented in certain domains of the "beautiful" where they were once denied entry, i.e., high fashion magazines. Reinscribed as spectacle, once again on display, the bodies of black women appearing in these magazines are not there to document the beauty of black skin, of black bodies, but rather to call attention to other concerns. They are represented so readers will notice that the magazine is racially inclusive even though their features are often distorted, their bodies contorted into strange and bizarre postures that make the images appear monstrous or grotesque. They seem to represent an anti-aesthetic, one that mocks the very notion of beauty.

Often black female models appear in portraits that make them look less like humans and more like mannequins or robots. Currently, black models whose hair is not straightened are often photographed wearing straight wigs; this seems to be especially the case if the models' features are unconventional, i.e., if she has large lips or particularly dark skin, which is not often featured in the magazine. The October 1989 issue of *Elle* presented a short profile of designer Azzedine Alaia. He stands at a distance from a black female body holding the sleeves of her dress. Wearing a ridiculous straight hair-do, she appears naked holding the dress in front of her body. The caption reads, "THEY ARE BEAUTIFUL AREN'T THEY!" His critical gaze is on the model and not the dress. As commentary it suggests that even black women can look beautiful in the right outfit. Of course when you read the piece, this statement is not referring to the model, but is a statement Alaia makes about his clothes. In contemporary postmodern fashion sense, the black female is the best medium for the showing of clothes because her image does not detract from the outfit; it is subordinated.

Years ago, when much fuss was made about the reluctance of fashion magazines to include images of black women, it was assumed that the presence of such representations would in and of themselves challenge racist stereotypes that imply black women are not beautiful. Nowadays, black women are included in magazines in a manner that tends to reinscribe prevailing stereotypes. Darker-skinned models are most likely to appear in photographs where their features are distorted. Biracial women tend to appear in sexualized images. Trendy catalogues like *Tweeds* and *J. Crew* make use of a racialized subtext in their layout and advertisements. Usually they are emphasizing the connection between a white European and American style. When they began to include darker-skinned models, they chose biracial or fair-skinned black women, particularly with blonde or light brown long hair. The nonwhite models appearing in these catalogues must resemble as closely as possible their white counterparts so as not to detract from the racialized subtext. A recent cover of *Tweeds* carried this statement:

> Color is, perhaps, one of the most important barometers of character and self-assurance. It is as much a part of the international language of clothes as silhouette. The message colors convey, however, should never over- whelm. They should speak as eloquently and intelligently as the wearer. Whenever colors have that intelligence, subtlety, and nuance we tend to call them European.

Given the racialized terminology evoked in this copy, it follows that when flesh is exposed in attire that is meant to evoke sexual desirability it is worn by a nonwhite model. As sexist/racist sexual mythology would have it, she is the embodiment of the best of the black female savage tempered by those elements of whiteness that soften this image, giving it an aura of virtue and innocence. In the racialized pornographic imagination, she is the perfect combination of virgin and whore, the ultimate vamp. The impact of this image is so intense that Iman, a highly paid black fashion model who once received worldwide acclaim because she was the perfect black clone of a white ice goddess beauty, has had to change. Postmodern notions that black female beauty is constructed, not innate or inherent, are personified by the career of Iman. Noted in the past for features this culture sees as "Caucasian"—thin nose, lips, and limbs—Iman appears in the October 1989 issue of *Vogue* "made over." Her lips and breasts are suddenly full. Having once had her "look" destroyed by a car accident and then remade, Iman now goes a step further. Displayed as the embodiment of a heightened sexuality, she now looks like the racial/sexual stereotype. In one full-page shot, she is naked, wearing only a pair of brocade boots, looking as though she is ready to stand on any street corner and turn a trick, or worse yet, as though she just walked off one of the pages of *Players* (a porn magazine for blacks). Iman's new image appeals to a culture that is eager to reinscribe the image of black woman as sexual primitive. This new representation is a response to con- temporary fascination with an ethnic look, with the exotic Other who promises to fulfill racial and sexual stereotypes, to satisfy longings. This image is but an extension of the edible black tit.

Currently, in the fashion world the new black female icon who is also gaining greater notoriety, as she assumes both the persona of sexually hot "savage" and white-identified black girl, is the Caribbean-born model Naomi Campbell. Imported beauty, she, like Iman, is almost constantly visually portrayed nearly nude against a sexualized background. Abandoning her "natural" hair for blonde wigs or everlengthening weaves, she has great crossover appeal. Labeled by fashion critics as the black Briget Bardot, she embodies an aesthetic that suggests black women, while appealingly "different," must resemble white women to be considered really beautiful.

Within literature and early film, this sanitized ethnic image was defined as that of the "tragic mulatto." Appearing in film, she was the vamp that white men feared. As Julie Burchill puts it outrageously in *Girls On Film*:

> In the mature Forties, Hollywood decided to get to grips with the meaty and messy topic of multiracial romance, but it was a morbid business. Even when the girls were gorgeous white girls—multiracial romance brought tears, traumas, and suicide. The message was clear: you intelligent white men suffer enough guilt because of what your grandaddy did—you want to suffer some more! Keep away from those girls.

Contemporary films portraying biracial stars convey this same message. The warning for women is different from that given men—we are given messages about the danger of asserting sexual desire. Clearly the message from *Imitation of Life* was that attempting to define oneself as sexual subject would lead to rejection and abandonment. In the film *Choose Me*, Rae Dawn Chong plays the role of the highly sexual black woman chasing and seducing the white man who does not desire her (as was first implied in *Imitation of Life*) but instead uses her sexually, beats her, then discards her. The biracial black woman is constantly "gaslighted" in contemporary film. The message her sexualized image conveys does not change even as she continues to chase the white man as if only he had the power to affirm that she is truly desirable.

European films like *Mephisto* and the more recent *Mona Lisa* also portray the almost white, black woman as tragically sexual. The women in the films can only respond to constructions of their reality created by the more powerful. They are trapped. Mona Lisa's struggle to be sexually self-defining leads her to choose lesbianism, even though she is desired by the white male hero. Yet her choice of a female partner does not mean sexual fulfillment as the object of her lust is a drug-addicted young white woman who is always too messed up to be sexual. Mona Lisa nurses and protects her. Rather than asserting sexual agency, she is once again in the role of mammy.

In a more recent film, *The Virgin Machine*, a white German woman obsessed by the longing to understand desire goes to California where she hopes to find a "paradise of black Amazons." However, when she arrives and checks out the lesbian scene, the black women she encounters are portrayed as mean fat grotesques, lewd and licentious. Contemporary films continue to place black women in two categories, mammy or slut, and occasionally a combination of the two. In *Mona Lisa*, one scene serves as powerful commentary on the way black sexuality is perceived in a racist and imperialist social context. The white male who desires the black prostitute Mona Lisa is depicted as a victim of romantic love who wishes to rescue her from a life of ruin. Yet he is also the conqueror, the colonizer, and this is most evident in the scene where he watches a video wherein she engages in fellatio with the black male pimp who torments her. Both the black man and the black woman are presented as available for the white male's sexual consumption. In the context of postmodern sexual practice, the masturbatory voyeuristic technologically based fulfillment of desire is more exciting than actually possessing any real Other.

There are few films or television shows that attempt to challenge assumptions that sexual relationships between black women and white men are not based solely on power relationships which mirror master/slave paradigms. Years ago, when soap operas first tried to portray romantic/sexual involvement between a black woman and a white man, the station received so many letters of protest from outraged viewers that they dropped this plot. Today many viewers are glued to the television screen watching the soap opera *All My Children* primarily to see if the black woman played by Debbie Morgan will win the white man she so desperately loves. These two lovers are never portrayed in bedroom scenes so common now in daytime soaps. Morgan's character is competing not just with an old white woman flame to get her white man, she is competing with a notion of family. And the story poses the question of whether white male desire for black flesh will prevail over commitments to blood and family loyalty.

Despite this plot of interracial sexual romance on the soaps, there is little public discussion of the connections between race and sexuality. In real life, it was the Miss America pageant where a black woman was chosen to represent beauty and therefore desirability which forced a public discussion of race and sex. When it was revealed that Vanessa Williams, the fair-skinned straightened-hair "beauty," had violated the representation of the Miss America girl as pure and virtuous by having posed nude in a series of photographs showing her engaged in sexual play with a white woman, she lost her crown but gained a different status. After her public "disgrace," she was able to remain in the limelight by appropriating the image of sexualized vamp and playing sexy roles in films. Unmasked by a virtuous white public, she assumed (according to their standards) the rightful erotic place set aside for black women in the popular imagination. The American public that had so brutally critiqued Williams and rejected her had no difficulty accepting and applauding her when she accepted the image of fallen woman. Again, as in the case of Tina Turner, Williams's bid for continued success necessitated her acceptance of conventional racist/sexist representations of black female sexuality.

The contemporary film that has most attempted to address the issue of black female sexual agency is Spike Lee's *She's Gotta Have It*. Sad to say, the black woman does not get "it." By the end of the film, she is still unable to answer the critical question, posed by one of her lovers as he rapes her, "whose pussy is this?" Reworded the question might be: How and when will black females assert sexual agency in ways that liberate us from the confines of colonized desire, of racist/sexist imagery and practice? Had Nola Darling been able to claim her sexuality and name its power, the film would have had a very different impact.

There are few films that explore issues of black female sexuality in ways that intervene and disrupt conventional representations. The short film *Dreaming Rivers*, by the British black film collective Sankofa, juxtaposes the idealized representation of black woman as mother with that of sexual subject, showing adult children facing their narrow notions of black female identity. The film highlights the autonomous sexual identity of a mature black woman which exists apart from her role as mother and caregiver. *Passion of Remembrance*, another film by Sankofa, offers exciting new representations of the black female body and black female sexuality. In one playfully erotic scene, two young black women, a lesbian couple, get dressed to go out. As part of their celebratory preparations they dance together, painting their lips, looking at their images in the mirror, exulting in their black female bodies. They shake to a song that repeats the refrain "let's get loose" without conjuring images of a rotgut colonized sexuality on display for the racist/sexist imagination. Their pleasure, the film suggests, emerges in a decolonized erotic context rooted in commitments to feminist and antiracist politics. When they look in the mirror and focus on specific body parts (their full thick lips and buttocks), the gaze is one of recognition. We see their pleasure and delight in themselves.

Films by African American women filmmakers also offer the most oppositional images of black female sexuality. Seeing for a second time Kathleen Collin's film *Losing Ground*, I was impressed by her daring, the way she portrays black female sexuality in a way that is fresh and exciting. Like *Passion of*

Remembrance it is in a domestic setting, where black women face one another (in Collin's film—as mother and daughter), that erotic images of black female sexuality surface outside a context of domination and exploitation. When daughter and mother share a meal, the audience watches as a radical sexual aesthetics emerges as the camera moves from woman to woman, focusing on the shades and textures of their skin, the shapes of their bodies, and the way their delight and pleasure in themselves is evident in their environment. Both black women discreetly flaunt a rich sensual erotic energy that is not directed outward, it is not there to allure or entrap; it is a powerful declaration of black female sexual subjectivity.

When black women relate to our bodies, our sexuality, in ways that place erotic recognition, desire, pleasure, and fulfillment at the center of our efforts to create radical black female subjectivity, we can make new and different representations of ourselves as sexual subjects. To do so we must be willing to transgress traditional boundaries. We must no longer shy away from the critical project of openly interrogating and exploring representations of black female sexuality as they appear everywhere, especially in popular culture. In *The Power of the Image: Essays on Representation and Sexuality*, Annette Kuhn offers a critical manifesto for feminist thinkers who long to explore gender and representation:

> In order to challenge dominant representations, it is necessary first of all to understand how they work, and thus where to seek points of possible productive transformation. From such understanding flow various politics and practices of oppositional cultural production, among which may be counted feminist interventions . . . there is another justification for a feminist analysis of mainstream images of women: may it not teach us to recognize inconsistencies and contradictions within dominant traditions of representation, to identify points of leverage for our own intervention: cracks and fissures through which may be captured glimpses of what in other circumstance might be possible, visions of "a world outside the order not normally seen or thought about?"

This is certainly the challenge facing black women, who must confront the old painful representations of our sexuality as a burden we must suffer, representations still haunting the present. We must make the oppositional space where our sexuality can be named and represented, where we are sexual subjects—no longer bound and trapped.

7

Foucault, Femininity, and the Modernization of Patriarchal Power

Sandra Lee Bartky

I

In a striking critique of modern society, Michel Foucault has argued that the rise of parliamentary institutions and of new conceptions of political liberty was accompanied by a darker countermovement, by the emergence of a new and unprecedented discipline directed against the body. More is required of the body now than mere political allegiance or the appropriation of the products of its labor: The new discipline invades the body and seeks to regulate its very forces and operations, the economy and efficiency of its movements.

The disciplinary practices Foucault describes are tied to peculiarly modern forms of the army, the school, the hospital, the prison, and the manufactory; the aim of these disciplines is to increase the utility of the body, to augment its forces:

What was then being formed was a policy of coercions that act upon the body, a calculated manipulation of its elements, its gestures, its behaviour. The human body was entering a machinery of power that explores it, breaks it down and rearranges it. A "political anatomy," which was also a "mechanics of power," was being born; it defined how one may have a hold over others' bodies, not only so that they may do what one wishes, but so that they may operate as one wishes, with the techniques, the speed and the efficiency that one determines. Thus, discipline produces subjected and practiced bodies, "docile" bodies.[1]

The production of "docile bodies" requires that an uninterrupted coercion be directed to the very processes of bodily activity, not just their result; this "microphysics of power" fragments and partitions the body's time, its space, and its movements.[2]

The student, then, is enclosed within a classroom and assigned to a desk he cannot leave; his ranking in the class can be read off the position of his desk in the serially ordered and segmented space of the classroom itself. Foucault tells us that "Jean-Baptiste de la Salle dreamt of a classroom in which the spatial distribution might provide a whole series of distinctions at once, according to the pupil's progress, worth, character, application, cleanliness, and parents' fortune."[3] The student must sit upright, feet upon the floor, head erect; he may not slouch or fidget; his animate body is brought into a fixed correlation with the inanimate desk.

The minute breakdown of gestures and movements required of soldiers at drill is far more relentless:

> Bring the weapon forward. In three stages. Raise the rifle with the right hand, bringing it close to the body so as to hold it perpendicular with the right knee, the end of the barrel at eye level, grasping it by striking it with the right hand, the arm held close to the body at waist height. At the second stage, bring the rifle in front of you with the left hand, the barrel in the middle between the two eyes, vertical, the right hand grasping it at the small of the butt, the arm outstretched, the trigger-guard resting on the first finger, the left hand at the height of the notch, the thumb lying along the barrel against the moulding. At the third stage. . . . [4]

These "body-object articulations" of the soldier and his weapon, the student and his desk, effect a "coercive link with the apparatus of production." We are far indeed from older forms of control that "demanded of the body only signs or products, forms of expression or the result of labor."[5]

The body's time, in these regimes of power, is as rigidly controlled as its space: The factory whistle and the school bell mark a division of time into discrete and segmented units that regulate the various activities of the day. The following timetable, similar in spirit to the ordering of my grammar school classroom, was suggested for French "écoles mutuelles" of the early nineteenth century:

> 8:45 entrance of the monitor, 8:52 the monitor's summons, 8:56 entrance of the children and prayer, 9:00 the children go to their benches, 9:04 first slate, 9:08 end of dictation, 9:12 second slate, etc.[6]

Control this rigid and precise cannot be maintained without a minute and relentless surveillance.

Jeremy Bentham's design for the Panopticon, a model prison, captures for Foucault the essence of the disciplinary society. At the periphery of the Panopticon, a circular structure; at the center, a tower with wide windows that open onto the inner side of the ring. The structure on the periphery is divided into cells, each with two windows, one facing the windows of the tower, the other facing the outside, allowing an effect of backlighting to make any figure visible within the cell. "All that is needed, then, is to place a supervisor in a central tower and to shut up in each cell a madman, a patient, a condemned man, a worker or a schoolboy."[7] Each inmate is alone, shut off from effective communication with his fellows, but constantly visible from the tower. The effect of this is "to induce in the inmate a state of conscious and permanent visibility that assures the automatic functioning of power"; each becomes to himself his own jailer.[8] This "state of conscious and permanent visibility" is a sign that the tight, disciplinary control of the body has gotten a hold on the mind as well. In the perpetual self-surveillance of the inmate lies the genesis of the celebrated "individualism" and heightened self-consciousness which are hallmarks of modern times. For Foucault, the structure and effects of the Panopticon resonate throughout society: Is it surprising that "prisons resemble factories, schools, barracks, hospitals, which all resemble prisons?"[9]

Foucault's account in *Discipline and Punish* of the disciplinary practices that produce the "docile bodies" of modernity is a genuine tour de force, incorporating a rich theoretical account of the ways in which instrumental reason takes hold of the body with a mass of historical detail. But Foucault treats the body throughout as if it were one, as if the bodily experiences of men and women did not differ and as if men and women bore the same relationship to the characteristic institutions of modern life. Where is the account of the disciplinary practices that engender the "docile bodies" of women, bodies more docile than the bodies of men? Women, like men, are subject to many of the same disciplinary practices Foucault describes. But he is blind to those disciplines that produce a modality of embodiment that is peculiarly feminine. To overlook the forms of subjection that engender the feminine body is to perpetuate the silence and powerlessness of those upon whom these disciplines have been imposed. Hence, even though a liberatory note is sounded in Foucault's critique of power, his analysis as a whole reproduces that sexism which is endemic throughout Western political theory.

We are born male or female, but not masculine or feminine. Femininity is an artifice, an achievement, "a mode of enacting and reenacting received gender norms which surface as so many styles of the flesh."[10] In what follows, I shall examine those disciplinary practices that produce a body which in gesture and appearance is recognizably feminine. I consider three categories of such practices: those that aim to produce a body of a certain size and general configuration; those that bring forth from this body a specific repertoire of gestures, postures, and movements; and those directed toward the display of this body as an ornamented surface. I shall examine the nature of these disciplines, how they are imposed, and by whom. I shall probe the effects of the imposition of such discipline on female identity and subjectivity. In the final section I shall argue that these disciplinary practices must be understood in the light of the modernization of patriarchal domination, a modernization that unfolds historically according to the general pattern described by Foucault.

II

Styles of the female figure vary over time and across cultures: they reflect cultural obsessions and preoccupations in ways that are still poorly understood. Today, massiveness, power, or abundance in a woman's body is met with distaste. The current body of fashion is taut, small-breasted, narrow-hipped, and of a slimness bordering on emaciation; it is a silhouette that seems more appropriate to an adolescent boy or a newly pubescent girl than to an adult woman. Since ordinary women have normally quite different dimensions, they must of course diet.

Mass-circulation women's magazines run articles on dieting in virtually every issue. The *Ladies' Home Journal* of February 1986 carries a "Fat-Burning Exercise Guide," while *Mademoiselle* offers to "Help Stamp Out Cellulite" with "Six Sleek-Down Strategies." After the diet-busting Christmas holidays and later, before summer bikini season, the titles of these features become shriller and more arresting. The reader is now addressed in the imperative mode: Jump into shape for summer! Shed ugly winter fat with the all-new Grapefruit Diet! More women than men visit diet doctors, while women greatly outnumber men in self-help groups such as Weight Watchers and Overeaters Anonymous—in the case of the latter, by well over 90 percent.[11]

Dieting disciplines the body's hungers: Appetite must be monitored at all times and governed by an iron will. Since the innocent need of the organism for food will not be denied, the body becomes one's enemy, an alien being bent on thwarting the disciplinary project. Anorexia nervosa, which has now assumed epidemic proportions, is to women of the late twentieth century what hysteria was to women of an earlier day: the crystallization in a pathological mode of a widespread cultural obsession.[12] A survey taken recently at UCLA is astounding: Of 260 students interviewed, 27.3 percent of the women but only 5.8 percent of men said they were "terrified" of getting fat: 28.7 percent of women and only 7.5 percent of men said they were obsessed or "totally preoccupied" with food. The body images of women and men are strikingly different as well: 35 percent of women but only 12.5 percent of men said they felt fat though other people told them they were thin. Women in the survey wanted to weigh ten pounds less than their average weight; men felt they were within a pound of their ideal weight. A total of 5.9 percent of women and no men met the psychiatric criteria for anorexia or bulimia.[13]

Dieting is one discipline imposed upon a body subject to the "tyranny of slenderness"; exercise is another.[14] Since men as well as women exercise, it is not always easy in the case of women to distinguish what is done for the sake of physical fitness from what is done in obedience to the requirements of femininity. Men as well as women lift weights, do yoga, calisthenics, and aerobics, though "jazzercise" is a largely female pursuit. Men and women alike engage themselves with a variety of machines, each designed to call forth from the body a different exertion: There are Nautilus machines, rowing machines, ordinary and motorized exercycles, portable hip and leg cycles, belt massagers, trampolines; treadmills, arm and leg pulleys. However, given the widespread female obsession with weight, one suspects that many women are working out with these apparatuses in the health club or at the gym with a different aim in mind and in quite a different spirit than the men.

But there are classes of exercises meant for women alone, these designed not to firm or to reduce the body's size overall, but to resculpture its various parts on the current model. M. J. Saffon, "international beauty expert," assures us that his twelve basic facial exercises can erase frown lines, smooth the forehead, raise hollow cheeks, banish crow's feet, and tighten the muscles under the chin.[15] There are exercises to build the breasts and exercises to banish "cellulite," said by "figure consultants" to be a special type of female fat. There is "spot-reducing," an umbrella term that covers dozens of punishing exercises designed to reduce "problem areas" like thick ankles or "saddlebag" thighs. The very idea of "spot-reducing" is both scientifically unsound and cruel, for it raises expectations in women that can never be realized: The pattern in which fat is deposited or removed is known to be genetically determined.

It is not only her natural appetite or unreconstructed contours that pose a danger to women: The very expressions of her face can subvert the disciplinary project of bodily perfection. An expressive face lines and creases more readily than an inexpressive one. Hence, if women are unable to suppress strong emotions, they can at least learn to inhibit the tendency of the face to register them. Sophia Loren recommends a unique solution to this problem: A piece of tape applied to the forehead or between the brows will tug at the skin when one frowns and act as a reminder to relax the face.[16] The tape is to be worn whenever a woman is home alone.

III

There are significant gender differences in gesture, posture, movement, and general bodily comportment: Women are far more restricted than men in their manner of movement and in their lived spatiality. In her classic paper on the subject, Iris Young observes that a space seems to surround women in imagination which they are hesitant to move beyond: This manifests itself both in a reluctance to reach, stretch, and extend the body to meet resistances of matter in motion —as in sport or in the performance of physical tasks—and in a typically constricted posture and general style of movement. Woman's space is not a field in which her bodily intentionality can be freely realized but an enclosure in which she feels herself positioned and by which she is confined.[17] The "loose woman" violates these norms: Her looseness is manifest not only in her morals, but in her manner of speech, and quite literally in the free and easy way she moves.

In an extraordinary series of over two thousand photographs, many candid shots taken in the street, the German photographer Marianne Wex has documented differences in typical masculine and feminine body posture. Women sit waiting for trains with arms close to the body, hands folded together in their laps, toes pointing straight ahead or turned inward, and legs pressed together.[18] The women in these photographs make themselves small and narrow, harmless; they seem tense; they take up little space. Men, on the other hand, expand into the available space; they sit with legs far apart and arms flung out at some distance from the body. Most common in these sitting male figures is what Wex calls the "proferring position": the men sit with legs thrown wide apart, crotch visible, feet pointing outward, often with an arm and casually dangling hand resting comfortably on an open, spread thigh.

In proportion to total body size, a man's stride is longer than a woman's. The man has more spring and rhythm to his step; he walks with toes pointed outward, holds his arms at a greater distance from his body, and swings them farther; he tends to point the whole hand in the direction he is moving. The woman holds her arms closer to her body, palms against her sides; her walk is circumspect. If she has subjected herself to the additional constraint of high-heeled shoes, her body is thrown forward and off-balance: The struggle to walk under these conditions shortens her stride still more.[19]

But women's movement is subjected to a still finer discipline. Feminine faces, as well as bodies, are trained to the expression of deference. Under male scrutiny, women will avert their eyes or cast them downward; the female gaze is trained to abandon its claim to the sovereign status of seer. The "nice" girl learns to avoid the bold and unfettered staring of the "loose" woman who looks at whatever and whomever she pleases. Women are trained to smile more than men, too. In the economy of smiles, as elsewhere, there is evidence that women are exploited, for they give more than they receive in return; in a smile elicitation study, one researcher found that the rate of smile return by women was 93 percent, by men only 67 percent.[20] In many typical women's jobs, graciousness, deference, and the readiness to serve are part of the work; this requires the worker to fix a smile on her face for a good part of the working day, whatever her inner state.[21] The economy of touching is out of balance, too: men touch women more often and on more parts of the body than women touch men: female secretaries, factory workers, and waitresses report that such liberties are taken routinely with their bodies.[22]

Feminine movement, gesture, and posture must exhibit not only constriction, but grace as well, and a certain eroticism restrained by modesty:

all three. Here is field for the operation for a whole new training: A woman must stand with stomach pulled in, shoulders thrown slightly back, and chest out, this to display her bosom to maximum advantage. While she must walk in the confined fashion appropriate to women, her movements must, at the same time, be combined with a subtle but provocative hip-roll. But too much display is taboo: Women in short, low-cut dresses are told to avoid bending over at all, but if they must, great care must be taken to avoid an unseemly display of breast or rump. From time to time, fashion magazines offer quite precise instructions on the proper way of getting in and out of cars. These instructions combine all three imperatives of women's movement: A woman must not allow her arms and legs to flail about in all directions; she must try to manage her movements with the appearance of grace—no small accomplishment when one is climbing out of the back seat of a Fiat—and she is well advised to use the opportunity for a certain display of leg.

All the movements we have described so far are self-movements; they arise from within the woman's own body. But in a way that normally goes unnoticed, males in couples may literally steer a woman everywhere she goes: down the street, around corners, into elevators, through doorways, into her chair at the dinner table, around the dance-floor. The man's movement "is not necessarily heavy and pushy or physical in an ugly way; it is light and gentle but firm in the way of the most confident equestrians with the best trained horses."[23]

IV

We have examined some of the disciplinary practices a woman must master in pursuit of a body of the right size and shape that also displays the proper styles of feminine motility. But woman's body is an ornamented surface too, and there is much discipline involved in this production as well. Here, especially in the application of make-up and the selection of clothes, art and discipline converge, though, as I shall argue, there is less art involved than one might suppose.

A woman's skin must be soft, supple, hairless, and smooth; ideally, it should betray no sign of wear, experience, age, or deep thought. Hair must be removed not only from the face but from large surfaces of the body as well, from legs and thighs, an operation accomplished by shaving, buffing with fine sandpaper, or foul-smelling depilatories. With the new high-leg bathing suits and leotards, a substantial amount of pubic hair must be removed too.[24] The removal of facial hair can be more specialized. Eyebrows are plucked out by the roots with a tweezer. Hot wax is sometimes poured onto the mustache and cheeks and then ripped away when it cools. The woman who wants a more permanent result may try electrolysis: This involves the killing of a hair root by the passage of an electric current down a needle which has been inserted into its base. The procedure is painful and expensive.

The development of what one "beauty expert" calls "good skin-care habits" requires not only attention to health, the avoidance of strong facial expressions, and the performance of facial exercises, but the regular use of skin-care preparations, many to be applied oftener than once a day: cleansing lotions (ordinary soap and water "upsets the skin's acid and alkaline balance"), wash-off cleansers (milder than cleansing lotions), astringents, toners, make-up removers, night creams, nourishing creams, eye creams, moisturizers, skin balancers, body lotions, hand creams, lip pomades, suntan lotions, sun screens, facial masks. Provision of the proper facial mask is complex: There are sulfur masks for pimples; hot or oil masks for dry areas; also cold masks for dry areas; tightening masks; conditioning masks; peeling masks; cleansing masks made of herbs, cornmeal, or almonds; mud packs. Black women may wish to use "fade creams" to "even skin tone." Skin-care preparations are never just sloshed onto the skin, but applied according to precise rules: Eye cream is dabbed on gently in movements toward, never away from, the nose; cleansing cream is applied in outward directions only, straight across the forehead, the upper lip, and the chin, never up but straight down the nose and up and out on the cheeks.[25]

The normalizing discourse of modern medicine is enlisted by the cosmetics industry to gain credibility for its claims. Dr. Christiaan Barnard lends his enormous prestige to the Glycel line of "cellular treatment activators"; these contain "glycosphingolipids" that can "make older skin behave and look like younger skin." The Clinique computer at any Clinique counter will select a combination of preparations just right for you. Ultima II contains "procollagen" in its anti-aging eye cream that "provides hydration" to "demoralizing lines." "Biotherm" eye cream dramatically improves the "biomechanical properties of the skin."[26] The Park Avenue clinic of Dr. Zizmor, "chief of dermatology at one of New York's leading hospitals," offers not only medical treatment such as dermabrasion and chemical peeling but "total deep skin cleansing" as well.[27]

Really good skin-care habits require the use of a variety of aids and devices: facial steamers; faucet filters to collect impurities in the water;

borax to soften it; a humidifier for the bedroom; electric massagers; back-brushes; complexion brushes; loofahs; pumice stones; blackhead removers. I will not detail the implements or techniques involved in the manicure or pedicure.

The ordinary circumstances of life as well as a wide variety of activities cause a crisis in skin-care and require a stepping up of the regimen as well as an additional laying on of preparations. Skin-care discipline requires a specialized knowledge: A woman must know what to do if she has been skiing, taking medication, doing vigorous exercise, boating, or swimming in chlorinated pools; if she has been exposed to pollution, heated rooms, cold, sun, harsh weather, the pressurized cabins on airplanes, saunas or steam rooms, fatigue or stress. Like the schoolchild or prisoner, the woman mastering good skin-care habits is put on a timetable: Georgette Klinger requires that a shorter or longer period of attention be paid to the complexion at least four times a day.[28] Hair-care, like skin-care, requires a similar investment of time, the use of a wide variety of preparations, the mastery of a set of techniques and again, the acquisition of a specialized knowledge.

The crown and pinnacle of good hair care and skin care is, of course, the arrangement of the hair and the application of cosmetics. Here the regimen of hair care, skin care, manicure, and pedicure is recapitulated in another mode. A woman must learn the proper manipulation of a large number of devices—the blow dryer, styling brush, curling iron, hot curlers, wire curlers, eye-liner, lipliner, lipstick brush, eyelash curler, mascara brush—and the correct manner of application of a wide variety of products—foundation, toner, covering stick, mascara, eye shadow, eye gloss, blusher, lipstick, rouge, lip gloss, hair dye, hair rinse, hair lightener, hair "relaxer," etc.

In the language of fashion magazines and cosmetic ads, making up is typically portrayed as an aesthetic activity in which a woman can express her individuality. In reality, while cosmetic styles change every decade or so and while some variation in make-up is permitted depending on the occasion, making up the face is, in fact, a highly stylized activity that gives little rein to self-expression. Painting the face is not like painting a picture; at best, it might be described as painting the same picture over and over again with minor variations. Little latitude is permitted in what is considered appropriate make-up for the office and for most social occasions; indeed, the woman who uses cosmetics in a genuinely novel and imaginative way is liable to be seen not as an artist but as an eccentric. Furthermore, since a properly made-up face is, if not a card of entrée, at least a badge of acceptability in most social and professional contexts, the woman who chooses not to wear cosmetics at all faces sanctions of a sort which will never be applied to someone who chooses not to paint a watercolor. *lack of agency*

V — *here come the "differences"*

Are we dealing in all this merely with sexual *difference*? Scarcely. The disciplinary practices I have described are part of the process by which the ideal body of femininity—and hence the feminine body-subject—is constructed; in doing this, they produce a "practiced and subjected" body, i.e., a body on which an inferior status has been inscribed. A woman's face must be made up, that is to say, made over, and so must her body: she is ten pounds overweight; her lips must be made more kissable; her complexion dewier; her eyes more mysterious. The "art" of make-up is the art of disguise, but this presupposes that a woman's face, unpainted, is defective. Soap and water, a shave, and routine attention to hygiene may be enough for *him*; for *her* they are not. The strategy of much beauty-related advertising is to suggest to women that their bodies are deficient, but even without such more or less explicit teaching, the media images of perfect female beauty which bombard us daily leave no doubt in the minds of most women that they fail to measure up. The technologies of femininity are taken up and practiced by women against the background of a pervasive sense of bodily deficiency: This accounts for what is often their compulsive or even ritualistic character.

The disciplinary project of femininity is a "set-up": It requires such radical and extensive measures of bodily transformation that virtually every woman who gives herself to it is destined in some degree to fail. Thus, a measure of shame is added to a woman's sense that the body she inhabits is deficient: she ought to take better care of herself; she might after all have jogged that last mile. Many women are without the time or resources to provide themselves with even the minimum of what such a regimen requires, e.g., a decent diet. Here is an additional source of shame for poor women who must *class* bear what our society regards as the more general shame of poverty. The burdens poor women bear in this regard are not merely psychological, since conformity to the prevailing standards of bodily acceptability is a known factor in economic mobility. *NJ fancy clothes salvation army*

The larger disciplines that construct a "feminine" body out of a female one are by no means race- or class-specific. There is little evidence that women of color or working-class women are in general less committed to the incarnation of an ideal femininity than their more privileged sisters. This is not to

i.e. white

deny the many ways in which factors of race, class, locality, ethnicity, or personal taste can be expressed within the kinds of practices I have described.
The rising young corporate executive may buy her cosmetics at Bergdorf-
Goodman while the counter-server at McDonald's gets hers at the K-Mart;
the one may join an expensive "upscale" health club, while the other may have
to make do with the $9.49 GFX Body-Flex II Home-Gym advertised in the
National Enquirer: Both are aiming at the same general result.[29]

   In the regime of institutionalized heterosexuality woman must make herself "object and prey" for the man: It is for him that these eyes are limpid
pools, this cheek baby-smooth.[30] In contemporary patriarchal culture, a
panoptical male connoisseur resides within the consciousness of most
women: They stand perpetually before his gaze and under his judgment.
Woman lives her body as seen by another, by an anonymous patriarchal
Other. We are often told that "women dress for other women." There is some
truth in this: Who but someone engaged in a project similar to my own can
appreciate the panache with which I bring it off? But women know for whom
this game is played: They know that a pretty young woman is likelier to
become a flight attendant than a plain one and that a well-preserved older
woman has a better chance of holding onto her husband than one who has "let
herself go."

   Here it might be objected that performance for another in no way signals
the inferiority of the performer to the one for whom the performance is
intended: The actor, for example, depends on his audience but is in no way
inferior to it; he is not demeaned by his dependency. While femininity is
surely something enacted, the analogy to theater breaks down in a number
of ways. First, as I argued earlier, the self-determination we think of as requisite to an artistic career is lacking here: Femininity as spectacle is something in which virtually every woman is required to participate. Second, the
precise nature of the criteria by which women are judged, not only the
inescapability of judgment itself, reflects gross imbalances in the social
power of the sexes that do not mark the relationship of artists and their audiences. An aesthetic of femininity, for example, that mandates fragility and a
lack of muscular strength produces female bodies that can offer little resistance to physical abuse, and the physical abuse of women by men, as we
know, is widespread. It is true that the current fitness movement has permitted women to develop more muscular strength and endurance than was
heretofore allowed; indeed, images of women have begun to appear in the
mass media that seem to eroticize this new muscularity. But a woman may by
no means develop more muscular strength than her partner; the bride who

would tenderly carry her groom across the threshold is a figure of comedy, not romance.[31] *hetero sexism + femininity*

Under the current "tyranny of slenderness" women are forbidden to become large or massive; they must take up as little space as possible. The very contours a woman's body takes on as she matures—the fuller breasts and rounded hips—have become distasteful. The body by which a woman feels herself judged and which by rigorous discipline she must try to assume is the body of early adolescence, slight and unformed, a body lacking flesh or substance, a body in whose very contours the image of immaturity has been inscribed. The requirement that a woman maintain a smooth and hairless skin carries further the theme of inexperience, for an infantilized face must accompany her infantilized body, a face that never ages or furrows its brow in thought. The face of the ideally feminine woman must never display the marks of character, wisdom, and experience that we so admire in men.

To succeed in the provision of a beautiful or sexy body gains a woman attention and some admiration but little real respect and rarely any social power. A woman's effort to master feminine body discipline will lack importance just because she does it: Her activity partakes of the general depreciation of everything female. In spite of unrelenting pressure to "make the most of what they have," women are ridiculed and dismissed for the triviality of their interest in such "trivial" things as clothes and make-up. Further, the narrow identification of woman with sexuality and the body in a society that has for centuries displayed profound suspicion toward both does little to raise her status. Even the most adored female bodies complain routinely of their situation in ways that reveal an implicit understanding that there is something demeaning in the kind of attention they receive. Marilyn Monroe, Elizabeth Taylor, and Farrah Fawcett have all wanted passionately to become actresses-artists and not just "sex objects."

But it is perhaps in their more restricted motility and comportment that the inferiorization of women's bodies is most evident: Women's typical body language, a language of relative tension and constriction, is understood to be a language of subordination when it is enacted by men in male status hierarchies. In groups of men, those with higher status typically assume looser and more relaxed postures: The boss lounges comfortably behind the desk while the applicant sits tense and rigid on the edge of his seat. Higher-status individuals may touch their subordinates more than they themselves get touched; they initiate more eye contact and are smiled at by their inferiors more than they are observed to smile in return.[32] What is announced in the comportment of superiors is confidence and ease, especially ease of access to the

Other. Female constraint in posture and movement is no doubt overdetermined: The fact that women tend to sit and stand with legs, feet, and knees close or touching may well be a coded declaration of sexual circumspection in a society that still maintains a double standard, or an effort, albeit unconscious, to guard the genital area. In the latter case, a woman's tight and constricted posture must be seen as the expression of her need to ward off real or symbolic sexual attack. Whatever proportions must be assigned in the final display to fear or deference, one thing is clear: Woman's body language speaks eloquently, though silently, of her subordinate status in a hierarchy of gender.

VI

If what we have described is a genuine discipline—a "system of micropower that is essentially non-egalitarian and asymmetrical"—who then are the disciplinarians?[33] Who is the top sergeant in the disciplinary regime of femininity? Historically, the law has had some responsibility for enforcement: In times gone by, for example, individuals who appeared in public in the clothes of the other sex could be arrested. While cross-dressers are still liable to some harassment, the kind of discipline we are considering is not the business of the police or the courts. Parents and teachers, of course, have extensive influence, admonishing girls to be demure and ladylike, to "smile pretty," to sit with their legs together. The influence of the media is pervasive, too, constructing as it does an image of the female body as spectacle, nor can we ignore the role played by "beauty experts" or by emblematic public personages such as Jane Fonda and Lynn Redgrave.

But none of these individuals—the skin-care consultant, the parent, the policeman— docs in fact wield the kind of authority that is typically invested in those who manage more straightforward disciplinary institutions. The disciplinary power that inscribes femininity in the female body is everywhere and it is nowhere; the disciplinarian is everyone and yet no one in particular. Women regarded as overweight, for example, report that they are regularly admonished to diet, sometimes by people they scarcely know. These intrusions are often softened by reference to the natural prettiness just waiting to emerge: "People have always said that I had a beautiful face and 'if you'd only lose weight you'd be really beautiful.'"[34] Here, "people"—friends and casual acquaintances alike—act to enforce prevailing standards of body size.

Foucault tends to identify the imposition of discipline upon the body with the operation of specific institutions, e.g., the school, the factory, the prison.

To do this, however, however, is to overlook the extent to which discipline can be institutionally *unbound* as well as institutionally bound.[35] The anonymity of disciplinary power and its wide dispersion have consequences which are crucial to a proper understanding of the subordination of women. The absence of a formal institutional structure and of authorities invested with the power to carry out institutional directives creates the impression that the production of femininity is either entirely voluntary or natural. The several senses of "discipline" are instructive here. On the one hand, discipline is something imposed on subjects of an "essentially inegalitarian and asymmetrical" system of authority. Schoolchildren, convicts, and draftees are subject to discipline in this sense. But discipline can be sought voluntarily as well, as, for example, when an individual seeks initiation into the spiritual discipline of Zen Buddhism. Discipline can, of course, be both at once: The volunteer may seek the physical and occupational training offered by the army without the army's ceasing in any way to be the instrument by which he and other members of his class are kept in disciplined subjection. Feminine bodily discipline has this dual character: On the one hand, no one is marched off for electrolysis at the end of a rifle, nor can we fail to appreciate the initiative and ingenuity displayed by countless women in an attempt to master the rituals of beauty. Nevertheless, insofar as the disciplinary practices of femininity produce a "subjected and practiced," an inferiorized, body, they must be understood as aspects of a far larger discipline, an oppressive and inegalitarian system of sexual subordination. This system aims at turning women into the docile and compliant companions of men just as surely as the army aims to turn its raw recruits into soldiers.

Now the transformation of oneself into a properly feminine body may be any or all of the following: a rite of passage into adulthood; the adoption and celebration of a particular aesthetic; a way of announcing one's economic level and social status; a way to triumph over other women in the competition for men or jobs; or an opportunity for massive narcissistic indulgence.[36] The social construction of the feminine body is all these things, but it is at base discipline, too, and discipline of the inegalitarian sort. The absence of formally identifiable disciplinarians and of a public schedule of sanctions serves only to disguise the extent to which the imperative to be "feminine" serves the interest of domination. This is a lie in which all concur: Making up is merely artful play; one's first pair of high-heeled shoes is an innocent part of growing up and not the modern equivalent of foot-binding.

Why aren't all women feminists? In modern industrial societies, women are not kept in line by fear of retaliatory male violence; their victimization is

not that of the South African black. Nor will it suffice to say that a false consciousness engendered in women by patriarchal ideology is at the basis of
female subordination. This is not to deny the fact that women are often subject to gross male violence or that women and men alike are ideologically
mystified by the dominant gender arrangements. What I wish to suggest
instead is that an adequate understanding of women's oppression will require
an appreciation of the extent to which not only women's lives but their very
subjectivities are structured within an ensemble of systematically duplicitous
practices. The feminine discipline of the body is a case in point: The practices
which construct this body have an overt aim and character far removed,
indeed radically distinct, from their covert function. In this regard, the system of gender subordination, like the wage-bargain under capitalism, illustrates in its own way the ancient tension, between what is and what appears:
The phenomenal forms in which it is manifested are often quite different
from the real relations which form its deeper structure.

VII *differences II? not quite*

The lack of formal public sanctions does not mean that a woman who is
unable or unwilling to submit herself to the appropriate body discipline will
face no sanctions at all. On the contrary, she faces a very severe sanction
indeed in a world dominated by men: the refusal of male patronage. For the
heterosexual woman, this may mean the loss of a badly needed intimacy; for
both heterosexual women and lesbians, it may well mean the refusal of a
decent livelihood.

As noted earlier, women punish themselves too for the failure to conform. The growing literature on women's body size is filled with wrenching
confessions of shame from the overweight:

> I felt clumsy and huge. I felt that I would knock over furniture, bump into
> things, tip over chairs, not fit into vw's, especially when people were try-
> ing to crowd into the back seat. I felt like I was taking over the whole
> room. . . . I felt disgusting and like a slob. In the summer I felt hot and
> sweaty and I knew people saw my sweat as evidence that I was too fat.
>
> I feel so terrible about the way I look that I cut off connection with my
> body. I operate from the neck up. I do not look in mirrors. I do not want
> to spend time buying clothes. I do not want to spend time with make-up
> because it's painful for me to look at myself.[37]

I can no longer bear to look at myself. Whenever I have to stand in front of a mirror to comb my hair I tie a large towel around my neck. Even at night I slip my nightgown on before I take off my blouse and pants. But all this has only made it worse and worse. It's been so long since I've really looked at my body.[38]

The depth of these women's shame is a measure of the extent to which all women have internalized patriarchal standards of bodily acceptability. A fuller examination of what is meant here by "internalization" may shed light on a question posed earlier: Why isn't every woman a feminist?

Something is "internalized" when it gets incorporated into the structure of the self. By "structure of the self" I refer to those modes of perception and of self-perception which allow a self to distinguish itself both from other selves and from things which are not selves. I have described elsewhere how a generalized male witness comes to structure woman's consciousness of herself as a bodily being.[39] This, then, is one meaning of "internalization." The sense of oneself as a distinct and valuable individual is tied not only to the sense of how one is perceived, but also to what one knows, especially to what one knows how to do; this is a second sense of "internalization." Whatever its ultimate effect, discipline can provide the individual upon whom it is imposed with a sense of mastery as well as a secure sense of identity. There is a certain contradiction here: While its imposition may promote a larger disempowerment, discipline may bring with it a certain development of a person's powers. Women, then, like other skilled individuals, have a stake in the perpetuation of their skills, whatever it may have cost to acquire them and quite apart from the question whether, as a gender, they would have been better off had they never had to acquire them in the first place. Hence, feminism, especially a genuinely radical feminism that questions the patriarchal construction of the female body, threatens women with a certain de-skilling, something people normally resist: Beyond this, it calls into question that aspect of personal identity which is tied to the development of a sense of competence.

Resistance from this source may be joined by a reluctance to part with the rewards of compliance; further, many women will resist the abandonment of an aesthetic that defines what they take to be beautiful. But there is still another source of resistance, one more subtle perhaps, but tied once again to questions of identity and internalization. To have a body felt to be "feminine"—a body socially constructed through the appropriate practices—is in most cases crucial to a woman's sense of herself as female and, since persons currently can *be* only as male or female, to her sense of herself as an existing individual. To possess such a body may also be essential to her sense of herself as a sexually desiring and desirable subject. Hence, any political project which aims to dismantle the machinery that turns a female body into a feminine one may well be apprehended by a woman as something that threatens her with desexualization, if not outright annihilation.

The categories of masculinity and femininity do more than assist in the construction of personal identities; they are critical elements in our informal social ontology. This may account to some degree for the otherwise puzzling phenomenon of homophobia and for the revulsion felt by many at the sight of female bodybuilders; neither the homosexual nor the muscular woman can be assimilated easily into the categories that structure everyday life. The radical feminist critique of femininity, then, may pose a threat not only to a woman's sense of her own identity and desirability but to the very structure of her social universe.

Of course, many women *are* feminists, favoring a program of political and economic reform in the struggle to gain equality with men.[40] But many "reform" or liberal feminists, indeed, many orthodox Marxists, are committed to the idea that the preservation of a woman's femininity is quite compatible with her struggle for liberation.[41] These thinkers have rejected a normative femininity based upon the notion of "separate spheres" and the traditional sexual division of labor while accepting at the same time conventional standards of feminine body display. If my analysis is correct, such a feminism is incoherent. Foucault has argued that modern bourgeois democracy is deeply flawed in that it seeks political rights for individuals constituted as unfree by a variety of disciplinary micropowers that lie beyond the realm of what is ordinarily defined as the "political." "The man described for us whom we are invited to free," he says, "is already in himself the effect of a subjection much more profound than himself."[42] If, as I have argued, female subjectivity is constituted in any significant measure in and through the disciplinary practices that construct the feminine body, what Foucault says here of "man" is perhaps even truer of "woman." Marxists have maintained from the first the inadequacy of a purely liberal feminism: We have reached the same conclusion through a different route, casting doubt at the same time on the adequacy of traditional Marxist prescriptions for women's liberation as well. Liberals call for equal rights for women, traditional Marxists for the entry of women into production on an equal footing with men, the socialization of housework and proletarian revolution: neither calls for the deconstruction of the categories of masculinity and femininity.[43] Femininity as a certain "style of the flesh" will have to be surpassed in the direction of something quite different, not masculinity, which is in many ways only its mirror opposite, but a radical and as yet unimagined transformation of the female body.

VIII

Foucault has argued that the transition from traditional to modern societies has been characterized by a profound transformation in the exercise of power, by what he calls "a reversal of the political axis of individualization."[44] In older authoritarian systems, power was embodied in the person of the monarch and exercised upon a largely anonymous body of subjects; violation of the law was seen as an insult to the royal individual. While the methods employed to enforce compliance in the past were often quite brutal, involving gross assaults against the body, power in such a system operated in a haphazard and discontinuous fashion; much in the social totality lay beyond its reach.

By contrast, modern society has seen the emergence of increasingly invasive apparatuses of power: These exercise a far more restrictive social and psychological control than was heretofore possible. In modern societies, effects of power "circulate through progressively finer channels, gaining access to individuals themselves, to their bodies, their gestures and all their daily actions."[45] Power now seeks to transform the minds of those individuals who might be tempted to resist it, not merely to punish or imprison their bodies. This requires two things: a finer control of the body's time and its movements—a control that cannot be achieved without ceaseless surveillance and a better understanding of the specific person, of the genesis and nature of his "case." The power these new apparatuses seek to exercise requires a new knowledge of the individual: Modern psychology and sociology are born. Whether the new modes of control have charge of correction, production, education, or the provision of welfare, they resemble one another; they exercise power in a bureaucratic mode—faceless, centralized, and pervasive. A reversal has occurred: Power has now become anonymous, while the project of control has brought into being a new individuality. In fact, Foucault believes that the operation of power constitutes the very subjectivity of the subject. Here, the image of the Panopticon returns: Knowing that he may be observed from the tower at any time, the inmate takes over the job of policing himself. The gaze which is inscribed in the very structure of the disciplinary institution is internalized by the inmate: Modern technologies of behavior are thus oriented toward the production of isolated and self-policing subjects.[46]

Women have their own experience of the modernization of power, one which begins later but follows in many respects the course outlined by Foucault. In important ways, a woman's behavior is less regulated now than it was in the past. She has more mobility and is less confined to domestic space. She enjoys what to previous generations would have been an unimaginable sexual liberty. Divorce, access to paid work outside the home, and the increasing secularization of modern life have loosened the hold over her of the traditional family and, in spite of the current fundamentalist revival, of the church. Power in these institutions was wielded by individuals known to her. Husbands and fathers enforced patriarchal authority in the family. As in the ancien régime a woman's body was subject to sanctions if she disobeyed. Not Foucault's royal individual but the Divine Individual decreed that her desire be always "unto her husband," while the person of the priest made known to her God's more specific intentions concerning her place and duties. In the days when civil and ecclesiastical authority were still conjoined, individuals formally invested with power were charged with the correction of recalcitrant women whom the family had somehow failed to constrain.

By contrast, the disciplinary power that is increasingly charged with the production of a properly embodied femininity is dispersed and anonymous; there are no individuals formally empowered to wield it; it is, as we have seen, invested in everyone and in no one in particular. This disciplinary power is peculiarly modern: It does not rely upon violent or public sanctions, nor does it seek to restrain the freedom of the female body to move from place to place. For all that, its invasion of the body is well-nigh total: The female body enters "a machinery of power that explores it, breaks it down and rearranges it." The disciplinary techniques through which the "docile bodies" of women are constructed aim at a regulation which is perpetual and exhaustive—a regulation of the body's size and contours, its appetite, posture, gestures, and general comportment in space and the appearance of each of its visible parts.

As modern industrial societies change and as women themselves offer resistance to patriarchy, older forms of domination are eroded. But new forms arise, spread, and become consolidated. Women are no longer required to be chaste or modest, to restrict their sphere of activity to the home, or even to realize their properly feminine destiny in maternity: Normative femininity is coming more and more to be centered on woman's body—not its duties and obligations or even its capacity to bear children, but its sexuality, more precisely, its presumed heterosexuality and its appearance. There is, of course, nothing new in women's preoccupation with youth and beauty. What is new is the growing power of the image in a society increasingly oriented toward the visual media. Images of normative femininity, it might be ventured, have replaced the religiously oriented tracts of the past. New too is the spread of this discipline to all classes of women and its deployment throughout the life cycle. What was formerly the speciality of the aristocrat or courtesan is now the routine obligation of every woman, be she a grandmother or a barely pubescent girl.

To subject oneself to the new disciplinary power is to be up-to-date, to be "with-it"; as I have argued, it is presented to us in ways that are regularly disguised. It is fully compatible with the current need for women's wage labor, the cult of youth and fitness, and the need of advanced capitalism to maintain high levels of consumption. Further, it represents a saving in the economy of enforcement: Since it is women themselves who practice this discipline on and against their own bodies, men get off scot-free.

The woman who checks her make-up half a dozen times a day to see if her foundation has caked or her mascara run, who worries that the wind or rain may spoil her hairdo, who looks frequently to see if her stockings have bagged at the ankle, or who, feeling fat, monitors everything she eats, has become, just as surely as the inmate of Panopticon, a self-policing subject, a self committed to a relentless self-surveillance. This self-surveillance is a form of obedience to patriarchy. It is also the reflection in woman's consciousness of the fact that *she* is under surveillance in ways that *he* is not, that whatever else she may become, she is importantly a body designed to please or to excite. There has been induced in many women, then, in Foucault's words, "a state of conscious and permanent visibility that assures the automatic functioning of power."[48] Since the standards of female bodily acceptability are impossible fully to realize, requiring as they do a virtual transcendence of nature, a woman may live much of her life with a pervasive feeling of bodily deficiency. Hence, a tighter control of the body has gained a new kind of hold over the mind.

Foucault often writes as if power constitutes the very individuals upon whom it operates:

> The individual is not to be conceived as a sort of elementary nucleus, a primitive atom, a multiple and inert material on which power comes to fasten or against which it happens to strike. . . . In fact, it is already one

of the prime effects of power that certain bodies, certain gestures, certain discourses, certain desires, come to be identified and constituted as individuals.[49]

Nevertheless, if individuals were wholly constituted by the power/knowledge regime Foucault describes, it would make no sense to speak of resistance to discipline at all. Foucault seems sometimes on the verge of depriving us of a vocabulary in which to conceptualize the nature and meaning of those periodic refusals of control which, just as much as the imposition of control, mark the course of human history.

Peter Dews accuses Foucault of lacking a theory of the "libidinal body," i.e., the body upon which discipline is imposed and whose bedrock impulse toward spontaneity and pleasure might perhaps become the locus of resistance.[50] Do women's "libidinal" bodies, then, not rebel against the pain, constriction, tedium, semistarvation, and constant self-surveillance to which they are currently condemned? Certainly they do, but the rebellion is put down every time a woman picks up her eyebrow tweezers or embarks upon a new diet. The harshness of a regimen alone does not guarantee its rejection, for hardships can be endured if they are thought to be necessary or inevitable.

While "nature," in the form of a "libidinal" body, may not be the origin of a revolt against "culture," domination and the discipline it requires are never imposed without some cost. Historically, the forms and occasions of resistance are manifold. Sometimes, instances of resistance appear to spring from the introduction of new and conflicting factors into the lives of the dominated: The juxtaposition of old and new and the resulting incoherence or "contradiction" may make submission to the old ways seem increasingly unnecessary. In the present instance, what may be a major factor in the relentless and escalating objectification of women's bodies—namely, women's growing independence—produces in many women a sense of incoherence that calls into question the meaning and necessity of the current discipline. As women (albeit a small minority of women) begin to realize an unprecedented political, economic, and sexual self-determination, they fall ever more completely under the dominating gaze of patriarchy. It is this paradox, not the "libidinal body," that produces, here and there, pockets of resistance.

In the current political climate, there is no reason to anticipate either widespread resistance to currently fashionable modes of feminine embodiment or joyous experimentation with new "styles of the flesh"; moreover, such novelties would face profound opposition from material and psychological sources identified earlier in this essay (see section VII). In spite of this, a number of oppositional discourses and practices have appeared in recent years. An increasing number of women are "pumping iron," a few with little concern for the limits of body development imposed by current canons of femininity. Women in radical lesbian communities have also rejected hegemonic images of femininity and are struggling to develop a new female aesthetic. A striking feature of such communities is the extent to which they have overcome the oppressive identification of female beauty and desirability with youth. Here, the physical features of aging—"character" lines and graying hair—not only do not diminish a woman's attractiveness, they may even enhance it. A popular literature of resistance is growing, some of it analytical and reflective, like Kim Chernin's *The Obsession*, some oriented toward practical self-help, like Marcia Hutchinson's recent *Transforming Body Image: Learning to Love the Body You Have*. This literature reflects a mood akin in some ways to that other and earlier mood of quiet desperation to which Betty Friedan gave voice in *The Feminine Mystique*. Nor should we forget that a mass-based women's movement is in place in this country, which has begun a critical questioning of the meaning of femininity, if not yet in this, then in other domains of life. We women cannot begin the re-vision of our own bodies until we learn to read the cultural messages we inscribe upon them daily and until we come to see that even when the mastery of the disciplines of femininity produce a triumphant result, we are still only women. *a bit of an ambivalent ending*

NOTES

1. Michel Foucault, *Discipline and Punish* (New York: Vintage, 1979), p. 138.

2. Ibid., p. 28.

3. Ibid., p. 147.

4. Ibid., p. 153. Foucault is citing an eighteenth-century military manual, "Ordonnance du Ier janvier 1766 . . ., titre XI, article 2."

5. Ibid., p. 153.

6. Ibid., p. 150.

7. Ibid., p. 200.

8. Ibid., p. 201.

9. Ibid., p. 228.

10. Judith Butler, "Embodied Identity in De Beauvoir's *The Second Sex*," unpublished manuscript, p. 11, presented to American Philosophical Association, Pacific Division, March 22, 1985. See also Butler's recent monograph *Gender Trouble: Feminism and the Subversion of Identity* (New York: Routledge, 1990).

11. Marcia Millman, *Such a Pretty Face: Being Fat in America* (New York: Norton, 1980), p. 46.

12. Susan Bordo, "Anorexia Nervosa: Psychopathology as the Crystallization of Culture," *Philosophical Forum* 17, no. 2 (Winter 1985–86): 73–104. See also Bordo's *Unbearable Weight: Feminism, Western Culture, and the Body* (Berkeley: University of California Press, 1993).

13. *USA Today*, May 30, 1985.

14. Phrase taken from the title of Kim Chernin's *The Obsession: Reflections on the Tyranny of Slenderness* (New York: Harper and Row, 1981), an examination from a feminist perspective of women's eating disorders and of the current female preoccupation with body size.

15. M. J. Saffon, *The 15-Minute-a-Day Natural Face Lift* (New York: Warner Books, 1981).

16. Sophia Loren, *Women and Beauty* (New York: William Morrow, 1984), p. 57.

17. Iris Young, "Throwing Like a Girl: A Phenomenology of Feminine Body Comportment, Motility, and Spatiality," *Human Studies* 3, (1980): 137–56.

18. Marianne Wex, *Let's Take Back Our Space: "Female" and "Male" Body Language as a Result of Patriarchal Structures* (Berlin: Frauenliteraturverlag Hermine Fees, 1979). Wex claims that Japanese women are still taught to position their feet so that the toes point inward, a traditional sign of submissiveness (p. 23).

19. In heels, the "female foot and leg are turned into ornamental objects and the impractical shoe, which offers little protection against dust, rain and snow, induces helplessness and dependence. . . . The extra wiggle in the hips, exaggerating a slight natural tendency, is seen as sexually flirtatious while the smaller steps and tentative, insecure tread suggest daintiness, modesty and refinement. Finally, the overall hobbling effect with its sadomasochistic tinge is suggestive of the restraining leg irons and ankle chains endured by captive animals, prisoners and slaves who were also festooned with decorative symbols of their bondage." Susan Brownmiller, *Femininity* (New York: Simon and Schuster, 1984), p. 184.

20. Nancy Henley, *Body Politics* (Englewood Cliffs, N. J.: Prentice-Hall, 1977), p. 176.

21. For an account of the sometimes devastating effects on workers, like flight attendants, whose conditions of employment require the display of a perpetual friendliness, see Arlie Hochschild, *The Managed Heart: The Commercialization of Human Feeling* (Berkeley: University of California Press, 1983).

22. Henley, *Body Politics*, p. 108.

23. Ibid., p. 149.

24. Clairol has just introduced a small electric shaver, the "Bikini," apparently intended for just such use.

25. Georgette Klinger and Barbara Rowes, *Georgette Klinger's Skincare* (New York: William Morrow, 1978), pp. 102, 105, 151, 188, and passim.

26. *Chicago Magazine*, March 1986, pp. 43, 10, 18, and 62.

27. *Essence*, April 1986, p. 25. I am indebted to Laurie Shrage for calling this to my attention and for providing most of these examples.

28. Klinger, *Skincare*, pp. 137–40.

29. In light of this, one is surprised to see a two-ounce jar of "Skin Regeneration Formula," a "Proteolytic Enzyme Cream with Bromelain and Papain," selling for $23.95 in the tabloid *Globe* (April 8, 1986, p. 29) and an unidentified amount of Tova Borgnine's "amazing new formula from Beverly Hills" (otherwise unnamed) going for $41.75 in the *National Enquirer* (April 8, 1986, p. 15).

30. "It is required of woman that in order to realize her femininity she must make herself object and prey, which is to say that she must renounce her claims as sovereign subject." Simone De Beauvoir, *The Second Sex* (New York: Bantam Books, 1968), p. 642.

31. The film *Pumping Iron II* portrays very clearly the tension for female bodybuilders (a tension that enters into formal judging in the sport) between muscular development and a properly feminine appearance.

32. Henley, *Body Politics*, p. 101, 153, and passim.

33. Foucault, *Discipline and Punish*, p. 222.

34. Millman, *Such a Pretty Face*, p. 80. These sorts of remarks are made so commonly to heavy women that sociologist Millman takes the most cliched as title of her study of the lives of the overweight.

35. I am indebted to Nancy Fraser for the formulation of this point.

36. See *Femininity and Domination: Studies in the Phenomenology of Oppression* (New York: Routledge, 1990), chap. 3.

37. Millman, *Such a Pretty Face*, pp. 80 and 195.

38. Chernin, *The Obsession*, p. 53.

39. See *Femininity and Domination*, chap. 3.

40. For a claim that the project of liberal or "mainstream" feminism is covertly racist, see bell hooks, *Ain't I Woman: Black Women and Feminism* (Boston: South End Press, 1981), chap. 4. For an authoritative general critique of liberal feminism, see Alison Jaggar, *Feminist Politics and Human Nature* (Totowa, N.J.: Rowman and Allanheld, 1983), chaps. 3 and 7.

41. See, for example, Mihailo Markovic, "Women's Liberation and Human Emancipation," in *Women and Philosophy*, ed. Carol C. Gould and Marx W. Wartofsky (New York: Putnam, 1976), pp. 165–66.

42. Foucault, *Discipline and Punish*, p. 30.

43. Some radical feminists have called for just such a deconstruction. See espe-

cially Monique Wittig, *The Lesbian Body* (New York: Avon, 1976), and Butler, *Gender Trouble*.

44. Foucault, *Discipline and Punish*, p. 44.

45. Foucault, Colin Gordon, ed., *Power/Knowledge* (New York: Pantheon, 1980), p. 151. Quoted in Peter Dews, "Power and Subjectivity in Foucault," *New Left Review* 144 (March–April 1984): 17.

46. Dews, "Power and Subjectivity," p. 77.

47. Foucault, *Discipline and Punish*, p. 138.

48. Ibid., p. 201.

49. Foucault, *Power/Knowledge*, p. 98. In fact, Foucault is not entirely consistent on this point. For an excellent discussion of contending Foucault interpretations and for the difficulty of deriving a consistent set of claims from Foucault's work generally, see Nancy Fraser, "Michel Foucault: A 'Young Conservative'?" *Ethics* 96, no. 9 (October 1985): 165–84.

50. Dews, "Power and Subjectivity," p. 92.

51. See Marcia Hutchinson, *Transforming Body Image: Learning to Love the Body You Have* (Trumansburg, N.Y.: Crossing Press, 1985). See also Bordo, "Anorexia Nervosa: Psychopathology as the Crystallization of Culture."

8

On Being the Object of Property

Patricia J. Williams

performative writing?

On Being Invisible

REFLECTIONS

For some time I have been writing about my great-great-grandmother. I have considered the significance of her history and that of slavery from a variety of viewpoints on a variety of occasions: in every speech, in every conversation, even in my commercial transactions class. I have talked so much about her that I finally had to ask myself what it was I was looking for in this dogged pursuit of family history. Was I being merely indulgent, looking for roots in the pursuit of some genetic heraldry, seeking the inheritance of being special, different, unique in all that primogeniture hath wrought?

I decided that my search was based in the utility of such a quest, not mere indulgence,

Patricia J. Williams, "On Being the Object of Property." Originally appeared in *Signs: Journal of Women in Culture and Society* 14:1 (1988) and is reprinted with permission from the University of Chicago Press and the author.

but a recapturing of that which had escaped historical scrutiny, which had been overlooked and underseen. I, like so many blacks, have been trying to pin myself down in history, place myself in the stream of time as significant, evolved, present in the past, continuing into the future. To be without documentation is too unsustaining, too spontaneously ahistorical, too dangerously malleable in the hands of those who would rewrite not merely the past but my future as well. So I have been picking through the ruins for my roots.

What I know of my mother's side of the family begins with my great-great-grandmother. Her name was Sophie and she lived in Tennessee. In 1850, she was about twelve years old. I know that she was purchased when she was eleven by a white lawyer named Austin Miller and was immediately impregnated by him. She gave birth to my great-grandmother Mary, who was taken away from her to be raised as a house servant.[1] I know nothing more of Sophie (she was, after all, a black single mother—in today's terms—suffering the anonymity of yet another statistical teenage pregnancy). While I don't remember what I was told about Austin Miller before I decided to go to law school, I do remember that just before my first day of class, my mother said, in a voice full of secretive reassurance, "The Millers were lawyers, so you have it in your blood."[2]

When my mother told me that I had nothing to fear in law school, that law was "in my blood," she meant it in a very complex sense. First and foremost, she meant it defiantly; she meant that no one should make me feel inferior because someone else's father was a judge. She wanted me to reclaim that part of my heritage from which I had been disinherited, and she wanted me to use it as a source of strength and self-confidence. At the same time, she was asking me to claim a part of myself that was the dispossessor of another part of myself; she was asking me to deny that disenfranchised little black girl of myself that felt powerless, vulnerable and, moreover, rightly felt so.

In somewhat the same vein, Mother was asking me not to look to her as a role model. She was devaluing that part of herself that was not Harvard and refocusing my vision to that part of herself that was hard-edged, proficient, and Western. She hid the lonely, black, defiled-female part of herself and pushed me forward as the projection of a competent self, a cool rather than despairing self, a masculine rather than a feminine self.

I took this secret of my blood into the Harvard milieu with both the pride and the shame with which my mother had passed it along to me. I found myself in the situation described by Marguerite Duras, in her novel *The Lover*: "We're united in a fundamental shame at having to live. It's here we are at the heart of our common fate, the fact that [we] are our mother's children, the children of a candid creature murdered by society. We're on the side of society which has reduced her to despair. Because of what's been done to our mother, so amiable, so trusting, we hate life, we hate ourselves."[3]

Reclaiming that from which one has been disinherited is a good thing. Self-possession in the full sense of that expression is the companion to self-knowledge. Yet claiming for myself a heritage the weft of whose genesis is my own disinheritance is a profoundly troubling paradox.

IMAGES

A friend of mine practices law in rural Florida. His office is in Belle Glade, an extremely depressed area where the sugar industry reigns supreme, where blacks live pretty much as they did in slavery times, in dormitories called slave ships. They are penniless and illiterate and have both a high birth rate and a high death rate.

My friend told me about a client of his, a fifteen-year-old young woman pregnant with her third child, who came seeking advice because her mother had advised a hysterectomy—not even a tubal ligation—as a means of birth control. The young woman's mother, in turn, had been advised of the propriety of such a course in her own case by a white doctor some years before. Listening to this, I was reminded of a case I worked on when I was working for the Western Center on Law and Poverty about eight years ago. Ten black Hispanic women had been sterilized by the University of Southern California—Los Angeles County General Medical Center, allegedly without proper consent, and in most instances without even their knowledge.[4] Most of them found out what had been done to them upon inquiry, after a much-publicized news story in which an intern charged that the chief of obstetrics at the hospital pursued a policy of recommending Caesarian delivery and simultaneous sterilization for any pregnant woman with three or more children and who was on welfare. In the course of researching the appeal in that case, I remember learning that one-quarter of all Navajo women of childbearing age—literally all those of childbearing age ever admitted to a hospital—have been sterilized.[5]

As I reflected on all this, I realized that one of the things passed on from slavery, which continues in the oppression of people of color, is a belief structure rooted in a concept of black (or brown, or red) anti-will, the antithetical embodiment of pure will. We live in a society in which the closest equivalent of nobility is the display of unremittingly controlled will-fulness. To be perceived as unremittingly will-less is to be imbued with an almost lethal trait.

Many scholars have explained this phenomenon in terms of total and infantilizing interdependency of dominant and oppressed.[6] Consider, for example, Mark Tushnet's distinction between slave law's totalistic view of personality and the bourgeois "pure will" theory of personality: "Social relations in slave society rest upon the interaction of owner with slave; the owner, having total dominion over the slave. In contrast, bourgeois social relations rest upon the paradigmatic instance of market relations, the purchase by a capitalist of a worker's labor power; that transaction implicates only a part of the worker's personality. Slave relations are total, engaging the master and slave in exchanges in which each must take account of the entire range of belief, feeling, and interest embodied by the other; bourgeois social relations are partial, requiring only that participants in a market evaluate their general productive characteristics without regard to aspects of personality unrelated to production."[7]

Although such an analysis is not objectionable in some general sense, the description of master-slave relations as "total" is, to me, quite troubling. Such a choice of words reflects and accepts—at a very subtle level, perhaps—a historical rationalization that whites had to, could do, and did do everything for these simple, above-animal subhumans. It is a choice of vocabulary that fails to acknowledge blacks as having needs beyond those that even the most "humane" or "sentimental" white slavemaster could provide.[8] In trying to describe the provisional aspect of slave law, I would choose words that revealed its structure as rooted in a concept of, again, black anti-will, the polar opposite of pure will. I would characterize the treatment of blacks by whites in whites' law as defining blacks as those who had no will. I would characterize that treatment not as total interdependency, but as a relation in which partializing judgments, employing partializing standards of humanity, impose generalized inadequacy on a race: if pure will or total control equals the perfect white person, then impure will and total lack of control equals the perfect black man or woman. Therefore, to define slave law as comprehending a "total" view of personality implicitly accepts that the provision of food, shelter, and clothing (again assuming the very best of circumstances) is the whole requirement of humanity. It assumes also either that psychic care was provided by slave owners (as though a slave or an owned psyche could ever be reconciled with mental health) or that psyche is not a significant part of a whole human.

Market theory indeed focuses attention away from the full range of human potential in its pursuit of a divinely willed, invisibly handed economic actor. Master-slave relations, however, focused attention away from the full range of black human potential in a somewhat different way: it pursued a vision of blacks as simple-minded, strong-bodied economic actants.[9] Thus, while blacks had an indisputable generative force in the marketplace, their presence could not be called activity; they had no active role in the market. To say, therefore, that "market relations disregard the peculiarities of individuals, whereas slave relations rest on the mutual recognition of the humanity of master and slave"[10] (no matter how dialectical or abstracted a definition of humanity one adopts) is to posit an inaccurate equation: if "disregard for the peculiarities of individuals" and "mutual recognition of humanity" are polarized by a "whereas," then somehow regard for peculiarities of individuals must equal recognition of humanity. In the context of slavery this equation mistakes whites' overzealous and oppressive obsession with projected specific peculiarities of blacks for actual holistic regard for the individual. It overlooks the fact that most definitions of humanity require something beyond mere biological sustenance, some healthy measure of autonomy beyond that of which slavery could institutionally or otherwise conceive. Furthermore, it overlooks the fact that both slave and bourgeois systems regarded certain attributes as important and disregarded certain others, and that such regard and disregard can occur in the same glance, like the wearing of horseblinders to focus attention simultaneously toward and away from. The experiential blinders of market actor and slave are focused in different directions, yet the partializing ideologies of each makes the act of not seeing an unconscious, alienating component of seeing. Restoring a unified social vision will, I think, require broader and more scattered resolutions than the simple symmetry of ideological bipolarity.

Thus, it is important to undo whatever words obscure the fact that slave law was at least as fragmenting and fragmented as the bourgeois worldview—in a way that has persisted to this day, cutting across all ideological boundaries. As "pure will" signifies the whole bourgeois personality in the bourgeois worldview, so wisdom, control, and aesthetic beauty signify the whole white personality in slave law. The former and the latter, the slave-master and the burgermeister, are not so very different when expressed in those terms. The reconciling difference is that in slave law the emphasis is really on the inverse rationale: that irrationality, lack of control, and ugliness signify the whole slave personality. "Total" interdependence is at best a polite way of rationalizing such personality splintering; it creates a bizarre sort of yin-yang from the dross of an oppressive schizophrenia of biblical dimension. I would just call it schizophrenic, with all the baggage that that connotes. That is what sounds right to me. Truly total relationships (as opposed

to totalitarianism) call up images of whole people dependent on whole people; an interdependence that is both providing and laissez-faire at the same
time. Neither the historical inheritance of slave law nor so-called bourgeois
law meets that definition.

None of this, perhaps, is particularly new. Nevertheless, as precedent to
anything I do as a lawyer, the greatest challenge is to allow the full truth of
partializing social constructions to be felt for their overwhelming reality—
reality that otherwise I might rationally try to avoid facing. In my search for
roots, I must assume, not just as history but as an ongoing psychological
force, that, in the eyes of white culture, irrationality, lack of control, and
ugliness signify not just the whole slave personality, not just the whole black
personality, but me.

VISION

Reflecting on my roots makes me think again and again of the young woman
in Belle Glade, Florida. She told the story of her impending sterilization,
according to my friend, while keeping her eyes on the ground at all times.
My friend, who is white, asked why she wouldn't look up, speak with him
eye to eye. The young woman answered that she didn't like white people seeing inside her.

My friend's story made me think of my own childhood and adolescence:
my parents were always telling me to look up at the world; to look straight
at people, particularly white people; not to let them stare me down; to hold
my ground; to insist on the right to my presence no matter what. They told
me that in this culture you have to look people in the eye because that's how
you tell them you're their equal. My friend's story also reminded me how
very difficult I had found that looking-back to be. What was hardest was not
just that white people saw me, as my friend's client put it, but that they
looked through me, that they treated me as though I were transparent.

By itself, seeing into me would be to see my substance, my anger, my vulnerability, and my wild raging despair—and that alone is hard enough to
show, to share. But to uncover it and to have it devalued by ignore-ance, to
hold it up bravely in the organ of my eyes and to have it greeted by an impassive stare that passes right through all that which is me, an impassive stare
that moves on and attaches itself to my left earlobe or to the dust caught in
the rusty vertical geysers of my wiry hair or to the breadth of my freckled
brown nose—this is deeply humiliating. It re-wounds, relives the early child-

hood anguish of uncensored seeing, the fullness of vision that is the permanent turning-away point for most blacks.

The cold game of equality-staring makes me feel like a thin sheet of glass: white people see all the worlds beyond me but not me. They come trotting at me with force and speed; they do not see me. I could force my presence, the real me contained in those eyes, upon them, but I would be smashed in the process. If I deflect, if I move out of the way, they will never know I existed.

Marguerite Duras, again in *The Lover*, places the heroine in relation to her family. "Every day we try to kill one another, to kill. Not only do we not talk to one another, we don't even look at one another. When you're being looked at you can't look. To look is to feel curious, to be interested, to lower yourself."[11]

To look is also to make myself vulnerable; yet not to look is to neutralize the part of myself which is vulnerable. I look in order to see, and so I must look. Without that directness of vision, I am afraid I will will my own blindness, disinherit my own creativity, and sterilize my own perspective of its embattled, passionate insight.

On Ardor

THE CHILD

One Saturday afternoon not long ago, I sat among a litter of family photographs telling a South African friend about Marjorie, my godmother and my mother's cousin. She was given away by her light-skinned mother when she was only six. She was given to my grandmother and my great-aunts to be raised among her darker-skinned cousins, for Marjorie was very dark indeed. Her mother left the family to "pass," to marry a white man—Uncle Frederick, we called him with trepidatious presumption yet without his ever knowing of our existence—an heir to a meat-packing fortune. When Uncle Frederick died thirty years later and the fortune was lost, Marjorie's mother rejoined the race, as the royalty of resentful fascination—Lady Bountiful, my sister called her—to regale us with tales of gracious upper-class living.

My friend said that my story reminded him of a case in which a swarthy, crisp-haired child was born, in Durban, to white parents. The Afrikaner government quickly intervened, removed the child from its birth home, and placed it to be raised with a "more suitable," browner family.

When my friend and I had shared these stories, we grew embarrassed somehow, and our conversation trickled away into a discussion of laissez-faire economics and governmental interventionism. Our words became a clear line, a railroad upon which all other ideas and events were tied down and sacrificed.

THE MARKET

As a teacher of commercial transactions, one of the things that has always impressed me most about the law of contract is a certain deadening power it exercises by reducing the parties to the passive. It constrains the lively involvement of its signatories by positioning enforcement in such a way that parties find themselves in a passive relationship to a document: it is the contract that governs, that "does" everything, that absorbs all responsibility and deflects all other recourse.

Contract law reduces life to fairy tale. The four corners of the agreement become parent. Performance is the equivalent of obedience to the parent. Obedience is dutifully passive. Passivity is valued as good contract-socialized behavior; activity is caged in retrospective hypotheses about states of mind at the magic moment of contracting. Individuals are judged by the contract unfolding rather than by the actors acting autonomously. Nonperformance is disobedience; disobedience is active; activity becomes evil in contrast to the childlike passivity of contract conformity.

One of the most powerful examples of all this is the case of Mary Beth Whitehead, mother of Sara—of so-called Baby M. Ms. Whitehead became a vividly original actor *after* the creation of her contract with William Stern; unfortunately for her, there can be no greater civil sin. It was in this upside-down context, in the picaresque unboundedness of breachor, that her energetic grief became hysteria and her passionate creativity was funneled, whorled, and reconstructed as highly impermissible. Mary Beth Whitehead thus emerged as the evil stepsister who deserved nothing.

Some time ago, Charles Reich visited a class of mine.[12] He discussed with my students a proposal for a new form of bargain by which emotional "items"—such as praise, flattery, acting happy or sad—might be contracted for explicitly. One student, not alone in her sentiment, said, "Oh, but then you'll just feel obligated." Only the week before, however (when we were discussing the contract which posited that Ms. Whitehead "will not form or attempt to form a parent-child relationship with any child or children"), this same student had insisted that Ms. Whitehead must give up her child, because she had *said* she would: "She was obligated!" I was confounded by the degree to which what the student took to be self-evident, inalienable gut reactions could be governed by illusions of passive conventionality and form.

It was that incident, moreover, that gave me insight into how Judge Harvey Sorkow, of New Jersey Superior Court, could conclude that the contract that purported to terminate Ms. Whitehead's parental rights was "not illusory."[13]

(As background, I should say that I think that, within the framework of contract law itself, the agreement between Ms. Whitehead and Mr. Stern was clearly illusory.[14] On the one hand, Judge Sorkow's opinion said that Ms. Whitehead was seeking to avoid her *obligations*. In other words, giving up her child became an actual obligation. On the other hand, according to the logic of the judge, this was a service contract, not really a sale of a child; therefore delivering the child to the Sterns was an "obligation" for which there was no consideration, for which Mr. Stern was not paying her.)

Judge Sorkow's finding the contract "not illusory" is suggestive not just of the doctrine by that name, but of illusion in general, and delusion, and the righteousness with which social constructions are conceived, acted on, and delivered up into the realm of the real as "right," while all else is devoured from memory as "wrong." From this perspective, the rhetorical tricks by which Sara Whitehead became Melissa Stern seem very like the heavy-worded legalities by which my great-great-grandmother was pacified and parted from her child. In both situations, the real mother had no say, no power; her powerlessness was imposed by state law that made her and her child helpless in relation to the father. My great-great-grandmother's powerlessness came about as the result of a contract to which she was not a party; Mary Beth Whitehead's powerlessness came about as a result of a contract that she signed at a discrete point of time—yet which, over time, enslaved her. The contract-reality in both instances was no less than magic: it was illusion transformed into not-illusion. Furthermore, it masterfully disguised the brutality of enforced arrangements in which these women's autonomy, their flesh and their blood, were locked away in word vaults, without room to reconsider—*ever*.

In the months since Judge Sorkow's opinion, I have reflected on the similarities of fortune between my own social positioning and that of Sara Melissa Stern Whitehead. I have come to realize that an important part of the complex magic that Judge Sorkow wrote into his opinion was a supposition that it is "natural" for people to want children "like" themselves. What this reasoning raised for me was an issue of what, exactly, constituted this "likeness"? (What would have happened, for example, if Ms. Whitehead had turned out to have been the "passed" descendant of my "failed" godmother Marjorie's mother? What if the child she bore had turned out to be recessively and visibly black? Would the sperm of Mr. Stern have been so powerful as to make this child "his" with the exclusivity that Judge Sorkow originally assigned?) What constitutes, moreover, the collective understanding of "un-likeness"?

These questions turn, perhaps, on not-so-subtle images of which mothers should be bearing which children. Is there not something unseemly, in our society, about the spectacle of a white woman mothering a black child? A white woman giving totally to a black child; a black child totally and demandingly dependent for everything, for sustenance itself, from a white woman. The image of a white woman suckling a black child; the image of a black child sucking for its life from the bosom of a white woman. The utter interdependence of such an image; the selflessness, the merging it implies; the giving up of boundary; the encompassing of other within self; the unbounded generosity, the interconnectedness of such an image. Such a picture says that there is no difference; it places the hope of continuous generation, of immortality of the white self in a little black face.

When Judge Sorkow declared that it was only to be expected that parents would want to breed children "like" themselves, he simultaneously created a legal right to the same. With the creation of such a "right," he encased the children conforming to "likeliness" in protective custody, far from whole ranges of taboo. Taboo about touch and smell and intimacy and boundary. Taboo about ardor, possession, license, equivocation, equanimity, indifference, intolerance, rancor, dispossession, innocence, exile, and candor. Taboo about death. Taboos that amount to death. Death and sacredness, the valuing of body, of self, of other, of remains. The handling lovingly in life, as in life; the question of the intimacy versus the dispassion of death.

In effect, these taboos describe boundaries of valuation. Whether something is inside or outside the marketplace of rights has always been a way of valuing it. When a valued object is located outside the market, it is generally understood to be too "priceless" to be accommodated by ordinary exchange relationships; when, in contrast, the prize is located within the marketplace, all objects outside become "valueless." Traditionally, the Mona Lisa and human life have been the sorts of subjects removed from the fungibility of commodification, as "priceless." Thus when black people were bought and sold as slaves, they were placed beyond the bounds of humanity. And thus, in the twistedness of our brave new world, when blacks have been thrust out of the market and it is white children who are bought and sold, black babies have become "worthless" currency to adoption agents—"surplus" in the salvage heaps of Harlem hospitals.

[handwritten annotation: what would W. say about move against interracial adoption to preserve cult. her. etc?]

THE IMAGINATION

"Familiar though his name may be to us, the storyteller in his living immediacy is by no means a present force. He has already become something remote from us and something that is getting even more distant. . . . Less and less frequently do we encounter people with the ability to tell a tale properly. . . . It is as if something that seemed inalienable to us, the securest among our possessions, were taken from us: the ability to exchange experiences."[15]

My mother's cousin Marjorie was a storyteller. From time to time I would press her to tell me the details of her youth, and she would tell me instead about a child who wandered into a world of polar bears, who was prayed over by polar bears, and in the end eaten. The child's life was not in vain because the polar bears had been made holy by its suffering. The child had been a test, a message from god for polar bears. In the polar bear universe, she would tell me, the primary object of creation was polar bears, and the rest of the living world was fashioned to serve polar bears. The clouds took their shape from polar bears, trees were designed to give shelter and shade to polar bears, and humans were ideally designed to provide polar bears with meat.[16]

The truth, the truth, I would laughingly insist as we sat in her apartment eating canned fruit and heavy roasts, mashed potatoes, pickles and vanilla pudding, cocoa, Sprite, or tea. What about roots and all that, I coaxed. But the voracity of her amnesia would disclaim and disclaim and disclaim; and she would go on telling me about the polar bears until our plates were full of emptiness and I became large in the space which described her emptiness and I gave in to the emptiness of words.

On Life and Death

SIGHING INTO SPACE

There are moments in my life when I feel as though a part of me is missing. There are days when I feel so invisible that I can't remember what day of the week it is, when I feel so manipulated that I can't remember my own name, when I feel so lost and angry that I can't speak a civil word to the people who love me best. Those are the times when I catch sight of my reflection in store windows and am surprised to see a whole person looking back. Those are the times when my skin becomes gummy as clay and my nose slides around on my face and my eyes drip down to my chin. I have to close my eyes at such times and remember myself, draw an internal picture that is smooth and whole; when all else fails, I reach for a mirror and stare myself down until the features reassemble themselves like lost sheep.

Two years ago, my godmother Marjorie suffered a massive stroke. As she lay dying, I would come to the hospital to give her her meals. My feeding her who had so often fed me became a complex ritual of mirroring and self-assembly. The physical act of holding the spoon to her lips was not only a rite of nurture and of sacrifice, it was the return of a gift. It was a quiet bowing to the passage of time and the doubling back of all things. The quiet woman who listened to my woes about work and school required now that I bend my head down close to her and listen for mouthed word fragments, sentence crumbs. I bent down to give meaning to her silence, her wandering search for words.

She would eat what I brought to the hospital with relish; she would reject what I brought with a turn of her head. I brought fruit and yogurt, ice cream and vegetable juice. Slowly, over time, she stopped swallowing. The mashed potatoes would sit in her mouth like cotton, the pudding would slip to her chin in slow sad streams. When she lost not only her speech but the power to ingest, they put a tube into her nose and down to her stomach, and I lost even that medium by which to communicate. No longer was there the odd but reassuring communion over taste. No longer was there some echo of comfort in being able to nurture one who nurtured me.

This increment of decay was like a little newborn death. With the tube, she stared up at me with imploring eyes, and I tried to guess what it was that she would like. I read to her aimlessly and in desperation. We entertained each other with the strange embarrassed flickering of our eyes. I told her stories to fill the emptiness, the loneliness, of the white-walled hospital room.

I told her stories about who I had become, about how I had grown up to know all about exchange systems, and theories of contract, and monetary fictions. I spun tales about blue-sky laws and promissory estoppel, the wispy-feathered complexity of undue influence and dark-hearted theories of unconscionability. I told her about market norms and gift economy and the thin razor's edge of the bartering ethic. Once upon a time, I rambled, some neighbors of mine included me in their circle of barter. They were in the

habit of exchanging eggs and driving lessons, hand-knit sweaters and computer programming, plumbing and calligraphy. I accepted the generosity of
their inclusion with gratitude. At first, I felt that, as a lawyer, I was worthless, that I had no barterable skills and nothing to contribute. What I came to
realize with time, however, was that my value to the group was not calculated
by the physical items I brought to it. These people included me because they
wanted me to be part of their circle, they valued my participation apart from
the material things I could offer. So I gave of myself to them, and they gave
me fruit cakes and dandelion wine and smoked salmon, and in their giving,
their goods became provisions. Cradled in this community whose currency
was a relational ethic, my stock in myself soared. My value depended on the
glorious intangibility, the eloquent invisibility of my just being *part* of the collective; and in direct response I grew spacious and happy and gentle.

My gentle godmother. The fragility of life; the cold mortuary shelf.

DISPASSIONATE DEATHS

The hospital in which my godmother died is now filled to capacity with
AIDS patients. One in sixty-one babies born there, as in New York City generally, is infected with AIDS antibodies.[17] Almost all are black or Hispanic.
In the Bronx, the rate is one in forty-three.[18] In Central Africa, experts esti-
mate that, of children receiving transfusions for malaria-related anemia,
"about 1000 may have been infected with the AIDS virus in each of the last
five years."[19] In Congo, 5 percent of the entire population is infected.[20] The
New York Times reports that "the profile of Congo's population seems to guarantee the continued spread of AIDS."[21]

In the Congolese city of Pointe Noir, "the annual budget of the sole public health hospital is estimated at about $200,000—roughly the amount of
money spent in the United States to care for four AIDS patients."[22]

The week in which my godmother died is littered with bad memories. In
my journal, I made note of the following:

> *Good Friday*: Phil Donahue has a special program on AIDS. The segues are:
>   a. from Martha, who weeps at the prospect of not watching her
>   children grow up
>   b. to Jim, who is not conscious enough to speak just now, who
>   coughs convulsively, who recognizes no one in his family
>   any more

  c. to Hugh who, at 85 pounds, thinks he has five years but whose
     doctor says he has weeks
  d. to an advertisement for denture polish ("If you love your
     Polident Green/then gimmeeya SMILE!")
  e. and then one for a plastic surgery salon on Park Avenue ("The
     only thing that's expensive is our address")
  f. and then one for what's coming up on the five o'clock news
     (Linda Lovelace, of *Deep Throat* fame, "still recovering from a
     double mastectomy and complications from silicone injections"
     is being admitted to a New York hospital for a liver transplant)
  g. and finally one for the miracle properties of all-purpose house
     cleaner ("Mr. Cleeean/is the man/behind the shine/is it wet or
     is it dry?" I note that Mr. Clean, with his gleaming bald head,
     puffy musculature and fever-bright eyes, looks like he is under-
     going radiation therapy). Now back to our show.
  h. "We are back now with Martha," (who is crying harder than
     before, sobbing uncontrollably, each jerking inhalation a deep
     unearthly groan). Phil says, "Oh honey, I hope we didn't make
     it worse for you."

Easter Saturday: Over lunch, I watch another funeral. My
office windows overlook a graveyard as crowded and still as a
rush-hour freeway. As I savor pizza and milk, I notice that one of
the mourners is wearing an outfit featured in the window of
Bloomingdale's (59th Street store) only since last weekend. This
thread of recognition jolts me, and I am drawn to her in sorrow;
the details of my own shopping history flash before my eyes as I
reflect upon the sober spree that brought her to the rim of this
earthly chasm, her slim suede heels sinking into the soft silt of
the graveside.

Resurrection Sunday: John D., the bookkeeper where I used to
work, died, hit on the head by a stray but forcefully propelled
hockey puck. I cried copiously at his memorial service, only to
discover, later that afternoon when I saw a black rimmed photograph, that I had been mourning the wrong person. I had cried
because the man I *thought* had died is John D. the office messenger,
a bitter unfriendly man who treats me with disdain; once I bought
an old electric typewriter from him which never worked. Though
he promised nothing, I have harbored deep dislike since then;
death by hockey puck is only one of the fates I had imagined for

him. I washed clean my guilt with buckets of tears at the news of what I thought was his demise.

The man who did die was small, shy, anonymously sweet-featured and innocent. In some odd way I was relieved; no seriously obligatory mourning to be done here. A quiet impassivity settled over me and I forgot my grief.

HOLY COMMUNION

A few months after my godmother died, my Great Aunt Jag passed away in Cambridge, at ninety-six the youngest and the last of her siblings, all of whom died at ninety-seven. She collapsed on her way home from the polling place, having gotten in her vote for "yet another Kennedy." Her wake was much like the last family gathering at which I had seen her, two Thanksgivings ago. She was a little hard of hearing then and she stayed on the outer edge of the conversation, brightly, loudly, and randomly asserting enjoyment of her meal. At the wake, cousins, nephews, daughters-in-law, first wives, second husbands, great-grand-nieces gathered round her casket and got acquainted all over again. It was pouring rain outside. The funeral home was dry and warm, faintly spicily clean-smelling; the walls were solid, dark, respectable wood; the floors were cool stone tile. On the door of a room marked "No Admittance" was a sign that reminded workers therein of the reverence with which each body was held by its family and prayed employees handle the remains with similar love and care. Aunt Jag wore yellow chiffon; everyone agreed that laying her out with her glasses on was a nice touch.

Afterward, we all went to Legal Seafoods, her favorite restaurant, and ate many of her favorite foods.

On Candor

ME

I have never been able to determine my horoscope with any degree of accuracy. Born at Boston's now-defunct Lying-In Hospital, I am a Virgo, despite a quite poetic soul. Knowledge of the hour of my birth, however, would determine not just my sun sign but my moons and all the more intimate specificities of my destiny. Once upon a time, I sent for my birth certificate, which was retrieved from the oblivion of Massachusetts microfiche. Said document revealed that an infant named Patricia Joyce, born of parents named Williams, was delivered into the world "colored." Since no one thought to put down the hour of my birth, I suppose that I will never know my true fate.

In the meantime, I read what text there is of me.

My name, Patricia, means patrician. Patricias are noble, lofty, elite, exclusively educated, and well mannered despite themselves. I was on the cusp of being Pamela, but my parents knew that such a me would require lawns, estates, and hunting dogs too.

I am also a Williams. Of William, whoever he was: an anonymous white man who owned my father's people and from whom some escaped. That rupture is marked by the dark-mooned mystery of utter silence.

Williams is the second most common surname in the United States; Patricia is *the* most common prename among women born in 1951, the year of my birth.

THEM

In the law, rights are islands of empowerment. To be un-righted is to be disempowered, and the line between rights and no rights is most often the line between dominators and oppressors. Rights contain images of power, and manipulating those images, either visually or linguistically, is central in the making and maintenance of rights. In principle, therefore, the more dizzyingly diverse the images that are propagated, the more empowered we will be as a society.

In reality, it was a lovely polar bear afternoon. The gentle force of the earth. A wide wilderness of islands. A conspiracy of polar bears lost in timeless forgetting. A gentleness of polar bears, a fruitfulness of polar bears, a silent black-eyed interest of polar bears, a bristled expectancy of polar bears. With the wisdom of innocence, a child threw stones at the polar bears. Hungry, they rose from their nests, inquisitive, dark-souled, patient with foreboding, fearful in tremendous awakening. The instinctual ferocity of the hunter reflected upon the hunted. Then, proud teeth and warrior claws took innocence for wilderness and raging insubstantiality for tender rabbit breath.

In the newspapers the next day, it was reported that two polar bears in the

Brooklyn Zoo mauled to death an eleven-year-old boy who had entered their cage to swim in the moat. The police were called and the bears were killed.[23]

In the public debate that ensued, many levels of meaning emerged. The rhetoric firmly established that the bears were innocent, naturally territorial, unfairly imprisoned, and guilty. The dead child (born into the urban jungle of a black, welfare mother and a Hispanic alcoholic father who had died literally in the gutter only six weeks before) was held to a similarly stern standard. The police were captured, in a widely disseminated photograph,[24] shooting helplessly, desperately, into the cage, through three levels of bars, at a pieta of bears; since this image, conveying much pathos, came nevertheless not in time to save the child, it was generally felt that the bears had died in vain.[25]

In the egalitarianism of exile, pluralists rose up as one body, with a call to buy more bears, control juvenile delinquency, eliminate all zoos, and confine future police.[26]

In the plenary session of the national meeting of the Law and Society Association, the keynote speaker unpacked the whole incident as a veritable laboratory of emergent rights discourse. Just seeing that these complex levels of meaning exist, she exulted, should advance rights discourse significantly.[27]

At the funeral of the child, the presiding priest pronounced the death of Juan Perez not in vain, since he was saved from growing into "a lifetime of crime." Juan's Hispanic-welfare-black-widow-of-an-alcoholic mother decided then and there to sue.

The Universe Between

How I ended up at Dartmouth College for the summer is too long a story to tell. Anyway, there I was, sharing the town of Hanover, New Hampshire, with about two hundred prepubescent males enrolled in Dartmouth's summer basketball camp, an all-white, very expensive, affirmative action program for the street-deprived.

One fragrant evening, I was walking down East Wheelock Street when I encountered about a hundred of these adolescents, fresh from the courts, wet, lanky, big-footed, with fuzzy yellow crew cuts, loping toward Thayer Hall and food. In platoons of twenty-five or so, they descended upon me, jostling me, smacking me, and pushing me from the sidewalk into the gutter. In a thoughtless instant, I snatched off my brown silk headrag, my flag of African femininity and propriety, my sign of meek and supplicatory place and presentation. I released the armored rage of my short nappy hair (the scalp gleaming bare between the angry wire spikes) and hissed: "Don't I exist for you?! See Me! And deflect, godammit!" (The quaint professionalism of my formal English never allowed the rage in my head to rise so high as to over-flow the edges of my text.)

They gave me wide berth. They clearly had no idea, however, that I was talking to them or about them. They skirted me sheepishly, suddenly polite, because they did know, when a crazed black person comes crashing into one's field of vision, that it is impolite to laugh. I stood tall and spoke loudly into their ranks: "I have my rights!" The Dartmouth Summer Basketball Camp raised its collective eyebrows and exhaled, with a certain tested nobility of exhaustion and solidarity.

I pursued my way, manumitted back into silence. I put distance between them and me, gave myself over to polar bear musings. I allowed myself to be watched over by bear spirits. Clean white wind and strong bear smells. The shadowed amnesia; the absence of being; the presence of polar bears. White wilderness of icy meat-eaters heavy with remembrance; leaden with undo-ing; shaggy with the effort of hunting for silence; frozen in a web of inten-tion and intuition. A lunacy of polar bears. A history of polar bears. A pride of polar bears. A consistency of polar bears. In those meandering pastel polar bear moments, I found cool fragments of white-fur invisibility. Solid, black-gummed, intent, observant. Hungry and patient, impassive and exquisitely timed. The brilliant bursts of exclusive territoriality. A complexity of mes-sages implied in our being.

NOTES

1. For a more detailed account of the family history to this point, see Patricia J. Williams, "Grandmother Sophie," *Harvard Blackletter* 3 (1986): 79.

2. Patricia J. Williams, "Alchemical Notes: Reconstructing Ideals from Deconstructed Rights," *Harvard Civil Rights—Civil Liberties Law Review* 22 (1987): 418.

3. Marguerite Duras, *The Lover* (New York: Harper and Row, 1985), p. 55.

4. *Madrigal v. Quilligan,* U.S. Court of Appeals, 9th Circuit, Docket no. 78-3187, October 1979.

5. This was the testimony of one of the witnesses. It is hard to find official con-firmation or this or any other sterilization statistic involving Native American women. Official statistics kept by the U.S. Public Health Service, through the

Centers for Disease Control in Atlanta, come from data gathered by the National Hospital Discharge Survey, which covers neither federal hospitals nor penitentiaries. Services to Native American women living on reservations are provided almost exclusively by federal hospitals. In addition, the U.S. Public Health Service breaks down its information into only three categories: "White," "Black," and "Other." Nevertheless, in 1988 the Women of All Red Nations Collective of Minneapolis, Minnesota, distributed a fact sheet entitled "Sterilization Studies of Native American Women," which claimed that as many as 50 percent of all Native American women of child-bearing age have been sterilized. According to "Surgical Sterilization Surveillance: Tubal Sterilization and Hysterectomy in Women Aged 15–44, 1979–1980," issued by the Centers for Disease Control in 1983, "In 1980, the tubal sterilization rate for black women . . . was 45 percent greater than that for white women" (7). Furthermore, a study released in 1984 by the Division of Reproductive Health of the Center for Health Promotion and Education (one of the Centers for Disease Control) found that, as of 1982, 48.8 percent of Puerto Rican women between the ages of 15 and 44 had been sterilized.

6. See, generally, Stanley Elkins, *Slavery* (New York: Grosset and Dunlap, 1963); Kenneth Stampp, *The Peculiar Institution* (New York: Vintage, 1956): Winthrop Jordan, *White over Black* (Baltimore: Penguin, 1968).

7. Mark Tushnet, *The American Law of Slavery* (Princeton, N.J.: Princeton University Press, 1981), p. 6. There is danger, in the analysis that follows, of appearing to "pick" on Tushnet. That is not my intention, nor is it to impugn the body of his research, most of which I greatly admire. The choice of this passage for analysis has more to do with the randomness of my reading habits; the fact that he is one of the few legal writers to attempt, in the context of slavery, a juxtaposition of political theory with psychoanalytic theories of personality; and the fact that he is perceived to be of the political left, which simplifies my analysis in terms of its presumption of sympathy, i.e., that the constructions of thought revealed are socially derived and unconscious rather than idiosyncratic and intentional.

8. In another passage, Tushnet observes: "The court thus demonstrated its appreciation of the ties of sentiment that slavery could generate between master and slave and simultaneously denied that those ties were relevant in the law" (67). What is noteworthy about the reference to "sentiment" is that it assumes that the fact that emotions could grow up between slave and master is itself worth remarking: slightly surprising, slightly commendable for the court to note (i.e., in its "appreciation")— although "simultaneously" with, and presumably in contradistinction to, the court's inability to take official cognizance of the fact. Yet, if one really looks at the ties that bound master and slave, one has to flesh out the description of master-slave with the ties of father-son, father-daughter, half-sister, half-brother, uncle, aunt, cousin, and

a variety of de facto foster relationships. And if one starts to see those ties as more often than not intimate family ties, then the terminology "appreciation of . . . sentiment . . . between master and slave" becomes a horrifying mockery of any true sense of family sentiment, which is utterly, utterly lacking. The court's "appreciation," from this enhanced perspective, sounds blindly cruel, sarcastic at best. And to observe that courts suffused in such "appreciation" could simultaneously deny its legal relevance seems not only a truism; it misses the point entirely.

9. "Actants have a kind of phonemic, rather than a phonetic role: they operate on the level of function, rather than content. That is, an actant may embody itself in a particular character (termed an acteur) or it may reside in the function of more than one character in respect of their common role in the story's underlying 'oppositional' structure. In short, the deep structure of the narrative generates and defines its actants at a level beyond that of the story's surface content" (Terence Hawkes, *Structuralism and Semiotics* [Berkeley: University of California Press, 1977], p. 89).

10. Tushnet, p. 69.

11. Duras, p. 54.

12. Charles Reich is author of *The Greening of America* (New York: Random House, 1970) and professor of law at the University of San Francisco Law School.

13. See, generally, In the Matter of Baby "M," A Pseudonym for an Actual Person, Superior Court of New Jersey, Chancery Division, Docket no. FM-25314-86E, March 31, 1987. This decision was appealed, and on February 3, 1988, the New Jersey Supreme Court ruled that surrogate contracts were illegal and against public policy. In addition to the contract issue, however, the appellate court decided the custody issue in favor of the Sterns but granted visitation rights to Mary Beth Whitehead.

14. "An illusory promise is an expression cloaked in promissory terms, but which, upon closer examination, reveals that the promisor has committed himself not at all" (J. Calamari and J. Perillo, *Contracts*, 3d ed. [St. Paul: West Publishing, 1987], p. 228).

15. Walter Benjamin, "The Storyteller," in *Illuminations*, ed. Hannah Arendt (New York: Schocken, 1969), p. 83.

16. For an analysis of similar stories, see Richard Levins and Richard Lewontin, *The Dialectical Biologist* (Cambridge: Harvard University Press, 1985), p. 66.

17. Lambert, "Study Finds Antibodies for AIDS in 1 in 61 Babies in New York City," *New York Times* (January 13, 1988), sec. A.

18. Ibid.

19. "Study Traces AIDS in African Children," *New York Times* (January 22, 1988), sec. A.

20. Brooke, "New Surge of AIDS in Congo May Be an Omen for Africa," *New York Times* (January 22, 1988), sec. A.

21. Ibid.

22. Ibid.

23. Barron, "Polar Bears Kill a Child at Prospect Park Zoo," *New York Times* (May 20, 1987), sec. A.

24. *New York Post* (May 22, 1987), p. 1.

25. Barron, "Officials Weigh Tighter Security at Zoos in Parks," *New York Times* (May 22, 1987), sec. B.

26. Ibid.

27. Patricia J. Williams, "The Meaning of Rights" (address to the annual meeting of the Law and Society Association, Washington, D.C., June 6, 1987).

9

Film and the Masquerade

THEORIZING THE FEMALE SPECTATOR

Mary Ann Doane

Heads in Hieroglyphic Bonnets

In his lecture on "Femininity," Freud forcefully inscribes the absence of the female spectator of theory in his notorious statement, "to those of you who are women this will not apply—you are yourselves the problem."[1] Simultaneous with this exclusion operated upon the female members of his audience, he invokes, as a rather strange prop, a poem by Heine. Introduced by Freud's claim concerning the importance and elusiveness of his topic—"Throughout history people have knocked their heads against the riddle of the nature of femininity"—are four lines of Heine's poem:

> Heads in hieroglyphic bonnets,
> Heads in turbans and black birettas,
> Heads in wigs and thousand other
> Wretched, sweating heads of humans[2]

Mary Ann Doane, "Film and the Masquerade: Theorizing the Female Spectator." *Screen* 23 (1982): 78–87. Reprinted with permission from the author and the publisher.

The effects of the appeal to this poem are subject to the work of overdetermination Freud isolated in the text of the dream. The sheer proliferation of heads and hats (and hence, through a metonymic slippage, minds), which are presumed to have confronted this intimidating riddle before Freud, confers on his discourse the weight of an intellectual history, of a tradition of interrogation. Furthermore, the image of hieroglyphics strengthens the association made between femininity and the enigmatic, the undecipherable, that which is "other." And yet Freud practices a slight deception here, concealing what is elided by removing the lines from their context, castrating, as it were, the stanza. For the question over which Heine's heads brood is not the same as Freud's—it is not "What is Woman?," but instead, "what signifies Man?" The quote is taken from the seventh section (entitled "Questions") of the second cycle of *The North Sea*. The full stanza, presented as the words of "a young man, / His breast full of sorrow, his head full of doubt," reads as follows:

> O solve me the riddle of life,
> The teasingly time-old riddle,
> Over which many heads already have brooded,
> Heads in hats of hieroglyphics,
> Turbaned heads and heads in black skull-caps,
> Heads in perrukes and a thousand other
> Poor, perspiring human heads—
> Tell me, what signifies Man?
> Whence does he come? Whither does he go?
> Who lives up there upon golden stars?[3]

The question in Freud's text is thus a disguise and a displacement of that other question, which in the pretext is both humanistic and theological. The claim to investigate an otherness is a pretense, haunted by the mirror-effect by means of which the question of the woman reflects only the man's own ontological doubts. Yet what interests me most in this intertextual misrepresentation is that the riddle of femininity is initiated from the beginning in Freud's text as a question in masquerade. But I will return to the issue of masquerade later.

More pertinently, as far as the cinema is concerned, it is not accidental that Freud's eviction of the female spectator/auditor is copresent with the invocation of a hieroglyphic language. The woman, the enigma, the hieroglyphic, the picture, the image—the metonymic chain connects with another: the cinema, the theatre of pictures, a writing in images of the woman

but not *for* her. For she *is* the problem. The semantic valence attributed to a
hieroglyphic language is two-edged. In fact, there is a sense in which the term
is inhabited by a contradiction. On the one hand, the hieroglyphic is summoned, particularly when it merges with a discourse on the woman, to con-
note an indecipherable language, a signifying system which denies its own
function by failing to signify anything to the uninitiated, to those who do not
hold the key. In this sense, the hieroglyphic, like the woman, harbors a mystery, an inaccessible though desirable otherness. On the other hand, the hieroglyphic is the most readable of languages. Its immediacy, its accessibility
are functions of its status as a *pictorial* language, a writing in images. For the
image is theorized in terms of a certain *closeness*, the lack of a distance or gap
between sign and referent. Given its iconic characteristics, the relationship
between signifier and signified is understood as less arbitrary in imagistic systems of representation than in language "proper." The intimacy of signifier
and signified in the iconic sign negates the distance which defines phonetic
language. And it is the absence of this crucial distance or gap which also,
simultaneously, specifies both the hieroglyphic and the female. This is precisely why Freud evicted the woman from his lecture on femininity. Too close
to herself, entangled in her own enigma, she could not step back, could not
achieve the necessary distance of a second look.[4]

Thus, while the hieroglyphic is an indecipherable or at least enigmatic language, it is also and at the same time potentially the most universally understandable, comprehensible, appropriable of signs.[5] And the woman shares
this contradictory status. But it is here that the analogy slips. For hieroglyphic
languages are *not* perfectly iconic. They would not achieve the status of languages if they were—due to what Todorov and Ducrot refer to as a certain
non-generalizability of the iconic sign:

> Now it is the impossibility of generalizing this principle of representation
> that has introduced even into fundamentally morphemographic writing
> systems such as Chinese, Egyptian, and Sumerian, the phonographic prin-
> ciple. We might almost conclude that every logography [the graphic sys-
> tem of language notation] grows out of *the impossibility of a generalized iconic
> representation*; proper nouns and abstract notions (including inflections)
> are then the ones that will be noted phonetically.[6]

The iconic system of representation is inherently deficient—it cannot disengage itself from the "real," from the concrete; it lacks the gap necessary for
generalizability (for Saussure, this is the idea that, "Signs which are arbitrary

realize better than others the ideal of the semiotic process."). The woman, too, is defined by such an insufficiency. My insistence upon the congruence between certain theories of the image and theories of femininity is an attempt to dissect the *episteme* which assigns to the woman a special place in cinematic representation while denying her access to that system.

The cinematic apparatus inherits a theory of the image which is not conceived outside of sexual specifications. And historically, there has always been a certain imbrication of the cinematic image and the representation of the woman. The woman's relation to the camera and the scopic regime is quite different from that of the male. As Noël Burch points out, the early silent cinema, through its insistent inscription of scenarios of voyeurism, conceives of its spectator's viewing pleasure in terms of that of the Peeping Tom, behind the screen, reduplicating the spectator's position in relation to the woman as screen.[7] Spectatorial desire, in contemporary film theory, is generally delineated as either voyeurism or fetishism, as precisely a pleasure in seeing what is prohibited in relation to the female body. The image orchestrates a gaze, a limit, and its pleasurable transgression. The woman's beauty, her very desirability, becomes a function of certain practices of imaging—framing, lighting, camera movement, angle. She is thus, as Laura Mulvey has pointed out, more closely associated with the surface of the image than its illusory depths, its constructed three-dimensional space which the man is destined to inhabit and hence control.[8] In *Now Voyager*, for instance, a single image signals the momentous transformation of the Bette Davis character from ugly spinster aunt to glamorous single woman. Charles Affron describes the specifically cinematic aspect of this operation as a "stroke of genius':

> The radical shadow bisecting the face in white/dark/white strata creates a visual phenomenon quite distinct from the makeup transformation of lipstick and plucked eyebrows. . . . This shot does not reveal what we commonly call acting, especially after the most recent exhibition of that activity, but the sense of face belongs to a plastique pertinent to the camera. The viewer is allowed a different perceptual referent, a chance to come down from the nerve-jarring, first sequence and to use his eyes anew.[9]

A "plastique pertinent to the camera" constitutes the woman not only as the image of desire but as the desirous image—one which the devoted cinéphile can cherish and embrace. To "have" the cinema is, in some sense, to "have" the woman. But *Now Voyager* is, in Affron's terms, a "tear-jerker," in others, a "woman's picture," that is, a film purportedly produced for a female audience. What, then, of the female spectator? What can one say about her desire in relation to this process of imaging? It would seem that what the cinematic institution has in common with Freud's gesture is the eviction of the female spectator from a discourse purportedly about her (the cinema, psychoanalysis)—one which, in fact, narrativizes her again and again.

A Lass But Not a Lack

Theories of female spectatorship are thus rare, and when they are produced, seem inevitably to confront certain blockages in conceptualization. The difficulties in thinking female spectatorship demand consideration. After all, even if it is admitted that the woman is frequently the object of the voyeuristic or fetishistic gaze in the cinema, what is there to prevent her from reversing the relation and appropriating the gaze for her own pleasure? Precisely the fact that the reversal itself remains locked within the same logic. The male striptease, the gigolo—both inevitably signify the mechanism of reversal itself, constituting themselves as aberrations whose acknowledgment simply reinforces the dominant system of aligning sexual difference with a subject/object dichotomy. And an essential attribute of that dominant system is the matching of male subjectivity with the agency of the look.

The supportive binary opposition at work here is not only that utilized by Laura Mulvey—an opposition between passivity and activity, but perhaps more importantly, an opposition between proximity and distance in relation to the image.[10] It is in this sense that the very logic behind the structure of the gaze demands a sexual division. While the distance between image and signified (or even referent) is theorized as minimal, if not nonexistent, that between the film and the spectator must be maintained, even measured. One need only think of Noël Burch's mapping of spectatorship as a perfect distance from the screen (two times the width of the image)—a point in space from which the filmic discourse is most accessible.[11]

But the most explicit representation of this opposition between proximity and distance is contained in Christian Metz's analysis of voyeuristic desire in terms of a kind of social hierarchy of the senses: "It is no accident that the main socially acceptable arts are based on the senses at a distance, and that those which depend on the senses of contact are often regarded as 'minor' arts (= culinary arts, art of perfumes, etc.)."[12] The voyeur, according to Metz, must maintain a distance between himself and the image—the cinéphile *needs* the gap which represents for him the very distance between desire and its object. In this sense, voyeurism is theorized as a type of metadesire:

> If it is true of all desire that it depends on the infinite pursuit of its absent object, voyeuristic desire, along with certain forms of sadism, is the only desire whose principle of distance symbolically and spatially evokes this fundamental rent.[13]

Yet even this status as metadesire does not fully characterize the cinema for it is a feature shared by other arts as well (painting, theatre, opera, etc.). Metz thus adds another reinscription of this necessary distance. What specifies the cinema is a further reduplication of the lack which prompts desire. The cinema is characterized by an illusory sensory plenitude (there is "so much to see") and yet haunted by the absence of those very objects which are there to be seen. Absence is an absolute and irrecoverable distance. In other words, Noël Burch is quite right in aligning spectatorial desire with a certain spatial configuration. The viewer must not sit either too close or too far from the screen. The result of both would be the same—he would lose the image of his desire.

It is precisely this opposition between proximity and distance, control of the image and its loss, which locates the possibilities of spectatorship within the problematic of sexual difference. For the female spectator there is a certain overpresence of the image—she *is* the image. Given the closeness of this relationship, the female spectator's desire can be described only in terms of a kind of narcissism—the female look demands a becoming. It thus appears to negate the very distance or gap specified by Metz and Burch as the essential precondition for voyeurism. From this perspective, it is important to note the constant recurrence of the motif of proximity in feminist theorist (especially those labeled "new French feminisms") which purport to describe a feminine specificity. For Luce Irigaray, female anatomy is readable as a constant relation of the self to itself, as an autoeroticism based on the embrace of the two lips which allow the woman to touch herself without mediation. Furthermore, the very notion of property, and hence possession of something which can be constituted as other, is antithetical to the woman: "*Nearness* however, is not foreign to woman, a nearness so close that any identification of one or the other, and therefore any form of property, is impossible. Woman enjoys a closeness with the other that is *so near she cannot possess it any more than she can possess herself*."[14] Or, in the case of female madness or delirium, "women do not manage to articulate their madness: they suffer it directly in their body."[15] The distance necessary to detach the signifiers of madness from the body in the construction of even a discourse which exceeds the boundaries of sense is lacking. In the words of Hélène Cixous, "More so than men who are coaxed toward social success, toward sublimation, women are body."[16]

This theme of the overwhelming presence-to-itself of the female body is elaborated by Sarah Kofman and Michèle Montrelay as well. Kofman describes how Freudian psychoanalysis outlines a scenario whereby the subject's passage from the mother to the father is simultaneous with a passage from the senses to reason, nostalgia for the mother henceforth signifying a longing for a different positioning in relation to the sensory or the somatic, and the degree of civilization measured by the very distance from the body.[17] Similarly, Montrelay argues that while the male has the possibility of displacing the first object of desire (the mother), the female must become that object of desire:

> Recovering herself as maternal body (and also as phallus), the woman can no longer repress, "lose," the first stake of representation. . . . From now on, anxiety, tied to the presence of this body, can only be insistent, continuous. This body, so close, which she has to occupy, is an object in excess which must be "lost," that is to say, repressed, in order to be symbolised.[18]

This body so close, so excessive, prevents the woman from assuming a position similar to the man's in relation to signifying systems. For she is haunted by the loss of a loss, the lack of that lack so essential for the realization of the ideals of semiotic systems.

Female specificity is thus theorized in terms of spatial proximity. In opposition to this "closeness" to the body, a spatial distance in the male's relation to his body rapidly becomes a temporal distance in the service of knowledge. This is presented quite explicitly in Freud's analysis of the construction of the "subject supposed to know." The knowledge involved here is a knowledge of sexual difference as it is organized in relation to the structure of the look, turning on the visibility of the penis. For the little girl in Freud's description, seeing and knowing are simultaneous—there is no temporal gap between them. In "Some Psychological Consequences of the Anatomical Distinction Between the Sexes," Freud claims that the girl, upon seeing the penis for the first time, "makes her judgment and her decision in a flash. She has seen it and knows that she is without it and wants to have it."[19] In the lecture on "Femininity" Freud repeats this gesture, merging perception and intellection: "They [girls] at once notice the difference and, it must be admitted, its significance too."[20]

The little boy, on the other hand, does not share this immediacy of understanding. When he first sees the woman's genitals he "begins by showing irresolution and lack of interest; he sees nothing or disowns what he has seen, he softens it down or looks about for expedients for bringing it into line with his expectations."[21] A second event, the threat of castration, is necessary to prompt a rereading of the image, endowing it with a meaning in relation to the boy's own subjectivity. It is in the distance between the look and the threat that the boy's relation to knowledge of sexual difference is formulated. The boy, unlike the girl in Freud's description, is capable of a revision of earlier events, a retrospective understanding which invests the events with a significance which is in no way linked to an immediacy of sight. This gap between the visible and the knowable, the very possibility of disowning what is seen, prepares the ground for fetishism. In a sense, the male spectator is destined to be a fetishist, balancing knowledge and belief.

The female, on the other hand, must find it extremely difficult, if not impossible, to assume the position of fetishist. That body which is so close continually reminds her of the castration which cannot be "fetishized away." The lack of a distance between seeing and understanding, the mode of judging "in a flash," is conducive to what might be termed as "overidentification" with the image. The association of tears and "wet wasted afternoons" (in Molly Haskell's words)[22] with genres specified as feminine (the soap opera, the "woman's picture") points very precisely to this type of overidentification, this abolition of a distance, in short, this inability to fetishize. The woman is constructed differently in relation to processes of looking. For Irigaray, this dichotomy between distance and proximity is described as the fact that:

> The masculine can partly look at itself, speculate about itself, represent itself and describe itself for what it is, whilst the feminine can try to speak to itself through a new language, but cannot describe itself from outside or in formal terms, except by identifying itself with the masculine, thus by losing itself.[23]

Irigaray goes even further: the woman always has a problematic relation to the visible, to form, to structures of seeing. She is much more comfortable with, closer to, the sense of touch.

The pervasiveness, in theories of the feminine, of descriptions of such a claustrophobic closeness, a deficiency in relation to structures of seeing and the visible, must clearly have consequences for attempts to theorize female spectatorship. And, in fact, the result is a tendency to view the female spectator as the site of an oscillation between a feminine position and a masculine position, invoking the metaphor of the transvestite. Given the structures of cinematic narrative, the woman who identifies with a female character must adopt a passive or masochistic position, while identification with the active hero necessarily entails an acceptance of what Laura Mulvey refers to as a certain "masculinization" of spectatorship: "As desire is given cultural materiality in a text, for women (from childhood onwards) trans-sex identification is a *habit* that very easily becomes *second Nature*. However, this Nature does not sit easily and shifts restlessly in its borrowed transvestite clothes."[24]

The transvestite wears clothes which signify a different sexuality, a sexuality which, for the woman, allows a mastery over the image and the very possibility of attaching the gaze to desire. Clothes make the man, as they say. Perhaps this explains the ease with which women can slip into male clothing. As both Freud and Cixous point out, the woman seems to be *more* bisexual than the man. A scene from Cukor's *Adam's Rib* graphically demonstrates this ease of female transvestism. As Katharine Hepburn asks the jury to imagine the sex role reversal of the three major characters involved in the case, there are three dissolves linking each of the characters successively to shots in which they are dressed in the clothes of the opposite sex. What characterizes the sequence is the marked facility of the transformation of the two women into men in contradistinction to a certain resistance in the case of the man. The acceptability of the female reversal is quite distinctly opposed to the male reversal which seems capable of representation only in terms of farce. Male transvestism is an occasion for laughter; female transvestism only another occasion for desire.

Thus, while the male is locked into sexual identity, the female can at least pretend that she is other—in fact, sexual mobility would seem to be a distinguishing feature of femininity in its cultural construction. Hence, transvestism would be fully recuperable. The idea seems to be this: it is understandable that women would want to be men, for everyone wants to be elsewhere than in the feminine position. What is not understandable within the given terms is why a woman might flaunt her femininity, produce herself as an excess of femininity, in other words, foreground the masquerade. Masquerade is not as recuperable as transvestism precisely because it constitutes an acknowledgement that it is femininity itself which is constructed as mask—as the decorative layer which conceals a nonidentity. For Joan

Riviere, the first to theorize the concept, the masquerade of femininity is a
kind of reaction-formation against the woman's trans-sex identification, her
transvestism. After assuming the position of the subject of discourse rather
than its object, the intellectual woman whom Riviere analyzes felt compelled
to compensate for this theft of masculinity by overdoing the gestures of feminine flirtation.

> Womanliness therefore could be assumed and worn as a mask, both to
> hide the possession of masculinity and to avert the reprisals expected if she
> was found to possess it—much as a thief will turn out his pockets and ask
> to be searched to prove that he has not the stolen goods. The reader may
> now ask how I define womanliness or where I draw the line between gen-
> uine womanliness and the masquerade. My suggestion is not, however,
> that there is any such difference; whether radical or superficial, they are
> the same thing.[25]

The masquerade, in flaunting femininity, holds it at a distance. Womanliness
is a mask which can be worn or removed. The masquerade's resistance to
patriarchal positioning would therefore lie in its denial of the production of
femininity as closeness, as presence-to-itself, as, precisely, imagistic. The
transvestite adopts the sexuality of the other—the woman becomes a man in
order to attain the necessary distance from the image. Masquerade, on the
other hand, involves a realignment of femininity, the recovery, or more accurately, simulation, of the missing gap or distance. To masquerade is to manufacture a lack in the form of a certain distance between oneself and one's
image. If, as Moustafa Safouan points out, "to wish to include in oneself as an
object the cause of the desire of the Other is a formula for the structure of
hysteria,"[26] then masquerade is antihysterical for it works to effect a separation between the cause of desire and oneself. In Montrelay's words, "the
woman uses her own body as a disguise."[27]

The very fact that we can speak of a woman "using" her sex or "using" her
body for particular gains is highly significant—it is not that a man cannot use
his body in this way but that he doesn't have to. The masquerade doubles representation; it is constituted by a hyperbolization of the accoutrements of
femininity. *Apropos* of a recent performance by Marlene Dietrich, Sylvia
Bovenschen claims, "we are watching a woman demonstrate the representation of a woman's body."[28] This type of masquerade, an excess of femininity,
is aligned with the *femme fatale* and, as Montrelay explains, is necessarily
regarded by men as evil incarnate: "It is this evil which scandalises whenever

woman plays out her sex in order to evade the word and the law. Each time she subverts a law or a word which relies on the predominantly masculine structure of the look."[29] By destabilizing the image, the masquerade confounds this masculine structure of the look. It effects a defamiliarization of female iconography. Nevertheless, the preceding account simply specifies masquerade as a type of representation which carries a threat, disarticulating male systems of viewing. Yet, it specifies nothing with respect to female spectatorship. What might it mean to masquerade as spectator? To assume the mask in order to see in a different way?

"Men Seldom Make Passes at Girls Who Wear Glasses"

The first scene in *Now Voyager* depicts the Bette Davis character as repressed, unattractive, and undesirable or, in her own words, as the spinster aunt of the family. ("Every family has one.") She has heavy eyebrows, keeps her hair bound tightly in a bun, and wears glasses, a drab dress, and heavy shoes. By the time of the shot discussed earlier, signalling her transformation into beauty, the glasses have disappeared, along with the other signifiers of unattractiveness. Between these two moments there is a scene in which the doctor who cures her actually confiscates her glasses (as a part of the cure). The woman who wears glasses constitutes one of the most intense visual clichés of the cinema. The image is a heavily marked condensation of motifs concerned with repressed sexuality, knowledge, visibility and vision, intellectuality, and desire. The woman with glasses signifies simultaneously intellectuality and undesirability; but the moment she removes her glasses (a moment which, it seems, must almost always be *shown* and which is itself linked with a certain sensual quality), she is transformed into spectacle, the very picture of desire. Now, it must be remembered that the cliché is a heavily loaded moment of signification, a social knot of meaning. It is characterized by an effect of ease and naturalness. Yet, the cliché has a binding power so strong that it indicates a precise moment of ideological danger or threat—in this case, the woman's appropriation of the gaze. Glasses worn by a woman in the cinema do not generally signify a deficiency in seeing but an active looking, or even simply the fact of seeing as opposed to being seen. The intellectual woman looks and analyzes, and in usurping the gaze she poses a threat to an entire system of representation. It is as if the woman had forcefully moved to the other side of the specular. The overdetermination of the image of the woman with glasses, its status as a cliché, is a crucial aspect of the cinematic alignment of structures of seeing and being seen with sexual difference. The cliché, in assuming an immediacy of understanding, acts as a mechanism for the naturalization of sexual difference.

But the figure of the woman with glasses is only an extreme moment of a more generalized logic. There is always a certain excessiveness, a difficulty associated with women who appropriate the gaze, who insist upon looking. Linda Williams has demonstrated how, in the genre of the horror film, the woman's active looking is ultimately punished. And what she sees, the monster, is only a mirror of herself—both woman and monster are freakish in their difference—defined by either "too much" or "too little."[30] Just as the dominant narrative cinema repetitively inscribes scenarios of voyeurism, internalizing or narrativizing the film-spectator relationship (in films like *Psycho*, *Rear Window*, *Peeping Tom*), taboos in seeing are insistently formulated in relation to the female spectator as well. The man with binoculars is countered by the woman with glasses. The gaze must be dissociated from mastery. In *Leave Her to Heaven* (John Stahl, 1945), the female protagonist's (Gene Tierney's) excessive desire and overpossessiveness are signaled from the very beginning of the film by her intense and sustained stare at the major male character, a stranger she first encounters on a train. The discomfort her look causes is graphically depicted. The Gene Tierney character is ultimately revealed to be the epitome of evil—killing her husband's crippled younger brother, her unborn child, and ultimately herself in an attempt to brand her cousin as a murderess in order to ensure her husband's future fidelity. In *Humoresque* (Jean Negulesco, 1946), Joan Crawford's problematic status is a result of her continual attempts to assume the position of spectator—fixing John Garfield with her gaze. Her transformation from spectator to spectacle is signified repetitively by the gesture of removing her glasses. Rosa, the character played by Bette Davis in *Beyond the Forest* (King Vidor, 1949), walks to the station every day simply to *watch* the train departing for Chicago. Her fascination with the train is a fascination with its phallic power to transport her to "another place." This character is also specified as having a "good eye"—she can shoot, both pool and guns. In all three films the woman is constructed as the site of an excessive and dangerous desire. This desire mobilizes extreme efforts of containment and unveils the sadistic aspect of narrative. In all three films the woman dies. As Claire Johnston points out, death is the "location of all impossible signs,"[31] and films demonstrate that the woman as subject of the gaze is clearly an impossible sign. There is a perverse rewriting of this logic of the gaze in *Dark Victory* (Edmund Goulding, 1939), where the woman's story achieves heroic and tragic proportions not only in blindness, but in a blindness which mimes sight—when the woman pretends to be able to see.

Out of the Cinema and into the Streets: The Censorship of the Female Gaze

This process of narrativizing the negation of the female gaze in the classical Hollywood cinema finds its perfect encapsulation in a still photograph taken in 1948 by Robert Doisneau, *Un Regard Oblique*. Just as the Hollywood narratives discussed above purport to center a female protagonist, the photograph appears to give a certain prominence to a woman's look. Yet, both the title of the photograph and its organization of space indicate that the real site of scopophiliac power is on the margins of the frame. The man is not centered; in fact, he occupies a very narrow space on the extreme right of the picture. Nevertheless, it is his gaze which defines the problematic of the photographs: it is his gaze which effectively erases that of the woman. Indeed, as subject of the gaze, the woman looks intently. But not only is the object of her look concealed from the spectator, her gaze is encased by the two poles defining the masculine axis of vision. Fascinated by nothing visible—a blankness or void for the spectator—unanchored by a "sight" (there is nothing "proper" to her vision—save, perhaps, the mirror), the female gaze is left free-floating, vulnerable to subjection. The faint reflection in the shop window of only the frame of the picture at which she is looking serves merely to rearticulate, *en abŷme* the emptiness of her gaze, the absence of her desire in representation.

On the other hand, the object of the male gaze is fully present, *there* for the spectator. The fetishistic representation of the nude female body, fully in view, insures a masculinization of the spectatorial position. The woman's look is literally outside the triangle which traces a complicity between the man, the nude, and the spectator. The feminine presence in the photograph, despite a diegetic centering of the female subject of the gaze, is taken over by the picture as object. And, as if to doubly "frame" her in the act of looking, the painting situates its female figure as a spectator (although it is not clear whether she is looking at herself in a mirror or peering through a door or window). While this drama of seeing is played out at the surface of the photograph, its deep space is activated by several young boys, out-of-focus, in front of a belt shop. The opposition out-of-focus/in-focus reinforces the supposed clarity accorded to the representation of the woman's "non-vision."

Un Regard Oblique by Robert Doisneau.

Furthermore, since this out-of-focus area constitutes the precise literal center of the image, it also demonstrates how the photograph makes figurative the operation of centering—draining the actual center point of significance in order to deposit meaning on the margins. The male gaze is centered, in control—although it is exercised from the periphery.

The spectator's pleasure is thus produced through the framing/negation of the female gaze. The woman is there as the butt of a joke—a "dirty joke" which, as Freud has demonstrated, is always constructed at the expense of a woman. In order for a dirty joke to emerge in its specificity in Freud's description, the object of desire—the woman—must be absent and a third person (another man) must be present as witness to the joke—"so that gradually, in place of the woman, the onlooker, now the listener, becomes the person to whom the smut is addressed."[32] The terms of the photograph's address as joke once again ensure a masculinization of the place of the spectator. The operation of the dirty joke is also inextricably linked by Freud to scopophilia and the exposure of the female body:

> Smut is like an exposure of the sexually different person to whom it is
> directed. By the utterance of the obscene words it compels the person
> who is assailed to imagine the part of the body or the procedure in ques-
> tion and shows her that the assailant is himself imagining it. It cannot be
> doubted that the desire to see what is sexual exposed is the original motive
> of smut.[33]

From this perspective, the photograph lays bare the very mechanics of the
joke through its depiction of sexual exposure and a surreptitious act of seeing (and desiring). Freud's description of the joke-work appears to constitute
a perfect analysis of the photograph's orchestration of the gaze. There is a
"voice-off" of the photographic discourse, however—a component of the
image which is beyond the frame of this little scenario of voyeurism. On the
far left-hand side of the photograph, behind the wall holding the painting of
the nude, is the barely detectable painting of a woman imaged differently, in
darkness—*out of sight* for the male, blocked by his fetish. Yet, to point to this
almost invisible alternative in imaging is also only to reveal once again the
analyst's own perpetual desire to find a not-seen that might break the hold of
representation. Or to laugh last.

There is a sense in which the photograph's delineation of a sexual politics
of looking is almost uncanny. But, to counteract the very possibility of such
a perception, the language of the art critic effects a naturalization of this joke
on the woman. The art-critical reception of the picture emphasizes a natural
but at the same time "imaginative" relation between photography and life,
ultimately subordinating any formal relations to a referential ground:
"Doisneau's lines move from right to left, directed by the man's glance; the
woman's gaze creates a line of energy like a hole in space. . . . The creation of
these relationships from life itself is imagination in photography."[34] "Life
itself," then, presents the material for an "artistic" organization of vision along
the lines of sexual difference. Furthermore, the critic would have us believe
that chance events and arbitrary clicks of the shutter cannot be the agents of
a generalized sexism because they are particular, unique—"Kertesz and
Doisneau depend entirely upon our recognition that they were present at the
instant of the unique intersection of events."[35] Realism seems always to
reside in the streets and, indeed, the out-of-focus boys across the street, at
the center of the photograph, appear to act as a guarantee of the "chance"
nature of the event, its arbitrariness, in short—its realism. Thus, in the discourse of the art critic the photograph, in capturing a moment, does not construct it; the camera finds a naturally given series of subject and object posi-

tions. What the critic does not consider are the conditions of reception of photography as an art form, its situation within a much larger network of representation. What is it that makes the photograph not only readable but pleasurable—at the expense of the woman? The critic does not ask what makes the photograph a negotiable item in a market of signification.

The Missing Look

The photograph displays insistently, in microcosm, the structure of the cinematic inscription of a sexual differentiation in modes of looking. Its process of framing the female gaze repeats that of the cinematic narratives described above, from *Leave Her to Heaven* to *Dark Victory*. Films play out scenarios of looking in order to outline the terms of their own understanding. And given the divergence between masculine and feminine scenarios, those terms would seem to be explicitly negotiated as markers of sexual difference. Both the theory of the image and its apparatus, the cinema, produce a position for the female spectator—a position which is ultimately untenable because it lacks the attribute of distance so necessary for an adequate reading of the image. The entire elaboration of femininity as a closeness, a nearness, as present-to-itself is not the definition of an essence but the delineation of a *place* culturally assigned to the woman. Above and beyond a simple adoption of the masculine position in relation to the cinematic sign, the female spectator is given two options: the masochism of overidentification or the narcissism entailed in becoming one's own object of desire, in assuming the image in the most radical way. The effectivity of masquerade lies precisely in its potential to manufacture a distance from the image, to generate a problematic within which the image is manipulable, producible, and readable by the woman. Doisneau's photograph is not readable by the female spectator—it can give her pleasure only in masochism. In order to "get" the joke, she must once again assume the position of transvestite.

It is quite tempting to foreclose entirely the possibility of female spectatorship, to repeat at the level of theory the gesture of the photograph, given the history of a cinema which relies so heavily on voyeurism, fetishism, and identification with an ego ideal conceivable only in masculine terms. And, in fact, there has been a tendency to theorize femininity and hence the feminine gaze as repressed, and in its repression somehow irretrievable, the enigma constituted by Freud's question. Yet, as Michel Foucault has demonstrated, the repressive hypothesis on its own entails a very limited and simplistic notion of the working of power.[36] The "no" of the father, the prohibition, is its only technique. In theories of repression there is no sense of the productiveness and positivity of power. Femininity is produced very precisely as a position within a network of power relations. And the growing insistence upon the elaboration of a theory of female spectatorship is indicative of the crucial necessity of understanding that position in order to dislocate it.

NOTES

1. Sigmund Freud, "Femininity," *The Standard Edition of the Complete Psychological Works of Sigmund Freud*, ed. James Strachey (London: The Hogarth Press and the Institute of Psycho-analysis, 1961), p. 113.

2. This is the translation given in a footnote in *The Standard Edition*, p. 113.

3. Heinrich Heine, *The North Sea*, trans. Vernon Watkins (New York: New Direction Books, 1951), p. 77.

4. In other words, the woman can never ask her own ontological question. The absurdity of such a situation within traditional discursive conventions can be demonstrated by substituting a "young woman" for the "young man" of Heine's poem.

5. As Oswald Ducrot and Tzvetan Todorov point out in *Encyclopedic Dictionary of the Science of Language*, trans. Catherine Porter (Baltimore and London: Johns Hopkins University Press, 1979), p. 195, the potentially universal understandability of the hieroglyphic is highly theoretical and can only be thought as the unattainable ideal of an imagistic system: "It is important of course not to exaggerate either the resemblance of the image with the object—the design is stylized very rapidly— or the "natural" and "universal" character of the signs: Sumerian, Chinese, Egyptian, and Hittite hieroglyphics for the same object have nothing in common."

6. Ibid., p. 194. Emphasis mine.

7. See Noël Burch's film, *Correction Please, or How We Got Into Pictures*.

8. Laura Mulvey, "Visual Pleasure and Narrative Cinema," *Screen* 16, no. 3 (Autumn 1975): 12–13.

9. Charles Affron, *Star Acting: Gish, Garbo, Davis* (New York, E. P. Dutton, 1977), pp. 281–82.

10. This argument focuses on the image to the exclusion of any consideration of the soundtrack primarily because it is the process of imaging which seems to constitute the major difficulty in theorizing female spectatorship. The image is also popularly understood as metonymic signifier for the cinema as a whole and for good reason: historically, sound has been subordinate to the image within the dominant classical system. For more on the image/sound distinction in relation to sexual

difference see my article, "The Voice in the Cinema: The Articulation of Body and Space," *Yale French Studies*, no. 60: 33–50.

11. Noël Burch, *Theory of Film Practice*, trans. Helen R. Lane (New York and Washington: Praeger, 1973), p. 35.

12. Christian Metz, "The Imaginary Signifier," *Screen* 16, no. 2 (Summer 1975): 60.

13. Ibid., p. 61.

14. Luce Irigaray, "This Sex Which Is Not One," *New French Feminisms*, ed. Elaine Marks and Isabelle de Courtivron (Amherst: University of Massachusetts Press, 1980), pp. 104–105.

15. Irigaray, "Women's Exile," *Ideology and Consciousness*, no. 1 (May 1977): 74.

16. Hélène Cixous, "The Laugh of the Medusa," *New French Feminisms*, p. 257.

17. Sarah Kofman, "Ex: The Woman's Enigma" *Enclitic* 4, no. 2 (Fall 1980): 20.

18. Michèle Montrelay, "Inquiry into Femininity," *mlf*, no. 1 (1978): 91–92.

19. Freud, "Some Psychological Consequences of the Anatomical Distinction Between the Sexes," *Sexuality and the Psychology of Love*, ed. Philip Rieff (New York: Collier, 1963), pp. 187–88.

20. Freud, "Femininity," p. 125.

21. Freud, "Some Psychological Consequences," p. 187.

22. Molly Haskell, *From Reverence to Rape* (Baltimore: Penguin, 1974), p. 154.

23. Irigaray, "Women's Exile," p. 65.

24. Mulvey, "Afterthoughts . . . inspired by Duel in the Sun," *Framework* (Summer 1981): 13.

25. Joan Riviere, "Womanliness as a Masquerade," *Psychoanalysis and Female Sexuality*, ed. Hendrik M. Ruitenbeek (New Haven: College and University Press, 1966), p. 213. My analysis of the concept of masquerade differs markedly from that of Luce Irigaray. See *Ce sexe qui n'en est pas un* (Paris: Les Editions de Minuit, 1977), pp. 131–32. It also diverges to a great extent from the very important analysis of masquerade presented by Claire Johnston in "Femininity and the Masquerade: Anne of the Indies," *Jacques Tourneur* (London: British Film Institute, 1975), pp. 36–44. I am indebted to her for the reference to Riviere's article.

26. Moustala Safouan, "Is the Oedipus Complex Universal?" *m/f* 5–6 (1981): 84–85.

27. Montrelay, "Inquiry into Femininity," p. 93.

28. Silvia Bovenschen, "Is There a Feminine Aesthetic?" *New German Critique*, no. 10 (Winter 1977): 129.

29. Montrelay, p. 93.

30. Linda Williams, "When the Woman Looks . . .," in *Revision: Feminist Essays in Film Analysis*, ed. Mary Ann Doane, Pat Mellencamp, and Linda Williams (Frederick, Md.: AFI-University Publications, 1984).

31. Johnston, "Femininity and the Masquerade," p. 40.

32. Freud, *Jokes and Their Relation to the Unconscious*, trans. James Strachey (New York: Norton, 1960), p. 99.

33. Ibid., p. 98.

34. Weston J. Naef, *Counterparts: Form and Emotion in Photographs* (New York: Dutton and the Metropolitan Museum of Art, 1982), pp. 48–49.

35. Ibid.

36. Michel Foucault, *The History of Sexuality*, trans. Robert Hurley (New York: Pantheon, 1978).

10

The Body and Cinema

SOME PROBLEMS FOR FEMINISM

Annette Kuhn

Critique doesn't have to be the premise of a deduction which concludes: this then is what needs to be done. It should be an instrument for those who fight, those who resist and refuse what is.

—Michel Foucault,
Ideology and Consciousness

It must be clear by now that representation— and visual representation in particular—poses certain problems for both feminist thinking and feminist politics. I want to take a look at one or two of these problems as they presented themselves to me in the context of a recent cinema-going experience. Early in 1986 I attended a commercial screening in London of a film called *Pumping Iron II—The Women*.[1] The screening was organized for an all-women audience and was followed by a discussion between the audience and a panel, consisting of two film critics and a bodybuilder. It is possible there were more critics and bodybuilders in the audience, but most of the women present apparently fell into neither category. Though, being mostly feminists, they were not the "ordinary women" of the populist Imaginary, either.

Annette Kuhn, "The Body and Cinema: Some Problems for Feminism." Appeared in *Grafts: Feminist Cultural Criticism*, edited by Susan Sheridan, 1988, and is reprinted with permission from the author.

Few "ordinary women"—if such beings exist—would in any case have the opportunity to see *Pumping Iron II*. Although the film received an enthusiastic critical reception on its U.S. and British releases, it has had no general release, nor as far as I know has it been shown on television in Britain. And the video version circulating in Britain for a while has now been withdrawn. None of this matters very much in the present context, since the film figures here largely as a peg or point of departure for a set of general observations on visual representation and feminism. My argument, in other words, is applicable to more than this one film: and an argument based on *Pumping Iron II* might even shed some light on cinema in general.

Nevertheless, a summary of the storyline of *Pumping Iron II* is probably in order here. The film is about a women's bodybuilding championship held in Las Vegas in 1984. It may be called "semi-documentary," in that while all the characters play "themselves," they are placed in situations set up expressly for the camera. Indeed, the contest was proposed in the first place by the film's director, George Butler: its initial raison d'être, therefore, was that a film would be made of it. Suffice it to say—without entering into debates about "truth" and "fiction" in cinema—that a certain fictionality underlies the film's cinéma vérité appearance. This double status makes it entirely appropriate to look at the film as a narrative in the classic mold.

The main protagonists are real-life bodybuilding champions Rachel McLish, Carla Dunlap (the only black contestant), and Australian weight-lifter-turned-bodybuilder Bev Francis. The first part of the film shows these and other women in the run-up to the contest—their training, their relationships with their (male) coaches and with each other. The film's climax is the competition itself, held in the plush surroundings of Caesar's Palace. The narrative hook is simple: Who will win? But there is more to the story than that: the competition and its outcome turn upon the question of what sort of body a female bodybuilder ought to have. Before the 1984 championship, women bodybuilders had produced lithe and sinewy, as opposed to overtly muscular, physiques. But in the film, Bev Francis's entry into competition challenges this order of things. For hers is a body so extremely muscular that it can only be seen as "masculine' by judges and contestants accustomed to previous competition "form." Francis clearly has more muscles than any of the other women in the contest: the question is, can she win on these grounds?

This question, which becomes crucial to the progress of the narrative, is addressed quite explicitly in the film. When all the contestants are assembled in Las Vegas for their final few days of training before the championship, several discussions on this very issue take place. First of all, a group of competitors—all minor characters—relax together in the pool at Caesar's Palace, surrounded by classical statuary. They are all more or less in agreement that the judges should stick with the "feminine look." This is followed by a scene in which these very judges—all but one male—confer on "the official [International Federation of Bodybuilding] analysis" of the word "femininity." Then, following a short scene in which Carla Dunlap, under the gaze of a facsimile Winged Victory, does some synchroswimming practice alone in the pool, she and Bev chat about the judging of the contest, muscles, and, again, "femininity." Finally, Rachel McLish is seen expressing doubt to an interviewer that the world is yet ready for Bev Francis. But although the question "Who will win?" is duly answered at the end of the film, the conundrum of the appropriate body for a female bodybuilder is never really resolved—a point to which I shall return.

On its British release, *Pumping Iron II* was hailed by some as *the* feminist film of the year, on the grounds that it holds up conventional notions about the relationship between femaleness, femininity, and the body not only to scrutiny, but also to a certain amount of ridicule: this feminist reading sanctioned the women-only screening which I attended. Aside from the all-female audience, this was an extraordinary event in a number of respects. Most unusual, perhaps, was the packed auditorium. And the audience behaved not in the customary (in Britain, at least) manner as a gathering of individuals, couples or small groups of friends on their separate night out at the pictures, but as a single social group: talking back to characters on the screen, cheering on the "goodies," booing the "baddies," and so on. All the viewers, it seemed, were having a wonderful time, enjoying both the film and the circumstances in which they were watching it. Although the potential of female or feminist audiences as *communities* is an issue of obvious relevance to questions of feminism and representation,[2] I want to concentrate more specifically here on the question of what is involved for audiences of this sort in the reception of a film like *Pumping Iron II*.

This question was raised quite forcefully after the screening was over, during discussion of the film. Many of those who spoke were critical of the film. Criticism tended to be expressed in terms of the nature and value of women's bodybuilding as a sport. In particular, the view was put forward that aside from being competitive (A Bad Thing), the sport was narcissistic (An Even Worse Thing). If criticism from this feminist audience was not directed at the sorts of things that preoccupy film theorists (the film text, the specifically cinematic, the spectator-text relationship, and so on), it did in a way highlight some key problems—not just for feminist thinking around cinema and visual representation in general, but for other feminist practices as well.

The apparently inconsistent responses of this audience—enjoyment during, negative criticism after, the screening—might well betoken a certain discomfort with the pleasures evoked by the film. In this context, viewers' references to narcissism could be regarded as symptomatic. In relation to activities represented on the screen, this invocation of narcissism assumes a certain transparency on behalf of the cinematic image: a "naive" reading from which critics and theorists of cinema would undoubtedly hasten to dissociate themselves. Yet narcissism also describes a potential mode of relation to the film text, and its invocation in this displaced manner may well be an expression of the difficulty of such a relation, highly foregrounded, perhaps, in this particular text, but by no means confined to it.

One of the central and most productive insights of feminist film theory concerns the ways in which sexual difference is constructed, and spectators addressed as male/masculine and female/feminine, within the cinematic apparatus. To summarize and grossly oversimplify a substantial body of work, it might be argued that the options on offer to spectators in cinema are basically either to take up a masculine subject position as, so the argument goes, is proposed by the huge number of films in which the enunciating instance is male/masculine; or to submit to a masochism of overidentification, as is evoked, for example, by the Hollywood "women's picture"; or to adopt the narcissistic position of taking the screen as mirror and becoming one's own object of desire.[3]

In their inscription within a complex and unstable libidinal economy, these spectator-text relations are not mutually exclusive; each is, in theory, available to all spectators, regardless of gender. However, in the social, historical, and ideological space inhabited and produced by cinema, certain constraints are imposed upon such polymorphy. For example, the Hollywood women's melodrama of the 1940s and 1950s, proposing a mode of identification culturally marked as characteristically feminine, was deliberately marketed to female audiences: in this instance, social relations and psychic relations intersect in the actual reception of films. Nevertheless, while the pleasures of cinema are obviously available to women as well as to men, I would contend that for women there is an additional degree of instability in the relations of subjectivity upon which these pleasures depend.

In *Pumping Iron II*, for instance, an important source of pleasure for female spectators must lie in its construction of the female body not only as strong but also as capable of being shaped and defined by women themselves. And

yet while this film might evoke such new and technological narcissistic identifications, the pleasure of this position may at the same time be undercut in
at least two ways: first of all, by a construction of the female body as potentially monstrous; and secondly, as a consequence, by the fact that, for a
woman, assenting to the pleasures afforded by cinema is tantamount to
becoming caught up (to use Foucauldian terminology, on which I shall elaborate later[4]) in certain relations of power, held in place by these relations and
by the constructs of sexuality they inscribe.

These power relations and their associated instabilities characterize a
good deal of classical cinema. *Pumping Iron II* is exceptional only in that it
brings such contradictions to the fore at the levels of both narrative and spectacle. For example, on both these levels the film is quite clearly "about" the
female body in ways that most films are not. That is to say, while—as feminist film theorists have argued—the female body may figure crucially in the
production of both meaning and pleasure in classical cinema, *Pumping Iron II*
transcends this inscription of the female body to interrogate that body and its
limits. The film's narrative, I have suggested, is governed by the question of
who will win the contest. But since in this context "who?" must mean "which
body?," the trajectory of the narrative is harnessed to a further set of questions: What is a woman's body? Is there a point at which a woman's body
becomes something else? What is the relationship between a certain type of
body and "femininity"?

These are challenging questions in a cultural context in which the body
figures as an irreducible sign of the natural, the given, the unquestionable.
Foremost among these cultural effectivities of the body is its function as a signifier of sexual difference. But the concept of sexual difference is itself an
ideological battleground: it holds together—or tries to—a range of discourses and meanings centering on biological sex, social gender, gender
identity, and sexual object choice. The encapsulation of all these within constructs of sexual difference is a historically grounded ideological project
which works to set up a heterogeneous and variably determinate set of biological, physical, social, psychological, and psychic constructs as a unitary,
fixed, and unproblematic attribute of human subjectivity. One of the effects
of this is that, at a social level at least, every human being gets defined as
either male or female. From this fundamental difference flows a succession
of discourses and powers centering upon identification and sexuality.
Pumping Iron II can be read if not as actually unraveling this discursive formation, certainly as unpicking it a little around the edges.

The film does this most distinctively by constructing the body in a particular manner as *performance*. Performance is an activity that connotes pretense, dissimulation, "putting on an act," assuming a role. In other words, in the notion of performance a distance of some sort is implied between the "act" and the "real self" concealed behind it. Performance proposes a subject which is at once both fixed in, and called into question by, this very distinction between assumed persona and authentic self. Performance, in other words, poses the possibility of a mutable self, of a fluid subjectivity. If performance proposes fluidity and the body connotes fixity, the combination of the two in the instance of bodybuilding confers a distinctly contradictory quality on the activity. For bodybuilding involves more than placing the body on display, more than simply passive exhibition. The fact that bodybuilding is an active production of the body, a process of acting upon and determining its contours, is impossible to ignore. In *Pumping Iron II*, for example, innumerable scenes emphasize the sheer hard work involved in the production of the women's bodies. In bodybuilding—the willed construction of a certain physique—nature becomes culture.

Performance and the body are instrumental in the operations of classical cinema as well; but rarely in ways which in the final instance challenge the natural order of the body and its inscription of sexual difference. For in cinema, performance is usually appropriated to the self-evidently cultural and mutable instances of clothing and gesture.[5] In bodybuilding, muscles function in much the same way as clothing does in other types of performance. But muscles, unlike clothes, are supposed to be natural. What happens, then, when muscles enter the cultural domain? In a sense, of course, they already do inhabit it, for muscles carry a heavy burden of cultural meanings. Not least among these are meanings centered upon sexual difference and its naturalness. Within such a discourse, muscles are constituted as "essentially" masculine.

Thus when women enter the arena of bodybuilding, a twofold challenge to the natural order is posed. Not only is the naturalness of the body called into question by its inscription within a certain kind of performance: but when women have the muscles, the natural order of gender is under threat as well. Muscles are rather like drag, for female bodybuilders especially: while muscles can be assumed, like clothing, women's assumption of muscles implies a transgression of the proper boundaries of sexual difference. In *Pumping Iron II* the limits of the female body are the object of obsessive concern, to the extent that the opposite poles of the issue are represented in the "feminine" body of Rachel McLish against the "masculine" body of Bev Francis.

The woman's body as muscular may also be regarded as tantamount to a

Carla Dunlap poses down in the final round.

fetish, a point which brings me back to the question of cinema. For it is an axiom of feminist film theory that one of the masculine subject positions available to the spectator in cinema is constructed through a fetishistic look, a look which effects a disavowal of the threat of castration posed by woman. The phallic woman imaged in this process of disavowal is either overvalued as a glamorous figure, or punished as a monstrosity.[6] Such an operation, it is argued, is characteristic of the spectator-text relations proposed by classical cinema. Again, this operation is foregrounded in *Pumping Iron II*. In particular, Bev Francis's body can only, within the terms of the body/gender/culture problematic, be seen as "masculine," or at least as "not-feminine." How is such a disturbing body to be looked at when translated on to the cinema screen? Indeed, can it be looked at?[7]

At the level of spectacle, then, the threatening quality of Bev's body can be neutralized by its construction—in a fetishistic look—as monstrous. And yet at the level of narrative, Bev figures as a key character—indeed as a sympathetic character—in the film. Whether she will receive her just narrative deserts as a "good person" or her just, "specular" deserts as a phallic woman is a question entirely central to the suspenseful trajectory of *Pumping Iron II*.

Bev Francis: the challenger.

In the end, Bev loses the championship, coming in at a humiliating eighth place. But ultrafeminine Rachel McLish does not win, either: and of these two it is Bev who, by her magnanimity in defeat, scores the moral victory.

First prize, in fact, goes to Carla Dunlap, whose body is represented in the film as a midpoint between Bev's and Rachel's. But there is more to this resolution than mere compromise. Carla is set up as an outsider, as different from the other contestants—and not just by virtue of race: she is the most articulate of the group, a self-sufficient loner, the only one with no man to coach her and provide moral support. Carla's dea ex machina win does not so much answer the film's central question, then, as sidestep it. The issue of the appropriate body for a female bodybuilder is not actually resolved: rather it is displaced on to a set of discourses centering on—but also skirting—race, femininity, and the body, a complex of discourses which the film cannot acknowledge, let alone handle. In *Pumping Iron II*'s terms, Carla's body can be "read" only as a compromise: other major issues are left dangling.

These contradictions overdetermine the ways in which *Pumping Iron II* foregrounds a number of dilemmas facing female spectators at the cinema. Most especially, the film makes it clear that to adopt a narcissistic position in relation to the cinematic image is to run the risks of identifying with woman-as-fetish: of identifying with her overidealization, certainly—and, more commonly, perhaps, in the cinema of the 1980s—with her victimization and punishment. The difficulties of such a mode of identification effectively become a topic of *Pumping Iron II*, so that the instability of femininity as a subject position, and the discomfort involved in identification with it, are liable to become evident in looking at this film in ways they are not when such relations are more embedded, more submerged in the text.

This brings me back to the question of the powers at work in cinema's relation of spectatorship: powers through which, it is argued, sexual difference—and indeed perhaps other kinds of difference, too[8]—are constructed. To take pleasure in cinema is to be seduced by these operations; to be subject to, to submit to, the powers they inscribe. The spectator becomes caught up in, and constituted by, a set of powers which produce (among other things) discursive constructs of femininity and masculinity. She/he is positioned, defined, set in place, within these powers and constructs. The gendered subjectivities so produced are not interchangeable, however. This is one reason—and a very important one—why visual representation presents special problems for feminist politics. In this context two questions present themselves: Is it possible for women/feminists to take pleasure in visual representation, particularly in cinema? And, more generally, what is to be done about the problems all this poses for feminism? Before tackling these issues, however, I want to subject the notion of the instrumentality of representation to a little more scrutiny, with a view to understanding it better in relation to women, to the feminine, indeed to feminism.

Representation, as I have suggested, sets in play certain relations of power through which, among other things, discourses around sexual difference and subjects in and for those discourses are ongoingly produced. In this sense, representation may be regarded, once more to adopt Foucauldian terminology, as a strategy of normalization. Representation participates in the various relations of power with which we are surrounded and in which we are always in one way or another implicated. Representation can be understood, then, as a form of regulation.

This theoretical position suggests that no one, no social group, no structure, can stand outside the powers and the normalizing instrumentality of representation. Therefore if "women" are positioned and produced through these powers in specific ways as social subjects, it follows that they are not excluded from these powers. Nor, in the classic sense of the term, can women be regarded as "oppressed" by them. For power, in this model, is not a thing, is not imposed from outside its subjects, but is rather a process, the outcome of a series of interacting and potentially contradictory relations in which these subjects are necessarily involved. If power operates in this way as a network of countervailing "force relations," then resistance becomes an integral part of processes of power. Given this, what kinds of resistance to the normalizing effectivities of representation are available to feminism? In current circumstances, three sets of feminist strategies of resistance present themselves: censorship, feminist practices of representation, and feminist critical practice. My main concern here is with feminist critical practice, but a few words on the other two are perhaps in order first.

If censorship deserves attention, this is not because (at least in its legal or quasilegal manifestations) it constitutes an important feminist strategy of resistance to the normalizing powers of representation: on the contrary, generally speaking it does not. However, since feminist protests against visual representations of women are often appropriated (in Britain and the U.S., at least) in support of prefeminist and even antifeminist arguments in favor of censorship, it might be worthwhile making a few distinctions here. While censorship—to the extent that it seeks to repress certain representations—can be regarded as a prohibitive operation, it can also be seen as productive.[9] At the most basic level, for example, it produces the "unrepresentable" precisely as a set of images that should not be seen. What censorship both prohibits and produces is most especially that category of representations named the "obscene."

However, constructs of femininity produced by representation cannot simply be mapped directly on to constructs of the obscene produced by censorship. On the contrary, in fact: in both psychic and economic terms, "femininity" may be regarded as exactly a condition of representation. If feminists and censors seem to be at one in objecting to certain images of women, the objects of their objections are in fact completely different. It might be added, moreover, that censorship, in inciting desire for the unrepresentable, in the final instance acknowledges and reinforces the power of the image. To this extent, censorship is complicit in those very normalizing processes which feminism seeks to resist.

Feminist practices of representation, on the other hand, embody—in the quest for a "new voice," a transformation of vision—a wholly understandable desire to stand outside these powers. This is not necessarily an essentialist project, though given the appeals often made to an authentic feminine voice, "writing the body" and suchlike, it certainly looks like it at times. A good deal of exciting and valuable work in film, as in other areas of cultural production, has appeared in recent years, some of it indeed claiming to speak a "feminine voice." Nevertheless, the search for new forms of expression is more productively seen in terms of resistance to the powers of representation than as taking place outside their "field of force."

This argument is more than just a corollary of the notion that power is all-pervasive: it also registers a discomfort with a distinction between feminist cultural production on the one hand and feminist theory and criticism on the other. Such a polarization perpetuates the assumption that while theory and criticism are of necessity implicated in "discourses which negate or objectify [women] through their representations,"[10] feminist cultural production is somehow capable of transcending these limitations. At stake here, of course, is a separation of theory and practices: precisely one of the dualisms of patriarchal thought which feminist thinking seeks to challenge.

This brings me to the third and final strategy of resistance, strategically termed in this context feminist critical practice. Feminist critics and theorists among my readers may be relieved to hear that, in arguing that criticism can be a political practice in its own right, I have masculine authority on my side. I refer here to the quotation from Foucault which heads this essay. If feminist critics can place themselves among those who, in Foucault's words, "resist and refuse what is," we might well then ask: Where lies the specificity of feminist as against other forms of oppositional cultural practice? Perhaps it resides in the possibility that feminist critical practice may constitute not only a resistance to the powers of visual representation, but also an attempt to bridge the gap between woman as spectacle, as object of the look, and women as historical subjects. Alongside feminist cultural production, then, feminist critical practice

> can be a fundamentally deconstructive strategy which questions the possibility of universals or absolute meanings and exposes the constitution of power at stake in their assertion.[11]

However, I shall not end with any fanfares, for one further question remains unanswered: can feminists (and indeed women in general) take pleasure in visual representations, and if so, how? I have suggested that the feminist audience at the screening of *Pumping Iron II* was uncomfortable with its own pleasure in the film. If this is so, then their discomfort was simultaneously expressed and dealt with in a process of disavowal. This is evident in the negative criticisms directed at—but actually missing—the film: and it may be seen in itself as a form of resistance to the film's powers of seduction and subjection. The question remains, though: Can there be a feminist critical position which neither refuses nor disavows the pleasures of cinema? Because I love cinema, I want to answer yes. In the end, though, perhaps a feminist critical practice can do no more than offer the—not inconsiderable—pleasure of resistance?

weak argument

NOTES

1. *Pumping Iron II—The Women* (U.S., 1985). Directed by George Butler; British distributor Blue Dolphin; video distributor Virgin. For commentary on the production of the film see *American Cinematographer* 65, no. 7 (1984): 76–81; *Film Comment* 21, no. 4 (1985): 60–64.

2. In "Illicit Pleasures: Feminist Spectators and *Personal Best*," *Wide Angle* 8, no. 2 (1986): 45–56, Elizabeth Ellsworth considers how the audience of another film about women's sport may behave as a community.

3. Judith Mayne, in "Feminist Film Theory and Criticism," *Signs* 11, no. 1 (1985): 81–100, offers the nonspecialist reader a lucid introduction to, and exposition of, these ideas.

4. See Hubert L. Dreyfus and Paul Rabinow, *Michel Foucault: Beyond Structuralism and Hermeneutics* (Chicago: University of Chicago Press, 1982), chapter 5, for an account of the Foucauldian understanding of power.

5. Annette Kuhn, "Sexual Disguise and Cinema," in *The Power of the Image: Essays on Representation and Sexuality* (London:Routledge and Kegan Paul, 1985), pp. 48–73, addresses the theme of cross-dressing in Hollywood films as a potential challenge to the "natural" order of sexual difference proposed by cinema.

6. Sigmund Freud, "Fetishism" (1927), in *The Standard Edition of the Complete PsychologicalWorks of Sigmund Freud*, vol. 21 (London: Hogarth Press, 1953–74), pp. 152–7; Laura Mulvey, "Visual Pleasure and Narrative Cinema," *Screen* 16, no. 3 (1975): 6–18; Linda Williams, "When the Woman Looks," in Mary Anne Doane *et al.*, eds, *Re-Vision: Essays in Feminist Film Criticism* (Frederick, Md.: University Publications of America, Los Angeles, Calif., in association with the American Film Institute, 1984), pp. 83–99.

7. It is significant that neither Bev nor—interestingly—Carla, are among the women featured on the poster for *Pumping Iron II*.

8. Teresa de Lauretis, in "Aesthetic and Feminist Theory: Rethinking Women's Cinema," *New German Critique*, no. 34 (1985): 154–75, discusses differences of race and class in this context. Both of these—but especially considerations of race—are of relevance to a reading of *Pumping Iron II*.

9. The productive potential of censorship is discussed in Annette Kuhn, *Cinema, Censorship, and Sexuality, 1909–1925* (London: Routledge, 1988), chapter 8.

10. De Lauretis, p. 154.

11. Biddy Martin, "Feminist Criticism and Foucault," *New German Critique* no. 27 (1982): 12–13.

Cinema and the Dark Continent

RACE AND GENDER IN POPULAR FILM

Tania Modleski

Issues of race, gender, and ethnicity come together in an especially bizarre manner in one of the earliest sound films, *The Jazz Singer*, at the end of which the Jewish son, played by Al Jolson, donning black face for a theatrical performance, hears "the call of the ages—the cry of my race," sings "Mammy" to his mother, and rushes home to his dying father, promising to take up momentarily the father's role as cantor. Subsequently—and the coda is added to the film version of the stage play—the son returns to his show-business career, thus being permitted the best of both worlds, old and new. Here, of course, are the familiar oedipal themes of Hollywood cinema: the son's accession to the role of the father entails a modification of the stern and unyielding patriarchal attitude, thereby, in the case of *The Jazz Singer*, accommodating the assimilationist ideologies of the period.

Tania Modleski, "Cinema and the Dark Continent: Race and Gender in Popular Film." Reprinted from *Feminism Without Women: Culture and Criticism in a "Postfeminist" Age* by Tania Modleski (1991), by permission of the publisher Routledge, New York.

only essay
this section (but little oks)
written in '90s

The mother is a key figure in the process of the hero's growth and acculturation, since in her unconditional love for her child she can serve as the mediating force between father and son, old world and new, the desire for cultural difference and the desire for cultural integration.[1]

But the mother in the film is not the only mediator, not the only person whose sole significance lies in the meaning she holds for the white man and *his* drama; the other such figure is, of course, the black man, metonymically summoned to represent the unalterable fact of "race," and thus to form one pole of the assimilationist continuum, at the other end of which stands the Jolson character's shiksa girlfriend. It is ironic, if utterly characteristic, that the essentialist notion of race the film draws upon is asserted through masquerade and in a space of illusionism, i.e., the theatre. That is to say, the jazz singer recognizes his supposed racial *authenticity* as a Semite in the process of *miming* another race—assuming black skin and black voice—so that the film is situated squarely in the realm of the fetish, whereby the notion of ineradicable racial difference (one which defies history and calls out across "the ages") is simultaneously affirmed and negated.

Recent work by Homi Bhabha has shown how colonialist discourse as a whole involves a process of mimicry that is related psychoanalytically to the mechanism of fetishization, the play of presence and absence. By mimicry, I take Bhabha to be referring to an imposition by one nation of its structures, values, and language upon the colonized nation, an imposition that rather than completely obliterating difference speaks of "a desire for a subject of a difference that is almost the same, but not quite" and hence is, Bhabha continually emphasizes, *ambivalent*.[2] Although Bhabha's terms of reference concern the British Empire, they apply equally to the American situation, for, as Thomas Cripps points out in his somewhat dated but still useful study of blacks in American film, the position of blacks in relation to the dominant culture and its representations has been an "ambivalent" one: blacks had "absorbed American culture but could not expect to be absorbed by it."[3] Moreover, Cripps himself points out that the British colonial system "resembled American racial arrangements" in the way "it encouraged cultural assimilation while denying social integration" (p. 313). One fairly ludicrous result of such "arrangements" was that, for example, in cinema what used to be called "race movies" often had to do without white people. "Without whites, the requirements of dramatic construction created a world in which black characters acceded to the white ideal of segregation, and unreal black cops, crooks, judges, and juries interacted in such a way as to blame black victims for their social plight." But the lack of verisimilitude, which Cripps sees as a problem, can cut two ways: for it is easy to see how how such copies of white cinema could easily reflect back on the model itself, mocking it, defamiliarizing it, casting doubt upon its accuracy as, in the words of one film concerned with the perennial theme of "passing," an "imitation of life" (pp. 322–23).

Eddie Murphy's *Coming to America* furnishes a contemporary example of a movie in which black mimicry of whites is both a source of humor and a fundamental structuring principle of the text. In this movie, Prince Akeem leaves Africa to come to America—to Queens—in order to find a queen of his own choosing, one with a "mind of her own" rather than the woman destined and trained from birth to be his wife. Although on his arrival Prince Akeem discovers a world where black poverty seems to be the rule, the film rapidly moves beyond this world to enter middle-class black society, represented by the owner of a hamburger stand called McDowell's. The owner, whose daughter becomes Akeem's choice for a wife, explains the differences between his business and the McDonald's franchise: "they have golden arches, we have golden arcs. . . . Their rolls have sesame seeds, ours don't, etc."—distinctions, in other words, without a difference. The joke here, in which mimicry itself is foregrounded, may be said to cut a variety of ways, potentially mocking the white model for black middle-class ambitions but also, at least in the eyes of prejudiced white audiences, affirming white capitalism as the "real thing" and appearing to expose black aspirations as ridiculous and pathetic.

There is also another sense in which mimicry operates throughout the text. Insofar as the film may be said to belong to a recognizable genre, the screwball comedy, the film participates in, mimes, a fantasy unreal enough when it concerns whites and doubly so in relation to blacks. In a gesture reminiscent of the classic screwball hero Godfrey of *My Man Godfrey*, Akeem disguises himself as a penniless floor-washer in order to win over the father of the (motherless) woman he loves. As the barber advises, "If you want to get in good with the daughter, you got to get in good with the father." The film is clearly situated squarely within the bounds of the oedipal drama, the only twist being that the arrival of Akeem's real father is the decisive event in winning over the future father-in-law, who is bowled over on discovering the richness and royalty of his daughter's suitor. The film's major conflict thus turns out to be not an interracial or class conflict but one between the wealthy black Americans and the even wealthier Africans. That the film resolves its conflict according to the traditional dictates of the genre by ending with a wedding (between Burger Queen and future African king) that promises the harmonious union of two worlds—a black imitation of white corporate America, represented by McDowell's, and a black African nation represented by its royal family—takes on a particularly sinister irony in light of the role played by American corporations in the destruction of the environment of Third World peoples.

The ending of *Coming to America* may be seen as an attempt to resolve at the level of fantasy the ambivalence or doubleness Bhabha sees operating in representations of race: the black man as alien, African other (an otherness always already denied because it is the familiar, Americanized Eddie Murphy who plays the lead role) and the black man as assimilated dreamer of the American dream. Such an ambivalence, according to Bhabha, is explosive; there is an incipient menace in mimicry, and from "a difference that is almost nothing but not quite" it is but a step to a "difference that is almost total but not quite."[4] Switching genres, from comedy to horror, we may note that the film *Alien Nation* provides a vivid illustration of the thesis. In this film a group of aliens from another planet have been residing in Los Angeles as an oppressed minority, clearly meant to serve as allegorical figures for blacks. (Here we see vividly illustrated the dominant culture's tendency to collapse all racial groups into one undifferentiated mass which serves as the "Other" of white society. For, clearly, the notion of an alien nation draws on the existence of the Latino population of illegal "aliens.") The aliens are almost like whites but "not quite" (they get drunk on sour milk; the males have larger penises than the Americans; their heads are strangely shaped, hairless, and mottled),[5] and in the liberal surface text, the bigoted white cop must learn to accept his new alien partner, Sam Francisco, as someone whose differences are in fact insignificant in the face of the men's overriding common humanity. The two are involved in tracing down a deadly drug that has nearly destroyed the people on the alien planet, and at one point Sam forces his partner to witness the hideous physical transformation of a victim who has overdosed so that he may see "just how monstrous" his people "are capable of becoming." Yet, plot details aside, is it not the case that the threat of monstrosity—that is, of black monstrosity—has been present all along in the film as a consequence of the decision to make it an allegory rather than to treat the situation of blacks directly? And has not the tendency of films from the very early days of cinema to cast white people in blackface served a similar function—i.e., to suggest that blackness may be so monstrous it can only be signified but not directly represented? When in *Birth of a Nation* we watch the lecherous man in blackface pursuing the young white girl to her death, do we need to know about, in order to feel the force of, Griffith's reason for casting mostly white actors in the film: i.e., to protect the purity of white womanhood on the set?[6]

We need, then, not just to analyze the function of mimicry on the part of the colonized people, but to understand its role in the life and art of the colonizer—to understand, that is, the function of minstrelsy. Bhabha writes of the way the "not quite/not white" element of difference displayed by colonized races is related to the psychoanalytic notion of the fetish: "black skin splits under the racist gaze, displaced into signs of bestiality, genitalia, grotesquerie, which reveal the phobic myth of the undifferentiated whole white skin."[7] Minstrelsy would be a method by which the white man may disavow—acknowledge and at the same time deny—difference at the level of the body; as a process of fetishism, it seeks, like all fetishes, to restore the wholeness and unity threatened by the sight of difference, yet because it enters into the game of mimicry it is condemned to keep alive the possibility that there may be "no presence or identity behind the mask."[8] The concept of fetishism enables us to understand why minstrelsy has never really died out—why it lives in a different form in the "trading places" and "black like me" plots with which Hollywood is enamored, the most recent example being Paul Mazursky's *Moon Over Parador* (actually an instance of "brownface"), in which the Richard Dreyfus character, an unemployed Hollywood actor, is pressed into masquerading as the leader of a Central American country and in effect winds up playing the "Tootsie" of Latin American dictators.

Some of Bhabha's discussion covers familiar territory for a feminist reader, since he draws on material elaborated in feminist theory. The problematics of difference and sameness have, for example, been brilliantly analyzed by Luce Irigaray in her readings of Freud's essay "On Femininity" and Plato's *Republic*. Irigaray shows that for all Western culture's emphasis on the difference between the sexes, there is an underlying negation of the difference—and the threat—posed by the female sex, a negation evidenced for example in Freud's theorizing of the woman as an inferior man, as bearer of the "lack."[9] In Freudian theory, of course, the fetish is precisely the means whereby "lack" and difference are disavowed—accepted and negated simultaneously. It is the means, in other words, whereby "a multiple belief" may be maintained and hence serves to support the wildly divergent stereotypical associations that accrue around the fetishized body. For it is not just the black who is marked in the dominant discourse as, in Homi Bhabha's words, "both savage . . . and yet the most obedient and dignified of servants; . . . the embodiment of rampant sexuality and yet innocent as a child; . . . mystical, primitive, simple-minded and yet the most worldly and accomplished liar, and manipulator of social forces."[10] Much of this description also applies to the representation of woman, who in the male Imaginary undergoes a primal splitting into virgin and whore.

The importance of Bhabha's work, like Fanon's before him, lies partly, for me, in the way it insists on understanding the psychosocial dynamics of colonialism and racism, bringing psychoanalysis to bear on questions that have unfortunately all too often been viewed as not susceptible to a psychoanalytic understanding. Yet, unaccountably, although Bhabha utilizes the very concepts originally developed in the theorization of sexual difference, he almost entirely neglects the issue of gender and slights feminist work. In virtually ignoring the "woman question," while retaining the terms in which it has been posed, Bhabha commits the same kind of error for which Freud can be and has been criticized. The latter was undoubtedly being both racist and sexist in designating "woman" as the dark continent. But the answer is surely not to reverse the proposition and implicitly posit the "dark continent" as woman—not, at the very least, without carefully theorizing the relation.

Although he does not examine how race and gender intersect, Bhabha nevertheless notes at one point, "Darkness signifies at once both birth and death; it is in all cases a desire to return to the fullness of the mother, a desire for an unbroken and undifferentiated line of vision and origin."[11] For the heart of the matter, the heart of darkness, is, after all, "Mammy"—she who, absent in her own right, is spoken by man as guarantor of his origin and identity. In the face of the male desire to collapse sexual and racial difference into oceanic plenitude, feminism needs to insist on the complex, "multiple and cross-cutting" nature of identity and to ask: how do we rid ourselves of the desire for a "line of origin," how avoid positing either sexuality or race as theoretically primary, while we at the same time undertake to understand the vicious circularity of patriarchal thought whereby darkness signifies femininity and femininity darkness? I would like in this essay to address this question by examining first the way our culture through its representations explores the highly charged taboo relationships between black men and white women (specifically focusing on *Gorillas in the Mist* and a scene from an early film, *Blonde Venus*) and then to focus on the representations of black women in popular film, looking especially at the ways in which the black woman functions as the site of the displacement of white culture's (including white women's) fears and anxieties.

In *Gorillas in the Mist*, the question of origins is posed at the outset by, of course, a white man—in this case the anthropologist Dr. Louis Leakey, who is seen in a large hall lecturing about gorillas: "I want to know who I am, and what it was that made me that way." As if conjured up by his words, Dian Fossey appears, the woman who will journey alone to the heart of darkest Africa and whose story may be viewed as a phantasmatic answer to the white man's question.

It is an old story, an updated, middlebrow version of the King Kong tale, which itself is part of a tradition of animal movies that have functioned as thinly disguised "allegories for black brutes."[12] Of the perennial popularity of the film *King Kong*, for example, X. J. Kennedy wrote:

> A Negro friend from Atlanta tells me that in movies houses in colored neighborhoods throughout the South, *Kong* does a constant business. They show the thing in Atlanta at least every year, presumably to the same audiences. Perhaps this popularity may simply be due to the fact that *Kong* is one of the most watchable movies ever constructed, but I wonder whether Negro audiences may not find some archetypical appeal in this serio-comic tale of a huge black powerful free spirit whom all the hardworking white policemen are out to kill.[13]

Putting aside the way this passage provides a textbook example of how white racism gets projected into the psyches of the black audience, we may note that Kennedy's remarks are paradoxically couched in a liberal frame which tacitly acknowledges the legitimacy of black political grievances while employing an ahistorical notion of "archetype," which would deny the humanity of blacks (imaged as beasts) and so function to prevent them from achieving social and political equality. This is not to say that Kennedy's response is idiosyncratic: on the contrary, films like *King Kong*, made by whites in a racist society, lend themselves to this kind of interpretation, which is situated in the space of disavowal characteristic of colonialist discourse (the fetish indeed being a means by which two apparently opposed beliefs, "one archaic and one progressive," may simultaneously be held). This is a space, as we shall see, increasingly occupied in a postfeminist, post-civil rights era by a mass culture that must on one level acknowledge the political struggles of the last few decades and on another, deeper level would ward off the threat these struggles pose to the white male power structure.

Thus, for example, *Gorillas in the Mist* seems to respect the notion of a woman sacrificing the opportunity for a husband and family in order to pursue a career, a career that, indeed, involves her living the sort of adventurous and dangerous life usually reserved for men in popular films and that also accords her the kind of single-minded dedication to a cause typically attributed to the *male* scientific investigator. But the film takes it all back, as it were, by "deprofessionalizing" Fossey, neglecting to mention her growth as a scientist who in the course of her research in the mountains of Rwanda earned a Ph.D. from Harvard. The film further subverts its apparently liberal attitude to woman's independence by suggesting that Dian is merely channeling and sublimating (or should it be *desublimating*, since she goes "back" to the apes?) her sexual desires and maternal instincts into her cause. In the last scene, for example, after her death, the image track shows the son of the slaughtered gorilla swinging in the trees—clearly *Fossey's* son, since her tryst with its father, the gorilla Digit (in which the romantic music swells as Dian lies on her back, smiling blissfully when the gorilla slowly takes her hand, leaving a precious little deposit of dirt in her palm) is followed by her coupling with the *National Geographic* photographer. The soundtrack records a conversation between her and Roz Carr, the plantation owner, in which Fossey remarks, "I expected to get married and have children," and her friend replies, "Instead there's a mountain full of gorillas who wouldn't be alive if it weren't for you." The titles at the end tell us that Fossey's work "contributed significantly to the survival of the species"— woman's function, after all, even if it isn't quite the right species.

The transfer of Fossey's affection from her fiancé to Digit and his "group" is visually marked by the film through its replacement of the photo of the fiancé, which we see early in the film placed on a little typing table outside Dian's hut, with photos of the gorillas ("gorilla porn," as one of my friends remarked) that she passionately kisses right before her murder, while a song of Peggy Lee's ("I'd take a million trips to your lips") plays on the phonograph. But perverse as all this may sound—and in my view *is*—the most remarkable aspect of the film is the way in which it manages to make its psychosexual dynamics seem innocent. Indeed, the very title of the film points to a kind of disavowal, suggesting a tamed, romanticized, "misty" view of beasts and bestiality: a film whose *own* sublimating efforts work on every level to deny the perversity of the gorilla/woman sexual coupling it continually evokes.

Black skin "splits" in this film, to recall Homi Bhabha's words, into images of monstrosity and bestiality on the one hand and of nobility and wisdom on the other. Fossey's tracker, Sembagare, represents the latter option; he is presented as a man whose family has been wiped out along with their tribe and

thus, having no story or plot of his own, he is free to live a life of self-sacrificing devotion to the white woman. It is impossible to overestimate the
importance of this character—a common type in Hollywood cinema—in
serving as a guide to the audience's interpretation and judgment of events,
and it is interesting to reflect on the fact that such a character's possession of
the gaze may be concomitant with a radical *dis*possession in relation to the
narrative. Throughout the film, the camera continually cuts to shots of
Sembagare, usually gazing approvingly on some action performed by the
heroine, but also, occasionally, registering disapproval and dismay. Mostly
what Sembagare cares about is that the heroine's sexual and romantic needs
be fulfilled, and this is made clear from the very outset when he first sees and
comments on the picture of the fiancé. By attributing a kind of maternal concern to the black male as well as granting him a degree of moral authority,
the film can appear to be, in liberal fashion, empowering the character while
at the same time relieving the audiences' anxieties about the proximity of
white womanhood and black manhood.

That fears about the threat posed by the black male to white woman are
not far beneath the surface can be seen in the film's treatment of all the other
black men, who are usually shown in menacing groups, surrounding our
heroine, gesturing and muttering in their "savage" languages, and touching
her hair in awe. Early in the film, some black soldiers come to Fossey's hut,
destroy her possessions, and evict her from their country. The film treats
African civil wars as nothing more than a nuisance impeding Fossey's crusade—a crusade aligned with the film's project of substituting a timeless,
pastoral "gorilla nation" for the eminently less important struggles of emerging black nations. Significantly, as the men attempt to force her to leave,
Fossey furiously tells them not to touch her, to get their hands off her. Now,
given that the big love scene with the gorilla involves Fossey holding hands
with him, and indeed that the love interest is given the name "Digit" by
Fossey because of the webbing of his fingers, and finally that the film is most
horrified by the castration of the gorillas' heads and hands, the latter made
into curio ashtrays for rich Americans, we might be justified in seeing in this
motif of the hand a condensation of the film's basic conflict: a pitting of animals *against* black men, with the former ultimately viewed as less physically
and morally repellent than the latter. Here we might note that we come full
circle to Griffith's film *Birth of a Nation*, which had intercut shots of Flora
being stalked by Gus with ones of squirrels framed in an iris. The black man
thus becomes, as Cripps observes, "a predator about to pounce upon a harmless animal" (p. 48). Thus it is that in *Gorillas in the Mist*, the machete-wield-

ing black men who earn their living destroying gorillas are depicted as *less* truly and movingly human than the tragic and noble gorillas—as was the case in *King Kong*, as well.

Of course, at the level of its script, the film suggests a more complicated view, and at one point the photographer Bob cautions an angry Fossey that the black men are simply pawns in an economic power game that chiefly benefits rich Americans. In this respect too, then, the film operates in the realm of disavowal, verbally disputing its own visual scapegoating of the black men *and*, moreover, projecting the scapegoating onto the character of Fossey, who at one point terrorizes a little black boy by pretending to be a witch and at another point conducts a mock lynching of a black male poacher.

It is the white man, then, who in the end seems to be the most fully human character, while the black men are either self-sacrificing servants or threatening monsters, and the white woman is at the same time both a noble savior of innocent creatures and a witch whose unholy alliance with the beasts of the forests turns her into a raving monomaniac. In other words, into the space hollowed out by the film's fetishistic splittings steps the white man, equipped with the photographic apparatus which apparently enables him to establish the proper voyeuristic distance from the perversity that surrounds him. Interestingly, since this is Dian Fossey's story, and most of the film is from her point of view, the film gives the point of view over to Bob on several occasions. I have already referred to one instance—when Bob stares in fascination at Dian's "mating" with Digit, the camera cutting to tight close-ups of him as he crouches near his photographic equipment and stares intently at the coming together of woman and ape. Another such moment occurs when he first arrives on the scene, and we see Dian squatting on the floor, imitating the gorillas' movements and noises. So vertiginous does the film's play with mimicry become that the woman is constantly shown copying the gorillas, aping the anthropomorphized apes; like the blacks, she seems to occupy a position one step below the animals, to be not quite capable of achieving the same degree of humanity attained by the beasts.

But while an analysis of the point-of-view structure of *Gorillas in the Mist* suggests that, like most Hollywood films, and despite its biographical claims, this one is largely concerned with white male fears and fantasies and seems designed to assure the white man of his full humanity in relation to the animals, the female sex, and other races, it is important to understand that the voyeuristic distance between the white male and his "others" ultimately collapses. Bob, it turns out, is drawn to gorillas too, and he gets to act out his bestial lusts vicariously when he and Dian become lovers after he sees her with Digit and during an elaborate verbal play in which references to the beauty of the animals serve as double entendres applying to Fossey herself. Here we encounter the perennial thematics of homosocial desire, according to which the woman functions in a triangular relationship between two males, the woman becoming attractive to the second male as a result of being sought after or possessed by the first: a matter of, in René Girard's words, *mimetic* desire—of, in the film's case, man imitating beast.[14] Thus, we might say, by the end of the twentieth century, homosocial desire, long the cornerstone of patriarchal society, has expanded to include the entire order of Primates.

In *Gorillas in the Mist*, then, woman serves to initiate man into the secrets of his origin, whereupon he goes off to a new job in the wider world, escaping the carnage and destruction visited on the other players. Such violence is made to seem an appropriate ending to a film that touches on so many taboo areas, situating itself at the shifting borders between man and woman, whites and blacks, humans and animals, nature and society. One might expect that because of its unsettling obsession with these taboos, its nearly uncontrollable play of iteration, audiences would be troubled by the film's perversity. Seldom, however, did reviewers even mention the film's bizarre psychosocial dynamics; instead, the main "controversy" surrounding *Gorillas in the Mist* had to do with its accuracy as representation of Fossey's life—a question, once again, of mimicry, or mimesis. It is tempting to speculate that this question arises as a response to the disturbances created *by* the film at a phantasmatic level, instilling in us a longing for an authentic human life to serve as ground and source of the film's meaning, just as the film itself attempts to foreclose the historical process and establish a natural, pastoral space which would pre-exist the struggles of feminists and black nationalists. Such a question would take on a special urgency precisely because the lines toed by the film are so thin that it comes perilously close to mocking its own quest, making monkeys of us all.

In his book *The Signifying Monkey: A Theory of Afro-American Literary Criticism*, Henry Louis Gates praises Jean Renoir's silent film *Sur un air de Charleston* for its parody of the literature of discovery popular in Renaissance and Enlightenment Europe. In the film, a black man in blackface discovers a post-holocaust Europe and its only survivors, "a scantily clad white Wild Woman . . . and her lascivious companion, an ape." Gates sees in this scenario a "master trope of irony," which operates a "fairly straightforward . . . reversal . . .

of common European allegations of the propensity of African women to prefer the company of male apes." That Gates can see nothing dubious in
Renoir's "surrealistic critique of . . . fundamental conventions of Western discourse on the black" and can entirely neglect to consider the potency of
myths like *King Kong* (which long precede the 1933 film) suggests a very
large blind spot indeed—blind, that is, to the way the female Other, regardless of race, has been frequently consigned to categories that put her outside
the pale of the fully human.[15] (Why, we might inquire, did it not occur to the
"master" ironist to depict a scantily clad white man lewdly gyrating with his
pet ape?)

   Most pertinently we need to ask if, given the fetishistic nature of discourses on race and gender, a politically effective representational strategy
can ever operate via "reversal." Gates's own lucid discussion of the complexity of black American "signifying," which he argues both participates in and
subtly undermines white discourse, implicitly repudiates the viability of
"straightforward reversal" as political critique. If, as Gates argues, blacks have
developed a double-edged discourse capable of responding to what W. E .B.
DuBois called the "twoness" of their existence in American culture, how
much more pertinent is the theorization of such a discourse for anyone concerned with understanding the complex articulations of race *and* gender in
American life and with avoiding the "reversals" that keep us continually veer-
ing between the Scylla of racism and the Charybdis of sexism.

   To illustrate this point, I want to return to a scene in a film by a director
whose presence is strongly felt at the "originary" moment of feminist psychoanalytic film theory: namely, Josef von Sternberg, the auteur who was the
focus of Laura Mulvey's comments on the way popular narrative cinema
tends to fetishize the female body.[16] The film—*Blonde Venus*—has been as riv-
eting to contemporary theorists of cinema as the sight of Dian Fossey lying
among the apes was to the character Bob in *Gorillas in the Mist*.[17] A still from
the scene to which I am referring graces the cover of an issue of *Cinema
Journal* which includes an article about the subversiveness of the film's treatment of female sexuality.[18] In the plot leading up to this scene, the heroine
Helen, played by Marlene Dietrich, has recently left her humble home and
her husband and son to return to a career on the stage; in the still, she has
just emerged from an ape costume, although hairy bits of the costume
remain around her genital area, her shoulders, and her derrière, and she is
about to sing "Hot Voodoo." On her head is a blonde Afro wig and behind her
stand a group of women in blackface holding spears and giant masks painted
with large mouths and teeth.

Nowhere does Sternberg more forcefully reveal himself to be the master fetishist of the female body than in this scene, which for an adequate reading requires us to apply the insights of *both* a Homi Bhabha and a Laura Mulvey. Too often feminist film critics have alluded only parenthetically to the film's racism while devoting themselves chiefly to considering whether the film is "progressive" in its emphasis on performance and spectacle, its subtle visual undermining of the domestic ideal that the narrative purports to uphold. Yet the racism is not an incidental, "odd" moment to be bracketed off in order to pursue more pressing concerns, but is, in fact, central to the evocation and manipulation of desire that begins with the Hot Voodoo number and continues up to and beyond Helen's flight south to increasingly exotic locales, the last of which is a Louisiana boarding house run by a black woman.

In the Hot Voodoo sequence, the fetishistic working of presence and absence, difference and sameness, depends, as it does in *Gorillas in the Mist*, on the interplay of the elements of white woman, ape, and blacks. If it can be said that the film draws on the stereotypical association, referred to by Gates, of apes and black women, it can also be that said the white woman *is* the ape. But then again, of course, she is not the ape. Part of the sexual charge of the spectacle derives from the disavowal, the doubleness, the contradictory belief structure whereby she is posited as *simultaneously* animal and human, as well as simultaneously white and not white (suggested by the blonde Afro wig). Similarly, the white women in blackface and black Afro wigs who stand behind Dietrich are also affirmed and denied as African "savages" (and are fetishized further in that the war paint on their faces resembles the painting on the masks they carry in front of the lower halves of their bodies—the teeth on these masks clearly symbolizing the *vagina dentata*). I think we can take this fully theatricalized image as emblematic of some of the complex interrelations of gender and race in popular representation.[19]

In doing so, however, we are forced to recognize that while everyone in this scenario (except for the white male, played by Cary Grant, who is looking on) is relegated to "the ideologically appointed place of the stereotype")[20], the black women in the film are in the *most* marginalized position. If it is true, to cite Claire Johnston's famous formulation, woman as woman has largely been absent from patriarchal cinema, this has obviously been much more literally the case for black women than for whites.[21] And if the white woman has usually served as the signifier of male desire (which is what Johnston meant when she spoke of the absence of woman *as* woman), the black woman, when present at all, has served as a signifier of (white) female sexuality or of the maternal ("Mammy"). In the last part of this essay I would like to explore the way in which black women in contemporary popular film are reduced to being the signifiers of signifiers.

The use of the black woman to signify sexuality is vividly illustrated in one of the most recent films in the tradition of *The Jazz Singer*. In this case, however, the protagonist is a *woman* who finds herself going back to her Jewish roots. In *Crossing Delancey*, directed by Joan Micklin Silver, Amy Irving plays Izzy, a thirty-three year-old white woman who lives alone in Manhattan, works in a prestigious bookstore organizing readings by the literati, and, vehement disclaimers to the contrary notwithstanding, is clearly desperate to find a man. Indeed, she is so desperate that after ridding herself of an infatuation with a self-absorbed and pretentious writer, she overcomes a strong distaste for a Jewish pickle salesman, who has been chosen for her by a marriage broker in collusion with Izzy's grandmother. In a brief scene occurring rather early in the film, Izzy is trying to decide whether or not to call the writer to ask him out, and she asks the advice of a friend as the two relax in the sauna after a workout in the gym. While the women recline in their towels, the camera pans down to reveal two black women, one of whom, a very large woman whose ample flesh spills out of a tight bathing suit, loudly recounts to her friend an anecdote about love-making in which while performing fellatio ("I'm licking it, I'm kissing it, he's moaning") she discovers a long—"I mean long"—blonde hair, which the man rather lamely tries to explain away. The camera tilts back up, as Izzy, having listened intently to the conversation, thoughtfully remarks, "Maybe I *will* call him."

Clearly the black woman, small as her role is, represents sexuality and "embodiment" in a film that never mentions sex at any other time (to be sure, the fact of sex is hinted at when Izzy spends an occasional night with a married male friend, but it is never shown or discussed). Even the framing of the scene we have been discussing suggests in amazingly exemplary fashion the hierarchical division between black and white women, with the uptown Manhattanite princess-"on-her-high-horse" (to quote the grandmother), who will be forced to accept as a lover a Jewish man from lower Manhattan, placed in the upper part of the frame and the sexualized black females situated, as always, on the bottom (a spatial metaphor with both social and psychic dimensions). The black woman's story not only hints at the threat of miscegenation—for, just as this woman's lover has strayed, so too is Izzy straying from her roots—but represents directly all those desires that this postfeminist film is disavowing: both a voracious sexuality and a voracious hunger in general, resulting from the deprivations suffered by single middle-class white women in the modern world. Thus the fact that the one sexual act mentioned in the film (which is about a woman's love for a pickle salesman, no less) is the act of fellatio is not surprising given the ubiquitous presence of food in the film (scenes of Izzy and her friend eating hotdogs on Izzy's birthday after she lies to her boss about going to a fancy restaurant [obviously women cannot nurture themselves or each other]; of lonely women picking at food in salad bars and eating Chinese takeout while watching television; of a baby nursing at his mother's breast while the heroine looks on in envy—envy *not*, it is quite clear, of the mother but of the suckling child; and finally, of the [as the film portrays her] obnoxiously loud female marriage broker continually gobbling down other people's food, eating with greasy fingers and talking with her mouth crammed full).

Elsewhere, I have written about the horror of the body expressed in contemporary culture, the anorexic mentality to which this horror gives rise, and the tendency on the part of men to deal with these fears by displacing them onto the body of the female; what we need to note here is the special role played by the woman of color as receptacle of these fears. The function of the fat, sexually voracious black woman in *Crossing Delancey* is to enable the white Jewish subculture, through its heterosexual love story, to represent itself in a highly sentimentalized, romanticized, and sublimated light, while disavowing the desires and discontents underlying the civilization it is promoting. (Once again, then, we see the need for feminist analysis to consider the ways in which ethnic and racial groups are played off against—and play themselves off against—one another.)[22]

If in *Crossing Delancey*—a film written and directed by *women*—the black female body is the sexualized body, in other films the black woman functions not only as the sexual other, but as the maternal body, as psychic surrogate for the white mother—in short, as "Mammy." Recent feminist theory has shown that the nursery maid in Freud's own time played an important, although largely unacknowledged, role in initiating the child into sexual knowledge.[23] In America, as black feminists have pointed out, the black woman has more often than not served a similar function in the acculturation of white children. *Clara's Heart*, starring Whoopi Goldberg, provides an unusually stark illustration of the process whereby the young white male achieves maturity through penetrating the mystery of the black woman—"her wisdom, her warmth, her secret," as the poster proclaims. That (returning to the metaphor of the dark continent) we are dealing here almost literally with the "heart of darkness" is suggested by Clara's last name, which *is*

"Heart"—an organ that turns out to be a euphemism for a more libidinally cathected body part.

For Clara's secret, which her young charge David, suffering from neglect at the hands of his narcissistic parents, attempts to discover, is that she has been raped by her own son. The horror, the horror, indeed. The black male thus literalizes the psychic reality of the bourgeois male, for the rape is in fact the logical result of the *white* boy's—and the narrative's—probing. At one point, for example, David sits at Clara's knee and begins slowly and sensually to feel her leg, moving inexorably upward until Clara screams at him—an "overreaction" explained when we learn of the son's rape. Moreover, David not only continually badgers Clara to reveal her story but reads in secret the letters he finds in a suitcase under her bed. Again, Clara reacts furiously, saying he has ruined their friendship, although at other times she says he can never do anything to destroy her affection. The intense aggression aroused by the promise and withholding of unconditional love ultimately finds expression in the revelation of incest and rape—a rape that is enacted by the sexually monstrous black male, who is presumably incapable of sublimating such feelings and thus destined to remain forever a casualty of Oedipus, while the recognition of his own desires in the mirror provided by the black male enables the white boy to rechannel his hostilities and become a man: previously unathletic, we now see him win a swimming championship under the approving eye of his father! Thus the black man comes to serve as as the white male's oedipal scapegoat, and the black woman is positioned, as in so many popular representations (like Spielberg's *The Color Purple*), as sexual victim—not of the white man, of course, the historical record notwithstanding—but of black men, including even their own sons.[24] And black people in general are once again consigned to the level of bestiality.

A more recent, enormously popular film in which Whoopi Goldberg again has a major role shows yet another way the black woman serves the function of embodiment. In *Ghost*, Whoopi Goldberg plays a spiritual medium, Oda Mae Brown, who stands in for the body of the white *male*, Sam, played by Patrick Swayze. Sam has died as a result of a mugging, which turns out to have been engineered by a coworker embezzling funds. When he learns of the plot and of his wife's danger at the hands of the mugger, he seeks out Oda Mae to help him communicate to his wife. After a great deal of mutual mistrust between the wife and Oda Mae, climaxed by a scene in which Oda Mae stands outside the door trying to convince the wife of her "authenticity," as it were, she is allowed inside the house, and the wife expresses a great longing to be able to touch her husband one last time. Oda Mae offers up her body up for the purpose, and Sam enters into it. The camera shows a close-up of the black woman's hands as they reach out to take those of the white woman, and then it cuts to a shot not of Oda Mae but of Sam, who in taking over her body has obliterated her presence entirely.

This sequence, in which Goldberg turns *into* a man may be seen as a kind of logical extension of all her comedic roles, for she is always coded in the comedies as more masculine than feminine. For example, there is a scene in *Jumping Jack Flash* in which she dresses up in a sexy evening dress that nearly gets chewed up by a shredding machine, and, as she climbs the stairs to her apartment at the end of the evening, she is heard muttering in anger because the taxi cab driver mistook her for a male transvestite. In *Fatal Beauty*, too, Goldberg's donning of women's clothes is seen to be a form of drag—of black female mimicry of (white) femininity, and when she dresses in such clothes she walks in an exaggeratedly awkward fashion like a man unaccustomed to female accoutrements.

Two important points need to be made here. First, the kind of "gender trouble" advocated by Judith Butler and others in which gender, anatomy, and performance are at odds with one another does not necessarily result in the subversive effects often claimed for it; on the contrary, in certain cases, such as those involving the woman of color who has often been considered, in Bhabha's words, "not quite" a woman, this kind of "play" may have extremely conservative implications. Second, when both extremes of the Whoopi Goldberg persona are considered together—those in which she represents the maternal/female body (as in *Clara's Heart*) and those in which she is coded as more or less male—we see that we are not all that far from the situation addressed by Sojourner Truth: The black woman is seen either as too literally a woman (reduced to her biology and her biological functions) or in crucial ways not really a woman at all.

I must acknowledge, however, although it places me in an uncomfortable position, that I personally find the Goldberg character in the comedies both attractive and empowering (and I know some young white girls who have made Goldberg a kind of cult heroine), and that part of this attraction for me lies in the way she represents a liberating departure from the stifling conventions of femininity. Yet I have to recognize as a white woman the extent to which these images are at least in part the creation of a racist mentality and to acknowledge how such images and my own reaction to them may serve to keep me and black women at odds (although I would also argue strongly that Goldberg's powerful acting allows her frequently to transcend some of the limitations of her material or else to bring out the subversive potential buried within the text).

It is urgent that white women come to understand the ways in which they themselves participate in racist structures not only of patriarchal cinema—as in *Crossing Delancey*—but also of contemporary criticism and theory. In an important article surveying the work of white women newly addressing issues of race, Valerie Smith points out that some white feminist theorists may be participating in an old tradition of forcing the black woman to serve the function of embodiment:

> It is striking that at precisely the moment when Anglo-American feminists and male Afro-Americanists begin to reconsider the material ground of their enterprise, they demonstrate their return to earth, as it were, by invoking the specific experiences of black women and the writings of black women. This association of black women with reembodiment resembles rather closely the association, in classic Western philosophy and in nineteenth-century cultural constructions of womanhood, of women of color with the body and therefore with animal passions and slave labor.[25]

What Smith's remarks clearly suggest is the black woman's need to refuse to function as either the man's *or* the white woman's bodily scapegoat, just as some white women are refusing any longer to function this way in male discourse.

I would like to end, however, with a fantasy, which involves reading the scene I have discussed in *Ghost* against the grain. This may be a fantasy that for many reasons black woman will not fully share, since it points in a utopian direction and wishes away some of the contradictions I have been analyzing. Without for a moment *forgetting* these contradictions, without denying the force of Hazel Carby's observation that feminist criticism (to say nothing of a "woman's film" like *Crossing Delancey*) has too often ignored "the hierarchical structuring of the relations between black and white women and often takes the concerns of middle-class, articulate white women as the norm," I nevertheless want to point to an alternative to the dominant fantasy expressed in *Ghost*.[26] If in the film the black woman exists solely to facilitate the white heterosexual romance, there is a sense in which we can shift our focus to read the white male as, precisely, the obstacle to the union of the two women, a union tentatively suggested in the image of the black and white hands as they reach toward one another. I like to think that despite the disturbing contradictions I have pointed out in this chapter, a time will come when we eliminate the locked door (to recall an image from *Ghost*) that separates women (a door, as we see in the film, easily penetrated by the white man), a time when we may join together to overthrow the ideology that, after all, primarily serves the interests of white heterosexual masculinity and is *ultimately* responsible for the persecutions suffered by people on account of their race, class, and gender. But since it is white women who in many cases have locked the door, it is their responsibility to open it up.

NOTES

1. See the discussion of the film in Patricia Erens, *The Jew in American Cinema* (Bloomington: Indiana University Press, 1984), pp. 101–6.

2. Homi K. Bhabha, "Of Mimicry and Man: The Ambivalence of Colonial Discourse," *October* 28 (Spring 1984): 131. Other texts by Bhabha that I draw on here include: "The Other Question: Difference, Discrimination, and the Discourse of Colonialism," in *Literature, Politics, and Theory: Papers from the Essex Conference 1976–84,* ed. Francis Barker, Peter Hulme, Margaret Iversen, and Diana Loxley (London: Methuen, 1986), pp. 148–72; "The Commitment to Theory," *New Formations* 5 (Summer 1988): 5–24; "Signs Taken for Wonders: Questions of Ambivalence and Authority Under a Tree Outside Delhi, May 1817," in *"Race," Writing, and Difference,* ed., Henry Louis Gates, Jr. (Chicago: University of Chicago Press, 1985), pp. 163–84.

3. Thomas Cripps, *Slow Fade to Black: The Negro in American Film, 1900–1942* (New York: Oxford University Press, 1977), p. 37.

4. Bhabha, "Of Mimicry and Man," p. 126.

5. One might note that for Bhabha mimicry is like camouflage, like being "mottled," "*not* harmonising." Ibid., p. 125.

6. For a discussion of this scene from the point of view of a black spectator, see Manthia Diawara, "Black Spectatorship: Problems of Identification and Resistance," *Screen* 29, no. 4 (Autumn 1988): 66–79.

7. Bhabha, "Of Mimicry and Man," p. 132. For other articles discussing the ambivalent nature of minstrelsy, see Sylvia Wynter, "Sambos and Minstrels," *Social Text* 1 (1979): 149–56; and Susan Willis "I Shop Therefore I Am: Is There a Place for Afro-American Culture in American Commodity Culture," in *Changing Our Own Words: Essays on Criticism, Theory, and Writing by Black Women,*ed. Cheryl Wall (New Brunswick, N.J.: Rutgers University Press, 1989), pp. 173–95.

8. Ibid., p. 128.

9. See Luce Irigaray, *Speculum of the Other Woman*, trans. Gillian C. Gill (Ithaca, N.Y.: Cornell University Press, 1985).

10. Bhabha, "The Other Question," p. 179.

11. Ibid., p. 170.

12. Cripps, *Slow Fade to Black*, p. 155.

13. X. J. Kennedy, "Who Killed King Kong?," in *Focus on the Horror Film*, ed. Roy Huss and T. J. Ross (Englewood Cliffs, N.J.: Prentice Hall, 1972), p. 109.

14. See René Girard, *Deceit, Desire, and the Novel: Self and Other in Literary Structure*, trans. Yvonne Freccero (Baltimore, Md.: Johns Hopkins University Press, 1972), and Eve Kosofsky Sedgwick's discussion of Girard's work in terms of "homosocial desire," in her *Between Men: English Literature and Male Homosocial Desire* (New York: Columbia University Press, 1985), pp. 21–25.

15. Henry Louis Gates, *The Signifying Monkey: A Theory of Afro-American Literary Criticism* (New York: Oxford University Press, 1988), pp. 108–09.

16. Laura Mulvey, "Visual Pleasure and Narrative Cinema," *Screen* 16, no. 3 (Autumn 1975): 6–18.

17. For examples, see Patricia Mellencamp, "Made in the Fade," *Ciné-Tracts* 3, no. 3 (Fall 1980): 13; Bill Nichols, *Ideology and the Image* (Bloomington: Indiana University Press, 1981), pp. 104–32; and E. Ann Kaplan, *Women and Film: Both Sides of the Camera* (New York and London: Methuen, 1983), pp. 49–59.

18. Lea Jacobs, "The Censorship of *Blonde Venus*: Textual Analysis and Historical Methods," *Cinema Journal* 27, no. 3 (Spring 1988): 21–31.

19. For a controversial discussion of race, gender, and spectacle, see Sander L. Gilman, "The Hottentot and the Prostitute: Toward an Iconography of Female Sexuality," in *Difference and Pathology: Stereotypes of Sexuality, Race, and Madness* (Ithaca, N.Y.: Cornell University Press, 1985), pp. 76–108.

20. Isaac Julien and Kobena Mercer, "De Margin and De centre," *Screen* 29, no. 4 (Autumn 1988): 5.

21. Claire Johnston, "Women's Cinema as Counter-Cinema," in *Sexual Strategems: The World of Women in Film,* ed. Patricia Erens (New York: Horizon Press, 1979), p. 136.

22. For a discussion of the complex relations between racism and anti-Semitism, see Elly Bulkin, Minnie Bruce Pratt, and Barbara Smith, *Yours in Struggle: Three Feminist Perspectives on Anti-Semitism and Racism* (New York: Long Haul Press, 1984).

23. For an interesting discussion of this, see Peter Stallybrass and Allon White, "Below Stairs: The Maid and the Family Romance," in their *The Politics and Poetics of Transgression* (Ithaca, N.Y.: Cornell University Press, 1986), pp. 149–70.

24. Jane Gaines, "White Privilege and Looking Relations: Race and Gender in Feminist Film Theory," *Screen* 29, no. 4 (Autumn 1988): 12–27. In this article, which

has a strong ideological axe to grind, since Gaines is attacking psychoanalytic film theory, Gaines tries to prove that psychoanalysis cannot be of use in discussing the issue of race. I hope I have shown that this is not necessarily the case, even though people who have *used* psychoanalysis may be racially biased: such bias is hardly sufficient to discredit the entire discipline.

25. Valerie Smith, "Black Feminist Theory and the Representation of the 'Other'," in *Changing Our Own Words: Essays on Criticism, Theory, and Writing by Black Women*, ed. Cheryl A. Wall (New Brunswick, N.J.: Rutgers University Press, 1989), p. 45.

26. Hazel Carby, *Reconstructing Womanhood: The Emergence of the Afro-American Woman Novelist* (New York: Oxford University Press, 1987), p. 17.

part 3

The Body Speaks

Your body must be heard.
—Hélène Cixous

12

Ain't I a Woman?

Sojourner Truth

Well, children, where there is so much racket
there must be something out of kilter. I think
that 'twixt the negroes of the South and the
women at the North, all talking about rights,
the white men will be in a fix pretty soon. But
what's all this here talking about?

That man over there says that women need
to be helped into carriages, and lifted over
ditches, and to have the best place everywhere.
Nobody ever helps me into carriages, or over
mud-puddles, or gives me any best place! And
ain't I a woman? Look at me! Look at my arm!
I have ploughed and planted, and gathered into
barns, and no man could head me! And ain't I a
woman? I could work as much and eat as much
as a man—when I could get it—and bear the
lash as well! And ain't I a woman? I have borne
thirteen children, and seen them most all sold
off to slavery, and when I cried out with my
mother's grief, none but Jesus heard me! And
ain't I a woman?

Sojourner Truth, "Ain't I A Woman?" Originally printed in *The
History of Woman Suffrage* (1881–1886). We gratefully acknowl-
edge Miriam Schneier's modernized version from *Feminism: The
Essential Historical Writings* (1972).

Then they talk about this thing in the head; what's this they call it? [Intellect, someone whispers.] That's it, honey. What's that got to do with women's rights or negro's rights? If my cup won't hold but a pint, and yours holds a quart, wouldn't you be mean not to let me have my little half-measure full?

Then that little man in black there, he says women can't have as much rights as men, 'cause Christ wasn't a woman! Where did your Christ come from? Where did your Christ come from? From God and a woman! Man had nothing to do with Him.

If the first woman God ever made was strong enough to turn the world upside down all alone, these women together ought to be able to turn it back, and get it right side up again! And now they is asking to do it, the men better let them.

Obliged to you for hearing me, and now old Sojourner ain't got nothing more to say.

13

La conciencia de la mestiza

TOWARDS A NEW CONSCIOUSNESS

polemically theoretical

Gloria Anzaldúa

*Por la mujer de mi raza
hablará el espíritu*

*ch. last
page*

Jose Vascocelos, Mexican philosopher, envisaged *una raza mestiza, una mezcla de razas afines, una raza de color—la primera raza sínetesis del globo*. He called it a cosmic race, *la raza cósmica*, a fifth race embracing the four major races of the world.[1] Opposite to the theory of the pure Aryan, and to the policy of racial purity that white America practices, his theory is one of inclusivity. At the confluence of two or more genetic streams, with chromosomes constantly "crossing over," this mixture of races, rather than resulting in an inferior being, provides hybrid progeny, a mutable, more malleable species with a rich gene pool. From this racial, ideological, cultural, and biological cross-pollinization, an "alien" consciousness is presently in the making—a new *mestiza* consciousness, *una conciencia de mujer*. It is a consciousness of the Borderlands.

Gloria Anzaldúa, "La conciencia de la mestiza: Towards a New Consciousness." From *Borderlands/La Frontera: The New Mestiza* © 1987. Reprinted with permission from Aunt Lute Books.

Una lucha de fronteras / A Struggle of Borders

Because I, a *mestiza*,
continually walk out of one culture
and into another,
because I am in all cultures at the same time,
alma entre dos mundos, tres, cuatro,
me zumba la cabeza con lo contradictorio.
Estoy norteada por todas las voces que me hablan
simultáneamente.

The ambivalence from the clash of voices results in mental and emotional states of perplexity. Internal strife results in insecurity and indecisiveness. The mestiza's dual or multiple personality is plagued by psychic restlessness.

In a constant state of mental nepantilism, an Aztec word meaning torn between ways, *la mestiza* is a product of the transfer of the cultural and spiritual values of one group to another. Being tricultural, monolingual, bilingual, or multilingual, speaking a patois, and in a state of perpetual transition, the *mestiza* faces the dilemma of the mixed breed: which collectivity does the daughter of a dark-skinned mother listen to?

El choque de un alma atrapado entre el mundo del espíritu y el mundo de la técnica a vecas la deja entullada. Cradled in one culture, sandwiched between two cultures, straddling all three cultures and their value systems, *la mestiza* undergoes a struggle of flesh, a struggle of borders, an inner war. Like all people, we perceive the version of reality that our culture communicates. Like others having or living in more than one culture, we get multiple, often opposing messages. The coming together of two self-consistent but habitually incompatible frames of reference[2] causes *un choque,* a cultural collision.

Within us and within *la cultura chicana,* commonly held beliefs of the white culture attack commonly held beliefs of the Mexican culture, and both attack commonly held beliefs of the indigenous culture. Subconsciously, we see an attack on ourselves and our beliefs as a threat and we attempt to block with a counter-stance.

But it is not enough to stand on the opposite riverbank, shouting questions, challenging patriarchal, white conventions. A counter-stance locks one into a duel of oppressor and oppressed; locked in mortal combat, like the cop and the criminal, both are reduced to a common denominator of violence. The counter-stance refutes the dominant culture's views and beliefs, and, for

Consciousness leads to →
what practice

this, it is proudly defiant. All reaction is limited by, and dependent on, what it is reacting against. Because the counter-stance stems from a problem with authority—outer as well as inner—it's a step toward liberation from cultural domination. But it is not a way of life. At some point, on our way to a new consciousness, we will have to leave the opposite bank, the split between the two mortal combatants somehow healed so that we are on both shores at once and, at once, see through serpent and eagle eyes. ① Or perhaps we will decide to disengage from the dominant culture, write it off altogether as a lost cause, and cross the border into a wholly new and separate ② territory. Or we might go another route. The possibilities are numerous once we decide to act and not react.

A Tolerance for Ambiguity

psychic

These numerous possibilities leave *la mestiza* floundering in uncharted seas. In perceiving conflicting information and points of view, she is subjected to a swamping of her psychological borders. She has discovered that she can't hold concepts or ideas in rigid boundaries. The borders and walls that are supposed to keep the undesirable ideas out are entrenched habits and patterns of behavior; these habits and patterns are the enemy within. Rigidity means death. Only by remaining flexible is she able to stretch the psyche horizontally and vertically. *La mestiza* constantly has to shift out of habitual formations; from convergent thinking, analytical reasoning that tends to use rationality to move toward a single goal (a Western mode), to divergent thinking,[3] characterized by movement away from set patterns and goals and toward a more whole perspective, one that includes rather than excludes.

The new *mestiza* copes by developing a tolerance for contradictions, a tolerance for ambiguity. She learns to be an Indian in Mexican culture, to be Mexican from an Anglo point of view. She learns to juggle cultures. She has a plural personality, she operates in a pluralistic mode—nothing is thrust out, the good the bad and the ugly, nothing rejected, nothing abandoned. Not only does she sustain contradictions, she turns the ambivalence into something else.

She can be jarred out of ambivalence by an intense, and often painful, emotional event that inverts or resolves the ambivalence. I'm not sure exactly how. The work takes place underground—subconsciously. It is work that the soul performs. That focal point or fulcrum, that juncture where the *mestiza* stands, is where phenomena tend to collide. It is where the possibility of uniting all that is separate occurs. This assembly is not one where severed or separated pieces merely come together. Nor is it a balancing of opposing powers. In attempting to work out a synthesis, the self has added a third element which is greater than the sum of its severed parts. That third element is a new consciousness—a *mestiza* consciousness—and though it is a source of intense pain, its energy comes from continual creative motion that keeps breaking down the unitary aspect of each new paradigm.

En unas pocas centurias, the future will belong to the *mestiza*. Because the future depends on the breaking down of paradigms, it depends on the straddling of two or more cultures. By creating a new mythos—that is, a change in the way we perceive reality, the way we see ourselves, and the ways we behave—*la mestiza* creates a new consciousness.

The work of *mestiza* consciousness is to break down the subject-object duality that keeps her a prisoner and to show in the flesh and through the images in her work how duality is transcended. The answer to the problem between the white race and the colored, between males and females, lies in healing the split that originates in the very foundation of our lives, our culture, our languages, our thoughts. A massive uprooting of dualistic thinking in the individual and collective consciousness is the beginning of a long struggle, but one that could, in our best hopes, bring us to the end of rape, of violence, of war.

La encrucijada / The Crossroads

A chicken is being sacrificed
at a crossroads, a simple mound of earth
a mud shrine for *Eshu*,
Yoruba god of indeterminacy,
who blesses her choice of path.
She begins her journey.

Su cuerpo es una bocacalle. La mestiza has gone from being the sacrificial goat to becoming the officiating priestess at the crossroads.

As a *mestiza* I have no country, my homeland cast me out; yet all countries are mine because I am every woman's sister or potential lover. (As a lesbian I have no race, my own people disclaim me; but I am all races because there is the queer of me in all races.) I am cultureless because, as a feminist, I challenge the collective cultural/religious male-derived beliefs of Indo-Hispanics and Anglos; yet I am cultured because I am participating in the cre-

ation of yet another culture, a new story to explain the world and our participation in it, a new value system with images and symbols that connect us
to each other and to the planet. *Soy un amasamiento*, I am an act of kneading,
of uniting and joining that not only has produced both a creature of darkness
and a creature of light, but also a creature that questions the definitions of
light and dark and gives them new meanings.

We are the people who leap in the dark, we are the people on the knees
of the gods. In our very flesh, (r)evolution works out the clash of cultures. It
makes us crazy constantly, but if the center holds, we've made some kind of
evolutionary step forward. *Nuestra alma el trabajo*, the opus, the great alchemical work; spiritual *mestizaje*, a "morphogenesis,"[4] an inevitable unfolding. We
have become the quickening serpent movement.

Indigenous like corn, like corn, the *mestiza* is a product of crossbreeding,
designed for preservation under a variety of conditions. Like an ear of
corn—a female seed-bearing organ—the *mestiza* is tenacious, tightly
wrapped in the husks of her culture. Like kernels she clings to the cob; with
thick stalks and strong brace roots, she holds tight to the earth—she will survive the crossroads.

Lavando y remojando el maíz en agua del cal, despojando el pellejo. Moliendo, mixte-
ando, amasando, haciendo tortillas de masa.[5] She steeps the corn in lime, it
swells, softens. With stone roller on *metate*, she grinds the corn, then grinds
again. She kneads and moulds the dough, pats the round balls into *tortillas*.

> We are the porous rock in the stone *metate*
> squatting on the ground.
> We are the rolling pin, *el maíz y agua*,
> *la masa harina. Somos el amasijo.*
> *Somos lo molido en el metate.*
> We are the *comal* sizzling hot,
> the hot *tortilla*, the hungry mouth.
> We are the coarse rock.
> We are the grinding motion,
> the mixed potion, *somos el molcajete.*
> We are the pestle, the *comino, ajo, pimienta,*
> We are the *chile colorado*,
> the green shoot that cracks the rock.
> We will abide.

EL CAMINO DE LA MESTIZA / THE MESTIZA WAY *practical processual*

Caught between the sudden contraction, the breath sucked in and the endless space, the brown woman stands still, looks at the sky. She decides to go down, digging her way along the roots of trees. Sifting through the bones, she shakes them to see if there is any marrow in them. Then, touching the dirt to her forehead, to her tongue, she takes a few bones, leaves the rest in their burial place.

She goes through her backpack, keeps her journal and address book, throws away the muni-bart metromaps. The coins are heavy and they go next, then the greenbacks flutter through the air. She keeps her knife, can opener and eyebrow pencil. She puts bones, pieces of bark, *hierbas*, eagle feather, snakeskin, tape recorder, the rattle and drum in her pack and she sets out to become the complete *tolteca*.[6]

Her first step is to take inventory. *Despojando, desgranando, quitando paja.* Just what did she inherit from her ancestors? This weight on her back —which is the baggage from the Indian mother, which the baggage from the Spanish father, which the baggage from the Anglo?

Pero es difícil differentiating between *lo heredado, lo adquirido, lo impuesto.* She puts history through a sieve, winnows out the lies, looks at the forces that we as a race, as women, have been a part of. *Luego bota lo que no vale, los desmientos, los desencuentros, el embrutecimiento. Aguarda el juicio, hondo y enraízado, de la gente antigua.* This step is a conscious rupture with all oppressive traditions of all cultures and religions. She communicates that rupture, documents the struggle. She reinterprets history and, using new symbols, she shapes new myths. She adopts new perspectives toward the dark-skinned, women, and queers. She strengthens her tolerance (and intolerance) for ambiguity. She is willing to share, to make herself vulnerable to foreign ways of seeing and thinking. She surrenders all notions of safety, of the familiar. Deconstruct, construct. She becomes a *nahual*, able to transform herself into a tree, a coyote, into another person. She learns to transform the small "I" into the total Self. *Se hace moldeadora de su alma. Según la concepción que tiene de sí misma, así será.*

Que no se nos olvide los hombres

"Tú no sirves pa' nada-
you're good for nothing.
Eres pura vieja."

"You're nothing but a woman" means you are defective. Its opposite is to be *un macho*. The modern meaning of the word "machismo," as well as the concept, is actually an Anglo invention. For men like my father, being "macho" meant being strong enough to protect and support my mother and us, yet being able to show love. Today's macho has doubts about his ability to feed and protect his family. His "machismo" is an adaptation to oppression and poverty and low self-esteem. It is the result of hierarchical male dominance. The Anglo, feeling inadequate and inferior and powerless, displaces or transfers these feelings to the Chicano by shaming him. In the Gringo world, the Chicano suffers from excessive humility and self-effacement, shame of self and self-deprecation. Around Latinos he suffers from a sense of language inadequacy and its accompanying discomfort; with Native Americans he suffers from a racial amnesia that ignores our common blood, and from guilt because the Spanish part of him took their land and oppressed them. He has an excessive compensatory hubris when around Mexicans from the other side. It overlays a deep sense of racial shame.

The loss of a sense of dignity and respect in the macho breeds a false machismo that leads him to put down women and even to brutalize them. Coexisting with his sexist behavior is a love for the mother which takes precedence over that of all others. Devoted son, macho pig. To wash down the shame of his acts, of his very being, and to handle the brute in the mirror, he takes to the bottle, the snort, the needle, and the fist.

Though we "understand" the root causes of male hatred and fear, and the subsequent wounding of women, we do not excuse, we do not condone, and we will no longer put up with it. From the men of our race, we demand the admission/acknowledgment/disclosure/testimony that they wound us, violate us, are afraid of us and of our power. We need them to say they will begin to eliminate their hurtful put-down ways. But more than the words, we demand acts. We say to them: We will develop equal power with you and those who have shamed us.

It is imperative that *mestizas* support each other in changing the sexist elements in the Mexican-Indian culture. As long as woman is put down, the Indian and the Black in all of us is put down. The struggle of the *mestiza* is above all a feminist one. As long as *los hombres* think they have to *chingar mujeres* and each other to be men, as long as men are taught that they are superior and therefore culturally favored over *la mujer*, as long as to be a *vieja* is a thing of derision, there can be no real healing of our psyches. We're halfway there—we have such love of the Mother, the good mother. The first step is to unlearn the *puta / virgen* dichotomy and to see *Coatalopeuh-Coatlicue* in the Mother, *Guadalupe*.

Tenderness, a sign of vulnerability, is so feared that it is showered on women with verbal abuse and blows. Men, even more than women, are fettered to gender roles. Women at least have had the guts to break out of bondage. Only gay men have had the courage to expose themselves to the woman inside them and to challenge the current masculinity. I've encountered a few scattered and isolated gentle straight men, the beginnings of a new breed, but they are confused, and entangled with sexist behaviors that they have not been able to eradicate. We need a new masculinity and the new man needs a movement.

Lumping the males who deviate from the general norm with man, the oppressor, is a gross injustice. *Asombra pensar que nos hemos quedado en ese pozo oscuro donde el mundo encierra a las lesbianas. Asombra pensar que hemos, como femenistas y lesbianas, cerrado nuestros corazónes a los hombres, a nuestros hermanos los jotos, desheredados y marginales como nosotros.* Being the supreme crossers of cultures, homosexuals have strong bonds with the queer white, Black, Asian, Native American, Latino, and with the queer in Italy, Australia, and the rest of the planet. We come from all colors, all classes, all races, all time periods. Our role is to link people with each other—the Blacks with Jews with Indians with Asians with whites with extraterrestrials. It is to transfer ideas and information from one culture to another. Colored homosexuals have more knowledge of other cultures; have always been at the forefront (although sometimes in the closet) of all liberation struggles in this country; have suffered more injustices and have survived them despite all odds. Chicanos need to acknowledge the political and artistic contributions of their queer. People, listen to what your *jotería* is saying.

The *mestizo* and the queer exist at this time and point on the evolutionary continuum for a purpose. We are a blending that proves that all blood is intricately woven together, and that we are spawned out of similar souls.

Somos una gente

Hay tantísimas fronteras
que dividen a la gente,
pero por cada frontera
existe también un puente.
    —Gina Valdés

relational sexuality to race...

Divided loyalties. Many women and men of color do not want to have any dealings with white people. It takes too much time and energy to explain to the downwardly mobile, white middle-class women that it's okay for us to want to own "possessions," never having had any nice furniture on our dirt floors or "luxuries" like washing machines. Many feel that whites should help their own people rid themselves of race hatred and fear first. I, for one, choose to use some of my energy to serve as mediator. I think we need to allow whites to be our allies. Through our literature, art, *corridos*, and folktales we must share our history with them so when they set up committees to help Big Mountain Navajos or the Chicano farmworkers or *los Nicaragüenses* they won't turn people away because of their racial fears and ignorances. They will come to see that they are not helping us but following our lead.

Individually, but also as a racial entity, we need to voice our needs. We need to say to white society: We need you to accept the fact that Chicanos are different, to acknowledge your rejection and negation of us. We need you to own the fact that you looked upon us as less than human, that you stole our lands, our personhood, our self-respect. We need you to make public restitution: to say that, to compensate for your own sense of defectiveness, you strive for power over us, you erase our history and our experience because it makes you feel guilty—you'd rather forget your brutish acts. To say you've split yourself from minority groups, that you disown us, that your dual consciousness splits off parts of yourself, transferring the "negative" parts onto us. (Where there is persecution of minorities, there is shadow projection. Where there is violence and war, there is repression of shadow.) To say that you are afraid of us, that to put distance between us, you wear the mask of contempt. Admit that Mexico is your double, that she exists in the shadow of this country, that we are irrevocably tied to her. Gringo, accept the doppelganger in your psyche. By taking back your collective shadow the intracultural split will heal. And finally, tell us what you need from us.

By Your True Faces We Will Know You

I am visible—see this Indian face—yet I am invisible. I both blind them with my beak nose and am their blind spot. But I exist, we exist. They'd like to think I have melted in the pot. But I haven't, we haven't.

The dominant white culture is killing us slowly with its ignorance. By taking away our self-determination, it has made us weak and empty. As a people we have resisted and we have taken expedient positions, but we have never been allowed to develop unencumbered—we have never been allowed to be fully ourselves. The whites in power want us people of color to barricade ourselves behind our separate tribal walls so they can pick us off one at a time with their hidden weapons; so they can whitewash and distort history. Ignorance splits people, creates prejudices. A misinformed people is a subjugated people.

Before the Chicano and the undocumented worker and the Mexican from the other side can come together, before the Chicano can have unity with Native Americans and other groups, we need to know the history of their struggle and they need to know ours. Our mothers, our sisters and brothers, the guys who hang out on street corners, the children in the playgrounds, each of us must know our Indian lineage, our afro-*mestisaje*, our history of resistance.

To the immigrant *mexicano* and the recent arrivals we must teach our history. The eighty million *mexicanos* and the Latinos from Central and South America must know of our struggles. Each one of us must know basic facts about Nicaragua, Chile, and the rest of Latin America. The Latinoist movement (Chicanos, Puerto Ricans, Cubans, and other Spanish-speaking people working together to combat racial discrimination in the marketplace) is good but it is not enough. Other than a common culture we will have nothing to hold us together. We need to meet on a broader communal ground.

The struggle is inner: Chicano, *indio*, American Indian, *mojado*, *mexicano*, immigrant Latino, Anglo in power, working-class Anglo, Black, Asian—our psyches resemble the bordertowns and are populated by the same people. The struggle has always been inner, and is played out in the outer terrains. Awareness of our situation must come before inner changes, which in turn come before changes in society. Nothing happens in the "real" world unless it first happens in the images in our heads.

El día de la Chicana

> I will not be shamed again
> Nor will I shame myself.

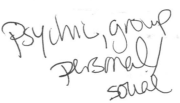

I am possessed by a vision: that we Chicanas and Chicanos have taken back or uncovered our true faces, our dignity and self-respect. It's a validation vision.

Seeing the Chicana anew in light of her history. I seek an exoneration, a seeing through the fictions of white supremacy, a seeing of ourselves in our true guises and not as the false racial personality that has been given to us and that we have given to ourselves. I seek our woman's face, our true features, the positive and the negative seen clearly, free of the tainted biases of male dominance. I seek new images of identity, new beliefs about ourselves, our humanity and worth no longer in question.

Estamos viviendo en la noche de la Raza, un tiempo cuando el trabajo se hace a lo quieto, en el oscuro. El día cuando aceptamos tal y como somos y para en donde vamos y porque—ese día será el día de la Raza. Yo tengo el conpromiso de expresar mi visión, mi sensibilidad, mi percepción de la revalidación de la gente mexicana, su mérito, estimación, honra, aprecio, y validez.

On December 2 when my sun goes into my first house, I celebrate *el día de la Chicana y el Chicano*. On that day I clean my altars, light my *Coatalopeuh* candle, burn sage and copal, take *el baño para espantar basura*, sweep my house. On that day I bare my soul, make myself vulnerable to friends and family by expressing my feelings. On that day I affirm who we are.

On that day I look inside our conflicts and our basic introverted racial temperament. I identify our needs, voice them. I acknowledge that the self and the race have been wounded. I recognize the need to take care of our personhood, of our racial self. On that day I gather the splintered and disowned parts of *la gente mexicana* and hold them in my arms. *Todas las partes de nosotros valen.*

On that day I say, "Yes, all you people wound us when you reject us. Rejection strips us of self-worth; our vulnerability exposes us to shame. It is our innate identity you find wanting. We are ashamed that we need your good opinion, that we need your acceptance. We can no longer camouflage our needs, can no longer let defenses and fences sprout around us. We can no longer withdraw. To rage and look upon you with contempt is to rage and be contemptuous of ourselves. We can no longer blame you, nor disown the white parts, the male parts, the pathological parts, the queer parts, the vulnerable parts. Here we are weaponless with open arms, with only our magic. Let's try it our way, the *mestiza* way, the Chicana way, the woman way.

On that day I search for our essential dignity as a people, a people with a sense of purpose—to belong and contribute to something greater than our *pueblo*. On that day I seek to recover and reshape my spiritual identity. *Anímate! Raza, a celebrar el día de la Chicana.*

El retorno

All movements are accomplished in six stages, and the seventh

brings return.

—I Ching[7]

Tanto tiempo sin verta casa mía,

mi cuna, mi hondo nido de la huerta.

—"Soledad"[8]

I stand at the river, watch the curving, twisting serpent, a serpent nailed to the fence where the mouth of the Rio Grande empties into the Gulf.

I have come back. *Tanto dolor me costó el alejamiento.* I shade my eyes and look up. The bone beak of a hawk slowly circling over me, checking me out as potential carrion. In its wake a little bird flickering its wings, swimming sporadically like a fish. In the distance the expressway and the slough of traffic like an irritated sow. The sudden pull in my gut, *la tierra, los aguaceros.* My land, *el viento soplando la arena, el lagartijo debajo de un nopalito. Me acuerdo como era antes. Una región desértica de vasta llanuras, costeras de baja altura, de escasa lluvia, de chaparrales formados por mesquites y huizaches.* If I look real hard I can almost see the Spanish fathers who were called "the cavalry of Christ" enter this valley riding their burros, see the clash of cultures commence.

Tierra natal. This is home, the small towns in the Valley, *los pueblitos* with chicken pens and goats picketed to mesquite shrubs. *En las colonias* on the other side of the tracks, junk cars line the front yards of hot pink and lavender-trimmed houses—Chicano architecture we call it, self-consciously. I have missed the TV shows where hosts speak in half and half, and where awards are given in the category of Tex-Mex music. I have missed the Mexican cemeteries blooming with artificial flowers, the fields of aloe vera and red pepper, rows of sugar cane, of corn hanging on the stalks, the cloud of *polvareda* in the dirt roads behind a speeding pickup truck, *el sabor de tamales de rez y venado.* I have missed *la yegua colorada* gnawing the wooden gate of her stall, the smell of horse flesh from Carito's corrals. *He hecho menos las noches calientes sin aire, noches de linternas y lechuzas* making holes in the night.

I still feel the old despair when I look at the unpainted, dilapidated, scrap lumber houses consisting mostly of corrugated aluminum. Some of the poorest people in the U.S. live in the Lower Rio Grande Valley, an arid and semi-arid land of irrigated farming, intense sunlight and heat, citrus groves next to chaparral and cactus. I walk through the elementary school I attended so long ago, which remained segregated until recently. I remember how the white teachers used to punish us for being Mexican.

How I love this tragic valley of South Texas, as Ricardo Sánchez calls it; this borderland between the Nueces and the Rio Grande. This land has survived possession and ill-use by five countries: Spain, Mexico, the Republic of Texas, the U.S., the Confederacy, and the U.S. again. It has survived Anglo-Mexican blood feuds, lynchings, burnings, rapes, pillage.

Today I see the valley still struggling to survive. Whether it does or not, it will never be as I remember it. The borderlands depression that was set off by the 1982 peso devaluation in Mexico resulted in the closure of hundreds of valley businesses. Many people lost their homes, cars, land. Prior to 1982, U.S. store owners thrived on retail sales to Mexicans who came across the border for groceries and clothes and appliances. While goods on the U.S. side have become ten, one hundred, one thousand times more expensive for Mexican buyers, goods on the Mexican side have become ten, one hundred, one thousand times cheaper for Americans. Because the valley is heavily dependent on agriculture and Mexican retail trade, it has the highest unemployment rates along the entire border region; it is the valley that has been hardest hit.[9]

"It's been a bad year for corn," my brother Nune says. As he talks, I remember my father scanning the sky for a rain that would end the drought, looking up into the sky, day after day, while the corn withered on its stalk. My father has been dead for twenty-nine years, having worked himself to death. The life span of a Mexican farm laborer is fifty-six—he lived to be thirty-eight. It shocks me that I am older than he. I, too, search the sky for rain. Like the ancients, I worship the rain god and the maize goddess, but unlike my father I have recovered their names. Now for rain (irrigation) one offers not a sacrifice of blood, but of money.

"Farming is in a bad way," my brother says. "Two to three thousand small and big farmers went bankrupt in this country last year. Six years ago the price of corn was $8.00 per hundred pounds," he goes on. "This year it is $3.90 per hundred pounds." And, I think to myself, after taking inflation into account, not planting anything puts you ahead.

I walk out to the back yard, stare at *los rosales de mamá*. She wants me to help her prune the rose bushes, dig out the carpet grass that is choking them.

Mamagrande Ramona también tenía rosales. Here every Mexican grows flowers. If they don't have a piece of dirt, they use car tires, jars, cans, shoe boxes. Roses are the Mexican's favorite flower. I think, how symbolic—thorns and all.

Yes, the Chicano and Chicana have always taken care of growing things and the land. Again I see the four of us kids getting off the school bus, changing into our work clothes, walking into the field with Papí and Mamí, all six of us bending to the ground. Below our feet, under the earth lie the watermelon seeds. We cover them with paper plates, putting *terremotes* on top of the plates to keep them from being blown away by the wind. The paper plates keep the freeze away. Next day or the next, we remove the plates, bare the tiny green shoots to the elements. They survive and grow, give fruit hundreds of times the size of the seed. We water them and hoe them. We harvest them. The vines dry, rot, are plowed under. Growth, death, decay, birth. The soil prepared again and again, impregnated, worked on. A constant changing of forms, *renacimientos de la tierra madre*.

> This land was Mexican once
> was Indian always
> and is.
> And will be again.

[handwritten: cyclical — Then why worry about white "supremacy"?]

[handwritten: Amen.]

[handwritten: cf. assertion of inclusivity p. 233]

NOTES

1. Jose Vasconcelos, *La raza cósmica: Misión de la raza Ibero-Americana* (México: Aguilar S.A. de Ediciones, 1961).

2. Arthur Koestler termed this "bisociation." Albert Rothenberg, *The Creative Process in Art, Science, and Other Fields* (Chicago: University of Chicago Press, 1979), p. 12.

3. In part, I derive my definitions for "convergent" and "divergent" thinking from Rothenberg, pp. 12–13.

4. To borrow chemist Ilya Prigogine's theory of "dissipative structures." Prigogine discovered that substances interact, not in predictable ways as it was taught in science, but in different and fluctuating ways to produce new and more complex structures, a kind of birth he called "morphogenesis," which created unpredictable innovations. Harold Gilliam, "Searching for a New World View," *This World* (January 1981): 23.

5. *Tortillas de masa harina*: corn tortillas are of two types, the smooth uniform ones made in a tortilla press and usually bought at a tortilla factory or supermarket,

and *gorditas*, made by mixing *masa* with lard or shortening or butter (my mother sometimes puts in bits of bacon or *chicharrones*).

6. Gina Valdés, *Puentes y fronteras: Coplas Chicanas* (Los Angeles: Castle Lithograph, 1982), p. 2.

7. Richard Wilhelm, *The I Ching, or Book of Changes*, trans. Cary F. Baynes (Princeton: Princeton University Press, 1950), p. 98.

8. *"Soledad"* is sung by the group, Haciendo Punto en Otro Son.

9. Out of the twenty-two border counties in the four border states, Hidalgo County (named for Father Hidalgo, who was shot in 1810 after instigating Mexico's revolt against Spanish rule under the banner of *la Virgen de Guadalupe*) is the most poverty-stricken county in the nation as well as the largest home base (along with Imperial in California) for migrant farm-workers. It was here that I was born and raised. I am amazed that both it and I have survived.

14

This Sex Which Is Not One

Luce Irigaray

Female sexuality has always been conceptualized on the basis of masculine parameters. Thus
the opposition between "masculine" clitoral
activity and "feminine" vaginal passivity, an
opposition which Freud—and many others—
saw as stages, or alternatives, in the development of a sexually "normal" woman, seems
rather too clearly required by the practice of
male sexuality. For the clitoris is conceived as
a little penis pleasant to masturbate so long
as castration anxiety does not exist (for the
boy child), and the vagina is valued for the
"lodging" it offers the male organ when the
forbidden hand has to find a replacement for
pleasure-giving.

In these terms, woman's erogenous zones
never amount to anything but a clitoris-sex that
is not comparable to the noble phallic organ, or
a hole-envelope that serves to sheathe and mas-

sage the penis in intercourse: a non-sex, or a masculine organ turned back upon itself, self-embracing.

About woman and her pleasure, this view of the sexual relation has nothing to say. Her lot is that of "lack," "atrophy" (of the sexual organ), and "penis envy," the penis being the only sexual organ of recognized value. Thus she attempts by every means available to appropriate that organ for herself: through her somewhat servile love of the father-husband capable of giving her one, through her desire for a child-penis, preferably a boy, through access to the cultural values still reserved by right to males alone and therefore always masculine, and so on. Woman lives her own desire only as the expectation that she may at last come to possess an equivalent of the male organ.

Yet all this appears quite foreign to her own pleasure, unless it remains within the dominant phallic economy. Thus, for example, woman's autoeroticism is very different from man's. In order to touch himself, man needs an instrument: his hand, a woman's body, language . . . And this self-caressing requires at least a minimum of activity. As for woman, she touches herself in and of herself without any need for mediation, and before there is any way to distinguish activity from passivity. Woman "touches herself" all the time, and moreover no one can forbid her to do so, for her genitals are formed of two lips in continuous contact. Thus, within herself, she is already two—but not divisible into one(s)—that caress each other.

This autoeroticism is disrupted by a violent break-in: the brutal separation of the two lips by a violating penis, an intrusion that distracts and deflects the woman from this "self-caressing" she needs if she is not to incur the disappearance of her own pleasure in sexual relations. If the vagina is to serve *also*, but *not only*, to take over for the little boy's hand in order to assure an articulation between autoeroticism and heteroeroticism in intercourse (the encounter with the totally other always signifying death), how, in the classic representation of sexuality, can the perpetuation of autoeroticism for woman be managed? Will woman not be left with the impossible alternative between a defensive virginity, fiercely turned in upon itself, and a body open to penetration that no longer knows, in this "hole" that constitutes its sex, the pleasure of its own touch? The more or less exclusive—and highly anxious—attention paid to erection in Western sexuality proves to what extent the imaginary that governs it is foreign to the feminine. For the most part, this sexuality offers nothing but imperatives dictated by male rivalry: the "strongest" being the one who has the best "hard-on," the longest, the biggest, the stiffest penis, or even the one who "pees the farthest" (as in little boys' contests). Or else one finds imperatives dictated by the enactment of sadomasochistic fantasies, these in turn governed by man's relation to his mother: the desire to force entry, to penetrate, to appropriate for himself the mystery of this womb where he has been conceived, the secret of his begetting, of his "origin." Desire/need, also to make blood flow again in order to revive a very old relationship—intrauterine, to be sure, but also prehistoric—to the maternal.

Woman, in this sexual imaginary, is only a more or less obliging prop for the enactment of man's fantasies. That she may find pleasure there in that role, by proxy, is possible, even certain. But such pleasure is above all a masochistic prostitution of her body to a desire that is not her own, and it leaves her in a familiar state of dependency upon man. Not knowing what she wants, ready for anything, even asking for more, so long as he will "take" her as his "object" when he seeks his own pleasure. Thus she will not say what she herself wants; moreover, she does not know, or no longer knows, what she wants. As Freud admits, the beginnings of the sexual life of a girl child are so "obscure," so "faded with time," that one would have to dig down very deep indeed to discover beneath the traces of this civilization, of this history, the vestiges of a more archaic civilization that might give some clue to woman's sexuality. That extremely ancient civilization would undoubtedly have a different alphabet, a different language . . . Woman's desire would not be expected to speak the same language as man's; woman's desire has doubtless been submerged by the logic that has dominated the West since the time of the Greeks.

Within this logic, the predominance of the visual, and of the discrimination and individualization of form, is particularly foreign to female eroticism. Woman takes pleasure more from touching than from looking, and her entry into a dominant scopic economy signifies, again, her consignment to passivity: she is to be the beautiful object of contemplation. While her body finds itself thus eroticized, and called to a double movement of exhibition and of chaste retreat in order to stimulate the drives of the "subject," her sexual organ represents *the horror of nothing to see*. A defect in this systematics of representation and desire. A "hole" in its scoptophilic lens. It is already evident in Greek statuary that this nothing-to-see has to be excluded, rejected, from such a scene of representation. Woman's genitals are simply absent, masked, sewn back up inside their "crack."

This organ which has nothing to show for itself also lacks a form of its own. And if woman takes pleasure precisely from this incompleteness of form which allows her organ to touch itself over and over again, indefinitely, by itself, that pleasure is denied by a civilization that privileges phallomorphism. The value granted to the only definable form excludes the one that is in play in female autoeroticism. The *one* of form, of the individual, of the (male) sexual organ, of the proper name, of the proper meaning . . . supplants, while separating and dividing, that contact of *at least two* (lips) which keeps woman in touch with herself, but without any possibility of distinguishing what is touching from what is touched.

Whence the mystery that woman represents in a culture claiming to count everything, to number everything by units, to inventory everything as individualities. *She is neither one nor two.* Rigorously speaking, she cannot be identified either as one person, or as two. She resists all adequate definition. Further, she has no "proper" name. And her sexual organ, which is not *one* organ, is counted as *none.* The negative, the underside, the reverse of the only visible and morphologically designatable organ (even if the passage from erection to detumescence does pose some problems): the penis.

But the "thickness" of that "form," the layering of its volume, its expansions and contractions and even the spacing of the moments in which it produces itself as form—all this the feminine keeps secret. Without knowing it. And if woman is asked to sustain, to revive, man's desire, the request neglects to spell out what it implies as to the value of her own desire. A desire of which she is not aware, moreover, at least not explicitly. But one whose force and continuity are capable of nurturing repeatedly and at length all the masquerades of "feminity" that are expected of her.

It is true that she still has the child, in relation to whom her appetite for touch, for contact, has free rein, unless it is already lost, alienated by the taboo against touching of a highly obsessive civilization. Otherwise her pleasure will find, in the child, compensations for and diversions from the frustrations that she too often encounters in sexual relations per se. Thus maternity fills the gaps in a repressed female sexuality. Perhaps man and woman no longer caress each other except through that mediation between them that the child—preferably a boy—represents? Man, identified with his son, rediscovers the pleasure of maternal fondling; woman touches herself again by caressing that part of her body: her baby-penis-clitoris.

What this entails for the amorous trio is well known. But the Oedipal interdiction seems to be a somewhat categorical and factitious law—although it does provide the means for perpetuating the authoritarian discourse of fathers—when it is promulgated in a culture in which sexual relations are impracticable because man's desire and woman's are strangers to each other. And in which the two desires have to try to meet through indirect means, whether the archaic one of a sense-relation to the mother's body, or the present one of active or passive extension of the law of the father. These are regressive emotional behaviors, exchanges of words too detached from the sexual arena not to constitute an exile with respect to it: "mother" and "father" dominate the interactions of the couple, but as social roles. The division of labor prevents them from making love. They produce or reproduce. Without quite knowing how to use their leisure. Such little as they have, such little indeed as they wish to have. For what are they to do with leisure? What substitute for amorous resource are they to invent? Still . . .

Perhaps it is time to return to that repressed entity, the female imaginary. So woman does not have a sex organ? She has at least two of them, but they are not identifiable as ones. Indeed, she has many more. Her sexuality, always at least double, goes even further: it is *plural*. Is this the way culture is seeking to characterize itself now? Is this the way texts write themselves/are written now? Without quite knowing what censorship they are evading? Indeed, woman's pleasure does not have to choose between clitoral activity and vaginal passivity, for example. The pleasure of the vaginal caress does not have to be substituted for that of the clitoral caress. They each contribute, irreplaceably, to woman's pleasure. Among other caresses . . . Fondling the breasts, touching the vulva, spreading the lips, stroking the posterior wall of the vagina, brushing against the mouth of the uterus, and so on. To evoke only a few of the most specifically female pleasures. Pleasures which are somewhat misunderstood in sexual difference as it is imagined—or not imagined, the other sex being only the indispensable complement to the only sex.

But *woman has sex organs more or less everywhere*. She finds pleasure almost anywhere. Even if we refrain from invoking the hystericization of her entire body, the geography of her pleasure is far more diversified, more multiple in its differences, more complex, more subtle, than is commonly imagined—in an imaginary rather too narrowly focused on sameness.

"She" is indefinitely other in herself. This is doubtless why she is said to be whimsical, incomprehensible, agitated, capricious . . . not to mention her language, in which "she" sets off in all directions leaving "him" unable to discern the coherence of any meaning. Hers are contradictory words, somewhat mad from the standpoint of reason, inaudible for whoever listens to them with ready-made grids, with a fully elaborated code in hand. For in what she says, too, at least when she dares, woman is constantly touching herself. She steps ever so slightly aside from herself with a murmur, an exclamation, a whisper, a sentence left unfinished . . . When she returns, it is to set off again from elsewhere. From another point of pleasure, or of pain. One would have to listen with another ear, as if hearing *an "other meaning" always in the process of weaving itself, of embracing itself with words, but also of getting rid of words in order not to become fixed, congealed in them.* For if "she" says something, it is not, it is already no longer, identical with what she means. What she says is never identical with anything, moreover; rather, it is contiguous. *It touches (upon).* And when it strays too far from that proximity, she breaks off and starts over at "zero": her body-sex.

It is useless, then, to trap women in the exact definition of what they mean, to make them repeat (themselves) so that it will be clear; they are already elsewhere in that discursive machinery where you expected to surprise them. They have returned within themselves. Which must not be understood in the same way as within yourself. They do not have the interiority that you have, the one you perhaps suppose they have. Within themselves means *within the intimacy of that silent, multiple, diffuse touch.* And if you ask them insistently what they are thinking about, they can only reply: Nothing. Everything.

Thus what they desire is precisely nothing, and at the same time everything. Always something more and something else besides that *one*—sexual organ, for example—that you give them, attribute to them. Their desire is often interpreted, and feared, as a sort of insatiable hunger, a voracity that will swallow you whole. Whereas it really involves a different economy more than anything else, one that upsets the linearity of a project, undermines the goal-object of a desire, diffuses the polarization toward a single pleasure, disconcerts fidelity to a single discourse . . .

Must this multiplicity of female desire and female language be understood as shards, scattered remnants of a violated sexuality? A sexuality denied? The question has no simple answer. The rejection, the exclusion of a female imaginary certainly puts woman in the position of experiencing herself only fragmentarily, in the little-structured margins of a dominant ideology, as waste, or excess, what is left of a mirror invested by the (masculine) "subject" to reflect himself, to copy himself. Moreover, the role of "femininity" is prescribed by this masculine specula(riza)tion and corresponds scarcely at all to woman's desire, which may be recovered only in secret, in hiding, with anxiety and guilt.

But if the female imaginary were to deploy itself, if it could bring itself into play otherwise than as scraps, uncollected debris, would it represent itself, even so, in the form of *one* universe? Would it even be volume instead of surface? No. Not unless it were understood, yet again, as a privileging of the maternal over the feminine. Of a phallic maternal, at that. Closed in upon the jealous possession of its valued product. Rivaling man in his esteem for productive excess. In such a race for power, woman loses the uniqueness of her pleasure. By closing herself off as volume, she renounces the pleasure that she gets from the *nonsuture of her lips*: she is undoubtedly a mother, but a virgin mother; the role was assigned to her by mythologies long ago. Granting her a certain social power to the extent that she is reduced, with her own complicity, to sexual impotence.

(Re-)discovering herself, for a woman, thus could only signify the possibility of sacrificing no one of her pleasures to another, of identifying herself with none of them in particular, *of never being simply one*. A sort of expanding universe to which no limits could be fixed and which would not be incoherence nonetheless—nor that polymorphous perversion of the child in which the erogenous zones would lie waiting to be regrouped under the primacy of the phallus.

Woman always remains several, but she is kept from dispersion because the other is already within her and is autoerotically familiar to her. Which is not to say that she appropriates the other for herself, that she reduces it to her own property. Ownership and property are doubtless quite foreign to the feminine. At least sexually. But not *nearness*. Nearness so pronounced that it makes all discrimination of identity, and thus all forms of property, impossible. Woman derives pleasure from what is *so near that she cannot have it, nor have herself*. She herself enters into a ceaseless exchange of herself with the other without any possibility of identifying either. This puts into question all prevailing economies: their calculations are irremediably stymied by woman's pleasure, as it increases indefinitely from its passage in and through the other.

However, in order for woman to reach the place where she takes pleasure as woman, a long detour by way of the analysis of the various systems of oppression brought to bear upon her is assuredly necessary. And claiming to fall back on the single solution of pleasure risks making her miss the process of going back through a social practice that *her* enjoyment requires.

For woman is traditionally a use-value for man, an exchange value among men; in other words, a commodity. As such, she remains the guardian of material substance, whose price will be established, in terms of the standard of their work and of their need/desire, by "subjects": workers, merchants, consumers. Women are marked phallically by their fathers, husbands, procurers. And this branding determines their value in sexual commerce. Woman is never anything but the locus of a more or less competitive exchange between two men, including the competition for the possession of mother earth.

How can this object of transaction claim a right to pleasure without removing her/itself from established commerce? With respect to other merchandise in the marketplace, how could this commodity maintain a relationship other than one of aggressive jealousy? How could material substance enjoy her/itself without provoking the consumer's anxiety over the disappearance of his nurturing ground? How could that exchange—which can in no way be defined in terms "proper" to woman's desire—appear as anything but a pure mirage, mere foolishness, all too readily obscured by a more sensible discourse and by a system of apparently more tangible values?

A woman's development, however radical it may seek to be, would thus not suffice to liberate woman's desire. And to date no political theory or political practice has resolved, or sufficiently taken into consideration, this historical problem, even though Marxism has proclaimed its importance. But women do not constitute, strictly speaking, a class, and their dispersion among several classes makes their political struggle complex, their demands sometimes contradictory.

There remains, however, the condition of underdevelopment arising from women's submission by and to a culture that oppresses them, uses them, makes of them a medium of exchange, with very little profit to them. Except in the quasi monopolies of masochistic pleasure, the domestic labor force, and reproduction. The powers of slaves? Which are not negligible powers, moreover. For where pleasure is concerned, the master is not necessarily well served. Thus to reverse the relation, especially in the economy of sexuality, does not seem a desirable objective.

But if women are to preserve and expand their autoeroticism, their homo-sexuality, might not the renunciation of heterosexual pleasure correspond once again to that disconnection from power that is traditionally theirs? Would it not involve a new prison, a new cloister, built of their own accord? For women to undertake tactical strikes, to keep themselves apart from men long enough to learn to defend their desire, especially through speech, to discover the love of other women while sheltered from men's imperious choices that put them in the position of rival commodities, to forge for themselves a social status that compels recognition, to earn their living in order to escape from the condition of prostitute . . . these are certainly indispensable stages in the escape from their proletarization on the exchange market. But if their aim were simply to reverse the order of things, even supposing this to be possible, history would repeat itself in the long run, would revert to sameness: to phallocratism. It would leave room neither for women's sexuality, nor for women's imaginary, nor for women's language to take (their) place.

15

Hysteria, Psychoanalysis, and Feminism

THE CASE OF ANNA O.

Dianne Hunter

We (Breuer and I) had often compared the symptomatology of hysteria with a pictographic script which has become intelligible after the discovery of a few bilingual inscriptions.

—Sigmund Freud,
Studies on Hysteria

Hysteria is not a pathological phenomenon, and can, in all respects, be considered as a supreme means of expression.

—Louis Aragon
and André Bréton,
La Révolution Surréaliste

I

The hysteric most often named and discussed by Freud, although he never met her, and never encountered a case like hers, was "Fräulein Anna O.," the inventor of the "talking cure," introduced in the first case history of *Studies on Hysteria*, published by Freud and Breuer in 1895. Anna O., whose real name was Bertha Pappenheim, inspired what may be called the "legend" of the origin of psychoanalysis, and later in her life became an important figure in the history of the German Jewish women's movement and in the history of modern institutionalized social work. She lived from 1859 to 1936, and in 1954, was honored by the Republic of West Germany as a "Helper of Humanity." Although feminists have recognized

Dianne Hunter, "Hysteria, Psychoanalysis, and Feminism: The Case of Anna O." Originally appeared in more extensive form in *Feminist Studies* 9, no. 3 (Fall 1983): 464–88, and was reprinted in *The (M)other Tongue: Essays in Feminist Psychoanalytic Interpretation*, edited by Shirley Nelson Garner, Claire Kahane, and Madelon Sprengnether, Cornell University Press, 1985.

Pappenheim for the philanthropic and political activities of her public life, we have given less attention to her role as a contributor to psychoanalytic theory and technique.[1]

The Anna O. described in psychoanalytic writings, an attractive, highly intelligent young woman, suffered an hysterical collapse at the age of twenty-one, during a period when she had been responsible for prolonged day and night nursing of her father, Siegmund, who was dying of tuberculosis. For nearly two years, during and after her father's illness, "Anna" was a patient of the well-known and respected Viennese physician Josef Breuer, who described her case as "the germ-cell of the whole of psychoanalysis."[2] Although Dr. Breuer never fully recognized the meaning of his encounter with Pappenheim, he found the case remarkable enough to report to his young friend and colleague Freud, who was profoundly impressed when he heard about Pappenheim's unusual treatment by verbalization and catharsis. That was in November of 1882.

Three years later, Freud was in Paris observing Jean-Martin Charcot's demonstrations of hypnosis and suggestion at the Salpêtrière hospital. At that time, Charcot's lessons on hysteria were as fashionable as the tirades of Sarah Bernhardt, and for much the same reason. In the late nineteenth century, hysteria was a chief subject in medical publications throughout Europe and in England. What Freud contributed to the work being done at this time in France was the idea of listening to what hysterics had to say. Bertha Pappenheim originated this technique, and another patient, "Elizabeth von R." (Ilona Weiss), refined it by suggesting to Freud the method of free association.

Although Breuer edited the story of Bertha Pappenheim's hysteria and suppressed her identity, we know her biography from later sources.[3] She was born in Vienna, the third child in a family that already had two daughters. (Her two sisters died in childhood.) Her birth was followed by that of the family's only son, Wilhelm, whose privileges Pappenheim came to resent. She attended a Catholic school, although her home was traditionally Jewish. Her grandfather, Wolf Pappenheim, a prominent personality of the Pressburg ghetto, devoted his fortune to the promotion of Jewish orthodoxy. Bertha's father, a wealthy grain merchant, cofounded the Jewish *Schiffschul* in Vienna. Bertha Pappenheim's mother, Recha, née Goldschmidt, described as rather authoritarian, was originally from Frankfurt-on-the-Main, Germany, where she later returned with her daughter. This city was a center of charitable activities among Bertha's relatives on her mother's side. These relatives, connected to artistic circles, included Heinrich Heine. Breuer remarks that some of Anna's more distant relatives had been psychotic, but she herself had been consistently healthy until her father's sickness in July 1880. She had received an education typical for girls of her class. She spoke perfect English, read French and Italian, and practiced embroidery and lacemaking, which remained a lifelong passion. There was a certain modernism about her training, however, since she rode horseback with her cousins. A photograph of Bertha in riding costume, dated 1882, Konstanz, Germany, bears little resemblance to the patient Breuer describes, although he does mention that she had used a horsewhip in his presence once when her pet dog attacked a cat. Breuer describes Anna as a willful, energetic, intuitive, and compassionate person, someone who took pleasure in caring for the poor and the sick. According to Breuer, Anna could be obstinate, but "sympathetic kindness" was one of her essential character traits. Breuer reports that Anna had a "powerful instinct" toward charity work, but he does not mention that such work was one of the few forms of activity women were traditionally permitted outside the home.

During the time Bertha Pappenheim nursed her father, she stopped eating. Her weight loss was such that she was forbidden to continue her nursing duties. She had also developed a cough which resembled her father's. At this point, Dr. Breuer was called in for the first time. Over the next three months, a very complex hysteria developed. Pappenheim suffered rigid paralyses of her arms, legs, and neck muscles, headaches, and somnambulism. First her right arm, then her right side, then her entire body suffered contracture. She was intermittently deaf. She had a convergent squint and severe, inexplicable disturbances of vision. She had temper tantrums during which she would throw things about the room, tear the buttons off her bedclothes, and grow distressed when relatives appeared.

Pappenheim in her hysteria experienced a profound disorganization of speech and, for a time, total aphasia. It is Pappenheim's aphasia and her use of her body as a signifier with which I am particularly concerned. Although many of what Freud refers to as Pappenheim's "museum of monuments" to "hyperaesthetic memories" have been richly and repeatedly analyzed, no one has sufficiently studied her unique use of languages. When she regained her ability to talk, Bertha Pappenheim was unable to understand or speak her native tongue although she proved surprisingly fluent in foreign languages, a circumstance Freud calls "strange" and other commentators call "bizarre." I would like to offer a psychoanalytic-feminist reading of Bertha's speechlessness and her communication in translation, gibberish, and pantomime. I think it is possible to see a liberating motive implicit in Pappenheim's linguistic disruptions, for speaking coherent German meant integration into a cultural identity Bertha Pappenheim wanted to reject.

She claimed to be divided into two selves: "a real one and an evil one which forced her to behave badly."[4] Two states of consciousness would alternate, one of which would interrupt while the other was speaking. Breuer refers to the pauses in Pappenheim's speech by the French term *absences*. This suggests that for Breuer as well as for Pappenheim, the abnormal states of consciousness represented foreign parts of the self, parts alien to signification in her native tongue.

In the afternoons Pappenheim would fall into a somnolent state. After sunset she would wake up, repeating the words "tormenting, tormenting." She was unable to speak a whole sentence, and her whole body was paralyzed. Breuer first noticed that she was at a loss for words and then that she had lost her command of grammar and syntax as well. She no longer conjugated verbs, and eventually used only infinitives, which, says Breuer, were "for the most part incorrectly formed from weak past participles."[5] Neither infinitives nor participles specify a person; as Breuer notes, "tormenting" is an impersonal form. Pappenheim also omitted both the definite and the indefinite article. In the process of time she became almost completely at a loss for words. When words failed her, she would put them together laboriously out of four or five languages and became nearly unintelligible. Here is a reconstruction of Pappenheim's linguistic mélange: "Jamais acht nobody bella mio please lieboehn nuit."[6] She tried to write the same mumbo jumbo.

For two weeks Bertha Pappenheim was completely silent, and at this point, Dr. Breuer recognized for the first time the psychical mechanism of his patient's disorder: "She had felt very much offended over something and had determined not to speak about it."[7] When Breuer guessed this and obliged her to talk about it during hypnosis, Pappenheim's linguistic inhibition disappeared, but she spoke only in English. In moments of extreme anxiety, her powers of speech either deserted her entirely or she used a mixture of languages. At the times when she felt most free, Pappenheim spoke French and Italian. She had amnesia between these times and the times when she spoke English. During her illness, she baffled her family and servants with discourses in languages they did not understand and astonished her doctors by producing a rapid, fluent extemporaneous English translation of any text in French or Italian she was asked to read aloud. Pappenheim also made up words: *gehäglich* for *behaglich*, meaning comfortable, and invented names in English for the process which she and Breuer had begun. She called it "chimney sweeping" when she was joking and "the talking cure" when she was being serious.

Freud and Breuer offer an inadequate explanation for Pappenheim's linguistic symptoms. We are told that one night while she was watching by her father's sickbed in a torment of anxiety, she fell into a twilight state, while her right arm, which was hanging over the back of the chair, went to sleep. Pappenheim was so terrified to find her arm paralyzed that she tried to pray, but could find no words. At length she remembered a child's prayer in English. Therefore when her hysteria developed, she spoke and wrote English. This recollection of the child's prayer seems to bear no relation to Pappenheim's determination to keep silent. Nor does it explain her inventive nomenclatures, polylingual jargon, or amazing speeches in French and Italian. All it tells us is that Bertha was so upset she forgot her mother tongue.

Although Breuer does not state what had offended Bertha, it is easy to infer that she resented and rejected her inferior position as a daughter in an orthodox Jewish family. Although her intellectual and poetic gifts were remarkable, and she was a lively and charming person, Bertha Pappenheim at twenty-one was assigned routine and monotonous household tasks. Her brother, a year younger than she and not nearly as bright, had recently entered the University of Vienna, an institution closed to women at that time. Breuer writes, "This girl, who was bubbling over with intellectual vitality, led an extremely monotonous existence in her puritanically-minded family. She embellished her life in a manner which probably influenced her decisively in the direction of her illness, by indulging in systematic day-dreaming, which she described as her 'private theatre.'"[8] Speculating on the origin of "hypnoid" (dissociated, split) states, Breuer and Freud note that these conditions often seem to grow out of the daydreams which are common even in healthy people, "and to which needlework and similar occupations render women especially prone."[9] That is, people left to embroidery are bound to embroider fantasies.

Pappenheim's daydreaming and her illness were heavily influenced by the necessity of spending hours tending her father's sickbed, a situation that cannot have failed to arouse wishes in such a lively and imaginative person, although Breuer does not mention this and seems not to have thought of it. Her squint developed while she was straining to see what time it was through her tears after she had waited up all night for a doctor who was late in arriving. In similar circumstances, Pappenheim hallucinated a black snake coming toward the sick man from the wall to bite him. When she tried to drive away the snake, she found her arm paralyzed and saw her hands turn into little snakes with death's-heads at the fingertips. Her cough developed when she heard dance music coming from a neighboring house, felt a sudden wish to leave her father's bedside, and was overcome with self-reproaches. Thereafter, she coughed nervously whenever she heard rhythmical music. Pappenheim hallucinated her father's face as a death's-head and then saw her own reflection in a mirror as the same image. Having lost her sisters to childhood deaths, and apparently wishing for the termination of her father's agonizing illness which she imitated with her cough, Pappenheim was preoccupied with skeletons. When Siegmund Pappenheim died, his daughter had to be removed to the country to protect her from suicidal impulses. Perhaps she wanted to join him in death, and perhaps she wanted to escape from guilt generated by what must have been a liberation and a relief. She had lost a patient "of whom she was passionately fond."

Pappenheim's hysteria arose from sources in her life history typical of her time. It was not uncommon in the nineteenth century for the potential of daughters to be sacrificed while sons were educated and privileged; it was also in keeping with prevailing customs for young women to be called upon to nurse aging and ill parents. Neither Pappenheim nor Breuer could consciously express the ambivalent emotions such situations would arouse. Although Breuer recognized Bertha's grief for her father's death as a cause of her symptoms, he overlooked the hostility, anger, guilt, and frustrated sexuality apparent to psychoanalysts.[10] Even a nonpsychoanalytic reading of the case indicates that Pappenheim found her existence lonely and tedious.

Late in her life Pappenheim thought of her lack of formal education as "defective spiritual nourishment,"[11] a reference that may illuminate the anorexic symptoms of her hysteria and her way of literalizing through her body her felt psychic condition. Breuer uses a similar metaphor of undernourishment to describe Anna O.: "She possessed a powerful intellect which would have been capable of digesting solid mental pabulum and which stood in need of it—though without receiving it after she had left school."[12] Once when Dr. Breuer interrupted his visits to her for several days because he had to leave Vienna, Bertha went entirely without food during his absence.

At the time she fell ill, Bertha Pappenheim must have wanted someone to talk with, someone to listen to her elaborate stories.[13] Breuer provided an audience for her mental creations. He increased by one the attendance at her "private theatre." Although Breuer had arrived as an old-fashioned physician with black bag in hand to treat Bertha Pappenheim's malady, she quickly changed the terms of the relationship by falling into autohypnosis and commencing to mutter in an apparently absent-minded state. She was clearly intrigued by the good looking and highly cultivated, successful doctor. Although Breuer does not say so, his account of Bertha Pappenheim's behavior suggests that she tried to seduce him, and that in a way she was successful. We are told about the various massages she received on her head and legs—standard procedures for treating paralysis. What was unusual, and the beginning of what developed into psychoanalysis, involved the long hours they spent in hypnosis together while Pappenheim told sad and fanciful stories and "talked herself out" until "she was clear in mind, calm, and cheerful." Breuer attributed her cheerfulness to the talking, not to his presence on the scene. During the course of their treatment Breuer spent a medically unprecedented amount of time in his patient's company, visiting her nearly every day between the end of 1880 and the middle of 1882, often more than once a day, listening to the most minute details of her present and past life, repeating set phrases from her stories to get her narratives started each session. Although Breuer states that Bertha Pappenheim was "astonishingly underdeveloped" sexually, every commentator has remarked upon her physical attractions. The case history suggests that Bertha fantasized a love affair with Breuer; and indeed, the infatuation seems to have been mutual, although unconscious on Breuer's part. Pappenheim failed to recognize her relatives and ignored all unwanted strangers, but she always had eyes for Breuer. According to Freud, her image of the treatment as "chimney sweeping" was a metaphor for sexual intercourse.[14] After many months of hearing reports of this fascinating patient, Mrs. Breuer finally grew jealous and angry. Surprised and probably feeling guilty as well, Breuer suddenly determined to end the treatment. He announced his intention to Pappenheim and prepared to depart on a trip to Venice with his wife. According to Freud, Pappenheim responded with an "untoward event."[15] She staged an hysterical childbirth to summon Breuer back for another session. He was shocked to find her in bed with abdominal cramps, which she explained with the words "Now Dr. Breuer's child is coming!"[16] He calmed her with hypnosis and then fled the house, abandoning her to a colleague. He never saw her again, and later when he heard that she was ill, he wished she would die and so cease to be miserable.[17] Breuer chose not to report the fantasy childbirth in the published version of the case history of Anna O., and he never acknowledged the erotic element in their attachment. This suppression might be explained by Breuer's fear of a scandal; and if he perceived that Pappenheim had been playing a role to allure him, he might have feared that publishing the story would not only compromise him, but make him appear foolish as well. However, his private obsession with the case after he had given it up, his reluctance to pre-

sent any account of it in public form, and his ultimate rejection of psychoanalysis indicate that there were other causes contributing to the absence of
the final scene from his report in *Studies on Hysteria*, which gives the false
impression that Anna's hysteria had disappeared.

George Pollock traces Breuer's anxiety to the loss of his young and attractive mother in childbirth when he was three or four years old. She, as well as
Breuer's oldest daughter, about eleven years old at the time of his relationship with the famous patient, was named Bertha.[18] When Freud began to
uncover the role of transference love in hypnosis and psychoanalysis, and to
stress the importance of sexuality in neuroses, Breuer dissociated himself
from his controversial colleague. Although Pappenheim had led the way to
the unconscious through her invention of the "talking cure" and her dramati-
zation of transference love in the doctor-patient relation, Breuer resisted the
implications of their encounter. Freud reports that Breuer repeatedly read to
him pieces of the case history during 1882 and 1883, but objected vehemently to publishing the story of the treatment. Freud decided to report the
case to Charcot, who listened but showed no interest. Ten years later Breuer
agreed to a joint publication because Freud convinced him that Pierre Janet's
work in French anticipated some of his results, such as the tracing back of
hysterical symptoms to events in the patient's life, and their removal by
means of hypnotic reproduction.

II

Although I think the oedipal configurations in Pappenheim's encounter
with Breuer are significant, I want to focus for a moment on the oral dimensions of their relationship. Leo Stone's discussion of transference wishes links
the unconscious meanings of the doctor-patient relation to the universal craving for the omnipotent mother of early infancy. Janet Malcolm summarizes:

> This craving . . . can be activated by doctors, politicians, clergymen, and
> teachers as well as by analysts. Stone draws a . . . distinction between the
> meaning of the primary transference generated by the physician and that
> generated by the analyst. While the physician's direct physical and emo-
> tional ministrations correspond to those of the "omniscient, omnipotent,
> and unintelligible" mother of the earliest period of infancy, the analyst's
> activities resemble (in unconscious reverberation) the not so agreeable
> ones of the mother in the months when the infant is learning to talk and

to separate from her—"that period of life where all the modalities of bodily intimacy and direct dependence on the mother are being relinquished or attenuated, *pari passu* with the rapid development of the great vehicle of communication by speech." It is in this state of "intimate separation," or "deprivation in intimacy," that analysis is conducted, deriving its mutative power from the tension between verbal closeness and emotional distance.[19]

In this stage of psychosexual development, linguistically constituted subjectivity ("I" versus "you," "he" versus "she," and syntactical relations) is superimposed upon our rhythmical, corporeal rapport with the mother. Prior to our accession to the grammatical order of language, we exist in a dyadic, semiotic world of pure sound and body rhythms, oceanically at one with our nurturer. Out of the infinite potential identities each newborn infant brings into the world, a single way of being is activated according to the way the mother behaves in oral symbiosis. The mother's style of relating communicates the unconscious significance the infant has for her. Through her body language—holding, nursing, caressing, bathing, dressing—and then through mirroring, through the image the child forms of itself as it sees itself reflected in the mother's face, especially in her eyes, the mother communicates an identity to the child. As Heinz Lichtenstein describes it, the mother "seduces the child into life," in the same way that the sun activates tropism in a plant and so shapes its form and direction.[20] Our sense of ourselves as separate beings, as "subjects," is bound up with our entry into the order of language in which speech becomes a substitute for bodily connection. The world we as children enter is always already constituted and governed by language. When we accede to the world where communication in words allows both separation and intimacy, we are relinquishing the immediacy of semiotic and corporeal rapport with our nurturer, from whom we recognize our separation.

A child reared in a family such as Bertha Pappenheim's makes her transition to speech as part of a process according to which she recognizes the father's privileged relation to the mother. In the order of language, "I" and "you" conceptualize and mark separate persons, as "she" and "he," "mother" and "father," differentiate genders and roles. Although it is usually the mother who activates an infant's capacity for speech in the oral, semiotic stage, subjectivity in the sense of being a separate, syntactical agent, a grammatical "subject," comes later in childhood, when, in the patriarchal family, the father's role is being recognized. Discovery of the father's role in the primal scene and recognition of male dominance in the social world conjoin with the integration of the patriarchal child into the systematic organization of language. The interlocking of linguistic with cultural rules suggests an equation between the organization of language and the systematic organization of patriarchal culture and its sexually differentiated, oedipal subjectivity. In patriarchal socialization, the power to formulate sentences coincides developmentally with a recognition of the power of the father.

In this light, Bertha Pappenheim's linguistic discord and conversion symptoms, her use of gibberish and gestures as means of expression, can be seen as a regression from the cultural order represented by her father as an orthodox patriarch. Bertha Pappenheim failed to speak her native language, but could be fluent in alien forms of expression. She failed to speak coherent German, but she succeeded in getting Dr. Breuer to speak her language and enter a world repressed by patriarchal consciousness. Breuer literally repeated Pappenheim's linguistic formulas; and in this way he came to an awareness of the unconscious. Bertha was twenty-one, on the brink of womanhood in a role offering little in the way of satisfaction or development of her intellectual gifts. When she looked into the mirror she saw a death's-head. Rejecting the cultural identity offered her, she tried to translate herself into another idiom. She regressed from the symbolic order of articulate German to the semiotic level of the body and the unintelligibility of foreign tongues. Her communication in signs, mutterings, and made-up jargon indicates an attempt to re-create the special semiotic babble that exists between an infant and its mother. Pappenheim reached the point of having to be fed by Breuer. She turned Breuer into a surrogate oral mother; in the sense that she took over his role as doctor, she turned him into an identity-giver as well. Her birth fantasy, which put Breuer to flight, can be read as a wish to bring a new identity and perhaps a new reality into the world.

Dr. Breuer was evidently not prepared for the idea that Pappenheim was giving birth to psychoanalysis. But he seems to have understood her situation admirably. Here is his analysis of the predisposing causes of her hysteria: "First, her monotonous family life and the absence of adequate intellectual occupation left her with an unemployed surplus of mental liveliness and energy, and this found an outlet in the constant activity of her imagination. Second, this led to a habit of daydreaming (her 'private theatre'), which laid the foundations for a dissociation of her mental personality."[21] In other words, Bertha Pappenheim was schizoid because she was bored and needed to both watch and put on shows. She was alienated, split between what Breuer began to call "the unconscious" or "secondary" state and her "normal" state. Breuer adds that although her two states were sharply separated, not only did the "secondary" (or 'hypnoid') state intrude into the first one, but also "a clear-sighted and calm observer sat, as she put it, in a corner of her brain and looked on at all the mad business." Thus, Pappenheim confessed to Breuer the persistence of clear thinking in the midst of her madness. After her conversion symptoms had ceased, and while she was passing through what Breuer called a temporary depression, Pappenheim told him that "the whole business had been simulated." He concludes:

> I have already described the astonishing fact that from the beginning to the end of the illness all the stimuli arising from the secondary state, together with their consequences, were permanently removed by being given verbal utterance in hypnosis, and I have only to add an assurance that this was not an invention of mine which I imposed on the patient by suggestion. It took me completely by surprise, and not until symptoms had been got rid of in this way in a whole series of instances did I develop a therapeutic technique out of it.[22]

Pappenheim actually treated herself, with Breuer as her student.

One may ask how it was that Bertha Pappenheim managed to achieve such a breakthrough. It seems that she was influenced by the widespread interest in catharsis that followed the publication of a book by the uncle of a friend of hers. This friend was Freud's future wife, Martha Bernays, whose uncle, Jacob Bernays, published a study of the Aristotelian concept of catharsis in 1880. Bernays's book was widely discussed by scholars and became an important topic of conversation in Viennese salons. Perhaps Pappenheim had been introduced to the concept of catharsis as a method of dramatizing and expelling emotions, and she then put it to use as a means of capturing and holding the attention of her scientifically minded physician.[23] Since women of Pappenheim's day remained outside the official cultural institutions transmitting knowledge, she was limited in her forms of discourse. She made a spectacle of herself in order to resolve the tension between her guilt and her desire to escape familial exploitation.[24] Her knowledge of the unconscious (her "clouds") was expressed in a distressed and distressing way. This knowledge had then to be *theorized* by men. She presented a startling and engaging demonstration of the psychological, affective causes of hysteria, but Dr. Breuer went away still believing in the somatic foundation of hysterical phenomena. It was left to Freud to complete the shift from physiological to psychological study and to articulate in a scientific way the central role of eros in therapeutic relationships, a major transition in the history of psychiatry.

Bertha Pappenheim invented the "talking cure" during an epoch that needed to tell itself its troubles. An important figure in the history of consciousness, she expressed in the language of the body what psychoanalysis says in words. I think we can regard her in the terms Erik H. Erikson has used to describe ideological leaders: "Individuals with an uncommon depth of conflict, they also have uncanny gifts, and uncanny luck with which they offer to the crisis of a generation the solution of their own crisis."[25]

In the process of talking herself out to Breuer, Pappenheim converted a nonverbal message, expressed in body language or pantomime and called an hysterical symptom, into a verbal language. That is, her narratives converted or translated a message from one language into another.[26] She was a psychodramatist, complete with appropriate scenic arrangements for the reproduction of crucial events; and she devised the method of narrating back piece by piece the story of each symptom to reach its source.[27] In a technique comparable to Shakespeare's in the play-within-the-play in *Hamlet*, Pappenheim put on a dumb show in distraction, muttered, and then spoke out the story behind the show. She restaged the origins of her symptoms in order to undo them. This is ritual as catharsis. Breuer said that the patient's symptoms disappeared as soon as the event which had given rise to them was reproduced in a trance, making it "possible to arrive at a therapeutic technical procedure which left nothing to be desired in its logical consistency and systematic application." Each individual symptom in her museum of "hyperaesthetic" memories was taken up separately, and the occasions on which it had appeared were described in reverse order, starting before the time when she became bedridden and going back to the event which had led to its first appearance. According to Breuer, "when this had been described the symptom was permanently removed."[28] In dramatizing her past, Pappenheim was also dramatizing the unconscious, and she was engaging her audience in an oedipal repetition in the form of Breuer's countertransference.

I have said that Pappenheim turned Breuer into a substitute oral mother, audience, and identity-giver in order to escape the crisis of cultural identity occasioned by her father's terminal illness, and I have described her as a psychodramatist who enacted the birth to consciousness of a new psychic reality. Through her clever manipulations of languages, she managed to avoid the role of dutiful orthodox daughter and find an intelligent, stimulating, and sympathetic listener. Pappenheim's entry into public life remains to be discussed.

III

She became a feminist in an epoch when women felt compelled to speak up against the abuses that paralyzed their development. In the same year that Freud and Breuer published their *Studies on Hysteria*, Pappenheim at the age of thirty-six became headmistress of an orphanage in Isenburg, Germany, near her mother's birthplace. This became the central headquarters for her forty-year career in philanthropic social work later commemorated by the West German government. She spent her life rescuing and sheltering abandoned and abused women and children. In linking the two phases of her career, Lucien Israël classifies Pappenheim as one of a number of celebrated hysterics who later led altruistic public lives, substituting themselves for a male mentor who failed them.[29] Israël analyzes such women as "successful hysterics," whom he sees as founding their vocations on a fantasy of universal love and a sense of rivalry with men. The Pappenheim case, claims Israël, demonstrates very clearly that the universal love embodied in her career as rescuer of women and children was originally directed at a specific person chosen as mentor. But the mentor, or more precisely, "master" *(maître)*, Breuer, failing to reciprocate her love, became an object of identification who was replaced by Pappenheim herself. Having discovered that the doctor is not all the patient had hoped, "successful hysterics" decide to incarnate his role as therapist, savior, "helper of humanity."

Israël's analysis overlooks the charity work tradition among Pappenheim's maternal relatives. Pappenheim chose to make Breuer the gift of her symptoms and their treatment because of what he stood for as a doctor. She chose him for a significant encounter involving issues that were bigger than both of them. Her identification with the role of savior is consistent with her status as an Eriksonian leader who forged her charisma out of her post-adolescent identity crisis, for Eriksonian ideological leaders feel that their lives must be made to count in the great historical movements of their day. The two great historical movements of Pappenheim's day were the discovery of the unconscious and the liberation of women, and she made herself heard in both of them. The range of her career as a reformer indicates that Bertha Pappenheim was "in love with activity on a large scale," a phrase Erikson adopts from Woodrow Wilson to describe the qualities of which charismatic leaders are made.[30]

The nature of Pappenheim's symptoms and their treatment connect her with several other remarkable women. Although it may be true that Pappenheim's performances for Breuer were inspired by a book she had read or heard about on catharsis, one must speculate about what currents might have been at work among her hysterical counterparts in Germany and France throughout the nineteenth century, and slightly later in Switzerland when psychoanalysis was introduced into the Burghölzli clinic in Zurich; and one must wonder what inspired Ilona Weiss to suggest the free associational method to Freud. As Henri Ellenberger observes, aspects of Pappenheim's hysteria have never been satisfactorily explained. First of all, between December 1881 and June 1882, Pappenheim's two personalities were sharply distinct, and Breuer was able to effect a shift from one to the other by holding up an orange, the food she had chiefly lived on during the previous year. While one part of Bertha existed in the present, another part relived the previous year precisely, day by day. Thanks to a diary Mrs. Pappenheim had kept, Breuer was able to verify that the events Bertha hallucinated had occurred, day by day, exactly one year earlier. Second, certain of Bertha's symptoms supposedly occurred without an incubation period and could be made to disappear simply by recalling the circumstances under which they had appeared the first time. Bertha had to recall each instance when the symptom had appeared, whatever the number, in exact chronological order, a unique feature of her treatment. These remarkable exercises in memory, and the idea of the patient dictating appropriate therapeutic procedures to the physician, although extraordinary in the 1880s in Vienna, were not unheard of in the history of medicine. Ellenberger links Pappenheim's case with the great exemplars of "magnetic illness" who achieved fame during the early part of the nineteenth century. Katharina Emmerich (1774–1824), a poor peasant and former nun from Dülmen, Westphalia, had dreams every night that followed one another in a regular sequence according to the cycle of the liturgical year, a mnemonic feat comparable to Pappenheim's hallucinations recalling each day of the previous year in exact sequence. Another subject, Friedericke Hauffe (1801–1829), "the Seeress of Prevorst," spoke frequently in an unknown language, and although uneducated and the daughter of a gamekeeper, she delivered recitatives in the purest High German instead of the Swabian dialect commonly spoken by the people around her. In her magnetic trances, the "Seeress" often prescribed treatments which unfailingly cured her exactly when predicted, just as Pappenheim predicted the date of her recovery to Breuer. Estelle L'Hardy (1825–1862), who fell ill upon her father's death, was cured of a dual personality through the dictations of a comforting angel appearing to her during "magnetic" sleep. Her doctor managed a gradual fusion of her normal and "magnetic" states by establishing an emotional rapport that challenged Estelle's dependency on her mother. Like Bertha, Estelle relied on a special relationship with her physician for her cure. Ellenberger sees Pappenheim as a kind of revenant of the "magnetic" patients who performed miraculous feats of memory, spoke in tongues, controlled the forms of their treatments, and predicted the dates of their "cures."[31] Another analogue to Bertha Pappenheim is her Parisian contemporary Blanche Wittmann, known as "queen of the hysterics" because of the impressive sculptural forms of her poses and the longevity of her tenure at the Salpêtrière hospital. The experiments with traumatic paralysis and their reproduction under hypnosis which Freud witnessed at the Salpêtrière are today regarded with skepticism, and Ellenberger concludes that Pappenheim's treatment was a clever trick. Yet her story and Charcot's séances at the Salpêtrière were major inspirations to Freud.

During her hysteria, Anna O. had taken up writing in a curious fashion. Her right hand being paralyzed, she wrote with her left hand and used Roman printed letters copied from her edition of Shakespeare. Such incorporation of foreign signifiers might have been linked to her desire for psychic integration and prefigures Pappenheim's later role as a translator. She resurrected and translated the memoirs of her ancestor Glückel of Hameln (1646–1724), who was "a born writer and storyteller." Wishing to transmit Jewish culture to a world ignorant of Yiddish, Pappenheim translated into German sagas and legends from the Talmud and Midrash, together with folk tales and *The Women's Bible*.[32] Special significance adheres to the sundry languages Pappenheim spoke in her hysteria and in later life because her use of translation as a verbal strategy reverberates in psychoanalytic preoccupation with the term and the process. Jacques Lacan, for example, calls psychotherapy the "repatriation of alienated signifiers."

Freud refers to the Anna O. case more than forty times in his collected works and frequently in his letters. The intensity of interest these references indicate suggests that she emblematized something essential for him. At the time he was working out his theory of hysteria, Freud was translating Hippolyte Bernheim and Charcot from French into German; his and Breuer's "Preliminary Communication" on the subject was immediately translated into Spanish, French, and English. Later on Freud conducted several analyses in translation, and psychoanalysis has been a multilingual movement.

Freud compared the symptomatology of hysteria to a "pictographic script which has become intelligible after the discovery of a few bilingual inscriptions."[33] Freud uses the word "translation" to discuss the work of psychoanalysis and the work of the unconscious. In the "dream-work," the latent wish is "translated" into the imagery of the manifest content of the dream. Freud writes: "The dream-thoughts and the dream-content are presented to us like two versions of the same subject-matter in two different languages. Or, more properly, the dream-content seems like a transcript of the dream-thoughts into another mode of expression, whose characters and syntactic laws it is our business to discover by comparing the original and the translation."[34] In hysteria, says Freud, psychic messages are "translated" into somatic expression. Analytic interventions he considered "translations" of the unconscious into the conscious. The "talking cure" is the "translation of affects into words." Repression for Freud was a "failure of translation." Thus the forms in which Anna O. communicated her distress and her shifts between languages to express levels of consciousness metaphorize what developed into what one may call a psychoanalytic concept of translation.[35]

Aragon and Bréton's celebration of nineteenth-century hysterics as fellow artists indicates that the surrealists recognized hysteria as an expressive discourse;[36] and we may add, it was a discourse of femininity addressed to patriarchal thought. Lucien Israël notes that the question of whether or not hysteria is an illness has received no answer. His own analysis of Bertha Pappenheim ventures close to the idea that feminism is transformed hysteria, or more precisely, that hysteria is feminism lacking a social network in the outer world. In popular culture the word "hysterical" has often been used in attempts to discredit feminist expression, for both hysterics and feminists are "out of control": neither hysterics nor feminists cooperate dutifully with patriarchal conventions. Attempts to discredit feminists as "hysterical" derive from a repressive impulse similar to the defense that creates hysterical symptoms in the first place: repudiation—of socially untoward feelings such as anger and resentment. Thus one may call hysteria a self-repudiating form of feminine discourse in which the body signifies what social conditions make it impossible to state linguistically.

Although hysteria had mainly been associated with women, Charcot and Freud demonstrated the existence of male hysteria and opened to analysis the repressed femininity of men. If we valorize hysteria as a form of making the unconscious conscious, we can call Bertha Pappenheim a forebear of psychoanalytic feminism. We note that psychoanalysis entered the history of consciousness in dialogue with feminine subjectivity, for Freud's discovery of the unconscious was a response to the body language of nineteenth-century hysterics. Thus, psychoanalysis can be read as a translation into theory of the language of hysteria.

Both psychoanalysis and hysteria subvert the reigning cultural order by exploding its linguistic conventions and decomposing its façade of orderly conduct. Both the psychoanalytic and the feminist movements have been international and interlingual. Thus the psychoanalysis of hysteria in Europe in the nineteenth century may be seen to contribute to the multi-lingualism, internationalism, and communication in translation of contemporary linguistic feminisms.[37] This theme finds its perfect metaphor in *The Dream of a Common Language*, where Adrienne Rich writes, "we are translations into different dialects/of a text still being written/in the original."[38] As a speaker in tongues and as a psychodramatist of the relationship between the body language of hysteria and psychoanalytic entrance into the history of consciousness, Anna O. represents a significant event in this unfolding multilingual text.

NOTES

1. See Marion A. Kaplan, *The Jewish Feminist Movement in Germany: The Campaign of the Judischer Frauenbund, 1904–1938* (Westport, Conn.: Greenwood Press, 1979).

2. Josef Breuer to Auguste Forel, November 21, 1907, quoted by George Pollock in "The Possible Significance of Childhood Object Loss in the Josef Breuer-Bertha Pappenheim (Anna O.)–Sigmund Freud Relationship," *Journal of the American Psychoanalytic Association* 16 (1968): 723.

3. Ernest Jones revealed Pappenheim's name. He writes: "Since she was the real discoverer of the cathartic method, her name . . . deserves to be commemorated." See *The Life and Work of Sigmund Freud*, 3 vols. (New York: Basic Books, 1953–57), 1: 223–26. But Jones's account of Pappenheim and Breuer contains errors. More accurate accounts of Pappenheim's life can be found in Dora Edinger, *Bertha Pappenheim: Freud's Anna O.* (Highland Park, Ill.: Congregation Solel, 1968); Henri Ellenberger, *The Discovery of the Unconscious* (New York: Basic Books, 1970), 480–84; Lucien Israël, *L'hystérique, le sexe, et le médecin* (Paris: Masson, 1980), 200–5; and Kaplan, *The Jewish Feminist Movement in Germany*.

4. Josef Breuer, "Fräulein Anna O.," *Studies on Hysteria*, in *Standard Edition of the Complete Works of Sigmund Freud* (hereafter *St. Ed.*), ed. and trans. James Strachey, 24 vols. (London: Hogarth Press, 1955), 2:24.

5. Ibid., 25.

6. Ann Elwood, "The Beginning of Psychoanalysis," in *The People's Almanac*, ed. David Wallechinsky and Irving Wallace (Garden City, N.Y.: Doubleday, 1975), 502. Neither Breuer nor Freud gives this sentence, although it is consistent with Breuer's description of Pappenheim's special use of languages.

7. Breuer, "Fräulein Anna O.," 25.

8. Ibid., 22.

9. Freud and Breuer, *Studies on Hysteria*, St. Ed., 2: 13.

10. See Pollock's article cited in n. 2, and another, "Pappenheim's Pathological Mourning: Possible Effects of Childhood Object Loss," *Journal of the American Psychoanalytic Association* 20 (1972): 476–93; Richard Karpe, "The Rescue Complex in Anna O.'s Final Identity," *Psychoanalytic Quarterly* 30 (1961): 1–27; and Marc Hollender, "The Case of Anna O.: A Reformulation," *American Journal of Psychiatry* 137 (July 1980): 797–800.

11. Ellen M. Jensen, "Anna O.: A Study of her Later Life," *Psychoanalytic Quarterly* 39 (1970): 277.

12. Breuer, "Fräulein Anna O.," 21.

13. In 1890 Pappenheim published a book of short stories called *In the Rummage Store*. She wrote under the pseudonym Paul Berthold, a disguise which reverses her initials and masculinizes her name.

14. Freud to Carl Jung, November 21, 1909, quoted by Pollock, "Object Loss," 732.

15. Freud, St. Ed., 14:12.

16. Reported by Sigmund Freud in a letter to Stephan Zweig, 1932, quoted by Pollock, "Object Loss," 716.

17. Jones, 1: 225.

18. Pollock, "Object Loss." In *The Story of Anna O.* (New York: Walker, 1972), Lucy Freeman recounts that the two Berthas, patient and daughter, once went for a springtime carriage ride together with Breuer. Freeman depicts Pappenheim as unresponsive during the trip and depressed afterward. See p. 26.

19. Janet Malcolm, "The Impossible Profession," *The New Yorker* 24 (November 1980): 104.

20. Heinz Lichtenstein, "Identity and Sexuality," *Journal of the American Psychoanalytic Association* 9 (1961): 179–260; D.W. Winnicott, "Mirror-role of Mother and Family in Child Development," in *The Predicament of the Family*, ed. Peter Lomas (London: Hogarth Press, 1972), 26–33.

21. Breuer, St. Ed., 2:41.

22. Ibid., 46.

23. Ellenberger, 484; Hollender, 797.

24. Compare Catherine Clément, *La Jeune Née* (Paris: Union Générale, 1975), 13, 22.

25. Erik H. Erikson, "Youth: Fidelity and Diversity," *Daedalus* 91, no. 1 (1962): 24.

26. Hollender, 798.

27. On the day Bertha Pappenheim regained her command of German, she did so by rearranging the furniture to resemble her father's sickroom. Having decided in advance that the date of her cure was at hand, Bertha reproduced on schedule the original scene when snakes appeared and she prayed in English. For this dramatic representation, she chose the anniversary of the day on which she had been moved to the country. Breuer (2:40) reports that this ritual freed Bertha from "innumerable disturbances."

28. Breuer, 2:35.

29. Israël, 204–5. Israël cites Mary Baker Eddy and several of Pierre Janet's patients as other examples; he states that a public career as a savior is one possible evolution of hysteria.

30. Erikson, 24.

31. Ellenberger, 484.

32. Jensen, 288.

33. Freud, *St. Ed.*, 2:129.

34. Freud, *The Interpretation of Dreams*, *St. Ed.*, 4:277.

35. In "Freud's Psychoanalytical Concept of Translation," a paper delivered at the Congress of the International Association for Semiotic Studies held in Vienna, July 1979, Patrick J. Mahony discussed the recurrence in psychoanalysis of the idea of translation. See Mahony's "Toward the Understanding of Translation in Psychoanalysis," *Journal of the American Psychoanalytic Association* 28, no. 2 (1980): 461–75.

36. Louis Aragon and André Bréton, "Le Cinquantenaire de L'Hystérie, 1878–1928," *La Révolution surréaliste*, no. 11 (1928): 20–22.

37. Anna O.'s attempt to change her world through manipulation of language on the level of the signifiers, as if language were omnipotent, prefigures some of the strategies of Mary Daly and certain contemporary French writers. See the Index of New Words in Daly's *Gyn/Ecology: The Metaethics of Radical Feminism* (Boston: Beacon Press, 1978); and the issue of *Les Cahiers du Grif* entitled "parlez-vous française?" (vol. 12, June 1976, published in Paris and Brussels.) This volume, which includes articles by Françoise Collin, Luce Irigaray, Jacqueline Aubenas et al., proposes various spoken and written languages of the female body and some ways of feminizing the French language. Viviane Forrester's novel *Vestiges* (Paris:

Seuil, 1978) is written in French and English. Hélène Cixous's *vivre l'orange* (Paris: des femmes, 1979), written in French and English, incorporates Brazilian, Italian, and German. Pappenheim's polylingualism prefigures the explosion of the conventions of language in contemporary feminist writing.

38. Adrienne Rich, "Sibling Mysteries," *The Dream of a Common Language* (New York: Norton, 1978), 51.

16

Uses of the Erotic

THE EROTIC AS POWER

Audre Lorde

There are many kinds of power, used and unused, acknowledged or otherwise. The erotic is a resource within each of us that lies in a deeply female and spiritual plane, firmly rooted in the power of our unexpressed or unrecognized feeling. In order to perpetuate itself, every oppression must corrupt or distort those various sources of power within the culture of the oppressed that can provide energy for change. For women, this has meant a suppression of the erotic as a considered source of power and information within our lives.

We have been taught to suspect this resource, vilified, abused, and devalued within Western society. On the one hand, the superficially erotic has been encouraged as a sign of female inferiority; on the other hand, women have been made to suffer and to feel both contemptible and suspect by virtue of its existence.

It is a short step from there to the false belief

Audre Lorde, "Uses of the Erotic." From *Sister Outsider*, © 1984 by Audre Lorde, The Crossing Press, Freedom, California, and reprinted by permission of the publisher.

that only by the suppression of the erotic within our lives and consciousness can women be truly strong. But that strength is illusory, for it is fashioned within the context of male models of power.

As women, we have come to distrust that power which rises from our deepest and nonrational knowledge. We have been warned against it all our lives by the male world, which values this depth of feeling enough to keep women around in order to exercise it in the service of men, but which fears this same depth too much to examine the possibilities of it within themselves. So women are maintained at a distant/inferior position to be psychically milked, much the same way ants maintain colonies of aphids to provide a life-giving substance for their masters.

But the erotic offers a well of replenishing and provocative force to the woman who does not fear its revelation, nor succumb to the belief that sensation is enough.

The erotic has often been misnamed by men and used against women. It has been made into the confused, the trivial, the psychotic, the plasticized sensation. For this reason, we have often turned away from the exploration and consideration of the erotic as a source of power and information, confusing it with its opposite, the pornographic. But pornography is a direct denial of the power of the erotic, for it represents the suppression of true feeling. Pornography emphasizes sensation without feeling.

The erotic is a measure between the beginnings of our sense of self and the chaos of our strongest feelings. It is an internal sense of satisfaction to which, once we have experienced it, we know we can aspire. For having experienced the fullness of this depth of feeling and recognizing its power, in honor and self-respect we can require no less of ourselves.

It is never easy to demand the most from ourselves, from our lives, from our work. To encourage excellence is to go beyond the encouraged mediocrity of our society. But giving in to the fear of feeling and working to capacity is a luxury only the unintentional can afford, and the unintentional are those who do not wish to guide their own destinies.

This internal requirement toward excellence which we learn from the erotic must not be misconstrued as demanding the impossible from ourselves nor from others. Such a demand incapacitates everyone in the process. For the erotic is not a question only of what we do; it is a question of how acutely and fully we can feel in the doing. Once we know the extent to which we are capable of feeling that sense of satisfaction and completion, we can then observe which of our various life endeavors bring us closest to that fullness.

The aim of each thing which we do is to make our lives and the lives of artistic?

our children richer and more possible. Within the celebration of the erotic in all our endeavors, my work becomes a conscious decision—a longed-for bed which I enter gratefully and from which I rise up empowered.

Of course, women so empowered are dangerous. So we are taught to separate the erotic demand from most vital areas of our lives other than sex. And the lack of concern for the erotic root and satisfactions of our work is felt in our disaffection from so much of what we do. For instance, how often do we truly love our work even at its most difficult?

The principal horror of any system which defines the good in terms of profit rather than in terms of human need, or which defines human need to the exclusion of the psychic and emotional components of that need—the principal horror of such a system is that it robs our work of its erotic value, its erotic power and life appeal and fulfillment. Such a system reduces work to a travesty of necessities, a duty by which we earn bread or oblivion for ourselves and those we love. But this is tantamount to blinding a painter and then telling her to improve her work, and to enjoy the act of painting. It is not only next to impossible, it is also profoundly cruel.

As women, we need to examine the ways in which our world can be truly different. I am speaking here of the necessity for reassessing the quality of all the aspects of our lives and of our work, and of how we move toward and through them.

The very word "erotic" comes from the Greek word *eros*, the personification of love in all its aspects—born of Chaos, and personifying creative power and harmony. When I speak of the erotic, then, I speak of it as an assertion of the lifeforce of women; of that creative energy empowered, the knowledge and use of which we are now reclaiming in our language, our history, our dancing, our loving, our work, our lives.

There are frequent attempts to equate pornography and eroticism, two diametrically opposed uses of the sexual. Because of these attempts, it has become fashionable to separate the spiritual (psychic and emotional) from the political, to see them as contradictory or antithetical. "What do you mean, a poetic revolutionary, a meditating gunrunner?" In the same way, we have attempted to separate the spiritual and the erotic, thereby reducing the spiritual to a world of flattened affect, a world of the ascetic who aspires to feel nothing. But nothing is farther from the truth. For the ascetic position is one of the highest fear, the gravest immobility. The severe abstinence of the ascetic becomes the ruling obsession. And it is one not of self-discipline but of self-abnegation.

Capacity for feeling (280) self-actualization
and erotic = self awareness?

The dichotomy between the spiritual and the political is also false, resulting from an incomplete attention to our erotic knowledge. For the bridge which connects them is formed by the erotic—the sensual—those physical, emotional, and psychic expressions of what is deepest and strongest and richest within each of us, being shared: the passions of love, in its deepest meanings.

Beyond the superficial, the considered phrase, "It feels right to me," acknowledges the strength of the erotic into a true knowledge, for what that means is the first and most powerful guiding light toward any understanding. And understanding is a handmaiden which can only wait upon, or clarify, that knowledge, deeply born. The erotic is the nurturer or nursemaid of all our deepest knowledge.

The erotic functions for me in several ways, and the first is in providing the power which comes from sharing deeply any pursuit with another person. The sharing of joy, whether physical, emotional, psychic, or intellectual, forms a bridge between the sharers which can be the basis for understanding much of what is not shared between them, and lessens the threat of their difference.

Another important way in which the erotic connection functions is the open and fearless underlining of my capacity for joy. In the way my body stretches to music and opens into response, hearkening to its deepest rhythms, so every level upon which I sense also opens to the erotically satisfying experience, whether it is dancing, building a bookcase, writing a poem, examining an idea.

That self-connection shared is a measure of the joy which I know myself to be capable of feeling, a reminder of my capacity for feeling. And that deep and irreplaceable knowledge of my capacity for joy comes to demand from all of my life that it be lived within the knowledge that such satisfaction is possible, and does not have to be called *marriage*, nor *god*, nor *an afterlife*.

This is one reason why the erotic is so feared, and so often relegated to the bedroom alone, when it is recognized at all. For once we begin to feel deeply all the aspects of our lives, we begin to demand from ourselves and from our life-pursuits that they feel in accordance with that joy which we know ourselves to be capable of. Our erotic knowledge empowers us, becomes a lens through which we scrutinize all aspects of our existence, forcing us to evaluate those aspects honestly in terms of their relative meaning within our lives. And this is a grave responsibility, projected from within each of us, not to settle for the convenient, the shoddy, the conventionally expected, nor the merely safe.

During World War II, we bought sealed plastic packets of white, uncolored margarine, with a tiny, intense pellet of yellow coloring perched like a topaz just inside the clear skin of the bag. We would leave the margarine out for a while to soften, and then we would pinch the little pellet to break it inside the bag, releasing the rich yellowness into the soft pale mass of margarine. Then taking it carefully between our fingers, we would knead it gently back and forth, over and over, until the color had spread throughout the whole pound bag of margarine, thoroughly coloring it.

I find the erotic such a kernel within myself. When released from its intense and constrained pellet, it flows through and colors my life with a kind of energy that heightens and sensitizes and strengthens all my experience.

We have been raised to fear the *yes* within ourselves, our deepest cravings. But, once recognized, those which do not enhance our future lose their power and can be altered. The fear of our desires keeps them suspect and indiscriminately powerful, for to suppress any truth is to give it strength beyond endurance. The fear that we cannot grow beyond whatever distortions we may find within ourselves keeps us docile and loyal and obedient, externally defined, and leads us to accept many facets of our oppression as women.

When we live outside ourselves, and by that I mean on external directives only rather than from our internal knowledge and needs, when we live away from those erotic guides from within ourselves, then our lives are limited by external and alien forms, and we conform to the needs of a structure that is not based on human need, let alone an individual's. But when we begin to live from within outward, in touch with the power of the erotic within ourselves, and allowing that power to inform and illuminate our actions upon the world around us, then we begin to be responsible to ourselves in the deepest sense. For as we begin to recognize our deepest feelings, we begin to give up, of necessity, being satisfied with suffering and self-negation, and with the numbness which so often seems like their only alternative in our society. Our acts against oppression become integral with self, motivated and empowered from within.

In touch with the erotic, I become less willing to accept powerlessness, or those other supplied states of being which are not native to me, such as resignation, despair, self-effacement, depression, self-denial.

And yes, there is a hierarchy. There is a difference between painting a back fence and writing a poem, but only one of quantity. And there is, for me, no difference between writing a good poem and moving into sunlight against the body of a woman I love.

This brings me to the last consideration of the erotic. To share the power of each other's feelings is different from using another's feelings as we would use a kleenex. When we look the other way from our experience, erotic or otherwise, we use rather than share the feelings of those others who participate in the experience with us. And use without consent of the used is abuse.

In order to be utilized, our erotic feelings must be recognized. The need for sharing deep feeling is a human need. But within the European-American tradition, this need is satisfied by certain proscribed erotic comings-together. These occasions are almost always characterized by a simultaneous looking away, a pretense of calling them something else, whether a religion, a fit, mob violence, or even playing doctor. And this misnaming of the need and the deed give rise to that distortion which results in pornography and obscenity—the abuse of feeling.

When we look away from the importance of the erotic in the development and sustenance of our power, or when we look away from ourselves as we satisfy our erotic needs in concert with others, we use each other as objects of satisfaction rather than share our joy in the satisfying, rather than make connection with our similarities and our differences. To refuse to be conscious of what we are feeling at any time, however comfortable that might seem, is to deny a large part of the experience, and to allow ourselves to be reduced to the pornographic, the abused, and the absurd.

The erotic cannot be felt secondhand. As a Black lesbian feminist, I have a particular feeling, knowledge, and understanding for those sisters with whom I have danced hard, played, or even fought. This deep participation has often been the forerunner for joint concerted actions not possible before.

But this erotic charge is not easily shared by women who continue to operate under an exclusively European-American male tradition. I know it was not available to me when I was trying to adapt my consciousness to this mode of living and sensation.

Only now, I find more and more women-identified women brave enough to risk sharing the erotic's electrical charge without having to look away, and without distorting the enormously powerful and creative nature of that exchange. Recognizing the power of the erotic within our lives can give us the energy to pursue genuine change within our world, rather than merely settling for a shift of characters in the same weary drama.

For not only do we touch our most profoundly creative source, but we do that which is female and self-affirming in the face of a racist, patriarchal, and antierotic society.

17

The Persistence of Vision

Donna Haraway

I would like to proceed by placing metaphorical reliance on a much maligned sensory system in feminist discourse: vision.[1] Vision can be good for avoiding binary oppositions. I would like to insist on the embodied nature of all vision and so reclaim the sensory system that has been used to signify a leap out of the marked body and into a conquering gaze from nowhere. This is the gaze that mythically inscribes all the marked bodies, that makes the unmarked category claim the power to see and not be seen, to represent while escaping representation. This gaze signifies the unmarked positions of Man and White, one of the many nasty tones of the word "objectivity" to feminist ears in scientific and technological, late-industrial, militarized, racist, and male-dominant societies, that is, here, in the belly of

Donna Haraway, "The Persistence of Vision" is an excerpt from "Situated Knowledges: The Science Question in Feminism and the Privilege of Partial Perspective," which appeared in *Feminist Studies*, 14, no. 3 (Fall 1988): 579–99, and is reprinted by permission of the publisher, *Feminist Studies*, Inc., c/o Women's Studies Program, University of Maryland, College Park, MD 20742.

the monster, in the United States in the late 1980s. I would like a doctrine of embodied objectivity that accommodates paradoxical and critical feminist science projects: Feminist objectivity means quite simply *situated knowledges*.

The eyes have been used to signify a perverse capacity—honed to perfection in the history of science tied to militarism, capitalism, colonialism, and male supremacy—to distance the knowing subject from everybody and everything in the interests of unfettered power. The instruments of visualization in multinationalist, postmodernist culture have compounded these meanings of disembodiment. The visualizing technologies are without apparent limit. The eye of any ordinary primate like us can be endlessly enhanced by sonography systems, magnetic resonance imaging, artificial intelligence-linked graphic manipulation systems, scanning electron microscopes, computed tomography scanners, color-enhancement techniques, satellite surveillance systems, home and office video display terminals, cameras for every purpose from filming the mucous membrane lining the gut cavity of a marine worm living in the vent gases on a fault between continental plates to mapping a planetary hemisphere elsewhere in the solar system. Vision in this technological feast becomes unregulated gluttony; all seems not just mythically about the god trick of seeing everything from nowhere, but to have put the myth into ordinary practice. And like the god trick, this eye fucks the world to make technomonsters. Zoe Sofoulis calls this the cannibaleye of masculinist extraterrestrial projects for excremental second birthing.

A tribute to this ideology of direct, devouring, generative, and unrestricted vision, whose technological mediations are simultaneously celebrated and presented as utterly transparent, can be found in the volume celebrating the one hundredth anniversary of the National Geographic Society. The volume closes its survey of the magazine's quest literature, effected through its amazing photography, with two juxtaposed chapters. The first is on "Space," introduced by the epigraph, "The choice is the universe—or nothing."[2] This chapter recounts the exploits of the space race and displays the color-enhanced "snapshots" of the outer planets reassembled from digitalized signals transmitted across vast space to let the viewer "experience" the moment of discovery in immediate vision of the "object."[3] These fabulous objects come to us simultaneously as indubitable recordings of what is simply there and as heroic feats of technoscientific production. The next chapter, is the twin of outer space: "Inner Space," introduced by the epigraph, "The stuff of stars has come alive."[4] Here, the reader is brought into the realm of the infinitesimal, objectified by means of radiation outside the

objectivity sort of a cypher is it a goal
or a means to an end in science?

wave lengths that are "normally" perceived by hominid primates, that is, the beams of lasers and scanning electron microscopes, whose signals are processed into the wonderful full-color snapshots of defending T cells and invading viruses.

But, of course, that view of infinite vision is an illusion, a god trick. I would like to suggest how our insisting metaphorically on the particularity and embodiment of all vision (although not necessarily organic embodiment and including technological mediation), and not giving in to the tempting myths of vision as a route to disembodiment and second-birthing allows us to construct a usable, but not an innocent, doctrine of objectivity. I want a feminist writing of the body that metaphorically emphasizes vision again, because we need to reclaim that sense to find our way through all the visualizing tricks and powers of modern sciences and technologies that have transformed the objectivity debates. We need to learn in our bodies, endowed with primate color and stereoscopic vision, how to attach the objective to our theoretical and political scanners in order to name where we are and are not, in dimensions of mental and physical space we hardly know how to name. So, not so perversely, objectivity turns out to be about particular and specific embodiment and definitely not about the false vision promising transcendence of all limits and responsibility. The moral is simple: only partial perspective promises objective vision. All Western cultural narratives about objectivity are allegories of the ideologies governing the relations of what we call mind and body, distance and responsibility. Feminist objectivity is about limited location and situated knowledge, not about transcendence and splitting of subject and object. It allows us to become answerable for what we learn how to see.

These are lessons that I learned in part walking with my dogs and wondering how the world looks without a fovea and very few retinal cells for color vision but with a huge neural processing and sensory area for smells. It is a lesson available from photographs of how the world looks to the compound eyes of an insect or even from the camera eye of a spy satellite or the digitally transmitted signals of space probe-perceived differences "near" Jupiter that have been transformed into coffee table color photographs. The "eyes" made available in modern technological sciences shatter any idea of passive vision; these prosthetic devices show us that all eyes, including our own organic ones, are active perceptual systems, building on translations and specific *ways* of seeing, that is, ways of life. There is no unmediated photograph or passive camera obscura in scientific accounts of bodies and machines; there are only highly specific visual possibilities, each with a wonderfully detailed, active, partial way of organizing worlds. All these pictures of the world should not be allegories of infinite mobility and interchangeability but of elaborate specificity and difference and the loving care people might take to learn how to see faithfully from another's point of view, even when the other is our own machine. That's not alienating distance; that's a *possible* allegory for feminist versions of objectivity. Understanding how these visual systems work, technically, socially, and psychically, ought to be a way of embodying feminist objectivity.

Many currents in feminism attempt to theorize grounds for trusting especially the vantage points of the subjugated; there is good reason to believe vision is better from below the brilliant space platforms of the powerful.[5] Building on that suspicion, this essay is an argument for situated and embodied knowledges and an argument against various forms of unlocatable, and so irresponsible, knowledge claims. Irresponsible means unable to be called into account. There is a premium on establishing the capacity to see from the peripheries and the depths. But here there also lies a serious danger of romanticizing and/or appropriating the vision of the less powerful while claiming to see from their positions. To see from below is neither easily learned nor unproblematic, even if "we" "naturally" inhabit the great underground terrain of subjugated knowledges. The positionings of the subjugated are not exempt from critical reexamination, decoding, deconstruction, and interpretation; that is, from both semiological and hermeneutic modes of critical inquiry. The standpoints of the subjugated are not "innocent" positions. On the contrary, they are preferred because in principle they are least likely to allow denial of the critical and interpretive core of all knowledge. They are knowledgeable of modes of denial through repression, forgetting, and disappearing acts—ways of being nowhere while claiming to see comprehensively. The subjugated have a decent chance to be on to the god trick and all its dazzling—and, therefore, blinding—illuminations. "Subjugated" standpoints are preferred because they seem to promise more adequate, sustained, objective, transforming accounts of the world. But *how* to see from below is a problem requiring at least as much skill with bodies and language, with the mediations of vision, as the "highest" technoscientific visualizations.

Such preferred positioning is as hostile to various forms of relativism as to the most explicitly totalizing versions of claims to scientific authority. But the alternative to relativism is not totalization and single vision, which is always finally the unmarked category whose power depends on systematic narrowing and obscuring. The alternative to relativism is partial, locatable, critical knowledges sustaining the possibility of webs of connections called

both Ansaldua + Harraway - views from below

solidarity in politics and shared conversations in epistemology. Relativism is a way of being nowhere while claiming to be everywhere equally. The "equality" of positioning is a denial of responsibility and critical inquiry. Relativism is the perfect mirror twin of totalization in the ideologies of objectivity; both deny the stakes in location, embodiment, and partial perspective; both make it impossible to see well. Relativism and totalization are both "god tricks" promising vision from everywhere and nowhere equally and fully, common myths in rhetorics surrounding Science. But it is precisely in the politics and epistemology of partial perspectives that the possibility of sustained, rational, objective inquiry rests.

So, with many other feminists, I want to argue for a doctrine and practice of objectivity that privileges contestation, deconstruction, passionate construction, webbed connections, and hope for transformation of systems of knowledge and ways of seeing. But not just any partial perspective will do; we must be hostile to easy relativisms and holisms built out of summing and subsuming parts. "Passionate detachment"[6] requires more than acknowledged and self-critical partiality. We are also bound to seek perspective from those points of view, which can never be known in advance, that promise something quite extraordinary, that is, knowledge potent for constructing worlds less organized by axes of domination. From such a viewpoint, the unmarked category would *really* disappear—quite a difference from simply repeating a disappearing act. The imaginary and the rational—the visionary and objective vision—hover close together. I think Harding's plea for a successor science and for postmodern sensibilities must be read as an argument for the idea that the fantastic element of hope for transformative knowledge and the severe check and stimulus of sustained critical inquiry are jointly the ground of any believable claim to objectivity or rationality not riddled with breathtaking denials and repressions. It is even possible to read the record of scientific revolutions in terms of this feminist doctrine of rationality and objectivity. Science has been utopian and visionary from the start; that is one reason "we" need it.

A commitment to mobile positioning and to passionate detachment is dependent on the impossibility of entertaining innocent "identity" politics and epistemologies as strategies for seeing from the standpoints of the subjugated in order to see well. One cannot "be" either a cell or molecule—or a woman, colonized person, laborer, and so on—if one intends to see and see from these positions critically. "Being" is much more problematic and contingent. Also, one cannot relocate in any possible vantage point without being accountable for that movement. Vision is *always* a question of the power to see—and perhaps of the violence implicit in our visualizing practices. With whose blood were my eyes crafted? These points also apply to testimony from the position of "oneself." We are not immediately present to ourselves. Self-knowledge requires a semiotic-material technology to link meanings and bodies. Self-identity is a bad visual system. Fusion is a bad strategy of positioning. The boys in the human sciences have called this doubt about self-presence the "death of the subject" defined as a single ordering point of will and consciousness. That judgment seems bizarre to me. I prefer to call this doubt the opening of nonisomorphic subjects, agents, and territories of stories unimaginable from the vantage point of the cyclopean, self-satiated eye of the master subject. The Western eye has fundamentally been a wandering eye, a traveling lens. These peregrinations have often been violent and insistent on having mirrors for a conquering self—but not always. Western feminists also *inherit* some skill in learning to participate in revisualizing worlds turned upside down in earth-transforming challenges to the views of the masters. All is not to be done from scratch.

The split and contradictory self is the one who can interrogate positionings and be accountable, the one who can construct and join rational conversations and fantastic imaginings that change history.[7] Splitting, not being, is the privileged image for feminist epistemologies of scientific knowledge. "Splitting" in this context should be about heterogeneous multiplicities that are simultaneously salient and incapable of being squashed into isomorphic slots or cumulative lists. This geometry pertains within and among subjects. Subjectivity is multidimensional; so, therefore, is vision. The knowing self is partial in all its guises, never finished, whole, simply there and original; it is always constructed and stitched together imperfectly, and *therefore* able to join with another, to see together without claiming to be another. Here is the promise of objectivity: a scientific knower seeks the subject position, not of identity but of objectivity, that is, partial connection. There is no way to "be" simultaneously in all, or wholly in any, of the privileged (i.e., subjugated) positions structured by gender, race, nation, and class. And that is a short list of critical positions. The search for such a "full" and total position is the search for the fetishized perfect subject of oppositional history, sometimes appearing in feminist theory as the essentialized Third World Woman.[8] Subjugation is not grounds for an ontology; it might be a visual clue. Vision requires instruments of vision; an optics is a politics of positioning. Instruments of vision mediate standpoints; there is no immediate vision from the standpoints of the subjugated. Identity, including self-identity, does not produce science; critical positioning does, that is, objectivity. Only those occupying

how to be the subject

recuping the split subject.   exploding metaphor of vision we open up delis a rational the positions of the dominators are self-identical, unmarked, disembodied, unmediated, transcendent, born again. It is unfortunately possible for the subjugated to lust for and even scramble into that subject position—and then disappear from view. Knowledge from the point of view of the unmarked is truly fantastic, distorted, and irrational. The only position from which objectivity could not possibly be practiced and honored is the standpoint of the master, the Man, the One God, whose Eye produces, appropriates, and orders all difference. No one ever accused the God of monotheism of objectivity, only of indifference. The god trick is self-identical, and we have mistaken that for creativity and knowledge, omniscience even.

Positioning is, therefore, the key practice in grounding knowledge organized around the imagery of vision, and much Western scientific and philosophic discourse is organized in this way. Positioning implies responsibility for our enabling practices. It follows that politics and ethics ground struggles for and contests over what may count as rational knowledge. That is, admitted or not, politics and ethics ground struggles over knowledge projects in the exact, natural, social, and human sciences. Otherwise, rationality is simply impossible, an optical illusion projected from nowhere comprehensively. Histories of science may be powerfully told as histories of the technologies. These technologies are ways of life, social orders, practices of visualization. Technologies are skilled practices. How to see? Where to see from? What limits to vision? What to see for? Whom to see with? Who gets to have more than one point of view? Who gets blinded? Who wears blinders? Who interprets the visual field? What other sensory powers do we wish to cultivate besides vision? Moral and political discourse should be the paradigm for rational discourse about the imagery and technologies of vision. Sandra Harding's claim, or observation, that movements of social revolution have most contributed to improvements in science might be read as a claim about the knowledge consequences of new technologies of positioning. But I wish Harding had spent more time remembering that social and scientific revolutions have not always been liberatory, even if they have always been visionary. Perhaps this point could be captured in another phrase: the science question in the military. Struggles over what will count as rational accounts of the world are struggles over *how* to see. The terms of vision: the science question in colonialism, the science question in exterminism,[9] the science question in feminism.

The issue in politically engaged attacks on various empiricisms, reductionisms, or other versions of scientific authority should not be relativism—but location. A dichotomous chart expressing this point might look like this:

universal rationality	ethnophilosophies
common language	heteroglossia
new organon	deconstruction
unified field theory	oppositional positioning
world system	local knowledges
master theory	webbed accounts

But a dichotomous chart misrepresents in a critical way the positions of embodied objectivity that I am trying to sketch. The primary distortion is the illusion of symmetry in the chart's dichotomy, making any position appear, first, simply alternative and, second, mutually exclusive. A map of tensions and reasonances between the fixed ends of a charged dichotomy better represents the potent politics and epistemologies of embodied, therefore accountable, objectivity. For example, local knowledges have also to be in tension with the productive structurings that force unequal translations and exchanges—material and semiotic—within the webs of knowledge and power. Webs *can* have the property of being systematic, even of being centrally structured global systems with deep filaments and tenacious tendrils into time, space, and consciousness, which are the dimensions of world history. Feminist accountability requires a knowledge tuned to reasonance, not to dichotomy. Gender is a field of structured and structuring difference, in which the tones of extreme localization, of the intimately personal and individualized body, vibrate in the same field with global high-tension emissions. Feminist embodiment, then, is not about fixed location in a reified body, female or otherwise, but about nodes in fields, inflections in orientations, and responsibility for difference in material-semiotic fields of meaning. Embodiment is significant prosthesis; objectivity cannot be about fixed vision when what counts as an object is precisely what world history turns out to be about.

How should one be positioned in order to see, in this situation of tensions, reasonances, transformations, resistances, and complicities? Here, primate vision is not immediately a very powerful metaphor or technology for feminist political-epistemological clarification, because it seems to present to consciousness already processed and objectified fields; things seem already fixed and distanced. But the visual metaphor allows one to go beyond fixed appearances, which are only the end products. The metaphor invites us to investigate the varied apparatuses of visual production, including the prosthetic technologies interfaced with our biological eyes and brains. And here we find highly particular machineries for processing regions of the electromagnetic spectrum into our pictures of the world. It is in the intricacies of these visualization technologies in which we are embedded that we will find metaphors and means for understanding and intervening in the patterns of objectification in the world—that is, the patterns of reality for which we must be accountable. In these metaphors, we find means for appreciating simultaneously *both* the concrete, "real" aspect and the aspect of semiosis and production in what we call scientific knowledge.

I am arguing for politics and epistemologies of location, positioning, and situating, where partiality and not universality is the condition of being heard to make rational knowledge claims. These are claims on people's lives. I am arguing for the view from a body, always a complex, contradictory, structuring, and structured body, versus the view from above, from nowhere, from simplicity. Only the god trick is forbidden. Here is a criterion for deciding the science question in militarism, that dream science/technology of perfect language, perfect communication, final order.

Feminism loves another science: the sciences and politics of interpretation, translation, stuttering, and the partly understood. Feminism is about the sciences of the multiple subject with (at least) double vision. Feminism is about a critical vision consequent upon a critical positioning in unhomogeneous gendered social space.[10] Translation is always interpretive, critical, and partial. Here is a ground for conversation, rationality, and objectivity—which is power-sensitive, not pluralist, "conversation." It is not even the mythic cartoons of physics and mathematics—incorrectly caricatured in antiscience ideology as exact, hypersimple knowledges—that have come to represent the hostile other to feminist paradigmatic models of scientific knowledge, but the dreams of the perfectly known in high-technology, permanently militarized scientific productions and positionings, the god trick of a Star Wars paradigm of rational knowledge. So location is about vulnerability; location resists the politics of closure, finality, or to borrow from Althusser, feminist objectivity resists "simplification in the last instance." That is because feminist embodiment resists fixation and is insatiably curious about the webs of differential positioning. There is no single feminist standpoint because our maps require too many dimensions for that metaphor to ground our visions. But the feminist standpoint theorists' goal of an epistemology and politics of engaged, accountable positioning remains eminently potent. The goal is better accounts of the world, that is, "science."

Above all, rational knowledge does not pretend to disengagement: to be from everywhere and so nowhere, to be free from interpretation, from being represented, to be fully self-contained or fully formalizable. Rational knowledge is a process of ongoing critical interpretation among "fields" of interpreters and decoders. Rational knowledge is power-sensitive conversation.[11] Decoding and transcoding plus translation and criticism; all are necessary. So science becomes the paradigmatic model, not of closure but of that which is contestable and contested. Science becomes the myth, not of what escapes human agency and responsibility in a realm above the fray but, rather, of accountability and responsibility for translations and solidarities linking the cacophonous visions and visionary voices that characterize the knowledges of the subjugated. A splitting of senses, a confusion of voice and sight, rather than clear and distinct ideas, becomes the metaphor for the ground of the rational. We seek not the knowledges ruled by phallogocentrism (nostalgia for the presence of the one true Word) and disembodied vision. We seek those ruled by partial sight and limited voice—not partiality for its own sake but, rather, for the sake of the connections and unexpected openings situated knowledges make possible. Situated knowledges are about communities, not about isolated individuals. The only way to find a larger vision is to be somewhere in particular. The science question in feminism is about objectivity as positioned rationality. Its images are not the products of escape and transcendence of limits (the view from above) but the joining of partial views and halting voices into a collective subject position that promises a vision of the means of ongoing finite embodiment, of living within limits and contradictions—of views from somewhere.

NOTES

This essay originated as a commentary on Sandra Harding's *The Science Question in Feminism*, at the Western Division meetings of the American Philosophical Association, San Francisco, March 1987. Support during the writing of this paper was generously provided by the Alpha Fund of the Institute for Advanced Study, Princeton, New Jersey. Thanks especially to Joan Scott, Judy Butler, Lila Abu-Lughod, and Dorinne Kondo.

1. John Varley's science fiction short story, "The Persistence of Vision," in *The Persistence of Vision* (New York: Dell, 1978), pp. 263–316, is part of the inspiration for this section. In the story, Varley constructs a utopian community designed and built by the deaf-blind. He then explores these people's technologies and other mediations of communication and their relations to sighted children and visitors. In the

story, "Blue Champagne," in *Blue Champagne* (New York: Berkeley, 1986), pp. 17–79,
Varley transmutes the theme to interrogate the politics of intimacy and technology
for a paraplegic young woman whose prosthetic device, the golden gypsy, allows her
full mobility. But because the infinitely costly device is owned by an intergalactic
communications and entertainment empire, for which she works as a media star
making "feelies," she may keep her technological, intimate, enabling, other self only
in exchange for her complicity in the commodification of all experience. What are
her limits to the reinvention of experience for sale? Is the personal political under
the sign of simulation? One way to read Varley's repeated investigations of finally
always limited embodiments, differently abled beings, prosthetic technologies, and
cyborgian encounters with their finitude, despite their extraordinary transcendence
of "organic" orders, is to find an allegory for the personal and political in the historical mythic time of the late twentieth century, the era of techno-biopolitics.
Prosthesis becomes a fundamental category for understanding our most intimate
selves. Prosthesis is semiosis, the making of meanings and bodies, not for transcendence but for power-charged communication.

[margin note: good ques.]

2. C. D. B Bryan, *The National Geographic Society: 100 Years of Adventure and
Discovery* (New York: Abrams, 1987), p. 352.

3. I owe my understanding of the experience of these photographs to Jim
Clifford, University of California at Santa Cruz, who identified their "land ho!"
effect on the reader.

4. Bryan, p. 454.

5. See Nancy Hartsock, "The Feminist Standpoint: Developing the Ground for
a Specifically Feminist Historical Materialism"; and Chela Sandoval, *Yours in Struggle:
Women Respond to Racism* (Oakland: Center for Third World Organizing, n.d.);
Harding; and Gloria Anzaldúa, *Borderlands/La Frontera* (San Francisco:
Spinsters/Aunt Lute, 1987).

6. Annette Kuhn, *Women's Pictures: Feminism and Cinema* (London: Routledge and
Kegan Paul, 1982), pp. 3–18.

7. Joan Scott reminded me that Teresa de Lauretis put it like this:

Differences among women may be better understood as differences within
women. . . . But once understood in their constitutive power—once it is
understood, that is, that these differences not only constitute each woman's
consciousness and subjective limits but all together define the *female subject of
feminism* in its very specificity, its inherent and at least for now irreconcilable
contradiction—these differences, then, cannot be again collapsed into a fixed
identity, a sameness of all women as Woman, or a representation of Feminism
as a coherent and available image.

See Theresa de Lauretis, "Feminist Studies/Critical Studies: Issues, Terms, and Contexts," in her *Feminist Studies/Critical Studies* (Bloomington: Indiana University Press, 1986), pp. 14–15.

8. Chandra Mohanty, "Under Western Eyes," *Boundary* 2 and 3 (1984): 333–58.

9. See Zoe Sofoulis, unpublished manuscript.

10. In *The Science Question in Feminism* (p. 18), Harding suggests that gender has three dimensions, each historically specific: gender symbolism, the social-sexual division of labor, and processes of constructing individual gendered identity. I would enlarge her point to note that there is no reason to expect the three dimensions to covary or codetermine each other, at least not directly. That is, extremely steep gradients between contrasting terms in gender symbolism may very well not correlate with sharp social-sexual divisions of labor or social power, but they may be closely related to sharp racial stratification or something else. Similarly, the processes of gendered subject formation may not be directly illuminated by knowledge of the sexual division of labor or the gender symbolism in the particular historical situation under examination. On the other hand, we should expect mediated relations among the dimensions. The mediations might move through quite different social axes of organization of both symbols, practice, and identity, such as race—and vice versa. I would suggest also that science, as well as gender or race, might be usefully broken up into such a multipart scheme of symbolism, social practice, and subject position. More than three dimensions suggest themselves when the parallels are drawn. The different dimensions of, for example, gender, race and science might mediate relations among dimensions on a parallel chart. That is, racial divisions of labor might mediate the patterns of connection between symbolic connections and formation of individual subject positions on the science or gender chart. Or formations of gendered or racial subjectivity might mediate the relations between scientific social division of labor and scientific symbolic patterns.

The chart below begins an analysis by parallel dissections. In the chart (and in reality?), both gender and science are analytically asymmetrical; that is, each term contains and obscures a structuring hierarchicalized binary opposition, sex/gender and nature/science. Each binary opposition orders the silent term by a logic of appropriation, as resource to product, nature to culture, potential to actual. Both poles of the opposition are constructed and structure each other dialectically. Within each voiced or explicit term, further asymmetrical splittings can be excavated, as from gender, masculine to feminine, and from science, hard sciences to soft sciences. This is a point about remembering how a particular analytical tool works, willy-nilly, intended or not. The chart reflects common ideological aspects of discourse on science and gender and may help as an analytical tool to crack open mystified units like Science or Woman.

	Gender	Science
1)	symbolic system	symbolic system
2)	social division of labor (by sex, by race, etc.)	social division of labor (e.g., by craft or industrial logics)
3)	individual identity/ subject position (desiring/ desired; autonomous/relational)	individual identity/ subject position (knower/ known; scientist/other)
4)	material culture (e.g., gender paraphernalia and daily gender technologies, the narrow tracks on which sexual difference runs)	material culture (e.g., laboratories, the narrow tracks on which facts run)
5)	dialectic of construction and discovery	dialectic of construction and discovery

11. Katie King, "Canons without Innocence" (Ph.D. diss., University of California at Santa Cruz, 1987).

18

Carnal Acts

Nancy Mairs

Inviting me to speak at her small liberal-arts college during Women's Week, a young woman set me a task: "We would be pleased," she wrote, "if you could talk on how you cope with your MS disability, and also how you discovered your voice as a writer." Oh, Lord, I thought in dismay, how am I going to pull this one off? How can I yoke two such disparate subjects into a coherent presentation, without doing violence to one, or the other, or both, or myself? This is going to take some fancy footwork, and my feet scarcely carry out the basic steps, let alone anything elaborate.

To make matters worse, the assumption underlying each of her questions struck me as suspect. To ask *how* I cope with multiple sclerosis suggests that I *do* cope. Now, "to cope," *Webster's Third* tells me, is "to face or encounter and to find necessary expedients to overcome problems and difficulties." In these terms, I have to confess, I don't feel like much of a coper. I'm likely to deal with my problems and difficulties by squawking and flapping around like that hysterical chicken who was convinced the sky was falling. Never mind that in my case the sky really *is* falling. In response to a clonk on the head, regardless of its origin, one might comport oneself with a grace and courtesy I generally lack.

As for "finding" my voice, the implication is that it was at one time lost or missing. But I don't think it ever was. Ask my mother, who will tell you a little wearily that I was speaking full sentences by the time I was a year old and could never be silenced again. As for its being a writer's voice, it seems to have become one early on. Ask Mother again. At the age of eight I rewrote the Trojan War, she will say, and what Nestor was about to do to Helen at the end doesn't bear discussion in polite company.

Faced with these uncertainties, I took my own teacherly advice, something, I must confess, I don't always do. "If an idea is giving you trouble," I tell my writing students, "put it on the back burner and let it simmer while you do something else. Go to the movies. Reread a stack of old love letters. Sit in your history class and take detailed notes on the Teapot Dome scandal. If you've got your idea in mind, it will go on cooking at some level no matter what else you're doing." "I've had an idea for my documented essay on the back burner," one of my students once scribbled in her journal, "and I think it's just boiled over!"

I can't claim to have reached such a flash point. But in the weeks I've had the themes "disability" and "voice" sitting around in my head, they seem to have converged on their own, without my having to wrench them together and bind them with hoops of tough rhetoric. They *are* related, indeed interdependent, with an intimacy that has for some reason remained, until now, submerged below the surface of my attention. Forced to juxtapose them, I yank them out of the depths, a little startled to discover how they were intertwined down there out of sight. This kind of discovery can unnerve you at first. You feel like a giant hand that, pulling two swimmers out of the water, two separate heads bobbling on the iridescent swells, finds the two bodies below, legs coiled around each other, in an ecstasy of copulation. You don't quite know where to turn your eyes.

Perhaps the place to start illuminating this erotic connection between who I am and how I speak lies in history. I have known that I have multiple sclerosis for about seventeen years now, though the disease probably started long before. The hypothesis is that the disease process, in which the protective covering of the nerves in the brain and spinal cord is eaten away and replaced by scar tissue, "hard patches," is caused by an autoimmune reaction to a slow-acting virus. Research suggests that I was infected by this virus, which no one has ever seen and which therefore, technically, doesn't even "exist," between the ages of four and fifteen. In effect, living with this mysterious mechanism feels like having your present self, and the past selves it embodies, haunted by a capricious and meanspirited ghost, unseen except for its footprints, which trips you even when you're watching where you're going, knocks glassware out of your hand, squeezes the urine out of your bladder before you reach the bathroom, and weights your whole body with a weariness no amount of rest can relieve. An alien invader must be at work. But of course it's not. It's your own body. That is, it's you.

This, for me, has been the most difficult aspect of adjusting to a chronic incurable degenerative disease: the fact that it has rammed my "self" straight back into the body I had been trained to believe it could, through high-minded acts and aspirations, rise above. The Western tradition of distinguishing the body from the mind and/or the soul is so ancient as to have become part of our collective unconscious, if one is inclined to believe in such a noumenon, or at least to have become an unquestioned element in the social instruction we impose upon infants from birth, in much the same way we inculcate, without reflection, the gender distinctions "female" and "male." I *have* a body, you are likely to say if you talk about embodiment at all; you don't say, I *am* a body. A body is a separate entity possessable by the "I"; the "I" and the body aren't, as the copula would make them, grammatically indistinguishable.

To widen the rift between the self and the body, we treat our bodies as subordinates, inferior in moral status. Open association with them shames us. In fact, we treat our bodies with very much the same distance and ambivalence women have traditionally received from men in our culture. Sometimes this treatment is benevolent, even respectful, but all too often it is tainted by outright sadism. I think of the bodybuilding regimens that have become popular in the last decade or so, with the complicated vacillations they reflect between self-worship and self-degradation: joggers and aerobic dancers and weightlifters all beating their bodies into shape. "No pain, no gain," the saying goes. "Feel the burn." Bodies get treated like wayward women who have to be shown who's boss, even if it means slapping them around a little. I'm not for a moment opposing rugged exercise here. I'm simply questioning the spirit in which it is often undertaken.

Since, as Hélène Cixous points out in her essay on women and writing, "Sorties,"[1] thought has always worked "through dual, hierarchical oppositions" (p. 64), the mind/body split cannot possibly be innocent. The utterance of an "I" immediately calls into being its opposite, the "not-I," Western discourse being unequipped to conceive "that which is neither 'I' nor 'not-I,'" "that which is both 'I' and 'not-I,'" or some other permutation which language doesn't permit me to speak. The "not-I" is, by definition, other. And we've never been too fond of the other. We prefer the same. We tend to ascribe to the other those qualities we prefer not to associate with our selves: it is the hidden, the dark, the secret, the shameful. Thus, when the "I" takes possession of the body, it makes the body into an other, direct object of a transitive verb, with all the other's repudiated and potentially dangerous qualities.

At the least, then, the body had best be viewed with suspicion. And a woman's body is particularly suspect, since so much of it is in fact hidden, dark, secret, carried about on the inside where, even with the aid of a speculum, one can never perceive all of it in the plain light of day, a graspable whole. I, for one, have never understood why anyone would want to carry all that delicate stuff around on the outside. It would make you awfully anxious, I should think, put you constantly on the defensive, create a kind of siege mentality that viewed all other beings, even your own kind, as threats to be warded off with spears and guns and atomic missiles. And you'd never get to experience that inward dreaming that comes when your flesh surrounds all your treasures, holding them close, like a sturdy shuttered house. Be my personal skepticism as it may, however, as a cultural woman I bear just as much shame as any woman for my dark, enfolded secrets. Let the word for my external genitals tell the tale: my pudendum, from the Latin infinitive meaning "to be ashamed."

It's bad enough to carry your genitals like a sealed envelope bearing the cipher that, once unlocked, might loose the chaotic flood of female pleasure—*jouissance*, the French call it—upon the world-of-the-same. But I have an additional reason to feel shame for my body, less explicitly connected with its sexuality: it is a crippled body. Thus it is doubly other, not merely by the homo-sexual standards of patriarchal culture but by the standards of physical desirability erected for every body in our world. Men, who are by definition exonerated from shame in sexual terms (this doesn't mean that an individual man might not experience sexual shame, of course; remember that I'm talking in general about discourse, not folks), may—more likely must—experience bodily shame if they are crippled. I won't presume to speak about the details of their experience, however. I don't know enough. I'll just go on telling what it's like to be a crippled woman, trusting that, since we're fellow creatures who've been living together for some thousands of years now, much of my experience will resonate with theirs.

I was never a beautiful woman, and for that reason I've spent most of my life (together with probably at least 95 percent of the female population of the United States) suffering from the shame of falling short of an unattainable standard. The ideal woman of my generation was . . . perky, I think you'd say, rather than gorgeous. Blond hair pulled into a bouncing ponytail. Wide blue eyes, a turned-up nose with maybe a scattering of golden freckles across it, a small mouth with full lips over straight white teeth. Her breasts were large but well harnessed high on her chest; her tiny waist flared to hips just wide enough to give the crinolines under her circle skirt a starting outward push. In terms of personality, she was outgoing, even bubbly, not pensive or mysterious. Her milieu was the front fender of a white Corvette convertible, surrounded by teasing crewcuts, dressed in black flats, a sissy blouse, and the letter sweater of the Corvette owner. Needless to say, she never missed a prom.

Ten years or so later, when I first noticed the symptoms that would be diagnosed as MS I was probably looking my best. Not beautiful still, but the ideal had shifted enough so that my flat chest and narrow hips gave me an elegantly attenuated shape, set off by a thick mass of long, straight, shining hair. I had terrific legs, long and shapely, revealed nearly to the pudendum by the fashionable miniskirts and hot pants I adopted with more enthusiasm than delicacy of taste. Not surprisingly, I suppose, during this time I involved myself in several pretty torrid love affairs.

The beginning of MS wasn't too bad. The first symptom, besides the pernicious fatigue that had begun to devour me, was "foot drop," the inability to raise my left foot at the ankle. As a consequence, I'd started to limp, but I could still wear high heels, and a bit of a limp might seem more intriguing than repulsive. After a few months, when the doctor suggested a cane, a crippled friend gave me quite an elegant wood-and-silver one, which I carried with a fair amount of panache. The real blow to my self-image came when I had to get a brace. As braces go, it's not bad: lightweight plastic molded to my foot and leg, fitting down into an ordinary shoe and secured around my calf by a Velcro strap. It reduces my limp and, more important, the danger of tripping and falling. But it meant the end of high heels. And it's ugly. Not as ugly as I think it is, I gather, but still pretty ugly. It signified for me, and perhaps still does, the permanence and irreversibility of my condition. The brace makes my MS concrete and forces me to wear it on the outside. As soon as I strapped the brace on, I climbed into trousers and stayed there (though not in the same trousers, of course). The idea of going around with my bare brace hanging out seemed almost as indecent as exposing my breasts. Not until 1984, soon after I won the Western States Book Award for poetry, did I put on a skirt short enough to reveal my plasticized leg. The connection between winning a writing award and baring my brace is not merely fortuitous; being affirmed as a writer really did embolden me. Since then, I've grown so accustomed to wearing skirts that I don't think about my brace any more than I think about my cane. I've incorporated them, I suppose: made them, in their necessity, insensate but fundamental parts of my body.

Meanwhile, I had to adjust to the most outward and visible sign of all, a three-wheeled electric scooter called an Amigo. This lessens my fatigue and increases my range terrifically, but it also shouts out to the world, "Here is a woman who can't stand on her own two feet." At the same time, paradoxically, it renders me invisible, reducing me to the height of a seven-year-old, with a child's attendant low status. "Would she like smoking or nonsmoking?" the gate agent assigning me a seat asks the friend traveling with me. In crowds I see nothing but buttocks. I can tell you the name of every type of designer jeans ever sold. The wearers, eyes front, trip over me and fall across my handlebars into my lap. "Hey!" I want to shout to the lofty world. "Down here! There's a person down here!" But I'm not, by their standards, quite a person anymore.

My self-esteem diminishes further as age and illness strip from me the features that made me, for a brief while anyway, a good-looking, even sexy, young woman. No more long, bounding strides: I shuffle along with the timid gait I remember observing, with pity and impatience, in the little old ladies at Boston's Symphony Hall on Friday afternoons. No more lithe, girlish figure: my belly sags from the loss of muscle tone, which also creates all kinds of intestinal disruptions, hopelessly humiliating in a society in which excretory functions remain strictly unspeakable. No more sex, either, if society had its way. The sexuality of the disabled so repulses most people that you can hardly get a doctor, let alone a member of the general population, to consider the issues it raises. Cripples simply aren't supposed to Want It, much less Do It. Fortunately, I've got a husband with a strong libido and a weak sense of social propriety, or else I'd find myself perforce practicing a vow of chastity I never cared to take.

Afflicted by the general shame of having a body at all, and the specific shame of having one weakened and misshapen by disease, I ought not to be able to hold my head up in public. And yet I've gotten into the habit of holding my head up in public, sometimes under excruciating circumstances. Recently, for instance, I had to give a reading at the University of Arizona.

Having smashed three of my front teeth in a fall onto the concrete floor of my screened porch, I was in the process of getting them crowned, and the temporary crowns flew out during dinner right before the reading. What to do? I wanted, of course, to rush home and hide till the dental office opened the next morning. But I couldn't very well break my word at this last moment. So, looking like Hansel and Gretel's witch, and lisping worse than the Wife of Bath, I got up on stage and read. Somehow, over the years, I've learned how to set shame aside and do what I have to do.

Here, I think, is where my "voice" comes in. Because, in spite of my demurral at the beginning, I do in fact cope with my disability at least some of the time. And I do so, I think, by speaking about it, and about the whole experience of being a body, specifically a female body, out loud, in a clear, level tone that drowns out the frantic whispers of my mother, my grandmothers, all the other trainers of wayward childish tongues: "Sssh! Sssh! Nice girls don't talk like that. Don't mention sweat. Don't mention menstrual blood. Don't ask what your grandfather does on his business trips. Don't laugh so loud. You sound like a loon. Keep your voice down. Don't tell. Don't tell. Don't tell." Speaking out loud is an antidote to shame. I want to distinguish clearly here between "shame," as I'm using the word, and "guilt" and "embarrassment," which, though equally painful, are not similarly poisonous. Guilt arises from performing a forbidden act or failing to perform a required one. In either case, the guilty person can, through reparation, erase the offense and start fresh. Embarrassment, less opprobrious though not necessarily less distressing, is generally caused by acting in a socially stupid or awkward way. When I trip and sprawl in public, when I wet myself, when my front teeth fly out, I feel horribly embarrassed, but, like the pain of childbirth, the sensation blurs and dissolves in time. If it didn't, every child would be an only child, and no one would set foot in public after the onset of puberty, when embarrassment erupts like a geyser and bathes one's whole life in its bitter stream. Shame may attach itself to guilt or embarrassment, complicating their resolution, but it is not the same emotion. I feel guilt or embarrassment for something I've done; shame, for who I am. I may stop doing bad or stupid things, but I can't stop being. How then can I help but be ashamed? Of the three conditions, this is the one that cracks and stifles my voice.

I can subvert its power, I've found, by acknowledging who I am, shame and all, and, in doing so, raising what was hidden, dark, secret about my life into the plain light of shared human experience. What we aren't permitted to utter holds us, each isolated from every other, in a kind of solipsistic thrall.

Without any way to check our reality against anyone else's, we assume that our fears and shortcomings are ours alone. One of the strangest consequences of publishing a collection of personal essays called *Plaintext* has been the steady trickle of letters and telephone calls saying essentially, in a tone of unmistakable relief, "Oh, me too! Me too!" It's as though the part I thought was solo has turned out to be a chorus. But none of us was singing loud enough for the others to hear.

Singing loud enough demands a particular kind of voice, I think. And I was wrong to suggest, at the beginning, that I've always had my voice. I have indeed always had *a* voice, but it wasn't *this* voice, the one with which I could call up and transform my hidden self from a naughty girl into a woman talking directly to others like herself. Recently, in the process of writing a new book, a memoir entitled *Remembering the Bone House*, I've had occasion to read some of my early writing, from college, high school, even junior high. It's not an experience I recommend to anyone susceptible to shame. Not that the writing was all that bad. I was surprised at how competent a lot of it was. Here was a writer who already knew precisely how the language worked. But the voice . . . oh, the voice was all wrong: maudlin, rhapsodic, breaking here and there into little shrieks, almost, you might say, hysterical. It was a voice that had shucked off its own body, its own homely life of Cheerios for breakfast and seventy pages of Chaucer to read before the exam on Tuesday and a planter's wart growing painfully on the ball of its foot, and reeled now wraithlike through the air, seeking incarnation only as the heroine who enacts her doomed love for the tall, dark, mysterious stranger. If it didn't get that part, it wouldn't play at all.

Among all these overheated and vaporous imaginings, I must have retained some shred of sense, because I stopped writing prose entirely, except for scholarly papers, for nearly twenty years. I even forgot, not exactly that I had written prose, but at least what kind of prose it was. So when I needed to take up the process again, I could start almost fresh, using the vocal range I'd gotten used to in years of asking the waiter in the Greek restaurant for an extra anchovy on my salad, congratulating the puppy on making a puddle outside rather than inside the patio door, pondering with my daughter the vagaries of female orgasm, saying goodbye to my husband, and hello, and goodbye, and hello. This new voice—thoughtful, affectionate, often amused—was essential because what I needed to write about when I returned to prose was an attempt I'd made not long before to kill myself, and suicide simply refuses to be spoken of authentically in high-flown romantic language. It's too ugly. Too shameful. Too strictly a bodily event. And, yes, too funny as well, though people are sometimes shocked to find humor shoved up against suicide. They don't like the incongruity. But let's face it, life (real life, I mean, not the edited-for-television version) is a cacophonous affair from start to finish. I might have wanted to portray my suicidal self as a languishing maiden, too exquisitely sensitive to sustain life's wounding pressures on her soul. (I didn't want to, as a matter of fact, but I might have.) The truth remained, regardless of my desires, that when my husband lugged me into the emergency room, my hair matted, my face swollen and gray, my nightgown streaked with blood and urine, I was no frail and tender spirit. I was a body, and one in a hell of a mess.

I "should" have kept quiet about that experience. I know the rules of polite discourse. I should have kept my shame, and the nearly lethal sense of isolation and alienation it brought, to myself. And I might have, except for something the psychiatrist in the emergency room had told my husband. "You might as well take her home," he said. "If she wants to kill herself, she'll do it no matter how many precautions we take. They always do." *They* always do. I was one of "them," whoever they were. I was, in this context anyway, not singular, not aberrant, but typical. I think it was this sense of commonality with others I didn't even know, a sense of being returned somehow, in spite of my appalling act, to the human family, that urged me to write that first essay, not merely speaking out but calling out, perhaps. "Here's the way I am," it said. "How about you?" And the answer came, as I've said: "Me too! Me too!"

This has been the kind of work I've continued to do: to scrutinize the details of my own experience and to report what I see, and what I think about what I see, as lucidly and accurately as possible. But because feminine experience has been immemorially devalued and repressed, I continue to find this task terrifying. "Every woman has known the torture of beginning to speak aloud," Cixous writes, "heart beating as if to break, occasionally falling into loss of language, ground and language slipping out from under her, because for woman speaking—even just opening her mouth—in public is something rash, a transgression" (p. 92).

The voice I summon up wants to crack, to whisper, to trail back into silence. "I'm sorry to have nothing more than this to say," it wants to apologize. "I shouldn't be taking up your time. I've never fought in a war, or even in a schoolyard free-for-all. I've never tried to see who could piss farthest up the barn wall. I've never even been to a whorehouse. All the important formative experiences have passed me by. I was raped once. I've borne two children. Milk trickling out of my breasts, blood trickling from between my legs. You don't want to hear about it. Sometimes I'm too scared to leave my house.

Not scared *of* anything, just scared: mouth dry, bowels writhing. When the fear got really bad, they locked me up for six months, but that was years ago. I'm getting old now. Misshapen, too. I don't blame you if you can't get it up. No one could possibly desire a body like this. It's not your fault. It's mine. Forgive me. I didn't mean to start crying. I'm sorry . . . sorry . . . sorry. . . ."

An easy solace to the anxiety of speaking aloud: this slow subsidence beneath the waves of shame, back into what Cixous calls "this body that has been worse than confiscated, a body replaced with a disturbing stranger, sick or dead, who so often is a bad influence, the cause and place of inhibitions. By censuring the body," she goes on, "breath and speech are censored at the same time" (p. 97). But I am not going back, not going under one more time. To do so would demonstrate a failure of nerve far worse than the depredations of ms have caused. Paradoxically, losing one sort of nerve has given me another. No one is going to take my breath away. No one is going to leave me speechless. To be silent is to comply with the standard of feminine grace. But my crippled body already violates all notions of feminine grace. What more have I got to lose? I've gone beyond shame. I'm shameless, you might say. You know, as in "shameless hussy"? A woman with her bare brace and her tongue hanging out.

I've "found" my voice, then, just where it ought to have been, in the body-warmed breath escaping my lungs and throat. Forced by the exigencies of physical disease to embrace my self in the flesh, I couldn't write bodiless prose. The voice is the creature of the body that produces it. I speak as a crippled woman. At the same time, in the utterance I redeem both "cripple" and "woman" from the shameful silences by which I have often felt surrounded, contained, set apart; I give myself permission to live openly among others, to reach out for them, stroke them with fingers and sighs. No body, no voice; no voice, no body. That's what I know in my bones.

NOTES

1. In *The Newly Born Woman*, translated by Betsy Wing (Minneapolis: University of Minnesota Press, 1986).

Part 4

Body on Stage

The opposite sex—
is neither!
—Kate Bornstein

19

One Is Not Born a Woman

Monique Wittig

A materialist feminist[1] approach to women's oppression destroys the idea that women are a "natural group": "a racial group of a special kind, a group perceived *as natural*, a group of men considered as materially specific in their bodies."[2] What the analysis accomplishes on the level of ideas, practice makes actual at the level of facts: by its very existence, lesbian society   ?
destroys the artificial (social) fact constituting women as a "natural group." A lesbian society[3] pragmatically reveals that the division from men of which women have been the object is a political one and shows that we have been ideologically rebuilt into a "natural group." In the case of women, ideology goes far since our bodies as well as our minds are the product of this manipulation. We have been compelled in our bodies and in our minds to correspond, feature by feature, with the *idea* of nature that has been established for us. Distorted to such

an extent that our deformed body is what they call "natural," what is supposed to exist as such before oppression. Distorted to such an extent that in
the end oppression seems to be a consequence of this "nature" within ourselves (a nature which is only an *idea*). What a materialist analysis does by reasoning, a lesbian society accomplishes practically: not only is there no natural
group "women" (we lesbians are living proof of it), but as individuals as well
we question "woman," which for us, as for Simone de Beauvoir, is only a
myth. She said: "One is not born, but becomes a woman. No biological, psychological, or economic fate determines the figure that the human female
presents in society: it is civilization as a whole that produces this creature,
intermediate between male and eunuch, which is described as feminine."[4]

However, most of the feminists and lesbian-feminists in America and elsewhere still believe that the basis of women's oppression *is biological as well as
historical*. Some of them even claim to find their sources in Simone de
Beauvoir.[5] The belief in mother right and in a "prehistory" when women created civilization (because of a biological predisposition) while the coarse and
brutal men hunted (because of a biological predisposition) is symmetrical
with the biologizing interpretation of history produced up to now by the class
of men. It is still the same method of finding in women and men a biological
explanation of their division, outside of social facts. For me this could never
constitute a lesbian approach to women's oppression, since it assumes that the
basis of society or the beginning of society lies in heterosexuality. Matriarchy
is no less heterosexual than patriarchy: it is only the sex of the oppressor that
changes. Furthermore, not only is this conception still imprisoned in the categories of sex (woman and man), but it holds onto the idea that the capacity
to give birth (biology) is what defines a woman. Although practical facts and
ways of living contradict this theory in lesbian society, there are lesbians who
affirm that "women and men are different species or races (the words are used
interchangeably): men are biologically inferior to women; male violence is a
biological inevitability."[6] By doing this, by admitting that there is a "natural"
division between women and men, we naturalize history, we assume that
"men" and "women" have always existed and will always exist. Not only do we
naturalize history, but also consequently we naturalize the social phenomena
which express our oppression, making change impossible. For example,
instead of seeing giving birth as a forced production, we see it as a "natural,"
"biological" process, forgetting that in our societies births are planned
(demography), forgetting that we ourselves are programmed to produce
children, while this is the only social activity "short of war"[7] that presents such
a great danger of death. Thus, as long as we will be "unable to abandon by will

or impulse a lifelong and centuries-old commitment to childbearing as *the* female creative act,"[8] gaining control of the production of children will mean much more than the mere control of the material means of this production: women will have to abstract themselves from the definition "woman" which is imposed upon them.

[handwritten: What's exactly a mark?]

A materialist feminist approach shows that what we take for the cause or origin of oppression is in fact only the *mark*[9] imposed by the oppressor: the "myth of woman,"[10] plus its material effects and manifestations in the appropriated consciousness and bodies of women. Thus, this mark does not predate oppression: Colette Guillaumin has shown that before the socioeconomic reality of black slavery, the concept of race did not exist, at least not in its modern meaning, since it was applied to the lineage of families. *[handwritten: meanings can change]* However, now, race, exactly like sex, is taken as an "immediate given," a "sensible given," "physical features," belonging to a natural order. But what we believe to be a physical and direct perception is only a sophisticated and mythic construction, an "imaginary formation,"[11] which reinterprets physical features (in themselves as neutral as any others but marked by the social system) through the network of relationships in which they are perceived. *[handwritten: What about blindness?]* (They are seen as *black*, therefore they *are* black; they are seen as *women*, therefore, they *are* women. But before being *seen* that way, they first had to be *made* that way.) Lesbians should always remember and acknowledge how "unnatural," compelling, totally oppressive, and destructive being "woman" was for us in the old days before the women's liberation movement. It was a political constraint, and those who resisted it were accused of not being "real" women. But then we were proud of it, since in the accusation there was already something like a shadow of victory: the avowal by the oppressor that "woman" is not something that goes without saying, since to be one, one has to be a "real" one. We were at the same time accused of wanting to be men. Today this double accusation has been taken up again with enthusiasm in the context of the women's liberation movement by some feminists and also, alas, by some lesbians whose political goal seems somehow to be becoming more and more "feminine." To refuse to be a woman, however, does not mean that one has to become a man. Besides, if we take as an example the perfect "butch," the classic example which provokes the most horror, whom Proust would have called a woman/man, how is her alienation different from that of someone who wants to become a woman? Tweedledum and Tweedledee. At least for a woman, wanting to become a man proves that she has escaped her initial programming. But even if she would like to, with all her strength, she

[handwritten: What? What is this "programming"?]

cannot become a man. For becoming a man would demand from a woman not only a man's external appearance but his consciousness as well, that is, the consciousness of one who disposes by right of at least two "natural" slaves during his life span. This is impossible, and one feature of lesbian oppression consists precisely of making women out of reach for us, since women belong to men. Thus a lesbian *has to* be something else, a not-woman, a not-man, a product of society, not a product of nature, for there is no nature in society.

The refusal to become (or to remain) heterosexual always meant to refuse to become a man or a woman, consciously or not. For a lesbian this goes further than the refusal of the *role* "woman." It is the refusal of the economic, ideological, and political power of a man. This, we lesbians, and nonlesbians as well, knew before the beginning of the lesbian and feminist movement. However, as Andrea Dworkin emphasizes, many lesbians recently "have increasingly tried to transform the very ideology that has enslaved us into a dynamic, religious, psychologically compelling celebration of female biological potential."[12] Thus, some avenues of the feminist and lesbian movement lead us back to the myth of woman which was created by men especially for us, and with it we sink back into a natural group. Having stood up to fight for a sexless society,[13] we now find ourselves entrapped in the familiar deadlock of "woman is wonderful." Simone de Beauvoir underlined particularly the false consciousness which consists of selecting among the features of the myth (that women are different from men) those which look good and using them as a definition for women. What the concept "woman is wonderful" accomplishes is that it retains for defining women the best features (best according to whom?) which oppression has granted us, and it does not radically question the categories "man" and "woman," which are political categories and not natural givens. It puts us in a position of fighting within the class "women" not as the other classes do, for the disappearance of our class, but for the defense of "woman" and its reenforcement. It leads us to develop with complacency "new" theories about our specificity: thus, we call our passivity "nonviolence," when the main and emergent point for us is to fight our passivity (our fear, rather, a justified one). The ambiguity of the term "feminist" sums up the whole situation. What does "feminist" mean? Feminist is formed with the word "femme," "woman," and means: someone who fights for women. For many of us it means someone who fights for women as a class and for the disappearance of this class. For many others it means someone who fights for woman and her defense—for the myth, then, and its reenforcement. But why was the word "feminist" chosen if it retains the least

gender = sex?.   Is passivity female or feminine?

You don't want ambiguous terms?
Then how can you have ambiguous categories?

ambiguity? We chose to call ourselves "feminists" ten years ago, not in order to support or reenforce the myth of woman, nor to identify ourselves with the oppressor's definition of us, but rather to affirm that our movement had a history and to emphasize the political link with the old feminist movement.

It is, then, this movement that we can put in question for the meaning that it gave to feminism. It so happens that feminism in the last century could never resolve its contradictions on the subject of nature/culture, woman/society. Women started to fight for themselves as a group and rightly considered that they shared common features as a result of oppression. But for them these features were natural and biological rather than social. They went so far as to adopt the Darwinist theory of evolution. They did not believe like Darwin, however, "that women were less evolved than men, but they did believe that male and female natures had diverged in the course of evolutionary development and that society at large reflected this polarization."[14] "The failure of early feminism was that it only attacked the Darwinist charge of female inferiority, while accepting the foundations of this charge—namely, the view of woman as 'unique.'"[15] And finally it was women scholars—and not feminists—who scientifically destroyed this theory. But the early feminists had failed to regard history as a dynamic process which develops from conflicts of interests. Furthermore, they still believed as men do that the cause (origin) of their oppression lay within themselves. And therefore after some astonishing victories the feminists of this first front found themselves at an impasse out of a lack of reasons to fight. They upheld the illogical principle of "equality in difference," an idea now being born again. They fell back into the trap which threatens us once again: the myth of woman.

Thus it is our historical task, and only ours, to define what we call oppression in materialist terms, to make it evident that women are a class, which is to say that the category "woman" as well as the category "man" are political and economic categories not eternal ones. Our fight aims to suppress men as a class, not through a genocidal, but a political struggle. Once the class "men" disappears, "women" as a class will disappear as well, for there are no slaves without masters. Our first task, it seems, is to always thoroughly dissociate "women" (the class within which we fight) and "woman," the myth. For "woman" does not exist for us: it is only an imaginary formation, while "women" is the product of a social relationship. We felt this strongly when everywhere we refused to be called a "*woman's* liberation movement." Furthermore, we have to destroy the myth inside and outside ourselves. "Woman" is not each one of us, but the political and ideological formation which negates "women" (the product of a relation of exploitation). "Woman"

the potential to have (bear) children does not make one heterosexual is there to confuse us, to hide the reality "women." In order to be aware of being a class and to become a class we first have to kill the myth of "woman" including its most seductive aspects (I think about Virginia Woolf when she said the first task of a woman writer is to kill "the angel in the house"). But to become a class we do not have to suppress our individual selves, and since no individual can be reduced to her/his oppression we are also confronted with the historical necessity of constituting ourselves as the individual subjects of our history as well. I believe this is the reason why all these attempts at "new" definitions of woman are blossoming now. What is at stake (and of course not only for women) is an individual definition as well as a class definition. For once one has acknowledged oppression, one needs to know and experience the fact that one can constitute oneself as a subject (as opposed to an object of oppression), that one can become *someone* in spite of oppression, that one has one's own identity. There is no possible fight for someone deprived of an identity, no internal motivation for fighting, since, although I can fight only with others, first I fight for myself.

The question of the individual subject is historically a difficult one for everybody. Marxism, the last avatar of materialism, the science which has politically formed us, does not want to hear anything about a "subject." Marxism has rejected the transcendental subject, the subject as constitutive of knowledge, the "pure" consciousness. All that thinks per se, before all experience, has ended up in the garbage can of history, because it claimed to exist outside matter, prior to matter, and needed God, spirit, or soul to exist in such a way. This is what is called "idealism." As for individuals, they are only the product of social relations, therefore their consciousness can only be "alienated." (Marx, in *The German Ideology*, says precisely that individuals of the dominating class are also alienated, although they are the direct producers of the ideas that alienate the classes oppressed by them. But since they draw visible advantages from their own alienation they can bear it without too much suffering.) There exists such a thing as class consciousness, but a consciousness which does not refer to a particular subject, except as participating in general conditions of exploitation at the same time as the other subjects of their class, all sharing the same consciousness. As for the practical class problems—outside of the class problems as traditionally defined—that one could encounter (for example, sexual problems), they were considered "bourgeois" problems that would disappear with the final victory of the class struggle. "Individualistic," "subjectivist," "petit bourgeois," these were the labels given to any person who had shown problems which could not be reduced to the "class struggle" itself.

[handwritten: What are the boundaries of this "class" of women?]

Thus Marxism has denied the members of oppressed classes the attribute of being a subject. In doing this, Marxism, because of the ideological and political power this "revolutionary science" immediately exercised upon the workers' movement and all other political groups, has prevented all categories of oppressed peoples from constituting themselves historically as subjects (subjects of their struggle, for example). This means that the "masses" did not fight for themselves but for *the* party or its organizations. And when an economic transformation took place (end of private property, constitution of the socialist state), no revolutionary change took place within the new society, because the people themselves did not change.

For women, Marxism had two results. It prevented them from being aware that they are a class and therefore from constituting themselves as a class for a very long time, by leaving the relation "women/men" outside of the social order, by turning it into a natural relation, doubtless for Marxists the only one, along with the relation of mothers to children, to be seen this way, and by hiding the class conflict between men and women behind a natural division of labor (*The German Ideology*). This concerns the theoretical (ideological) level. On the practical level, Lenin, *the* party, all the communist parties up to now, including all the most radical political groups, have always reacted to any attempt on the part of women to reflect and form groups based on their own class problem with an accusation of divisiveness. By uniting, we women are dividing the strength of the people. This means that for the Marxists women *belong* either to the bourgeois class or to the proletariat class, in other words, to the men of these classes. In addition, Marxist theory does not allow women any more than other classes of oppressed people to constitute themselves as historical subjects, because Marxism does not take into account the fact that a class also consists of individuals one by one. Class consciousness is not enough. We must try to understand philosophically (politically) these concepts of "subject" and "class consciousness" and how they work in relation to our history. When we discover that women are the objects of oppression and appropriation, at the very moment that we become able to perceive this, we become subjects in the sense of cognitive subjects, through an operation of abstraction. Consciousness of oppression is not only a reaction to (fight against) oppression. It is also the whole conceptual reevaluation of the social world, its whole reorganization with new concepts, from the point of view of oppression. It is what I would call the science of oppression created by the oppressed. *[handwritten: really?]* This operation of understanding reality has to be undertaken by every one of us: call it a subjective, cognitive practice. The movement back and forth between the levels of reality (the conceptual real-how does erasing sex & replacing it with class change things?

316   MONIQUE WITTIG

ity and the material reality of oppression, which are both social realities) is accomplished through language.

It is we who historically must undertake the task of defining the individual subject in materialist terms. This certainly seems to be an impossibility since materialism and subjectivity have always been mutually exclusive. Nevertheless, and rather than despairing of ever understanding, we must recognize the *need* to reach subjectivity in the abandonment by many of us to the myth "woman" (the myth of woman being only a snare that holds us up). This real necessity for everyone to exist as an individual, as well as a member of a class, is perhaps the first condition for the accomplishment of a revolution, without which there can be no real fight or transformation. But the opposite is also true; without class and class consciousness there are no real subjects, only alienated individuals. For women to answer the question of the individual subject in materialist terms is first to show, as the lesbians and feminists did, that supposedly "subjective," "individual," "private" problems are in fact social problems, class problems; that sexuality is not for women an individual and subjective expression, but a social institution of violence. But once we have shown that all so-called personal problems are in fact class problems, we will still be left with the question of the subject of each singular woman—not the myth, but each one of us. At this point, let us say that a new personal and subjective definition for all humankind can only be found beyond the categories of sex (woman and man) and that the advent of individual subjects demands first destroying the categories of sex, ending the use of them, and rejecting all sciences which still use these categories as their fundamentals (practically all social sciences).

use Marx but not really?

To destroy "woman" does not mean that we aim, short of physical destruction, to destroy lesbianism simultaneously with the categories of sex, because lesbianism provides for the moment the only social form in which we can live freely. Lesbian is the only concept I know of which is beyond the categories of sex (woman and man), because the designated subject (lesbian) is *not* a woman, either economically, or politically, or ideologically. For what makes a woman is a specific social relation to a man, a relation that we have previously called servitude,[16] a relation which implies personal and physical obligation as well as economic obligation ("forced residence,"[17] domestic corvée, conjugal duties, unlimited production of children, etc.), a relation which lesbians escape by refusing to become or to stay heterosexual. We are escapees from our class in the same way as the American runaway slaves were

offensive

MacKinnon, anyone?

when escaping slavery and becoming free. For us this is an absolute necessity; our survival demands that we contribute all our strength to the destruction of the class of women within which men appropriate women. This can be accomplished only by the destruction of heterosexuality as a social system which is based on the oppression of women by men and which produces the doctrine of the difference between the sexes to justify this oppression.

NOTES

1. Christine Delphy, "Pour un féminisme matérialiste," *L'Arc* 61 (1975). Translated as "For a Materialist Feminism," *Feminist Issues* 1, no. 2 (Winter 1981).

2. Colette Guillaumin, "Race et nature: Système des marques, idée de groupe naturel, et rapports sociaux," *Pluriel*, no. 11 (1977). Translated as "Race and Nature: The System of Marks, the Idea of a Natural Group and Social Relationships," *Feminist Issues* 8, no. 2 (Fall 1988).

3. I use the word "society" with an extended anthropological meaning; strictly speaking, it does not refer to societies, in that lesbian societies do not exist completely autonomously from heterosexual social systems.

4. Simone de Beauvoir, *The Second Sex* (New York: Bantam, 1952), p. 249.

5. Redstockings, *Feminist Revolution* (New York: Random House, 1978), p. 18.

6. Andrea Dworkin, "Biological Superiority: The World's Most Dangerous and Deadly Idea," *Heresies* 6:46.

7. Ti-Grace Atkinson, *Amazon Odyssey* (New York: Links Books, 1974), p. 15.

8. Dworkin, "Biological Superiority."

9. Guillaumin, "Race et nature."

10. de Beauvoir, "*The Second Sex.*"

11. Guillaumin, "Race et nature."

12. Dworkin, "Biological Superiority."

13. Atkinson, *Amazon Odyssey*, p. 6: "If feminism has any logic at all, it must be working for a sexless society."

14. Rosalind Rosenberg, "In Search of Woman's Nature," *Feminist Studies* 3, no. 1/2 (1975): 144.

15. Ibid., p. 146.

16. In an article published in *L'Idiot international* (mai 1970), whose original title was "Pour un mouvement de libération des femmes" ("For a Women's Liberation Movement").

17. Christiane Rochefort, *Les stances à Sophie* (Paris: Grasset, 1963).

20

Female Grotesques

CARNIVAL AND THEORY

Mary Russo

Pretext

There is a phrase that still resonates from childhood. Who says it? The mother's voice—not
my own mother's, perhaps, but the voice of an
aunt, an older sister, or the mother of a friend.
It is a harsh, matronizing phrase, and it is directed toward the behavior of other women:

This assumes a shared experience

"She" [the other woman] is making a spectacle out of herself.

Making a spectacle out of oneself seemed a
specifically feminine danger. The danger was of
an exposure. Men, I learned somewhat later in
life, "exposed themselves," but that operation
was quite deliberate and circumscribed. For a
woman, making a spectacle out of herself had
more to do with a kind of inadvertency and loss
of boundaries: the possessors of large, aging,

Mary Russo, "Female Grotesques: Carnival and Theory." From
Feminist Issues / Critical Issues, ed. Teresa de Lauretis, 1986. Reprinted with permission from Indiana University Press.

and dimpled thighs displayed at the public beach, of overly rouged cheeks, of a voice shrill in laughter, or of a sliding bra strap—a loose, dingy bra strap especially—were at once caught out by fate and blameworthy. It was my impression that these women had done something wrong, had stepped, as it were, into the limelight out of turn—too young or too old, too early or too late—and yet anyone, any *woman*, could make a spectacle out of herself if she was not careful. It is a feature of my own history and education that in contemplating these dangers, I grew to admire both the extreme strategies of the cool, silent, and cloistered St. Clare (enclosed, with a room of her own) and the lewd, exuberantly parodistic Mae West. *extremes*

Although the models, of course, change, there is a way in which radical negation, silence, withdrawal, and invisibility, and the bold affirmations of feminine performance, imposture, and masquerade (purity and danger) have suggested cultural politics for women.

Theory of Carnival and the Carnival of Theory

These extremes are not mutually exclusive, and in various and interesting ways they have figured round each other. Feminist theory and cultural production more generally have most recently brought together these strategies in approaching the questions of difference and the reconstruction or counterproduction of knowledge. In particular, the impressive amount of work across the discourse of carnival, or, more properly, the carnivalesque—much of it in relation to the work of the Russian scholar Mikhail Bakhtin[1]—has translocated the issues of bodily exposure and containment, disguise and gender masquerade, abjection and marginality, parody and excess, to the field of the social constituted as a symbolic system. Seen as a productive category, affirmative and celebratory (a Nietzschean gay science), the discourse of carnival moves away from modes of critique that would begin from some Archimedean point of authority without, to models of transformation and counterproduction situated within the social system and symbolically at its margins.[2]

The reintroduction of the body and categories of the body (in the case of carnival, the "grotesque body") into the realm of what is called the political has been a central concern of feminism. What would seem to be of great interest at this critical conjuncture in relation to this material would be an assessment of how the materials on carnival as historical performance may be configured with the materials on carnival as semiotic performance; in other words, how the relation between the symbolic and cultural constructs of femininity and Womanness and the experience of *women* (as variously identified and subject to multiple determinations) might be brought together toward a dynamic model of a new social subjectivity. The early work of Julia Kristeva on semiotics, subjectivity, and textual revolution and the more recent contributions of Teresa de Lauretis in mapping the terrain of a genuinely sociological and feminist semiotics are crucial to this undertaking.[3] This project is the grand one. More modestly, an examination of the materials on carnival can also recall limitations, defeats, and indifferences generated by carnival's complicitous place in dominant culture. There are especial dangers for women and other excluded or marginalized groups within carnival, though even the double jeopardy that I will describe may suggest an ambivalent redeployment of taboos around the female body as grotesque (the pregnant body, the aging body, the irregular body) and as unruly when set loose in the public sphere.

I would begin by citing briefly some of the important work on carnival in various fields (I could not pretend to be exhaustive, since the volume of recent work on Bakhtin alone is staggering). Here, I can only indicate some major lines of interest and weakness in the theory of carnival and cite some similar instances in what might be called the carnival of theory, that is, in the rhetorical masking, gesturing, and mise-en-scène of contemporary writing.

Not at all surprisingly, much of the early work on carnival in anthropology and social history dates from the late sixties, when enactments of popular protest, counterculture, experimental theatre, and multimedia art were all together suggestive of the energies and possibilities of unlimited cultural and social transformation. In many ways this essay is generated from the cultural surplus of that era. The work of Mary Douglas and Victor Turner, which was as influential in social history as, more recently, the work of Clifford Geertz, saw in the human body the prototype of society, the nation-state, and the city, and in the social dramas of transition and "rituals of status reversal" evidence of the reinforcement of social structure, hierarchy, and order through inversion. In liminal states, thus, temporary loss of boundaries tends to redefine social frames, and such topsy-turvy or time-out is inevitably set right and on course.[4] This structural view of carnival as essentially conservative is both strengthened and enlarged by historical analysis, which tends, of course, to be the political history of domination. The extreme difficulty of producing lasting social change does not diminish the usefulness of these symbolic models of transgression, and the histories of subaltern and counterproductive cultural activity are never as neatly closed as structural models might suggest.

Natalie Davis, in what remains the most interesting piece on carnival and gender, "Women on Top," argues dialectically that in early modern Europe, carnival and the image of the carnivalesque woman "undermined as well as reinforced" the renewal of existing social structure:

> The image of the disorderly woman did not always function to keep women in their place. On the contrary, it was a multivalent image that could operate, first, to widen behavioral options for women within and even outside marriage, and second, to sanction riot and political disobedience for both men and women in a society that allowed the lower orders few formal means of protest. Play with an unruly woman is partly a chance for temporary release from the traditional and stable hierarchy; but it is also part of the conflict over efforts to change the basic distribution of power within society.[5]

Among Davis's very interesting examples of the second possibility—that is, that the image of the unruly or carnivalesque woman actually worked to incite and embody popular uprisings—is the Wiltshire enclosure riots of 1641, where rioting men were led by male cross-dressers who called themselves "Lady Skimmington" (a skimmington was a ride through the streets mocking a henpecked husband, the name probably referring to the big skimming ladle that could be used for husband beatings).[6] The projection of the image of the fierce virago onto popular movements, especially a movement such as this one, involving the transgression of boundaries, is suggestive from the point of view of social transformation. What may it tell us about the construction of the female subject in history within this political symbology? Merely to sketch out the obvious problems in working toward an answer to this question, one might begin with the assumption that the history of the enclosure riots and the image of the unruly woman are not direct reflections of one another; both contain ambiguities and gender asymmetries that require historical and textual readings.

These readings are difficult in both areas. First, the history of popular movements has been largely the history of men; a stronger history of women in mixed and autonomous uprisings is needed to assess the place of women as historical subjects in relation to such uprisings. Second, as a form of representation, masquerade of the feminine (what psychoanalytic theory will insist is femininity par excellence) has its distinct problems. The carnivalized woman such as Lady Skimmington, whose comic female masquerade of those "feminine" qualities of strident wifely aggression, behind whose skirts men are protected and provoked to actions, is an image that, however counterproduced, perpetuates the dominant (and in this case misogynistic) representation of women by men. In the popular tradition of this particular example, Lady Skimmington is mocked alongside her henpecked husband, for she embodies the most despised aspects of "strong" femininity, and her subordinate position in society is in part underlined in this enactment of power reversal.

Furthermore, although the origins of this image in male-dominated culture may be displaced, there remain questions of enactment and gender-layering. Are women who have taken on this role (as opposed to men cross-dressing) as effective as male cross-dressers? Or is it, like the contemporary "straight" drag of college boys in the amateur theatricals of elite universities, a clear case of sanctioned play for men, while it is something always risking self-contempt for women to put on "the feminine"? In addition, one must ask of any representation other questions—questions of style, genre, and contextuality which may cut across the issue of gender. Is the parodistic and hyperbolic style of Lady Skimmington as a leader of men a sign of insurgency and lower-class solidarity for women and men? Does this comic female style work to free women from a more confining aesthetic? Or are women again so identified with style itself that they are as estranged from its liberatory and transgressive effects as they are from their own bodies as signs in culture generally? In what sense can women really produce or make spectacles out of themselves?

Historical inquiry may yield instances of performance (symbolic and political) that may bypass the pessimism of psychoanalytically oriented answers to this last question, but only if that history begins to understand the complexity of treating signifying systems and "events" together. In this regard, even the work on female political iconography and social movements by very distinguished historians, such as Maurice Agulhon and Eric Hobsbawm, remains problematic.[7] This methodological difficulty does not prevent historians from becoming increasingly aware of gender differences in relation to the carnivalesque. Other social historians have documented the insight of the anthropologist Victor Turner that the marginal position of women and others in the "indicative" world makes their presence in the "subjunctive" or possible world of the topsy-turvy carnival "quintessentially" dangerous; in fact, as Emmanuel Le Roy Ladurie shows in *Carnival at Romans*, Jews were stoned, and there is evidence that women were raped, during carnival festivities.[8] In other words, in the everyday indicative world, women and their bodies, certain bodies, in certain public framings, in certain public spaces, are always already transgressive—dangerous, and in danger.

With these complexities no doubt in mind, Davis concluded her brilliant article with the hope that "the woman on top might even facilitate innovation in historical theory and political behavior" (p. 131). Since the writing of her article, the conjuncture of a powerful women's movement and feminist scholarship has facilitated further interrogation of the relationship between symbology and social change. The figure of the female transgressor as public spectacle is still powerfully resonant, and the possibilities of redeploying this representation as a demystifying or utopian model have not been exhausted.

The Carnivalesque Body

Investigation of linguistic and cultural contexts in relation to categories of carnival and the body has been recently inspired by a new reception in English-speaking countries of the work of the Russian scholar and linguist Mikhail Bakhtin. Like the work of Davis and Le Roy Ladurie, Bakhtin's work on carnival is at one level a historical description of carnival in early modern Europe. It offers, as well, a proscriptive model of a socialist collectivity.

In his introduction to his study of Rabelais, Bakhtin enumerates three forms of carnival folk culture: ritual spectacles (which include feasts, pageants, and marketplace festivals of all kinds); comic verbal compositions, parodies both oral and written; and various genres of billingsgate (curses, oaths, profanations, marketplace speech). The laughter of carnival associated with these spectacles and unconstrained speech in the Middle Ages was for Bakhtin entirely positive. The Romantic period, in contrast, saw laughter "cut down to cold humour, irony, sarcasm" (*RW*, pp. 37–38). The privatism and individualism of this later humor make it unregenerative and lacking in communal hilarity. Without pretense to historical neutrality, Bakhtin's focus on carnival in early modern Europe contains a critique of modernity and its stylistic effects as a radical diminishment of the possibilities of human freedom and cultural production. He considers the culture of modernity to be as austere and bitterly isolating as the official religious culture of the Middle Ages, which he contrasts with the joy and heterogeneity of carnival and the carnivalesque style and spirit. Bakhtin's view of Rabelais and carnival is in some ways nostalgic for a socially diffuse oppositional context which has been lost, but which is perhaps more importantly suggestive of a future social horizon

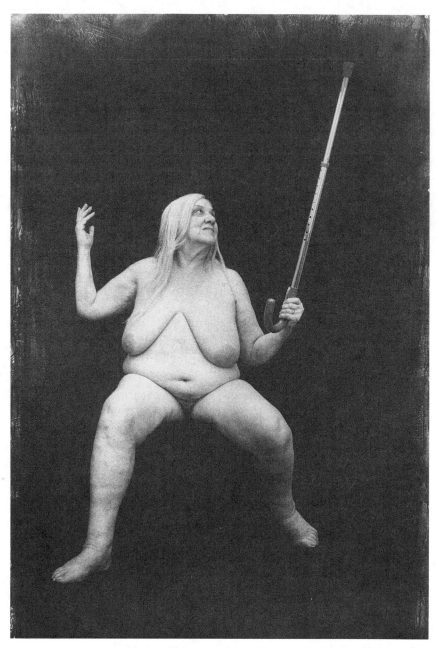

Figure Model Series. Unique silver gelatin print, 84" × 52". Photo by Jacqueline Hayden.

that may release new possibilities of speech and social performance.

The categories of carnivalesque speech and spectacle are heterogeneous, in that they contain the protocols and styles of high culture in and from a position of debasement. The masks and voices of carnival resist, exaggerate, and destabilize the distinctions and boundaries that mark and maintain high culture and organized society. It is as if the carnivalesque body politic had ingested the entire corpus of high culture and, in its bloated and irrepressible state, released it in fits and starts in all manner of recombination, inversion, mockery, and degradation. The political implications of this heterogeneity are obvious: it sets carnival apart from the merely oppositional and reactive; carnival and the carnivalesque suggest a redeployment or counterproduction of culture, knowledge, and pleasure. In its multivalent oppositional play, carnival refuses to surrender the critical and cultural tools of the dominant class, and in this sense, carnival can be seen above all as a site of insurgency, and not merely withdrawal.

The central category under which Bakhtin organizes his reading of Rabelais as a carnivalesque text is "grotesque realism," with particular emphasis on the grotesque body. The grotesque body is the open, protruding, extended, secreting body, the body of becoming, process, and change. The grotesque body is opposed to the classical body, which is monumental, static, closed, and sleek, corresponding to the aspirations of bourgeois individualism; the grotesque body is connected to the rest of the world. Significantly, Bakhtin finds his concept of the grotesque embodied in the Kerch terracotta figurines of senile, pregnant hags. Here is Bakhtin describing the figurines: "This is typical and very strongly expressed grotesque. It is ambivalent. It is pregnant death, a death that gives birth. There is nothing completed, nothing calm and stable in the bodies of these old hags. They combine senile, decaying, and deformed flesh with the flesh of new life, conceived but as yet unformed" (*RW*, pp. 25–26). "Moreover," he writes, "the old hags are laughing" (*RW*, p. 25).

Homologously, the grotesque body is the figure of the socialist state to come, a state unfinished, which, as it "outgrows itself, transgresses its own limits" (*RW*, p. 26). For Bakhtin, this body is, as well, a model for carnival language; a culturally productive linguistic body in constant semiosis. But for the feminist reader, this image of the pregnant hag is more than ambivalent. It is loaded with all of the connotations of fear and loathing associated with the biological processes of reproduction and of aging. Bakhtin, like many other social theorists of the nineteenth and twentieth centuries, fails to acknowledge or incorporate the social relations of gender in his semiotic model of the body politic, and thus his notion of the Female Grotesque remains, in all directions, repressed and undeveloped.

Yet, Bakhtin's description of these ancient crones is at least exuberant. Almost to prove his point about the impossibility of collective mirth over such images in the period of late capitalism, here is a version of the same female grotesque in the voice of Paul Céline:

> Women you know, they wane by candlelight, they spoil, melt, twist, ooze! [. . . The end of tapers is a horrible sight, the end of ladies too. . . .]⁹

Quoted and glossed by Julia Kristeva as a portrait of "a muse in the true tradition of the lowly genres—apocalyptic, Menippean, and carnevalesque," this passage suggests the dark festival of transgression that she charts in *Powers of Horror*. This book, which contrasts in tone with Kristeva's indispensable application of Bakhtin in, for instance, "Word, Dialogue, and the Novel" and *Polylogue*, draws on Mary Douglas's categories of purity and defilement to arrive, through the analytical processes of transference, at the brink of abjection.

Through the convolutions of Céline's relentlessly misogynist and anti-Semitic writing, Kristeva as author and problematized subject has projected herself toward the grotesque, which she sees as the "undoer of narcissism and of all imaginary identity as well" (p. 208). Her study is richly intertextual. As Kristeva focuses on Céline, her own text increasingly takes on his rhetoric of abjection, which interestingly comes to rest in the category of the maternal. Kristeva writes: "Abject . . . the jettisoned object, is radically excluded and draws me toward the place where meaning collapses . . . on the edge of non-existence and hallucination" (p. 2). And elsewhere: "Something maternal . . . bears upon the uncertainty of what I call abjection" (p. 208). The fascination with the maternal body in childbirth, the fear of and repulsion from it throughout the chosen texts of Céline, constitutes it here again as a privileged sight of liminality and defilement. Kristeva writes:

> When Céline locates the ultimate of abjection—and thus the supreme and sole interest of literature—in the birth-giving scene, he makes amply clear which fantasy is involved: something horrible to see at the impossible doors of the invisible—the mother's body. The scene of scenes is here not the so-called primal scene but the one of giving birth, incest turned inside out, flayed identity. Giving birth: the height of bloodshed and life, scorching moment of hesitation (between inside and outside, ego and

other, life and death), horror and beauty, sexuality and the blunt negation
of the sexual. . . . At the doors of the feminine, at the doors of abjection,
as I defined the term earlier, we are also, with Céline, given the most daring X-ray of the "drive foundations" of fascism.[10]

While there are many general reasons for questioning the use of the maternal in recent French criticism, here, I think, the point may be that the accu-
mulated horror and contempt that these descriptions of the maternal body
suggest generate a subliminal defense of the maternal, which then reemerges
in Kristeva as an idealized category far from the realities of motherhood,
either as a construction or as a lived experience.[11] Jews, unlike mothers,
would seem to merely drop out of the field of abjection, as the anti-Semitism
of Céline becomes for Kristeva a problem of maintaining the categorical
imperatives of identity and the political.[12]

The book ends on a note of mystical subjectivity: near "the quiet shore of
contemplation" (p. 210), far from the polis. On the verge, at the limit of this
avant-garde frontier, there remains, for Kristeva, only writing.[13] Peter
Stallybrass and Allon White, in their book on the politics and poetics of transgression, have called the exclusion of the already marginalized in moves such
as these "displaced abjection."[14] As I have argued, both in the history of carnival and in its theory, the category of the female body as grotesque (in, for
instance, pregnancy or aging) brings to light just such displacements. How
this category might be used affirmatively to destabilize the idealizations of
female beauty or to realign the mechanisms of desire, would be the subject
of another study.

Carnival of Theory

There has been, as well, a carnival of theory at the discursive level, in the poetics of postmodernist criticism and feminist writing. It has included all manner
of textual travesty, "mimetic rivalry," semiotic delinquency, parody, teasing,
posing, flirting, masquerade, seduction, counterseduction, tight-rope walking, and verbal aerialisms of all kinds. Performances of displacement, double
displacements, and more have permeated much feminist writing in our
attempts to survive or muscle in on the discourses of Lacanian psychoanalysis, deconstruction, avant-garde writing, and postmodernist visual art. It
could even be said, with reservation, that in relation to academic institutions,
what has come to be called "theory" has constituted a kind of carnival space.

The practice of criticism informed by this theory has taken great license stylistically, and in its posing posed a threat of sorts.

It is interesting to consider the discourse of carnival and poststructuralism together. In 1980, Michèle Richman, in her essay entitled "Sex and Signs: Language of French Feminist Criticism," saw in the proliferation of literature on festival in France a reaction primarily to structuralism and to the structuralist economy of exchange within which, as Lévi-Strauss described it, women circulate as signs but are not theorized as sign producers.[15] The festival or carnival discourse drew upon the work of Marcel Mauss (and, as importantly, on the writing of Georges Bataille) on the gift or *dépense* as that which exceeds this linguistically modeled economy. As Richman indicates, the discussion of *dépense* was relocated within a more general libidinal economy of desire. The generosity of femininity and feminine writing (*écriture féminine*) is privileged over male *dépense*, which is understood as being simultaneously a demand. The female body is the site of this desirous excess.

In terms strikingly similar to Bakhtin's formulation of the grotesque body as continuous process, Hélène Cixous calls this body "the body without beginning and without end."[16] Female sexuality and especially the mother's body, as it figures simultaneously demarcation and dissolution of identity, serve this cultural project of disrupting the political economy of the sign as it is produced in dominant discourse. This *écriture féminine*, which has been admirably discussed elsewhere by many American feminists, can be and has been done by men (in fact, modernist writers such as Joyce are often mentioned as models); how the male-authored or travestied "feminine" is different, and how the inscription of the female body in the texts produced by women may be usefully contextualized elsewhere are still important and unanswered questions, although the critiques of this feminization of writing as essentialist must be taken into account in reconsiderations of these topics.[17]

Beyond essentialism, there are, as I have indicated earlier, other historical and anthropological warnings to heed. Even within France there have been critiques of the feminine textual festival. Annie Leclerc has chided the "delirious adultors of the festival," and Catherine Clément in *La jeune née* parallels the carnivalesque with hysterical crisis. In terms similar to earlier critiques of carnival, she sees the cultural category of hysteria as

> the only form of contestation possible in certain types of social organization, within the context of the village community; it is also a safety valve. This lan-

guage not yet at the point of verbal expression, restrained within the bond of the body . . . remains convulsive. Men look but they do not hear.[18]

Historically, Clément is right: hysterics and madwomen generally have ended up in the attic or in the asylum, their gestures of pain and defiance having served only to put them out of circulation. As a figure of representation, however, hysteria may be less recuperable. The famous photographs commissioned by Charcot, which chart the various stages of hysteria in the patients of Salpêtrière, fix in attitude and gesture, in grimaces and leaps, a model of performance not unlike the fashionable histrionics of the great Romantic actresses and circus artists of the late nineteenth century. These paid performers were, like women hysterics, "seen but not heard," in one sense, since the scene of their livelihood, their context, it can be argued, was arranged by and for the male viewer. Nonetheless, they used their bodies in public, in extravagant ways that could have only provoked wonder and ambivalence in the female viewer, as such latitude of movement and attitude was not permitted most women without negative consequences.

This hyperbolic style, this "overacting," like the staged photographs of Salpêtrière (whatever Charcot's claims were to scientific documentation), can be read as double representations: as mimicries of the somatizations of the women patients whose historical performances were lost to themselves and recuperated into the medical science and medical discourse which maintain their oppressive hold on women. The photographs of Salpêtrière especially strike us as uncanny because of the repetitiveness of the hysterical performance. It is not only the content of hysterical behavior that strikes us as grotesque but its representation: if hysteria is a dis-play, these photographs display the display. If hysteria is understood as feminine in its image, accoutrements, and stage business (rather than in its physiology), then it may be used to rig us up (for lack of the phallic term) into discourse. The possibility, indeed the necessity, of using the female body in this sense allows for the distance necessary for articulation. Luce Irigaray describes this provisional strategy as follows:

> To play with mimesis is thus, for a woman, to try to recover the place of her exploitation by discourse, without allowing herself simply to be reduced to it. It means to resubmit herself—inasmuch as she is on the side of "perceptible," of "matter"—to "ideas," in particular to ideas about herself, that are elaborated in/by masculine logic, but so as to make "visible," by an effect of playful repetition, what was supposed to remain invisible:

the cover-up of a possible operation of the feminine in language. It also means to "unveil" the fact that, if women are such good mimics, it is because they are not simply reabsorbed into this function.[19]

What is called mimesis here is elsewhere, with various modifications, called masquerade. (Irigaray herself reserves the latter term to refer negatively to the false position of women experiencing desire only as male desire for them.) Female sexuality as masquerade is a well-noted psychoanalytic category. Jacques Lacan, a great *poseur* himself, has written of female sexuality as masking a lack, pretending to hide what is in fact not there:

> Paradoxical as this formulation might seem, I would say that it is in order to be the phallus, that is to say, the signifier of the desire of the Other, that the woman will reject an essential part of her femininity, notably all its attributes through masquerade. It is for what she is not that she expects to be desired as well as loved.[20]

The mask here is seen as feminine (for men and women) rather than something that hides a stable feminine identity. Femininity is a mask which masks nonidentity. According to Lacan, that produces an unexpected side effect for the man anxious to appear manly:

> The fact that femininity takes refuge in this mask, because of the *Verdrangung* inherent to the phallic mark of desire, has the strange consequence that, in the human being, virile display itself appears as feminine.[21]

In film theory, Mary Ann Doane has problematized the female spectator, using the essay of Joan Riviere on "Womanliness and Masquerade."[22] Her argument is that masquerade can "manufacture a distance from the image, to generate a problematic within which the image is manipulable, producible, and readable by the women."[23] It is, in other words, a way around the theorization of the spectator only in terms of the male gaze and male categories of voyeurism and fetishistic pleasure. More generally, her discussion of Riviere is extremely useful in explaining the asymmetries of transvestism, which for a woman has always been necessary in some sense in order for her to take part in a man's world. For a woman to dress, act, or position herself in discourse as a man is easily understandable and culturally compelling. To "act like a woman" beyond narcissism and masochism is, for psychoanalytic theory, trickier. That is the critical and hopeful power of the masquerade.

Deliberately assumed and foregrounded, femininity as mask, for a man, is a take-it-or-leave-it proposition; for a woman, a similar flaunting of the feminine is a take-it-*and*-leave-it *possibility*. To put on femininity with a vengeance suggests the power of taking it off.

These considerations account for some of the interest in masquerade for those contemporary artists and critics whose work on imposture and dissimulation tends to stress the constructed, the invented, and (to use Gayatri Spivak's wonderful phrase) the "scrupulously fake."[24] Spivak reads Nietzsche's characterization of female sexual pleasure as masquerade ("they 'give themselves,' even when they—give themselves. The female is so artistic") as an originary displacement, occluding "an unacknowledged envy: a man cannot fake an orgasm."[25] Reading Derrida, she sees the figure of woman displaced twice over. "Double displacement," she suggests, might be undone in carefully fabricated "useful and scrupulous fake readings in place of the passively active fake orgasm." Such readings may suggest new ways of making new spectacles of oneself.

Other work on masquerade has a more explicitly sociopolitical dimension, which greatly enriches psychoanalytic and deconstructive approaches to the material (I am thinking, for instance, of Dick Hebdige's work on subculture and Homi Bhabha's recent work on mimicry and the colonial subject).[26] For feminist theory, particularly, a more specifically historical and social use of masquerade may be needed, perhaps in the context of larger discussions of social groups and categories of the feminine mask in colonized and subcultural contexts, or in relation to other guises of the carnivalesque body. Nonetheless, the hyperboles of masquerade and carnival suggest, at least, some preliminary "acting out" of the dilemmas of femininity.

General Laughter and the Laughter of Carnival

Feminist theory itself has been travestied, hidden, and unacknowledged in many discussions of subjectivity and gender. It is part of what Elaine Showalter has called "critical cross-dressing."[27] The fathers of French theory alluded to here are in fact all masters of mise-en-scène. Even Derrida, whose persona has been more diffidently drawn in his writings, has been recently showcased as a carnival master.

The interview with Derrida published in *Critical Exchange*, in which he speaks of women and feminism, is quite as interesting for what he says about feminists as for the mise-en-scène.[28] Derrida restates his reservations about feminism as a form of phallogocentrism (fair enough). Later, he says that feminism is tantamount to phallogocentrism (not so fair).[29] James Creech, who edited and translated the interview, states that he attempted "to reproduce its conversational tone, with interruptions, ellipses, suspensions, and laughter that marked a very cordial and freeform discussion. Essentially nothing has been edited out, and the reader can follow the subtext of associations which lead from one moment of discussion to another" (p. 30). The transcription is punctuated by parenthetical laughter and occasionally, in bold face, "General Laughter." For instance:

> Certain feminists, certain women struggling in the name of feminism—may see in deconstruction only what will not allow itself to be feminist. That's why they try to constitute a sort of target, a silhouette, a shooting gallery almost, where they spot phallocentrism and beat up on it [*tappent dessus*]. Just as Said and others constitute an enemy in the image [*laughter*] of that against which they have ready arms, in the same way, I think certain feminists as they begin to read certain texts, focus on particular themes out of haste and say, "Well, there you have it. . . ." (I don't know exactly who one could think of in this regard, but I know it goes on.) In France I recall a very violent reaction from a feminist who upon reading *Spurs* and seeing the multiplication of phallic images—spurs, umbrellas, etc.—said, "So, it's a phallocentric text," and started kicking up a violent fuss, charging about like a bull perhaps. . . . [*general laughter*] (p. 30)

This is a startling scene—the feminist as raging bull ("I don't know exactly who one can think of in this regard, but I know it goes on"). The bull in the shooting gallery, spotting and targeting, "kicking up a violent fuss, charging about." Is this textual spotting and targeting a reverse image? Is phallogocentrism really tantamount to feminism here? Is this a male dressed as a female dressing as a male? What kind of drag is this? Who is waving the red flag? And, who must join this "general laughter"? The laughter of carnival is communal and spontaneous, but general laughter in this context is coercive, participated in, like much comedy, by the marginalized only in an effort to pass. But it can be heard from another position.

A counter scene is offered in the films of Yvonne Rainer, whose past as a performance artist puts her in a particularly good position to stage theory and intellectual comedy. In her film *The Man Who Envied Women* (1985) ("I don't know exactly who one can think of in this regard, but I know it goes on"), the man stands behind a female student, his hands gripping her shoulders as she asks the difference between the subject-in-process and the everyday individual with choices and identifications to make. He replies (paraphrasing Foucault): in the very enactment of the power relations that are being almost simultaneously affirmed and denied.

In another film, *Journeys from Berlin / 1971* (1980), the joke is Jean-Paul Sartre's in another interview. Reference is made to Sartre's trip to West Germany to visit the imprisoned terrorists awaiting trial. When asked why he visited only the cell of Andreas Baader and not that of his accomplice Ulrike Meinhof, he replies, "The gang is called Baader-Meinhof not Meinhof-Baader, isn't it?" In the voice-over, two people laugh, the man because he is pleased with the old intellectual's intellectual prowess, the woman because she hears the joke as on Sartre himself in decadence.

What Rainer stages is a dialogical laughter, the laughter of intertext and multiple identifications. It is the conflictual laughter of social subjects in a classist, racist, ageist, sexist society. It is the laughter we have now: other laughter for other times. Carnival and carnival laughter remain on the horizon with a new social subjectivity.

For now, right now, as I acknowledge the work of feminists in reconstituting knowledge, I imagine us going forward, growing old (I hope), or being grotesque in other ways. I see us viewed by ourselves and others, in our bodies and in our work, in ways that are continuously shifting the terms of viewing, so that looking at us, there will be a new question, the question that never occurred to Bakhtin in front of the Kerch terracotta figurines—

Why are these old hags laughing?

NOTES

I wish to thank Nancy Fitch and Catherine Portuges for their careful readings of an earlier version of this essay.

1. Mikhail Bakhtin, *Rabelais and His World*, trans. Helene Iswolsky (Bloomington: Indiana University Press, 1984). An earlier edition of this translation was published in 1968 by MIT Press. References to *Rabelais and His World* are identified as *RW*. Also important for discussions of language and carnival are *The Dialogical Imagination: Four Essays*, ed. Michael Holquist (Austin: University of Texas Press, 1981), and *Problems of Dostoevskii's Poetics*, trans. R. W. Rotsel (Ann Arbor: University of Michigan Press,

1973). For other works attributed to Bakhtin, see P. N. Medvedev and M. M. Bakhtin, *The Formal Method in Literary Scholarship: A Critical Introduction to Sociological Poetics*, trans. Albert J. Wehrle (Baltimore: Johns Hopkins University Press, 1978), and V. N. Volosinov, *Freudianism: A Marxist Critique* (New York; Academic Press, 1976).

2. I am indebted to Peter Stallybrass, whose book with Allon White, *The Politics and Poetics of Transgression* (Ithaca, N.Y.: Cornell University Press, 1986), contains a rigorous historical and critical introduction to carnival as political discourse.

3. See Julia Kristeva, *La Révolution du langage poétique: L'avant-garde à la fin du 19e siècle: Lautréamont et Mallarmé* (Paris: Seuil, 1977) and *Polylogue* (Paris: Seuil, 1977); and Teresa de Lauretis, *Alice Doesn't: Feminism, Semiotics, Cinema* (Bloomington: Indiana University Press, 1984).

4. Mary Douglas, *Purity and Danger; An Analysis of Concepts of Pollution and Taboo* (London: Routledge and Kegan Paul, 1966); Victor Turner, *From Ritual to Theater; The Human Seriousness of Play* (New York: Performing Arts Journal Publications, 1982) and *The Ritual Process: Structure and Anti-structure* (Chicago: University of Chicago Press, 1968). Clifford Geertz, *The Interpretation of Cultures* (New York: Basic Books, 1973).

5. Natalie Zemon Davis, "Women on Top," in her *Society and Culture in Early Modern France* (Stanford: Stanford University Press, 1965), pp. 124–52. I am quoting from p. 131.

6. Ibid., p. 148. As Davis points out, this image of the "strong woman" is problematic: "The unruly woman not only directed some of the male festive organizations; she was sometimes their butt. The village scold or the domineering wife might be ducked in the pond or pulled through the streets muzzled or branked or in creel" (p. 140).

7. Maurice Agulhon, *Marianne into Battle: Republican Imagery and Symbolism in France, 1789–1880* (Cambridge: Cambridge University Press, 1981); Eric Hobsbawm, "Man and Woman in Socialist Iconography," *History Workshop: A Journal of Socialist Historians* 6 (Autumn 1978): 107–21. See also replies to Hobsbawm by Maurice Agulhon and by feminist historians Sally Alexander, Anna Davin, and Eve Hostettler in *History Workshop* 8 (Autumn 1978): 167–83. For an interesting exchange on the topic, see Neil Hertz, "Medusa's Head: Male Hysteria under Political Pressure," *Representations* 4 (Fall 1983): 55–73, and the comments that follow it by Catherine Gallagher and Joel Fineman, pp. 55–72.

8. Victor Turner, "Frame, Flow, and Reflection: Ritual and Drama as Public Liminality," in *Performance in Postmodern Culture*, ed. Michel Benamou and Charles Caramello, Center for Twentieth Century Studies, Theories of Contemporary Culture, vol. 1 (Madison: Coda Press, 1977), pp. 35–55. As Turner puts it, "The danger here is not simply that of female 'unruliness.' This unruliness itself is the mark of the ultraliminal, of the perilous realm of possibility of 'anything *may* go' which threatens any social order and seems the more threatening, the *more* that order *seems*

rigorous and secure. . . . The subversive potential of the carnivalized feminine principle becomes evident in times of social change when its manifestations move out of the liminal world of Mardi Gras into the political arena itself" (pp. 41–42). Emmanuel Le Roy Ladurie, *Carnival at Romans*, trans. Mary Feeneg (New York: Braziller, 1979).

9. Paul Céline, quoted in Julia Kristeva, *Powers of Horror: An Essay on Abjection*, trans. Leon S. Roudiez (New York: Columbia University Press, 1982), p. 169.

10. Kristeva, *Powers of Horror*, pp. 155–56. See also chapter 8, "Those Females Who Can Wreck the Infinite" (pp. 157–73).

11. I am grateful to Ann Rosalind Jones for this insight. For an excellent critique of Kristeva's most recent work, see her "Julia Kristeva on Femininity: The Limits of a Semiotic Politics," *Feminist Review* 18 (Winter 1984): 56–73.

12. "His fascination with Jews, which was full of hatred and which he maintained to the end of his life, the simple-minded anti-Semitism that besots the tumultuous pages of the pamphlets, are no accident; they thwart the disintegration of identity that is coextensive with a scription that affects the most archaic distinctions, that bridges the gaps insuring life and meaning. Céline's anti-Semitism, like political commitment, for others—like, as a matter of fact, any political commitment, to the extent that it settles the subject within a socially justified illusion—is a security blanket" (Kristeva, *Powers of Horror*, pp. 136–37).

13. Writing, or "literature," is a "vision of the apocalypse that seems to me rooted no matter what its socio-historical condition might be, on the fragile border (borderline cases) where identities (subject/object, etc.) do not exist or only barely so—doubly, fuzzy, heterogeneous, animal, metamorphosed, altered, abject" (ibid., p. 207).

14. Stallybrass and White, *Politics and Poetics*, p. 21.

15. Michèle Richman, "Sex and Signs: The Language of French Feminist Criticism," *Language and Style* 13 (Fall 1980): 62–80.

16. Hélène Cixous, quoted in ibid., p. 74. The work of Luce Irigaray and Michèle Montrelay is especially important to this discussion.

17. The dangers of essentialism in posing the female body, whether in relation to representation or in relation to "women's history," have been well stated, so well stated, in fact, that "antiessentialism" may well be the greatest inhibition to work in cultural theory and politics at the moment, and must be displaced. For an account of recent debates around the female body and film, see Constance Penley, "Feminism, Film, and Theory and the Bachelor Machine," *M/F* 10 (1985): 39–61.

18. Catherine Clément, quoted in Richman, "Sex and Signs," p. 69.

19. Luce Irigaray, *The Sex Which Is Not One*, trans. Catherine Porter (Ithaca: Cornell University Press, 1985): 76.

20. Jacques Lacan, *Feminine Sexuality: Jacques Lacan and the "Ecole Freudienne,"* ed., Juliet Mitchell and Jacqueline Rose, trans. Jacqueline Rose (New York: Norton, 1982), p. 84.

21. Ibid., p. 85.

22. Mary Ann Doane, "Film and Masquerade: Theorizing the Female Spectator," *Screen* 23, nos. 3/4 (Sept./Oct. 1982): 74–87, and "Woman's Stake: Filming the Female Body," *October* 17 (Summer 1981): 23–36. See also Kaja Silverman, "*Historie d'O:* The Construction of a Female Subject," in *Pleasure and Danger: Exploring Female Sexuality*, ed. Carole S. Vance (Boston: Routledge and Kegan Paul, 1984), pp. 320–49, and "Changing the Fantasmatic Scene," *Framework* 20 (1983): 27–36. For a discussion of masquerade in relation to postmodernism, see Craig Owens, "Posing," in *Difference: On Representation and Sexuality Catalog* (New York; New Museum of Contemporary Art, 1985).

23. Doane, "Film and Masquerade," p. 87.

24. Gayatri Spivak, "Displacement and the Discourse of Woman," in *Displacement: Derrida and After*, ed. Mark Krupnick, Center for Twentieth Century Studies, Theories of Contemporary Culture, vol. 4 (Bloomington: Indiana University Press, 1983), p. 186.

25. Spivak, p. 170. As Spivak quotes Derrida, "She is twice model, in a contradictory fashion, at once lauded and condemned. . . . (First), like writing. . . . But, insofar as she does not believe, herself, in truth . . . she is again the model, this time the good model, or rather the bad model as good model: she plays dissimulation, ornament, lying, art, the artistic philosophy" (p. 171).

26. Dick Hebdige, *Subculture: The Meaning of Style* (London: Methuen, 1979); Homi Bhabha, "Of Mimicry and Man: The Ambivalence of Colonial Discourse," *October* 28 (Spring 1984): 125–33. Conversely, both Hebdige and Bhabha have largely ignored gender difference.

27. Elaine Showalter, "Critical Cross-Dressing: Male Feminists and the Woman of the Year," *Raritan* 3, no. 2 (Fall 1983): 130–49.

28. James Creech, Peggy Kamuf, and Jane Todd, "Deconstruction in America: An Interview with Jacques Derrida," *Critical Exchange* 17 (Winter 1985): 30. I wish to thank Theodore M. Norton for alerting me to the hilarious possibilities of this interview.

29. Derrida says, "So let's just say that the most insistent and the most organized motif in my texts is neither feminist nor phallocentric. And that at a certain point I try to show that the two are tantamount to the same thing" (ibid., p. 31).

21

The Empire Strikes Back

A POSTTRANSSEXUAL MANIFESTO

Sandy Stone

Frogs into Princesses

The verdant hills of Casablanca look down on homes and shops jammed chockablock against narrow, twisted streets filled with the odors of spices and dung. Casablanca is a very old city, passed over by Lawrence Durrell perhaps only by a geographical accident as the winepress of love. In the more modern quarter, located on a broad, sunny boulevard, is a building otherwise unremarkable except for a small brass nameplate that identifies it as the clinic of Dr. Georges Burou. It is predominantly devoted to obstetrics and gynecology, but for many years has maintained another reputation quite unknown to the stream of Moroccan women who pass through its rooms.

Dr. Burou is being visited by journalist James Morris. Morris fidgets in an anteroom reading

Sandy Stone, "The Empire Strikes Back: A Posttranssexual Manifesto." Originally appeared in *Body Guards*, 1991, edited by Julia Epstein and Kristina Straub. Reprinted with permission from Routledge, New York.

Elle and *Paris-Match* with something less than full attention, because he is on an errand of immense personal import. At last the receptionist calls for him, and he is shown to the inner sanctum. He relates:

> I was led along corridors and up staircases into the inner premises of the clinic. The atmosphere thickened as we proceeded. The rooms became more heavily curtained, more velvety, more voluptuous. Portrait busts appeared, I think, and there was a hint of heavy perfume. Presently I saw, advancing upon me through the dim alcoves of this retreat, which distinctly suggested to me the allure of a harem, a figure no less recognizably odalesque. It was Madame Burou. She was dressed in a long white robe, tasseled I think around the waist, which subtly managed to combine the luxuriance of a caftan with the hygiene of a nurse's uniform, and she was blonde herself, and carefully mysterious. . . . Powers beyond my control had brought me to Room 5 at the clinic in Casablanca, and I could not have run away then even if I had wanted to. . . . I went to say good-bye to myself in the mirror. We would never meet again, and I wanted to give that other self a long last look in the eye, and a wink for luck. As I did so a street vendor outside played a delicate arpeggio upon his flute, a very gentle merry sound which he repeated, over and over again, in sweet diminuendo down the street. Flights of angels, I said to myself, and so staggered . . . to my bed, and oblivion.[1]

Exit James Morris, enter Jan Morris, through the intervention of late twentieth-century medical practices in this wonderfully "oriental," almost religious narrative of transformation. The passage is from *Conundrum*, the story of Morris' "sex change" and the consequences for her life. Besides the wink for luck, there is another obligatory ceremony known to male-to-female transsexuals which is called "wringing the turkey's neck," although it is not recorded whether Morris performed it as well. I will return to this rite of passage later in more detail.

Making History

Imagine now a swift segue from the moiling alleyways of Casablanca to the rolling green hills of Palo Alto. The Stanford Gender Dysphoria Program occupies a small room near the campus in a quiet residential section of this affluent community. The program, which is a counterpart to Georges Burou's clinic in Morocco, has been for many years the academic focus of

Western studies of gender dysphoria syndrome, also known as transsexualism. Here are determined etiology, diagnostic criteria, and treatment.

The program was begun in 1968, and its staff of surgeons and psychologists first set out to collect as much history on the subject of transsexualism as was available. Let me pause to provide a very brief capsule of their results. A transsexual is a person who identifies his or her gender identity with that of the "opposite" gender. Sex and gender are quite separate issues, but transsexuals commonly blur the distinction by confusing the performative character of gender with the physical "fact" of sex, referring to their perceptions of their situation as being in the "wrong body." Although the term "transsexual" is of recent origin, the phenomenon is not. The earliest mention of something which we can recognize ex post facto as transsexualism, in light of current diagnostic criteria, was of the Assyrian king Sardanapalus, who was reported to have dressed in women's clothing and spun with his wives.[2] Later instances of something very like transsexualism were reported by Philo of Judea, during the Roman Empire. In the eighteenth century the Chevalier d'Eon, who lived for thirty-nine years in the female role, was a rival of Madame Pompadour for the attention of Louis XV. The first colonial governor of New York, Lord Cornbury, came from England fully attired as a woman and remained so during his time in office.[3]

Transsexualism was not accorded the status of an "official disorder" until 1980, when it was first listed in the *American Psychiatric Association Diagnostic and Statistical Manual*. As Marie Mehl points out, this is something of a Pyrrhic victory.[4]

Prior to 1980, much work had already been done in an attempt to define criteria for differential diagnosis. An example from the 1970s is this one, from work carried out by Leslie Lothstein and reported in Walters and Ross's *Transsexualism and Sex Reassignment*[5]:

> Lothstein, in his study of ten ageing transsexuals [average age fifty-two], found that psychological testing helped to determine the extent of the patients' pathology [*sic*] . . . [he] concluded that [transsexuals as a class] were depressed, isolated, withdrawn, schizoid individuals with profound dependency conflicts. Furthermore, they were immature, narcissistic, egocentric and potentially explosive, while their attempts to obtain [professional assistance] were demanding, manipulative, controlling, coercive, and paranoid.[6]

Here's another:

In a study of 56 transsexuals the results on the schizophrenia and depression scales were outside the upper limit of the normal range. The authors
see these profiles as reflecting the confused and bizarre life styles of the
subjects.[7]

These were clinical studies, which represented a very limited class of subjects. However, the studies were considered sufficiently representative for
them to be reprinted without comment in collections such as that of
Walters and Ross. Further on in each paper, though, we find that each
investigator invalidates his results in a brief disclaimer which is reminiscent
of the fine print in a cigarette ad: In the first, by adding "It must be admitted that Lothstein's subjects could hardly be called a typical sample as nine
of the ten studied had serious physical health problems" (this was a study
conducted in a health clinic, not a gender clinic), and in the second, with
the afterthought that "82 per cent of [the subjects] were prostitutes and
atypical of transsexuals in other parts of the world."[8] Such results might
have been considered marginal, hedged about as they were with markers of
questionable method or excessively limited samples. Yet they came to represent transsexuals in medicolegal/psychological literature, disclaimers
and all, almost to the present day.

   During the same period, feminist theoreticians were developing their
own analyses. The issue quickly became, and remains, volatile and divisive.
Let me quote an example.

   Rape . . . is a masculinist violation of bodily integrity. All transsexuals rape
   women's bodies by reducing the female form to an artifact, appropriating
   this body for themselves. . . . Rape, although it is usually done by force,
   can also be accomplished by deception.

This quote is from Janice Raymond's 1979 book *The Transsexual Empire: The
Making of The She-Male*, which occasioned the title of this paper. I read
Raymond to be claiming that transsexuals are constructs of an evil phallocratic empire and were designed to invade women's spaces and appropriate
women's power. Though *Empire* represented a specific moment in feminist
analysis and prefigured the appropriation of liberal political language by a
radical right, here in 1991, on the twelfth anniversary of its publication, it
is still the definitive statement on transsexualism by a genetic female academic.[9] To clarify my stakes in this discourse let me quote another passage
from *Empire*:

Masculine behavior is notably obtrusive. It is significant that transsexually constructed lesbian-feminists have inserted themselves into the positions of importance and/or performance in the feminist community. Sandy Stone, the transsexual engineer with Olivia Records, an 'all-women' recording company, illustrates this well. Stone is not only crucial to the Olivia enterprise but plays a very dominant role there. The . . . visibility he achieved in the aftermath of the Olivia controversy . . . only serves to enhance his previously dominant role and to divide women, as men frequently do, when they make their presence necessary and vital to women. As one woman wrote: "I feel raped when Olivia passes off Sandy . . . as a real woman. After all his male privilege, is he going to cash in on lesbian feminist culture too?"

This paper, "The *Empire* Strikes Back," is about morality tales and origin myths, about telling the "truth" of gender. Its informing principle is that "technical arts are always imagined to be subordinated by the ruling artistic idea, itself rooted authoritatively in nature's own life."[10] It is about the image and the real mutually defining each other through the inscriptions and reading practices of late capitalism. It is about postmodernism, postfeminism, and (dare I say it) posttranssexualism. Throughout, the paper owes a large debt to Donna Haraway.

"All of reality in late capitalist culture lusts to become an image for its own security"[11]

Let's turn to accounts by the transsexuals themselves. During this period virtually all of the published accounts were written by male-to-females. I want to briefly consider four autobiographical accounts of male-to-female transsexuals, to see what we can learn about what they think they are doing. (I will consider female-to-male transsexuals in another paper.)

The earliest partially autobiographical account in existence is that of Lili Elbe in Niels Hoyer's book *Man Into Woman* (1933).[12] The first fully autobiographical book was the paperback *I Changed My Sex!* (not exactly a quiet, contemplative title), written by the striptease artist Hedy Jo Star in the mid-1950s.[13] Christine Jorgensen, who underwent surgery in the early 1950s and is arguably the best known of the recent transsexuals, did not publish her autobiography until 1967; instead, Star's book rode the wave of publicity surrounding Jorgensen's surgery. In 1974 *Conundrum* was published, written by the popular English journalist Jan Morris. In 1977 there was *Canary*, by musician and performer Canary Conn.[14] In addition, many transsexuals keep something they call by the argot term "O.T.F.": The Obligatory Transsexual File. This usually contains newspaper articles and bits of forbidden diary entries about "inappropriate" gender behavior. Transsexuals also collect auto-biographical literature. According to the Stanford gender dysphoria pro-gram, the medical clinics do not, because they consider autobiographical accounts thoroughly unreliable. Because of this, and since a fair percentage of the literature is invisible to many library systems, these personal collec-tions are the only source for some of this information. I am fortunate to have a few of them at my disposal.

What sort of subject is constituted in these texts? Hoyer (representing Jacobson representing Elbe, who is representing Wegener who is represent-ing Sparre),[15] writes:

> A single glance of this man had deprived her of all her strength. She felt as if her whole personality had been crushed by him. With a single glance he had extinguished it. Something in her rebelled. She felt like a schoolgirl who had received short shrift from an idolized teacher. She was conscious of a peculiar weakness in all her members . . . it was the first time her woman's heart had trembled before her lord and master, before the man who had constituted himself her protector, and she understood why she then submitted so utterly to him and his will.[16]

We can put to this fragment all of the usual questions: Not by whom but *for* whom was Lili Elbe constructed? Under whose gaze did her text fall? And consequently what stories appear and disappear in this kind of seduction? It may come as no surprise that all of the accounts I will relate here are similar in their description of "woman" as male fetish, as replicating a socially enforced role, or as constituted by performative gender. Lili Elbe faints at the sight of blood.[17] Jan Morris, a world-class journalist who has been around the block a few times, still describes her sense of herself in relation to makeup and dress, of being on display, and is pleased when men open doors for her:

> I feel small, and neat. I am not small in fact, and not terribly neat either, but femininity conspires to make me feel so. My blouse and skirt are light, bright, crisp. My shoes make my feet look more delicate than they are, besides giving me . . . a suggestion of vulnerability that I rather like.

My red and white bangles give me a racy feel, my bag matches my shoes and makes me feel well organized . . . When I walk out into the street I feel consciously ready for the world's appraisal, in a way that I never felt as a man.[18]

Hedy Jo Star, who was a professional stripper, says in *I Changed My Sex!*: "I wanted the sensual feel of lingerie against my skin, I wanted to brighten my face with cosmetics. I wanted a strong man to protect me." Here in 1991 I have also encountered a few men who are brave enough to echo this sentiment for themselves, but in 1955 it was a proprietary feminine position.

Besides the obvious complicity of these accounts in a Western white male definition of performative gender, the authors also reinforce a binary, oppositional mode of gender identification. They go from being unambiguous men, albeit unhappy men, to unambiguous women. There is no territory between.[19] Further, each constructs a specific narrative moment when their personal sexual identification changes from male to female. This moment is the moment of neocolporraphy—that is, of gender reassignment or "sex change surgery."[20] Jan Morris, on the night preceding surgery, wrote: "I went to say good-bye to myself in the mirror. We would never meet again, and I wanted to give that other self a last wink for luck."[21]

Canary Conn writes: "I'm not a *muchacho* . . . I'm a *muchacha* now . . . a girl [*sic*]."[22]

Hedy Jo Star writes: "In the instant that I awoke from the anaesthetic, I realized that I had finally become a woman."[23]

Even Lili Elbe, whose text is second-hand, used the same terms: "Suddenly it occurred to him that he, Andreas Sparre, was probably undressing for the last time." Immediately on awakening from first-stage surgery (castration in Hoyer's account), Sparre writes a note. "He gazed at the card and failed to recognize the writing. It was a woman's script." Inger carries the note to the doctor: "What do you think of this, Doctor. No man could have written it?" "No," said the astonished doctor; "no, you are quite right"—an exchange which requires the reader to forget that orthography is an acquired skill. The same thing happens with Elbe's voice: "the strange thing was that your voice had completely changed . . . You have a splendid soprano voice! Simply astounding."[24] Perhaps as astounding now as then but for different reasons, since in light of present knowledge of the effects (and more to the point, the noneffects) of castration and hormones none of this could have happened. Neither has any effect on voice timbre. Hence, incidentally, the jaundiced eyes with which the clinics regard historical accounts.

If Hoyer mixes reality with fantasy and caricatures his subjects besides ("Simply astounding!"), what lessons are there in *Man Into Woman*? Partly what emerges from the book is how Hoyer deploys the strategy of building barriers within a single subject, strategies that are still in gainful employment today. Lili displaces the irruptive masculine self, still dangerously present within her, onto the God-figure of her surgeon/therapist Werner Kreutz, whom she calls The Professor, or The Miracle Man. The Professor is He Who Molds and Lili that which is molded:

> what the Professor is now doing with Lili is nothing less than an emotional moulding, which is preceding the physical moulding into a woman. Hitherto Lili has been like clay which others had prepared and to which the Professor has given form and life . . . by a single glance the Professor awoke her heart to life, a life with all the instincts of woman.[25]

The female is immanent, the female is bone-deep, the female is instinct. With Lili's eager complicity, The Professor drives a massive wedge between the masculine and the feminine within her. In this passage, reminiscent of the "oriental" quality of Morris's narrative, the male must be annihilated or at least denied, but the female is that which exists to be *continually* annihilated:

> It seemed to her as if she no longer had any responsibility for herself, for her fate. For Werner Kreutz had relieved her of it all. Nor had she any longer a will of her own . . . there could be no past for her. Everything in the past belonged to a person who . . . was dead. Now there was only a perfectly humble woman, who was ready to obey, who was happy to submit herself to the will of another . . . her master, her creator, her Professor. Between [Andreas] and her stood Werner Kreutz. She felt secure and salvaged.[26]

Hoyer has the same problems with purity and denial of mixture that recur in many transsexual autobiographical narratives. The characters in his narrative exist in an historical period of enormous sexual repression. How is one to maintain the divide between the "male" self, whose proper object of desire is Woman, and the "female" self, whose proper object of desire is Man?

> "As a man you have always seemed to me unquestionably healthy. I have, indeed, seen with my own eyes that you attract women, and that is the clearest proof that you are a genuine fellow." He paused, and then placed his hand on Andreas' shoulder. "You won't take it amiss if I ask you a frank

question? . . . Have you at any time been interested in your own kind? You know what I mean."

Andreas shook his head calmly. "My word on it, Niels; never in my life. And I can add that those kind of creatures have never shown any interest in me."

"Good, Andreas! That's just what I thought."[27]

Hoyer must separate the subjectivity of "Andreas," who has never felt anything for men, and "Lili," who, in the course of the narrative, wants to marry one. This salvaging procedure makes the world safe for "Lili" by erecting and maintaining an impenetrable barrier between her and "Andreas," reinforced again and again in such ways as two different handwriting styles and two different voices. The force of an imperative—a natural state toward which all things tend—to deny the potentialities of mixture, acts to preserve "pure" gender identity: at the dawn of the Nazi-led love affair with purity, no "creatures" tempt Andreas into transgressing boundaries with his "own kind."

"I will honestly and plainly confess to you, Niels, that I have always been attracted to women. And to-day as much as ever. A most banal confession!"[28]

—banal only so long as the person inside Andreas's body who voices it is Andreas, rather than Lili. There is a lot of work being done in this passage, a microcosm of the work it takes to maintain the same polar personae in society in the large. Further, each of these writers constructs his or her account as a narrative of redemption. There is a strong element of drama, of the sense of struggle against huge odds, of overcoming perilous obstacles, and of mounting awe and mystery at the breathtaking approach and final apotheosis of the Forbidden Transformation. Oboy.

The first operation . . . has been successful beyond all expectations. Andreas has ceased to exist, they said. His germ glands—oh, mystic words—have been removed.[29]

Oh, mystic words. The *mysterium tremendum* of deep identity hovers about a physical locus; the entire complex of male engenderment, the mysterious power of the Man-God, inhabits the "germ glands" in the way that the soul was thought to inhabit the pineal. Maleness is in the you-know-whats. For that matter, so is the ontology of the subject. Therefore Hoyer can demonstrate in the coarsest way that femaleness is lack:

> The operation which has been performed here [that is, castration] enables
> me to enter the clinic for women [exclusively for women].[30]

On the other hand, either Niels or Lili can be constituted by an act of *insin-
uation*, what the New Testament calls *endeuein*, or the putting on of the god,
inserting the physical body within a shell of cultural signification:

> Andreas Sparre . . . was probably undressing for the last time . . . For a life-
> time these coverings of coat and waistcoat and trousers had enclosed him.[31]
>   It is now Lili who is writing to you. I am sitting up in my bed in a silk
> nightdress with lace trimming, curled, powdered, with bangles, necklace,
> and rings.[32]

All these authors replicate the stereotypical male account of the constitution
of woman: Dress, makeup, and delicate fainting at the sight of blood. Each of
these adventurers passes directly from one pole of sexual experience to the
other. If there is any intervening space in the continuum of sexuality, it is
invisible. And nobody *ever* mentions wringing the turkey's neck.

No wonder feminist theorists have been suspicious. Hell, *I'm* suspicious.

How do these accounts converse with the medical/psychological texts? In
a time in which more interactions occur through texts, computer conferences, and electronic media than by personal contact, and consequently when
individual subjectivity can be constituted through inscription more often than
through personal association, there are still moments of embodied "natural
truth" that cannot be avoided. In the time period of most of these books, the
most critical of these moments was the intake interview at the gender dysphoria clinic when the doctors, who were all males, decided whether the person was eligible for gender reassignment surgery. The origin of the gender
dysphoria clinics is a microcosmic look at the construction of criteria for gender. The foundational idea for the gender dysphoria clinics was first, to study
an interesting and potentially fundable human aberration; second, to provide
help, as they understood the term, for a "correctable problem."

Some of the early nonacademic gender dysphoria clinics performed
surgery on demand, which is to say regardless of any judgment on the part of
the clinic staff regarding what came to be called appropriateness to the gender of choice. When the first academic gender dysphoria clinics were started
on an experimental basis in the 1960s, the medical staff would not perform
surgery on demand, because of the professional risks involved in performing
experimental surgery on "sociopaths." At this time there were no official

diagnostic criteria; "transsexuals" were, *ipso facto*, whoever signed up for assistance. Professionally this was a dicey situation. It was necessary to construct the category "transsexual" along customary and traditional lines, to construct plausible criteria for acceptance into a clinic. Professionally speaking, a test or a differential diagnosis was needed for transsexualism that did not depend on anything as simple and subjective as feeling that one was in the wrong body. The test needed to be objective, clinically appropriate, and repeatable. But even after considerable research, no simple and unambiguous test for gender dysphoria syndrome could be developed.[33]

The Stanford clinic was in the business of helping people, among its other agendas, as its members understood the term. Therefore the final decisions of eligibility for gender reassignment were made by the staff on the basis of an individual *sense* of the "appropriateness of the individual to their gender of choice." The clinic took on the additional role of "grooming clinic" or "charm school" because, according to the judgment of the staff, the men who presented as wanting to be women did not always "behave like" women. Stanford recognized that gender roles could be learned (to an extent). Their involvement with the grooming clinics was an effort to produce not simply anatomically legible females, but *women* . . . i.e., *gendered* females. As Norman Fisk remarked, "I now admit very candidly that . . . in the early phases we were avowedly seeking candidates who would have the best chance for success."[34] In practice this meant that the candidates for surgery were evaluated on the basis of their *performance* in the gender of choice. The criteria constituted a fully acculturated, consensual definition of gender, and *at the site of their enactment we can locate an actual instance of the apparatus of production of gender.*

This raises several sticky questions, the chief two being: Who is telling the story for whom, and how do the storytellers differentiate between the story they tell and the story they hear?

One answer is that they differentiate with great difficulty. The criteria which the researchers developed and then applied were defined recursively through a series of interactions with the candidates. The scenario worked this way: Initially, the only textbook on the subject of transsexualism was Harry Benjamin's definitive work *The Transsexual Phenomenon* (1966).[35] (Note that Benjamin's book actually postdates *I Changed My Sex!* by about ten years.) When the first clinics were constituted, Benjamin's book was the researchers' standard reference. And when the first transsexuals were evaluated for their suitability for surgery, their behavior matched up gratifyingly with Benjamin's criteria. The researchers produced papers which reported on this, and which were used as bases for funding.

It took a surprisingly long time—several years—for the researchers to realize that the reason the candidates' behavioral profiles matched Benjamin's so
well was that the candidates, too, had read Benjamin's book, which was passed
from hand to hand within the transsexual community, and they were only too
happy to provide the behavior that led to acceptance for surgery.[36] This sort of
careful repositioning created interesting problems. Among them was the
determination of the permissible range of expressions of physical sexuality.
This was a large gray area in the candidates' self-presentations, because
Benjamin's subjects did not talk about any erotic sense of their own bodies.
Consequently nobody else who came to the clinics did either. By textual
authority, physical men who lived as women and who identified themselves as
transsexuals, as opposed to male transvestites for whom erotic penile sensation
was permissible, could not experience penile pleasure. Into the 1980s there
was not a single preoperative male-to-female transsexual for whom data was
available who experienced genital sexual pleasure while living in the "gender
of choice."[37] The prohibition continued postoperatively in interestingly trans-
muted form, and remained so absolute that no postoperative transsexual
would admit to experiencing sexual pleasure through masturbation either. Full
membership in the assigned gender was conferred by orgasm, real or faked,
accomplished through heterosexual penetration.[38] "Wringing the turkey's
neck," the ritual of penile masturbation just before surgery, was the most secret
of secret traditions. To acknowledge so natural a desire would be to risk "crash
landing"; that is, "role inappropriateness" leading to disqualification.[39]

It was necessary to retrench. The two groups, on one hand the researchers
and on the other the transsexuals, were pursuing separate ends. The
researchers wanted to know what this thing they called gender dysphoria
syndrome was. They wanted a taxonomy of symptoms, criteria for differential diagnosis, procedures for evaluation, reliable courses of treatment, and
thorough follow-up. The transsexuals wanted surgery. They had very clear
agendas regarding their relation to the researchers, and considered the doctors' evaluation criteria merely another obstacle in their path—something to
be overcome. In this they unambiguously expressed Benjamin's original criterion in its simplest form: The sense of being in the "wrong" body.[40] This
seems a recipe for an uneasy adversarial relationship, and it was. It continues
to be, although with the passage of time there has been considerable dialogue
between the two camps. Partly this has been made possible by the realization
among the medical and psychological community that the expected criteria
for differential diagnosis did not emerge. Consider this excerpt from a paper
by Marie Mehl, written in 1986:

> There is no mental nor psychological test which successfully differentiates
> the transsexual from the so-called normal population. There is no more psy-
> chopathology in the transsexual population than in the population at large,
> although societal response to the transsexual does pose some insurmount-
> able problems. The psychodynamic histories of transsexuals do not yield any
> consistent differentiation characteristics from the rest of the population.[41]

These two accounts, Mehl's statement and that of Lothstein, in which he
found transsexuals to be depressed, schizoid, manipulative, controlling, and
paranoid, coexist within a span of less than ten years. With the achievement
of a diagnostic category in 1980—one which, after years of research, did not
involve much more than the original sense of "being in the wrong body"—
and consequent acceptance by the body police, i.e., the medical establishment, clinically "good" histories now exist of transsexuals in areas as widely
dispersed as Australia, Sweden, Czechoslovakia, Vietnam, Singapore, China,
Malaysia, India, Uganda, Sudan, Tahiti, Chile, Borneo, Madagascar, and the
Aleutians.[42] (This is not a complete list.) It is a considerable stretch to fit
them all into some plausible theory. Were there undiscovered or untried
diagnostic techniques that would have differentiated transsexuals from the
"normal" population? Were the criteria wrong, limited, or short-sighted? Did
the realization that criteria were not emerging just naturally appear as a
result of "scientific progress," or were there other forces at work?

Such a banquet of data creates its own problems. Concomitant with the
dubious achievement of a diagnostic category is the inevitable blurring of
boundaries as a vast heteroglossic account of difference, heretofore invisible
to the "legitimate" professions, suddenly achieves canonization and simultaneously becomes homogenized to satisfy the constraints of the category.
Suddenly the old morality tale of the truth of gender, told by a kindly white
patriarch in New York in 1966, becomes pancultural in the 1980s. Emergent
polyvocalities of lived experience, never represented in the discourse but
present at least in potential, disappear; the *berdache* and the stripper, the
tweedy housewife and the *mujerado*, the *mah'u* and the rock star, are still the
same story after all, if we only try hard enough.

Whose Story Is This, Anyway?

I wish to point out the broad similarities which this peculiar juxtaposition
suggests to aspects of colonial discourse with which we may be familiar:

The initial fascination with the exotic, extending to professional investigators; denial of subjectivity and lack of access to the dominant discourse; followed by a species of rehabilitation. Raising these issues has complicated life in the clinics.

"Making" history, whether autobiographic, academic, or clinical, is partly a struggle to ground an account in some natural inevitability. Bodies are screens on which we see projected the momentary settlements that emerge from ongoing struggles over beliefs and practices within the academic and medical communities. These struggles play themselves out in arenas far removed from the body. Each is an attempt to gain a high ground which is profoundly moral in character, to make an authoritative and final explanation for the way things are and consequently for the way they must continue to be. In other words, each of these accounts is culture speaking with the voice of an individual. The people who have no voice in this theorizing are the transsexuals themselves. As with males theorizing about women from the beginning of time, theorists of gender have seen transsexuals as possessing something less than agency. As with "genetic" "women," transsexuals are infantilized, considered too illogical or irresponsible to achieve true subjectivity, or clinically erased by diagnostic criteria; or else, as constructed by some radical feminist theorists, as robots of an insidious and menacing patriarchy, an alien army designed and constructed to infiltrate, pervert and destroy "true" women. In this construction as well, the transsexuals have been resolutely complicit by failing to develop an effective counterdiscourse.

Here on the gender borders at the close of the twentieth century, with the faltering of phallocratic hegemony and the bumptious appearance of heteroglossic origin accounts, we find the epistemologies of white male medical practice, the rage of radical feminist theories and the chaos of lived gendered experience meeting on the battlefield of the transsexual body: a hotly contested site of cultural inscription, a meaning machine for the production of ideal type. Representation at its most magical, the transsexual body is perfected memory, inscribed with the "true" story of Adam and Eve as the ontological account of irreducible difference, an essential biography which is part of nature. A story which culture tells itself, the transsexual body is a tactile politics of reproduction constituted through textual violence. The clinic is a technology of inscription.

Given this circumstance in which a minority discourse comes to ground in the physical, a counterdiscourse is critical. But it is difficult to generate a counterdiscourse if one is programmed to disappear. The highest purpose of the transsexual is to erase him/herself, to fade into the "normal" population as soon as possible. Part of this process is known as *constructing a plausible history*—learning to lie effectively about one's past. What is gained is acceptability in society. What is lost is the ability to authentically represent the complexities and ambiguities of lived experience, and thereby is lost that aspect of "nature" which Donna Haraway theorizes as Coyote—the Native American spirit animal who represents the power of continual transformation which is the heart of engaged life. Instead, authentic experience is replaced by a particular kind of story, one that supports the old constructed positions. This is expensive, and profoundly disempowering. Whether desiring to do so or not, transsexuals do not grow up in the same ways as "GGs," or genetic "naturals."[43] Transsexuals do not possess the same history as genetic "naturals," and do not share common oppression prior to gender reassignment. I am not suggesting a shared discourse. I am suggesting that in the transsexual's erased history we can find a story disruptive to the accepted discourses of gender, which originates from within the gender minority itself and which can make common cause with other oppositional discourses. But the transsexual currently occupies a position which is nowhere, which is outside the binary oppositions of gendered discourse. For a transsexual, *as a transsexual*, to generate a true, effective and representational counterdiscourse is to speak from outside the boundaries of gender, beyond the constructed oppositional nodes which have been predefined as the only positions from which discourse is possible. How, then, can the transsexual speak? If the transsexual were to speak, what would s/he say?

A Posttranssexual Manifesto

To attempt to occupy a place as speaking subject within the traditional gender frame is to become complicit in the discourse which one wishes to deconstruct. Rather, we can seize upon the textual violence inscribed in the transsexual body and turn it into a reconstructive force. Let me suggest a more familiar example. Judith Butler points out that the lesbian categories of "butch" and "femme" are not simple assimilations of lesbianism back into terms of heterosexuality. Rather, Butler introduces the concept of *cultural intelligibility*, and suggests that the contextualized and resignified "masculinity" of the butch, seen against a culturally intelligible "female" body, invokes a dissonance that both generates a sexual tension and constitutes the object of desire. She points out that this way of thinking about gendered objects of desire admits of much greater complexity than the example suggests. The lesbian butch or femme both recall the heterosexual scene but simultaneously displace it. The idea that butch and femme are "replicas" or "copies" of heterosexual exchange underestimates the erotic power of their internal dissonance.[44] In the case of the transsexual, the varieties of performative gender, seen against a culturally intelligible gendered body *which is itself a medically constituted textual violence*, generate new and unpredictable dissonances which implicate entire spectra of desire. In the transsexual as text we may find the potential to map the refigured body onto conventional gender discourse and thereby disrupt it, to take advantage of the dissonances created by such a juxtaposition to fragment and reconstitute the elements of gender in new and unexpected geometries. I suggest we start by taking Raymond's accusation that "transsexuals divide women" beyond itself, and turn it into a productive force to multiplicatively divide the old binary discourses of gender—as well as Raymond's own monistic discourse. To foreground the practices of inscription and reading which are part of this deliberate invocation of dissonance, I suggest constituting transsexuals not as a class or problematic "third gender," but rather as a *genre*—a set of embodied texts whose potential for *productive* disruption of structured sexualities and spectra of desire has yet to be explored.

In order to effect this, the genre of visible transsexuals must grow by recruiting members from the class of invisible ones, from those who have disappeared into their "plausible histories." The most critical thing a transsexual can do, the thing that *constitutes* success, is to "pass."[45] Passing means to live successfully in the gender of choice, to be accepted as a "natural" member of that gender. Passing means the denial of mixture. One and the same with passing is effacement of the prior gender role, or the construction of a plausible history. Considering that most transsexuals choose reassignment in their third or fourth decade, this means erasing a considerable portion of their personal experience. It is my contention that this process, in which both the transsexual and the medicolegal/psychological establishment are complicit, forecloses the possibility of a life grounded in the *intertextual* possibilities of the transsexual body.

To negotiate the troubling and productive multiple permeabilities of boundary and subject position that intertextuality implies, we must begin to rearticulate the foundational language by which both sexuality and transsexuality are described. For example, neither the investigators nor the transsexuals have taken the step of problematizing "wrong body" as an adequate descriptive category. In fact "wrong body" has come, virtually by default, to *define* the syndrome.[46] It is quite understandable, I think, that a phrase whose lexicality suggests the phallocentric, binary character of gender differentiation should be examined with deepest suspicion. So long as we, whether academics, clinicians, or transsexuals, ontologize both sexuality and transsexuality in this way, we have foreclosed the possibility of analyzing desire and motivational complexity in a manner which adequately describes the multiple contradictions of individual lived experience. We need a deeper analytical language for transsexual theory, one which allows for the sorts of ambiguities and polyvocalities which have already so productively informed and enriched feminist theory.

Judith Shapiro points out that "To those . . . who might be inclined to diagnose the transsexual's focus on the genitals as obsessive or fetishistic, the response is that they are, in fact, simply conforming to *their culture's* criteria for gender assignment" (emphasis mine).[47] This statement points to deeper workings, to hidden discourses and experiential pluralities within the transsexual monolith. They are not yet clinically or academically visible, and with good reason. For example, in pursuit of differential diagnosis a question sometimes asked of a prospective transsexual is "Suppose that you could be a man [or woman] in every way except for your genitals; would you be content?" There are several possible answers, but only one is clinically correct.[48] Small wonder, then, that so much of these discourses revolves around the phrase "wrong body." Under the binary phallocratic founding myth by which Western bodies and subjects are authorized, only one body per gendered subject is "right." All other bodies are wrong.

As clinicians and transsexuals continue to face off across the diagnostic battlefield which this scenario suggests, the transsexuals for whom gender identity is something different from *and perhaps irrelevant to* physical genitalia are occulted by those for whom the power of the medical/psychological establishments, and their ability to act as gatekeepers for cultural norms, is the final authority for what counts as a culturally intelligible body. This is a treacherous area, and were the silenced groups to achieve voice we might well find, as feminist theorists have claimed, that the identities of individual, embodied subjects were far less implicated in physical norms, and far more diversely spread across a rich and complex structuration of identity and desire, than it is now possible to express. And yet in even the best of the current debates, the standard mode is one of relentless totalization. The most egregious example in this paper, Raymond's stunning "All transsexuals rape women's bodies" (what if she had said, e.g., "all blacks rape women's bodies"), is no less totalizing than Kates's "transsexuals . . . take on an exaggerated and sterotypical female role," or Bolin's "transsexuals try to forget their male history." There are no subjects in these discourses, only homogenized, totalized objects—fractally replicating earlier histories of minority discourses in the large. So when I speak the forgotten word, it will perhaps wake memories of other debates. The word is *some*.

Transsexuals who pass seem able to ignore the fact that by creating totalized, monistic identities, forgoing physical and subjective intertextuality, they have foreclosed the possibility of authentic relationships. Under the principle of passing, denying the destabilizing power of being "read," relationships begin as lies—and passing, of course, is not an activity restricted to transsexuals. This is familiar to the person of color whose skin is light enough to pass as white, or to the closet gay or lesbian . . . or to anyone who has chosen invisibility as an imperfect solution to personal dissonance. In essence I am rearticulating one of the arguments for solidarity which has been developed by gays, lesbians, and people of color. The comparison extends further. To deconstruct the necessity for passing implies that transsexuals must take responsibility for *all* of their history, to begin to rearticulate their lives not as a series of erasures in the service of a species of feminism conceived from within a traditional frame, but as a political action begun by reappropriating difference and reclaiming the power of the refigured and reinscribed body. The disruptions of the old patterns of desire that the multiple dissonances of the transsexual body imply produce not an irreducible alterity but a myriad of alterities, whose unanticipated juxtapositions hold what Donna Haraway has called the promises of monsters—physicalities of constantly shifting figure and ground that exceed the frame of any possible representation.[49]

The essence of transsexualism is the act of passing. A transsexual who passes is obeying the Derridean imperative: "Genres are not to be mixed. I will not mix genres."[50] I could not ask a transsexual for anything more inconceivable than to forgo passing, to be consciously "read," to read oneself aloud—and by this troubling and productive reading, to begin to *write oneself* into the discourses by which one has been written—in effect, then, to become a (look out—dare I say it again?) posttranssexual.[51] Still, transsexuals know that silence can be an extremely high price to pay for acceptance. I want to speak directly to the brothers, sisters and others who may read/"read" this and say: I ask all of us to use the strength which brought us through the effort of restructuring identity, and which has also helped us to live in silence and denial, for a re-visioning of our lives. I know you feel that most of the work is behind you and that the price of invisibility is not great. But, although *individual* change is the foundation of all things, it is not the end of all things. Perhaps it's time to begin laying the groundwork for the next transformation.

NOTES

Thanks to Gloria Anzaldúa, Laura Chernaik, Ramona Fernandez, Thyrza Goodeve, and John Hartigan for their valuable comments on earlier drafts of this paper, Judy Van Maasdam and Donald Laub of the Stanford Gender Dysphoria Program for their uneasy help, Wendy Chapkis; Nathalie Magan; the Olivia Records Collective, for whose caring in difficult times I am deeply grateful; Janice Raymond, for playing Luke Skywalker to my Darth Vader; Graham Nash and David Crosby; and to Christy Staats and Brenda Warren for their steadfastness. In particular, I thank Donna Haraway, whose insight and encouragement continue to inform and illuminate this work.

1. Jan Morris, *Conundrum* (New York: Harcourt Brace Jovanovich, 1974), p. 155.

2. William A. W. Walters, and Michael W. Ross, *Transsexualism and Sex Reassignment* (Oxford: Oxford University Press, 1986).

3. This capsule history is related in the introduction to Richard Docter's *Transvestites and Transsexuals: Toward a Theory of Cross-Gender Behavior* (New York: Plenum Press, 1988). It is also treated by Judith Shapiro, "Transsexualism: Reflections on the Persistence of Gender and the Mutability of Sex," in Julia Epstein and Kristina Straub, ed., *Body Guards: The Cultural Politics of Gender Ambiguity* (New York: Routledge, 1991), as well as by Janice Irvine in *Disorders of Desire: Sex and Gender in Modern American Sexology* (Philadelphia: Temple University Press, 1990).

4. In Mehl's introduction to Betty Steiner, ed., *Gender Dysphoria Syndrome: Development, Research, Management* (New York: Plenum Press, 1985).

5. Walters and Ross, *Transsexualism*.

6. From Don Burnard and Michael W. Ross, "Psychosocial Aspects and Psychological Theory: What Can Psychological Testing Reveal?" in Walters and Ross, *Transsexualism*, 58.

7. Ibid., 58.

8. Ibid, 58.

9. Janice Raymond, *The Transsexual Empire: The Making of the She-Male* (Boston: Beacon, 1979). There is some hope to be taken that Judith Shapiro's work will supercede Raymond's as such a definitive statement. Shapiro's accounts seem excellently balanced, and she is aware that there are more accounts from transsexual scholars that have not yet entered the discourse.

10. This wonderful phrase is from Donna Haraway's "Teddy Bear Patriarchy: Taxidermy in the Garden Of Eden, New York City, 1908–1936," in *Social Text* 2. no. 2:20.

11. Haraway, "Teddy Bear Patriarchy." The anecdotal character of this section is

supported by field notes which have not yet been organized and coded. A thoroughly definitive and perhaps ethnographic version of this paper, with appropriate citations of both professionals and their subjects, awaits research time and funding.

12. Niels Hoyer (pseud. for Enst Ludwig Harthern Jacobsen), ed., *Man Into Woman: An Authentic Record of a Change of Sex. The True Story of the Miraculous Transformation of the Danish Painter EinarWegener [Andreas Sparre]*, trans. H. J. Stenning (New York: Dutton, 1933). The British sexologist Norman Haine wrote the introduction, thus making Hoyer's book a semimedical contribution.

13. Hedy Jo Star (Carl Rollins Hammonds), 1955. *I Changed My Sex! (From an O.T. F.)*. Star's book has disappeared from history, and I have been unable to find reference to it in any library catalog. Having held a copy in my hand, I am sorry I didn't hold tighter.

14. There was at least one other book published during this period, Renée Richards's *Second Serve*, which is not treated here.

15. Niels Hoyer was a pseudonym for Ernst Ludwig Harthern Jacobson; Lili Elbe was the female name chosen by the artist Einar Wegener, whose given name was Andreas Sparre. This lexical profusion has rich implications for studies of self and its constructions, in literature and also in such emergent social settings as computer conferences, where several personalities grounded in a single body are as much the rule as the exception.

16. Hoyer, *Man IntoWoman*, p. 163.

17. Ibid., p. 147.

18. Morris, *Conundrum*, p. 174.

19. In *Conundrum*, Morris does describe a period in her journey from masculine to feminine (from a few years before surgery to immediately afterward) during which her gender was perceived, by herself and others, as ambiguous. She is quite unambiguous, though, about the moment of transition from *male* to *female*.

20. Gender reassignment is the correct disciplinary term. In current medical discourse, sex is taken as a natural physical fact and cannot be changed.

21. Morris, *Conundrum*, p. 115. I was reminded of this account on the eve of my own surgery. Gee, I thought on that occasion, it would be interesting to magically become another person in that binary and final way. So I tried it myself—going to the mirror and saying goodbye to the person I saw there—and unfortunately it didn't work. A few days later, when I could next get to the mirror, the person looking back at me was still me. I still don't understand what I did wrong.

22. Canary Conn, *Canary: The Story of a Transsexual* (New York: Bantam, 1977), p. 271. Conn had her surgery at the clinic of Jesus Maria Barbosa in Tijuana. In this excerpt she is speaking to a Mexican nurse; hence the Spanish terms.

23. Star, *I Changed My Sex*.

24. I admit to being every bit as astounded as the good Doctor, since except for Hoyer's account there are no other records of change in vocal pitch or timbre following administration of hormones or gender reassignment surgery. If transsexuals do succeed in altering their vocal characteristics, they do it gradually and with great difficulty. But there are more than sufficient problems with Lili Elbe's "true story," not the least of which is the scene in which Elbe finally "becomes a woman" by virtue of her physician's *implanting into her abdominal cavity a set of human ovaries*. The attention given by the media in the past decade to heart transplants and diseases of the immune system have made the lay public more aware of the workings of the human immune response, but even in 1936 Hoyer's account would have been recognized by the medical community as questionable. Tissue rejection and the dream of mitigating it were the subjects of speculation in fiction and science fiction as late as the 1940s; e.g., the miracle drug "collodiansy" in H. Beam Piper's *One Leg Too Many* (1949).

25. Hoyer, *Man Into Woman*, p.165.

26. Ibid., p. 170. For an extended discussion of texts that transmute submission into personal fulfillment cf. Sandy Stone, forthcoming, "Sweet Surrender: Gender, Spirituality, and the Ecstasy of Subjection; Pseudo-transsexual Fiction in the 1970s."

27. Hoyer, *Man Into Woman*, p. 53.

28. Ibid.

29. Hoyer, *Man Into Woman*, p. 134.

30. Ibid., p. 139. Lili Elbe's sex change took place in 1930. In the United States today, the juridical view of successful male-to-female sex change is still based upon lack; e.g., a man is a woman when "the male generative organs have been totally and irrevocably destroyed." (From a clinic letter authorizing a name change on a passport, 1980).

31. Ibid., p. 125.

32. Ibid., p. 139. I call attention in both preceding passages to the Koine Greek verb ἐνδέυειν, referring to the moment of baptism, when the one being baptized enters into and is entered by the Word; *endeuein* may be translated as "to enter into" but also "to put on, to insinuate oneself into, like a glove"; viz. "He (*sic*) who is baptized into Christ shall have put on Christ." In this intense homoerotic vein in which both genders are present but collapsed in the sacrifi(c)ed body cf. such examples as Fray Bernardino de Sahagun's description of rituals during which the officiating priest puts on the flayed skin of a young woman (in Sir James George Frazer, *The Golden Bough:A Study in Magic and Religion* [London: Macmillan, 1911], pp. 589–91).

33. The evolution and management of this problem deserves a paper in itself. It is discussed in capsule form in Donald R. Laub and Patrick Gandy, eds., *Proceedings of the Second Interdisciplinary Symposium on Gender Dysphoria Syndrome* (Stanford:

Division of Reconstructive and Rehabilitation Surgery, Stanford Medical Center, 1973) and in Irvine, *Disorders Of Desire*.

34. Laub and Gandy, *Proceedings*, p. 7. Fisk's full remarks provide an excellent description of the aims and procedures of the Stanford group during the early years, and the tensions of conflicting agendas and various attempts at resolution are implicit in his account. For additional accounts cf. both Irvine, *Disorders of Desire*, and Shapiro, *Transsexualism*.

35. Harry Benjamin, *The Transsexual Phenomenon* (New York: Julian Press, 1966). The paper which was the foundation for the book was published as "Transsexualism and Transvestism as Psycho-somatic and Somato-Psychic Syndromes" in the *American Journal of Psychotherapy* 8 (1954): 219–30. A much earlier paper by D. O. Cauldwell, "Psychopathia transexualis," in *Sexology* 16 (1949): 274–80, does not appear to have had the same effect within the field, although John Money still pays homage to it by retaining Cauldwell's single-s spelling of the term. In early documents by other workers one may sometimes trace the influence of Cauldwell or Benjamin by how the word is spelled.

36. Laub and Gandy, *Proceedings*, pp. 8, 9 *passim*.

37. The problem here is with the ontology of the term "genital," in particular with regard to its definition for such activities as pre- and postoperative masturbation. Engenderment ontologizes the erotic economy of body surface; as Judith Butler and others (e.g., Foucault) point out, engenderment polices which parts of the body have their erotic components switched off or on. Conflicts arise when the *same* parts become multivalent; e.g., when portions of the (physical male) urethra are used to construct portions of the (gendered female in the physical male) neoclitoris. I suggest that we use this vertiginous idea as an example of ways in which we can refigure multivalence as intervention into the constitution of binary gendered subject positions; in a binary erotic economy, "Who" experiences erotic sensation associated with these areas? (Judith Shapiro raises a similar point in her essay "Transsexualism" in *Body Guards*, pp. 260–62. I have chosen a site geographically quite close to the one she describes, but hopefully more ambiguous, and therefore more dissonant in these discourses in which dissonance can be a powerful and productive intervention.)

38. This act in the borderlands of subject position suggests a category missing from Marjorie Garber's excellent paper "Spare Parts: The Surgical Construction of Gender," *differences* 1 (1990): 137–59; it is an intervention into the dissymmetry between "making a man" and "making a woman" that Garber describes. To a certain extent it figures a collapse of those categories within the transsexual imaginary, although it seems reasonable to conclude that this version of the coming-of-age story is still largely male—the male doctors and patients telling each other the sto-

ries of what Nature means for both Man and Woman. Generally female (female-to-male) patients tell the same stories from the other side.

39. The terms "wringing the turkey's neck" (male masturbation), "crash landing" (rejection by a clinical program), and "gaff" (an undergarment used to conceal male genitalia in preoperative m/f transsexuals), vary slightly in different geographical areas but are common enough to be recognized across sites.

40. Based upon Norman Fisk's remarks in Laub and Gandy, *Proceedings*, p. 7, as well as my own notes. Part of the difficulty, as I discuss in this essay, is that the investigators (not to mention the transsexuals) have failed to problematize the phrase "wrong body" as an adequate descriptive category.

41. In Walters and Ross, *Transsexualism*.

42. I use the word "clinical" here and elsewhere while remaining mindful of the "Pyrrhic victory" of which Marie Mehl spoke. Now that transsexualism has the uneasy legitimacy of a diagnostic category in the DSM, how do we begin the process of getting it *out* of the book?

43. The actual meaning of "GG," a m/f transsexual slang term, is "genuine girl," (*sic*) also called "genny."

44. Judith Butler, *Gender Trouble* (New York: Routledge, 1990).

45. The opposite of passing, being *read*, provocatively invokes the inscription practices to which I have referred.

46. I am suggesting a starting point, but it is necessary to go much further. We will have to question not only how *body* is defined in these discourses, but to more critically examine who gets to say *what "body" means*.

47. Shapiro, "Transsexualism."

48. In case the reader is unsure, let me supply the clinically correct answer: "No."

49. For an elaboration of this concept cf. Donna Haraway, "The Promises Of Monsters: A Regenerative Politics for Inappropriate/d Others," in Paula Treichler, Cary Nelson, and Larry Grossberg, eds. *Cultural Studies* (New York: Routledge, 1991).

50. Jacques Derrida, "La Loi Du Genre/The Law Of Genre," trans. Avital Ronell in *Glyph* 7 (1980): 176 (French); 202 (English).

51. I also call attention to Gloria Anzaldúa's theory of the mestiza, an illegible subject living in the borderlands between cultures, capable of partial speech in each but always only partially intelligible to each. Working against the grain of this position, Anzaldúa's "new mestiza" attempts to overcome illegibility partly by seizing control of speech and inscription and writing herself into cultural discourse. The stunning "Borderlands" is a case in point; cf. Gloria Anzaldúa, *Borderlands/La Frontera: The New Mestiza* (San Francisco: Spinsters/Aunt Lute, 1987).

22

A Provoking Agent

THE PORNOGRAPHY AND
PERFORMANCE ART OF
ANNIE SPRINKLE

Linda Williams

My feminist mother used to come into my room and joke whether I would grow up to be a whore or an artist. She was exactly right!

—Annie Sprinkle,
Love Magazine

The career of Annie Sprinkle is a peculiarly American success story. Beginning her professional performance career as a masseuse, soon after becoming a whore, Sprinkle next expanded into burlesque and live sex shows, then to writing for sex magazines and performing in pornographic films and videos (where she eventually became a director). In a later stage of her career she moved to such venues as the Franklin Furnace, Performing Garage, and other avantgarde performance spaces. In her recent one-woman show entitled *Post-Post Porn Modernist*, she performs a parodic show-and-tell of her life as a sexual performer. This show includes inviting audience members to shine a flashlight at her cervix through a speculum. In 1990, while she was giving this performance in Cleveland, the municipal vice squad forced her to omit the speculum component of her act. It is a fascinat-

Linda Williams, "A Provoking Agent: The Pornography and Performance Art of Annie Sprinkle." Originally appeared in *Dirty Looks:Women, Pornography, Power*, edited by Pamela Church Gibson and Roma Gibson, 1993. Reprinted by permission of the author.

ing comment on American culture that when Annie Sprinkle performed live sex shows in that same city she was never visited by the vice squad.[1]

Performance artists, especially women performers whose gendered and sexed bodies serve as the basic material of the performance, are often vulnerable to vice squads, or to NEA censorship, because their art and thought occurs through the body. Defenders of performance art have thus often found it necessary to distinguish this art from pornography.[2] While I agree that this art is not pornography, I am suspicious of attempts to draw the line too vigorously between performance art on the one hand and pornography on the other.[3] My tactic in this essay, therefore, will not be to establish the precise moment when Annie Sprinkle became a performance artist, nor to argue, as Chuck Kleinhans has done, that Sprinkle has always been a performance artist,[4] but rather to show how her myriad sexual performances tend to blur the boundaries between the two. This, I shall argue, is the particular genius, as well as the limitation, of Annie Sprinkle's postmodern feminist agency.

Annie Sprinkle's work demonstrates that the political context in which we ponder the questions of art and obscenity is no longer one in which a secure category of sexual obscenity can be safely confined to the wings of sexual representation. For as gender and sexual identities have become more politicized, and as "speaking sex" has become as important to gay, lesbian, bisexual, transsexual, and sadomasochist activists as it has to Jesse Helms, drawing clear lines between what is dirty and what is clean, what is properly brought on scene and what should be kept off (ob)scene, no longer seems the crux of a feminist sexual politics.[5]

A recent reviewer of *Post-Post Porn Modernist* claims, mistakenly I think, that Sprinkle's performance "strips away all porn," as if the vehement denial of all pornographic elements purified the art.[6] Such a claim relies on the kind of hierarchical binary opposition between art and pornography, and between artist and whore, that Annie Sprinkle's art *and* pornography challenges. The phenomenon of Annie Sprinkle forces us to ask: What is the political value, in terms of women's agency, of not drawing a firm line between obscene pornography on the one hand and legitimate art on the other?

As the quotation at the beginning of this essay suggests, Annie Sprinkle has a way of defusing and going beyond, rather than directly confronting, familiar oppositions. In this quotation the feminist mother poses the question of her daughter's vocation as an opposition: will her daughter be an artist *or* a whore? Without confronting the mother directly, the "postfeminist," "postporn" daughter counters her either/or with a destabilizing agreeability: "My mother was right!" The daughter unsettles the familiar opposition: she is neither artist *nor* whore but artist *and* whore.

Can Annie Sprinkle's performance of the postmodern, "post-feminist" sexual role "woman" accomplish the feminist goal of being *for women*? Does she represent a new permutation of feminist agency that moves beyond some of feminism's most troubling binary oppositions—beyond, for example, the opposition that posits pornography as inimical to women; beyond the opposition that posits pornography as inimical to art; beyond the opposition that posits women as powerless victims of male sexual power and thus as colonized in their desires? Or is Annie Sprinkle more simply a symptom of a "postfeminism" that has been accused, most recently by Tania Modleski, of being an end to feminism, a reversion to prefeminism?[7]

How, in other words, shall we interpret this postfeminist sensibility emerging so agreeably from the "depths" of a misogynist mass culture? Like Modleski, I reject postfeminism if it is taken to mean that the goals of feminism are either irrelevant or already achieved. However, I understand the political and social realities that have led many women to reject the term "feminism," to claim to be beyond it, when to my way of thinking they are still embedded within its struggles. One of the reasons for this rejection has been the association of feminism with an all-or-nothing understanding of what *is* good for women, with often self-righteous positions that know for sure on which side of any binary opposition a "proper" feminism belongs.

Sex workers, we know, have often found themselves on the "wrong" side of these binaries. For sex workers have all too often been regarded by feminists as objectified victims of an aggressive, sadistic, masculine sexuality rather than as sexual agents themselves. Antipornography feminists in particular have gone so far as to define pornography as "the graphic sexually explicit subordination of women" in which women are dehumanized sexual objects "presented as whores by nature."[8] To the Dworkin-MacKinnon antipornography faction, agency can only be located in resistance. Yet in Annie Sprinkle we encounter a whore turned pornographer turned performance artist with more of a stake in the "post" than in the "antis" that constitute so much feminist position-taking on this subject. This essay suggests that we take seriously the whore side of Annie Sprinkle's performances by examining, first, her early work as a whore and then how this whore persona informed her later work as a pornographer and performance artist. My hope is that this examination may help us to clarify the nature of a postfeminist sexual agency that has brought obscenity so aggressively on scene.

Another hope is that the case of Annie Sprinkle may be used to clarify a larger argument on the essentialist or nonessentialist meaning of the name "woman.' In *Am I that Name?*, Denise Riley has argued the value of a poststructuralist refusal of the name "woman" as reducing women to fixed identities which then work to reduce women's agency.[9] Feminism does not need the fixed category "woman," Riley argues. Against this poststructuralist position Tania Modleski has argued the importance of keeping the name "woman" as an essential category.[10] Modleski points out that Riley's title, a quotation from *Othello* in which Desdemona asks Iago if she is the name her husband has given her, ignores the fact that the name Othello actually gave Desdemona was not woman but "whore." Riley's point is that the name "woman" has become an essentialist trap. Her poststructuralist argument is that women lose agency if reduced to the singularity of this name. Modleski, however, suggests that Riley's elision of that other name, "whore," is an example of why the feminist use of the essentialist name "woman" is politically important. "Although women have had to take up the term 'women' emphatically to rescue it from opprobrium, they have done so in opposition to patriarchy's tendency to 'saturate' us with our sex" (pp. 16–17).

My interest in Annie Sprinkle is that she represents one possible feminist position of agency arising out of the embrace of this saturation. For Annie Sprinkle the postmodern, postfeminist, postporn performance artist has not eschewed the term "whore" or the sexual saturation of "woman." Rather, her sexual performances, firmly rooted within the specific conventions of pornography and the persona of "whore," are provocative instances of agency that draw upon the performative traditions of the sexually saturated "woman," without simply duplicating them. By performing sex differently, though still within the conventional rhetoric and form of the genre, Annie Sprinkle demonstrated a provocative feminist agency that would fruitfully contribute to her later feminist performance work.

From Masseuse to Whore

Let's begin with Annie Sprinkle's first sexual performances, the ones she writes about in her early sex magazines, then later in her book *Post Porn Modernist* (not to be confused with her performance piece *Post-Post Porn Modernist*) and in her interview in *Angry Women*. These writings are all versions of Annie Sprinkle's life story, which she has been writing and performing, initially for specialized sex magazines, since the early 70s. In every version of this story, Annie Sprinkle tells us that she did not know she was a prostitute until she was linguistically hit over the head—or in Althusser's terms, "hailed" or "interpellated"—by this discourse.

> I was working in a massage parlor. For 3 months I worked and didn't even know I was a hooker—I was having such a good time! The men I saw were referred to as "clients" or "massages." But finally, after about 3 months one woman used the word "trick" and I realized, "Ohmigod—they're *tricks*! Oh shit—I'm a *hooker*!"[11]

At first she believed the performance for which she was paid was the massage. The money "was for the massage plus a tip," while the sex "was just something I threw in for fun!"[12] "I just thought of myself as a horny masseuse. I liked having sex with the guys after I gave them a brief massage. When it finally did occur to me that I was a hooker, and I got over the initial shock, I enjoyed the idea."[13]

Now we could interpret this reasoning as the false consciousness often attributed to sex workers by antipornography feminists. But false consciousness assumes the existence of a "true" or authentic consciousness betrayed by the persona of the "happy hooker." It is this idea of an "authentic," "true" self that Annie Sprinkle's account of her experience contradicts. For she only recognized herself as a whore—one who performs sex for money—in the word "trick." She never chose—in any liberal, Enlightenment sense of the exercise of free will—to become a whore. Annie Sprinkle found herself "hailed" by an entire system of signification.[14] But her inability to choose does not necessarily mean that she is discursively constructed by a misogynist system over which she has no control, or that she is the victim of misogynist false consciousness. In what sense, then, *can* we speak of Annie Sprinkle's agency in the deeds that make her, first a whore and then, later, an artist?

The answer involves the thorny question of how and in what way there can be agency in the absence of a subject who preexists the discourses in which he or she is situated. In other words, if there is no subjectivity prior to discourse, if subjects are constructed in and by an already existing cultural field, and if, as in Annie Sprinkle's case, that cultural field "interpellates" the woman who performs sex for money as having the identity of "whore," then what hope is there for that woman's ability to "act otherwise" if she doesn't act *against* the system that constructs women as whores and objects of pornography?

Feminist postmodern theorist Judith Butler offers one answer to this problem when she writes that "the question of agency is not to be answered through recourse to an 'I' that pre-exists signification."[15] Rather, Butler argues, agency needs to be reformulated as a question of how agents construct their identities through *resignification*. The rules that enable and restrict the intelligible assertion of an "I"—rules, Butler reminds us, that are structured by gender hierarchy and compulsory heterosexuality—operate through repetition. Signification itself is "*not a founding act, but a regulated process of repetition* that both conceals itself and enforces its rules precisely through the production of substantializing effects." Agency is "located within the possibility of a variation on that repetition." In other words, there is no self prior to the convergence of discursive injunctions to be something (whore, mother, heterosexually desirable object, and so on). There is only, Butler writes, "a taking up of the tools where they lie" (p. 145).

For Annie Sprinkle these tools were initially the remarkable opportunity for repetition in the sexual acts performed by a whore. If, as Butler argues, the self is constructed out of the repetition of performances, and if agency occurs within the possibility of variation, then Annie Sprinkle's repetitious performances of sex acts have been the locus of her construction of self throughout her career. In this first instance of sexual performances in which she first wasn't, and then was, "hailed" as a whore, we can see the discovery of an agency that is not opposed to, but rooted in, the discourse that constructs her. Her agency could be said to consist in the fact that in the repetition of the performance of sex, first for free, then for money, she realizes that "whore" does not fully name who she is. Annie Sprinkle neither denies that she is a whore nor fights the system that so names her. Rather, she accepts the nomination; but in that acceptance also sees room for what Butler calls "subversive repetition." This subversive repetition becomes an articulation of something that is not named in "whore": her own desire. There is no other scene of Annie Sprinkle's agency; the scene of the ob-scene is the place where she is able both to "act otherwise" and still "be herself."

A whore performs sex for pay, usually for a single customer. The sexual performances must please the customer and not necessarily the performer, who may or may not be caught up in its art or excitement. Because the performer is so restricted in the nature of the performance, remarkably little is said about the quality of performance within the customer-whore transaction. Though it is often acknowledged that this performance can be either perfunctory or inspired, it is not an area of performance that is taken very seriously by the traditions of Western art. It is, however, taken seriously in an Eastern, Tantric tradition to which Sprinkle has recently been drawn, as well

Photo by Amy Artry. Art direction by Leslie Berany. Overpainting by Ryszard Wojtynski.

as in the narratives of pornographic films and videos which are almost obses-
sively about the quality and quantities of sexual performance.

All of Annie Sprinkle's performances begin by taking this performance of
sex for the pleasure of a customer or viewer very seriously and by linking this
performance to the fundamental contract by which the whore agrees to
please the john by showing him her "secrets." When Annie describes herself as

a "hooker with a heart of gold," she does so without mockery, without intending to demean the profession of whore or to subvert the whore's basic function of performing sexual acts that give pleasure.[16] She does not rail against the basic dichotomy that divides women into good girls and whores.[17] The art of her performance consists in what she can do by way of subversive repetition within this basic contract, not in refusing or opposing it but in finding her desire cultivated and satisfied within it. In the "whore" phase of Annie Sprinkle's career, these subversive repetitions consist of an ever-widening range of sexual acts, or "perversions" which expand the notion of what sexual performance is, and sexual objects, conventionally not regarded as a acceptable objects of desire—dwarves, burn victims, transsexuals, persons with AIDS, amputees—which allow her to explore her desires in new ways.

From Whore to Pornographer

Deep Inside Annie Sprinkle, the 1981 porno film which Sprinkle wrote and directed, is consistent with her early writings as well as her later performance work in its first-person direct address in the persona of the whore speaking to the client. "Hi, I'm Annie. I'm glad you came to see me. I want us to become very intimate." Intimacy here consists, as in the discourse of the whore, in showing and telling sexual secrets that please. Yet intimacy with a flesh and blood client is the one thing that is not possible within the mediated form of porno film and video; the whore-client relation of proximity is necessarily replaced, and in a sense compensated for, by the ideal visibility of sexual performers who are not physically there with the spectators viewing the film. Yet the woman who performs with another performer for the camera remains a kind of whore, replacing sexual performance with and for the pleasure of one with sexual performance for an audience of many. In most contemporary feature-length hard-core film and video this shift to the audience of many entails the abandonment of the female sexual performer's address to the client.[18]

Annie Sprinkle, however, maintains the paradoxical, quasiparodic rhetoric of intimate address to the client who is no longer really there, in the introduction to each of this film's numbers. Her pornography thus makes a point of retaining the literal voice of the whore whose name is inscribed in the Greek word "pornography," literally, whore-writing: the *graphos* (writing or representations) by *pornei* (whores). This word needs some explanation.

Though Andrea Dworkin has made much of the word's continuity from antiquity,[19] in fact our contemporary notion of pornography, as writing or images depicting sexual activities with the aim of arousal, bears little relation to the meaning of the word in antiquity. Classicist Holt N. Parker writes that *pornographos* was simply a subcategory of biography—tales of the lives of the courtesans—which may not contain any obscene material at all.[20] Parker notes, however, that another subspecies of literature—*anaiskhunto-graphoi*, literally writers of shameless things—more properly corresponds to the erotic content of contemporary pornography. These works, known today only secondarily and from fragments, correspond to our contemporary sex manuals. They were putatively based on the writer's personal experience describing various methods of heterosexual intercourse.[21]

Though the writing of these manuals was ascribed to women, this was not because of any proven female authorship but because the excesses of sexuality—to the Greeks this included pleasures that rendered participants ecstatically out of control and out of possession of themselves—were conceived in antiquity as feminine. Active, in-control sexuality was associated with the free man who "penetrated, who moved, who fucked" and who could also abstain from doing so if he chose. Women, on the other hand, like slaves and boys, were the passive penetrated, who did not move, who were fucked, and who had no power to abstain. Thus while women were the authorities on shameless things, they had no real authority or agency in speaking them because they were lacking the ultimate cultural value of self-control.[22] Parker borrows Joanna Russ's formulation of the classic double bind applied to this literature: "No proper woman writes about sex; therefore the writing is not by a woman. And if she does write, she's not a proper woman.'[23] Since this class of writing about shameless things most closely corresponds to the kind of advice-giving that Annie Sprinkle, speaking from her whore persona, offers in *Deep Inside Annie Sprinkle*, it is worth considering whether this same double bind erasing women's sexual agency still operates today.

In traditional pornography, "whores" (whether literally so or simply women who, because they speak of sex, are automatically "shameless') write of their experience of sex for the pleasure of men. These experiences must be presented as pleasurable for the genre to function. A whole generation of feminist performance artists has aggressively and angrily broken the contract to provide pleasure and thus grounded their performance art in an attack on pleasure that uses the tools of obscenity. Annie Sprinkle differs from these performers in that she does not rupture the whore's contract to provide pleasure. Instead, she goes back to its roots. In taking on the persona and address of the "whore" hailed by misogynist culture, she opens up a field of acting otherwise through subversive repetitions of the role. Moving-image pornography, like prostitution, offers the perfect occasion for repetition since it requires some variation of sexual performances to relieve the monotony of the seven-to-ten numbers conventionally offered by the feature-length form.

In this film Annie Sprinkle, self-designated "porn star," tells the conventional pornographic narrative of her sexual evolution from shy, nonglamorous, nonsexual "Ellen" to the sexually fulfilled, exhibitionist Annie. The basic structure of this narrative, which is full of advice about what positions are the most pleasurable, thus assumes the educative function that extends back to the sex manuals of antiquity. What is different in Annie Sprinkle's "whore-writing," however, is that she injects elements into this narrative that disrupt the active male, passive female paradigm of conventional pornography.

She begins by displaying a scrapbook with photos which are the "real" pictures of herself as an awkward girl growing up. These pictures of the ordinary, nonglamorous woman are unsettling. Whereas they do not suggest that this is the true woman while the fetishized Annie is false, nor do they suggest, as conventional "whore-writing" does, that the "true" woman is the fetishized desirable one. Instead, they suggest the very constructedness of the woman's identity and Annie's ability to manipulate the codes of glamour. The film also introduces an unusual note of social reality, with photos of Mom and Dad and the family and mention of their efforts to accept Annie's role in the "sex business."[24]

Having established that the persona who addresses us is not "naturally" glamorous and sexy, Annie next asks her absent client-viewer if "he" would like to see "what I would love to do to two husky men right now?" Happening across two husky naked men arm-wrestling before a fireplace, she admires their bodies, kisses their muscles, and inserts herself between them to initiate a threeway number that ends with the conventional porno "money shot"—external, and therefore visible, ejaculation by the male.[25] This threesome is perfectly conventional for 80s porn. What isn't conventional is the homoerotic context of the display of glistening male muscles, Annie's verbally articulated delight in their bodies, and her active control of the situation ("what I would like to do").

Moving on to the next number, still addressing an absent "client," Annie asks if he likes "big tits." "You may have noticed I have rather large ones." She then introduces Sassy, a "girlfriend who loves big tits." The number with Sassy is the conventional "lesbian" duo interrupted and completed by a male intruder. What isn't conventional is Sassy's very short stature—her mouth reaches as high as Annie's breasts—Annie's use of her breast to stimulate Sassy's clitoris, and Sassy's sustained, body-shuddering (performance of) orgasm, which takes place before the man arrives.

The third number introduces anal intercourse performed on Annie and ending in a conventional "money shot" on her lower back. What is different in this number is the fact that it begins in Annie's verbal celebration of anal eroticism, in this case her pleasure taken in a man's ass: "You ever wonder why I keep my middle nail short? Now take this ass for example." Though we never see the man's face, Annie continues her "dirty talk" instructions for fingering a man's ass while performing the deed. Only after she has completed her play with his anus does his play with hers commence.

Annie's "objectification" of the man's ass and her instructions on how to give anal pleasure to a man are unconventional preludes to her own more conventional anal penetration. It is possible to see this as simple table-turning: the objectified woman fragments and objectifies the male body in turn. But perhaps more challenging to the conventional porno form is the fact that here too Annie maintains the first-person address to a hypothetical client, speaking to the camera and thus raising new questions about the gendered nature of her address. Is she telling and showing a hypothetical "him" how to finger another man's ass? If so, the film insidiously transgresses "normal" heterosexual taboos against males penetrating males. Is she telling and showing "him" how *she* likes to finger a man's ass? If so, the pleasure depicted casts her in the role of active penetrator and him in the role of penetrated, again a switch in expectations for the conventionally posited heterosexual male viewer. Or is she perhaps telling and showing a hypothetical "her" how to finger a man's anus? After all, this is 80s porn and women are included in its address. If so, the original rhetoric of the female-whore addressing the male-client breaks down. Any way you look at it, Annie has played with the conventions of who gives pleasure to whom.

The fourth number is even less conventional; it constitutes one of Annie's specialities, and at least one source of her name. We could call it the female money shot. Annie performs it first alone, then after intercourse with a male partner. This partner performs his money shot as the conventional climax to intercourse while Annie does hers before his, on her own so to speak, and then as a kind of topper after. This exhibitionist display of female pleasures that are usually, in post-70s moving image pornography, internal and invisible is clearly based on the male-competitive "mine is bigger than yours" or "anything you can do I can do better" model. "You want visible proof of my orgasms measured against the standard of yours?" Annie seems to say, "Well here it is!" In this most spectacular of her performances, the female body might be said to parody the male body's obsession with measurable quantities of ejaculate and the projective force of expulsion, except that, if it is a parody, it is not one that automatically destroys the erotic terms of the performance.

We have seen that Annie Sprinkle's performances take as their starting point the role of the whore, whose first commitment is to deliver the goods: the performance of "sex" in a culture in which such performances can be bought. I have argued in *Hard Core* that contemporary hard-core film and video pornography particularly locates the climactic pay-off of those goods in the invisible interior of women's bodies. The genre's "frenzy of the visible" is thus a contradictory desire to see the involuntary, convulsive proof that a woman's pleasure is taking place measured against the standard of a male "norm."

However, since "normally" the woman's pleasure is not seen and measured in this same quantitative way as the man's, and since visual pornography also wants to show visual evidence of pleasure, the genre has given rise to the enduring fetish of the male money shot. One of the first "corrections" of the new pornography by and for women was to eliminate this convention. The films of the Femme production group offered clean sheets, handsome men, and no money shots. Annie Sprinkle's directorial contribution to this effort—a half-hour segment of *Rites of Passions* (Annie Sprinkle and Veronica Vera, 1987) called *The Search for the Ultimate Sexual Experience*—conformed to this standard as well. But suppression of the masculine standard for the exhibition of pleasure is only one strategy of acting otherwise. Annie Sprinkle's strategy here, in this earlier work, as well as later in *The Sluts and Goddesses Video Workshop, or How to be a Sex Goddess in 101 Easy Steps* (Annie Sprinkle and Maria Beatty, 1992), where she exhibits not only a female money shot but also the performance of a six-minute orgasm, would seem to so spectacularly imitate the male standard of the pornographic evidence of pleasure as to destabilize and denaturalize its "normal" meaning.

Anyone with experience of hard-core film and video must marvel at these orgasmic performances. We might say that, in an adaptation of Luce Irigaray's terms, recognizing the extent to which orgasm is one of the basic "goods" of porno, Annie Sprinkle decided to market her goods with a difference. This difference is measured in the degree of discrepancy and de-formation produced in repetitions that destabilize the very sense of what delivering the "goods" is.[26]

At the Society for Cinema Studies Panel on Annie Sprinkle ("Sprinkle, Sprinkle Little Star: Permutations of a Porn Star," May 1992) there was considerable debate about the nature of Sprinkle's orgasmic performances. While I argued that Sprinkle had performed a female version of a money shot, fellow panelist Chuck Kleinhans insisted that I had misconstrued "golden showers" as female ejaculation.[27] Kleinhans maintained that Sprinkle tells us we are seeing ejaculation for primarily legal reasons, since public urination is legally actionable in some localities. Another panelist, Chris Straayer, also perceived that the liquid was ejaculate but argued a different significance than I had: a liberatory return of the repressed of female ejaculation. Why, Straayer asked, has women's ejaculation been censored in the very pornography that has placed so much emphasis on visible proof of pleasure, if not as a means of continuing to reproduce female "lack"?

The debate suggests how insistently pornography catches its viewers in the impossible question of the ontological real of pleasure. Each of us has a fantasy of this real corresponding to our ideological investments in pleasure. I see Sprinkle playing with the conventions of the hard-core "frenzy of the visible" and exhibiting agency in the parody of masculine money shots; Kleinhans sees a greater affirmation of agency in the greater taboo of golden showers; Straayer sees a greater agency in the exhibition of a self-sufficient female sexuality in female ejaculation. The important point, however, is not to determine the truth of what the female body experiences but, rather, the variety of different truths that can be constructed and the fact that they are constructed here by a female pornographer who is clearly in control. Pornography is all about the supposedly true and natural but actually constructed bodily confessions of pleasure. Annie Sprinkle shows the extent to which even the whore locked in the contract to please the customer, making confession of the "shameless things" of sex, can speak differently—not necessarily more truthfully—of these things.

In a broader sense, however, we might consider the basic marketing of the "shameless goods" of Annie Sprinkle herself. Sprinkle is the fetishized woman *par excellence*. Though she will later metamorphose into an oscillation between the two equally valued states of slut and goddess, in this earlier pornography the self-conscious masquerade of femininity is of the whore who aims to please. But as we have seen, there is enough of a Mae West-style exaggeration in this persona to alert us to an element of parody. The gap-toothed, big-breasted, slightly chubby woman who addresses us in her sexiest voice and who has already shown us the pre-whore, preporn body out of which this new persona was constructed, presents herself as an effect of per-

ANATOMY OF A PIN UP Photo:

• False Eyelashes

• Mandatory Fake beauty mark.

• eyebrows penciled in

• Hair dyed to cover some gray.

• Breasts are real but sag. Bra lifts breasts.

• Extra Blush

• Red lipstick

• Hair put into HOT Rollers for curling but it creats dryness+ split ends.

• Pucker gives suggestion of a blow job

• Lungs restricted. I cannot brethe

• Bra is a size too small to make breasts look bigger.

• Body make-up.

• Hemeroids don't show, thank goodness.

• Corset hides a very big belly.

• Corset makes my waist 4½" smaller, but I can't brethe.

• I need assistance to hook all these garters, and to lace back of corset.

• Extra tall stockings make my legs look longer.

• Black stockings make legs look thinner.

• I never wear gloves except in pin-up photos.

• Gloves cover tattoos for a more All American girl effect. Barrowed from Antionette.

• Boots take 19 minutes to lace up. I need assistance to lace them because I can't bend over in the corset.

• I can't walk and can barely hobble.

• A plexiglass square keeps the white seemless paper from smudging.

• These heels are excruciatingly high.

• Boots are 1½ sizes too small. Barrowed and worn only for this shoot.

• My feet are killing me.

(In spite of it all, I'm sexually excited AND feeling great.)

Anatomy of a Pinup Photo. Photo by Zorro 1981. Drawing and idea by Annie Sprinkle 1991.

formance. As in her later how-to-do-it diagrams in which she draws arrows to parts of her body to show how a particular fetish effect was achieved, or in the famous bosom ballet in which she performs a dance with painted, yin/yang breasts, she invites us to admire a performance the truth of which is always elusive.

The gap between the performed imitation of the sex goddess and the "original" on which that imitation is based creates an effect not unlike that of the drag queen. Although Sprinkle "is" a woman and doesn't perform otherwise, her exaggeratedly fetishized femme appearance is offered as a performative achievement, not as natural. Judith Butler writes that "in imitating gender, drag implicitly reveals the imitative structure of gender itself.'[28] Sex and gender are denaturalized in drag by a performance which avows their distinctness and dramatizes the cultural mechanism of their fabricated unity.

In a recent documentary about Tantric sexual seekers, *Sacred Sex* (Cynthia Connop, 1992), Annie Sprinkle tells us in an interview that in her *Post-Post Porn Modernist* performance piece she takes on the persona of a "porno bimbo character." This could sound as if she performs a demeaning imitation of such a character, as if the parodic repetition criticizes the unauthenticity of the original. However, in neither of the performances of this role does Annie Sprinkle assume that there is a "proper" or "normal" female identity from which this construction diverges. Her parody of gender and desirability thus reveals, as Butler puts it about drag, "that the original identity after which gender fashions itself is an imitation without an origin."[29]

Parody causes laughter. But this laughter does not chide the imitative failure of this character with reference to a better, "truer" woman. It might be more appropriate, then, to speak of Annie Sprinkle's parody—her subversive repetitions of sexual performances, her "porno bimbo character" played to the hilt—as more properly a form of pastiche. The term has been invoked in a manner critical of postmodernism by Fredric Jameson, who argues that our contemporary postmodern condition is replete with parodies that have lost their ability to criticize and hence their ability to laugh. Such parodies degenerate to mere pastiche: imitations that mock the very notion of an original. Jameson argues that without the feeling that there exists something normal compared to which what is being imitated is comic, pastiche becomes blank parody, "parody that has lost its humor."[30]

It is precisely this notion of "norm," and "original," however, that is at issue in a postmodern world of sexual identities and representations.

We have seen that laughter at sexual pleasures which diverge from a "norm" are familiar features of contemporary culture. All the more reason, then, to welcome the pastiche with humor that does not posit a corrective norm but continuously plays with the terms of norm and perversion. This is what Annie Sprinkle does best. Sprinkle is proof, as Judith Butler puts it, that "the loss of the sense of 'the normal' . . . can be its own occasion for laughter, especially when "the normal' 'the original' is revealed to be a copy . . . an ideal that no one *can* embody."[31]

From Pornographer to Performance Artist (a Sketch)

These, then, are some examples of the strategy of the "post'—postmodern, poststructuralist, postfeminist—in the early work of Annie Sprinkle. While this work is not yet performance art and not yet "postporn," we can see in it the seeds of an evolution that is beyond, but never against, porn. Annie Sprinkle's persona will go on to include the sex educator, the sex therapist, the sexual fairy godmother, and the sex goddess—all personae which are reworked into the *Post-Post Porn Modernist* theatre piece.

In each new permutation, Sprinkle never denies or criticizes her whore-porn origins. For example, in *The Sluts and Goddesses Video Workshop, or How to be a Sex Goddess in 101 Easy Steps* Sprinkle becomes a "legitimate" sex educator proffering more knowledge than pleasure. Yet the interest of the tape is its combination of clinical knowledge and raunchy enjoyment, the participatory hands-on, pornographic nature of this particular sex educator's "show and tell." Once again Sprinkle has gone to the roots of the form —sex manual advice on the best positions—and transformed it without directly opposing it.

If, as the classicists tell us, pornographic sex manuals by putative women for the pleasure of men are the true origins of what today we call pornography, then this "workshop" exclusively by and discursively addressed to women, yet still imbued with all the naughtiness of conventional pornography, is its reappropriation. This reappropriation is certainly not free of the conventions of pornographic sex manuals for men. In this video, for example, Sprinkle repeats her performance of the female money shot, and goes on to measure the duration of an orgasm with a graphic insert of a digital clock (five minutes and ten seconds).

This image of the sex-educator flexing her orgasmic muscles is still similar to the whore-pornographer in *Deep Inside Annie Sprinkle*. In both cases duration and ejaculation are emphasized. In both cases a parody pastiche of masculine conventions dominates. Yet in this video, orgasm is no longer performed for the pleasure of a discursively addressed male viewer. Other women in the video facilitate the orgasm and function as audience cheerleaders. In the *Post-Post Porn Modernist* performance piece, the orgasm is a solo and the point is the self-sufficiency of the female body.

We have seen that Annie Sprinkle's spectacular orgasms are the constant feature of each of her pornographic, educative, or art performances. We have also seen the subtle ways in which these orgasms take on new meanings in different contexts. The point about these orgasms is never whether they are real or performed, showered with ejaculate or urine, parodic or sincere, since with Annie Sprinkle there is never an either/or but always a this/and.

These orgasms can be taken as indices of a very different sexual agency from that which obtained for the whore-writers of antiquity. For the Greeks, the rigid dichotomy between passive penetrated and active penetrator corresponded to the feminine and the masculine positions. Pleasure was always on the side of the uncontrolled female and, as in the famous argument between Zeus and Hera about who had the most pleasure in sex, always operated to the detriment of female agency in the social sphere. The woman's pleasure, quantified as inherently greater than the male's, was out of control and in excess, while the masculine pleasure of penetrator was capable of control and not in excess.

The female body remains today the one more "saturated" with sex. The insatiable, "excessively" pleasuring woman remains caught in the familiar double bind by which her knowledge of sex invalidates other forms of authority—we can think, for example, of Arlen Specter and the Senate Judiciary Committee's dismissal of Anita Hill's charges against Clarence Thomas as sexual fantasy and displaced desire. Nevertheless, despite the very real operation of this harmful double standard, the sphere of the sexual now occupies so much greater an area of social concern and social power that participation in sexual pleasure no longer automatically signifies the same powerlessness it did for the Greeks. This is why it is important not to conflate today's pornography with that of the ancients, or indeed, with that of any other time. And this is why sex-positive Annie Sprinkle and her spectacular orgasms can suggest quite another strategy for "acting otherwise."

I would make no claim for the resisting, subversive potential of Annie Sprinkle's strategies outside the realm of the sexual. And certainly sexual performance is *not* the solution to a great many of the problems of women. But Annie Sprinkle shows that, within the realm of the sexual, performances of bosom ballets, female money shots, and six-minute orgasms can sometimes work wonders. For sexuality today is a thoroughly commodified arena of self-help and self-fulfillment requiring levels of self-control and agency that would have baffled the Greeks. While it was once the case that a mind/body split relegated men to the realm of the spirit, women to the realm of the body, placing the blame of male lust on women, today sexual pleasure is far too important a commodity for women not to seek in it their own desire and agency.

NOTES

1. Cindy Carr, "War on Art: The Sexual Politics of Censorship," *Village Voice*, June 5, 1990, p. 28. Sprinkle called her performance piece, at the Cleveland Performance Art Festival, a demystification of the female body. She describes the burlesque club where she performed live sex as the "wildest" place she ever worked, commenting that the vice squad was unconcerned about that obscenity because it was confined to "the porn ghetto." "But now that it's something for me . . ." (Carr, p. 27).

2. Art critic Linda Burnham writes, for example, "I went to Cleveland for this performance [Annie Sprinkle's performance at the Cleveland Performance Art Festival], and performance art critics don't come any more credentialed than I do, and I declare it: Annie Sprinkle is a performance artist and this performance was art, not pornography." *High Performance* (1990): 13. In his paper at the 1992 Society for Cinema Studies conference, "When Did Annie Sprinkle Become an Artist?: Female Performance Art, Male Performance Anxiety, Art as Alibi, and Labial Art," Chuck Kleinhans has shown that Burnham's defense of Sprinkle is based both on an appeal to authority and on the location of a specific point in Sprinkle's career when she ceased to be pornographic and became art. Something of the same discriminating assertion occurs in performance artist Linda Montano's "baptism" of Annie Sprinkle and Veronica Vera as artists while the two were in attendance at Montano's upstate New York summer camp in 1987. See Linda Montano, "Summer Saint Camp 1987," *The Drama Review* 33 no. 1 (Spring 1989). The assumption in these defenses is that Annie Sprinkle became a performance artist when she began to deconstruct sexiness rather than simply to arouse. I hope to show, however, that Annie Sprinkle's performances never obey such simple dichotomies.

3. This line drawing, like the line drawing between the erotic and the pornographic, almost always depends on who you are and what turns you on (or off): pornography, as Robbe-Grillet once said, is the eroticism of the "other." In other words, if it turns me on it's erotic; if it turns you on it's pornographic. Performance art as a whole has been condemned by the New Right philistines as pornography on the assumption that some creep, not me, gets turned on by the material, or as bogus art. Here is Tony Kornheiser in a recent piece in the *Washington Post* (February 9,

1992): "I'm not exactly sure what it is—other than it seems like everybody who does it gets naked. Does that mean when I'm taking a shower, I'm a performance artist? Because if that's the case I want the NEA to spring for the soap." At the other extreme of this position is the condemnation of performance art as pornography. Attacks on performance art, like attacks on pornography, oscillate between the assumption that any engagement of the body is excessively obscene (showing what should never be shown) or excessively ordinary (the naked body in the shower).

4. "When Did Annie Sprinkle Become an Artist? Female Performance Art, Male Performance Anxiety, Art as Alibi, and Labial Art." Paper given at the Society for Cinema Studies conference, May 1992.

5. See "Pornographies On/Scene, or "Diff'rent Strokes for Diff'rent Folks'," in Lynne Segal and Mary McIntosh, eds., Sex Exposed: Sexuality and the Pornography Debate (London: Virago, 1992). In this article I suggest that the word "obscene," which literally means "off scene," no longer functions to refer to genuinely hidden things, sexual or otherwise. In our contemporary sexual politics the more proper term is on/scene.

6. Quoted in the documentary film Sacred Sex (Cynthia Connop, 1992).

7. Tania Modleski, Feminism Without Women: Culture and Criticism in a "Postfeminist" Age (New York: Routledge, 1991), p. 8.

8. These are excerpts from the Minneapolis Ordinance authored by Andrea Dworkin and Catharine MacKinnon. In "Appendix II" of Varda Burstyn, ed., Women against Censorship (Vancouver: Douglas and MacIntyre, 1985), p. 206.

9. Denise Riley, Am I that Name? Feminism and the Category of "Women" in History (Minneapolis: University of Minnesota Press, 1988).

10. Modleski, Feminism without Women, pp. 16–17.

11. Andrea Juno and V. Vale, Angry Women: Re/Search Publication (San Francisco, 1991), p. 24.

12. Ibid., p. 26.

13. Annie Sprinkle, Post Porn Modernist (Amsterdam: Torch Books, 1991), p. 13.

14. Louis Althusser, "Ideology and Ideological State Apparatuses (Notes towards an Investigation)," in Lenin and Philosophy and Other Essays, trans. Ben Brewster (London: New Left Books, 1971), pp. 122–73.

15. Judith Butler, Gender Trouble: Feminism and the Subversion of Identity (New York and London: Routledge, 1990), p. 143.

16. Juno and Vale, Angry Women, p. 26.

17. This is why she is out of place in an anthology called Angry Women.

18. Many stag films, however, still retain this discursive address. See Linda Williams, Hard Core: Power, Pleasure, and the "Frenzy of the Visible" (Berkeley: University of California Press, 1989), pp. 58–92.

19. Andrea Dworkin, *Pornography: Men Possessing Women* (Chicago: University of Chicago Press, 1979).

20. Holt Parker, "Love's Body Anatomized: The Ancient Erotic Handbooks and the Rhetoric of Sexuality," in Amy Richlin, ed., *Pornography and Representation in Greece and Rome* (New York: Oxford University Press, 1992), p. 91.

21. Ibid.

22. Ibid., p. 99

23. Dworkin, *Pornography*, p. 93.

24. It is worth noting that this shot of Mom and Dad is held so briefly that their faces are not actually discernible, apparently out of consideration for their feelings.

25. I discuss the form and function of this money shot in Chapter 4 of *Hard Core*.

26. I am alluding here to Luce Irigaray's notion, in the essay "When the Goods Get Together," that women as commodities have been prostituted to men as "goods." Irigaray suggests that these goods should refuse to go to market. However, she also raises another possibility—which she goes on to reject—that the goods might "go to market on their own . . . enjoy their own worth among themselves, to speak to each other, to desire each other, free from the control of seller-buyer-consumer subjects." In Luce Irigaray, *This Sex which is not One*, trans. Catherine Porter and Carolyn Burke (Ithaca: Cornell University Press, 1985), p. 197. I have suggested in *Hard Core* that the Femme Productions group of female pornographers, to which Annie Sprinkle belongs, represents a form of the "goods" getting together to market themselves differently (pp. 248–50). I am suggesting here that Annie Sprinkle's marketing offers a subtle revision of what these goods are.

27. His argument was based on his perception that liquid emerged from the urethra and not, as I thought, the vagina.

28. Butler, *Gender Trouble*, p. 137.

29. Ibid., p. 138.

30. Fredric Jameson, "Postmodernism and Consumer Society," in Hal Foster, ed., *The Anti-Aesthetic: Essays on Postmodern Culture* (Port Townsend, Wash.: Bay Press, 1983), p. 114.

31. Butler, *Gender Trouble*, pp. 138–39.

23

Tracking the Vampire

Sue-Ellen Case

In my teens, when I experienced the beginnings of fierce desire and embracing love for
other women, the only word I knew to describe my desire and my feelings was "queer"—
a painful term hurled as an insult against developing adolescents who were, somehow,
found to be unable to ante up in the heterosexist economy of sexual and emotional trade.
"Queer" was the site in the discourse at which I
felt both immediate identification and shame—
a contradiction that both established my social
identity and required me to render it somehow
invisible. At the same time, I discovered a book
on the life of Arthur Rimbaud. I was astounded
to find someone who, at approximately my
same age, embraced such an identity and even
made it the root of his poetic language. Thus,
while brimming with a desire and longing that
forced me to remain socially silent, I found in
Rimbaud an exquisite language—a new way

Sue-Ellen Case, "Tracking the Vampire." Appeared in *Differences:
A Journal of Feminist Cultural Studies* 3:2 (1991): 1–20. Reprinted
with permission of the publisher.

for language to mean, based on reveling in an illegitimate, homosexual state of desire.

This adolescent phase in the construction of my social identity is still marked in the word "queer" for me, with its plenitude and pain, its silence and poetry, and its cross-gender identification. For I became queer through my readerly identification with a male homosexual author. The collusion of the patriarchy and the canon made Rimbaud more available to me than the few lesbian authors who had managed to make it into print. Later, a multitude of other experiences and discourses continued to enhance my queer thinking. Most prominent among them was the subcultural discourse of camp which I learned primarily from old dykes and gay male friends I knew in San Francisco, when I lived in the ghetto of bars—before the rise of feminism. Then there was feminism, both the social movement and the critique, which became my social and theoretical milieu—after the bars. And finally, my young lesbian students and friends who have taught me how, in many ways, my life and my writing reflect a lesbian "of a certain age." My construction of the following queer theory, then, is historically and materially specific to my personal, social, and educational experience, and hopefully to others who have likewise suffered the scourge of dominant discourse and enjoyed these same strategies of resistance. It is in no way offered as a general truth or a generative model.

My adolescent experience still resonates through the following discursive strategies: the pain I felt upon encountering heterosexist discourse here becomes a critique of heterosexism within feminist theory—a way of deconstructing my own milieu to ease the pain of exclusion as well as to confront what we have long, on the street, called "the recreational use of the lesbian"; the identification with the insult, the taking on of the transgressive, and the consequent flight into invisibility are inscribed in the figure of the vampire; the discovery of Rimbaud and camp enables a theory that reaches across lines of gender oppression to gay men and, along with feminist theory, prompts the writing itself—ironically distanced and flaunting through metaphor. By imploding this particular confluence of strategies, this queer theory strikes the blissful wound into ontology itself, to bleed the fast line between living and dead.

But I am rushing headlong into the pleasure of this wound, an acceleration instigated by the figure that haunts this introduction, the figure that appears and disappears—the vampire. Like the actor peeking out at the audience from the wings before the curtain rises, she rustles plodding, descriptive prose into metaphors whose veiled nature prompts her entrance. Her discursive retinue whets my desire to flaunt, to camp it up a bit, to trans-invest the tropes. But first, the necessary warm-up act of exposition.

The Relationship Between Queer Theory and Lesbian Theory: or, "Breaking Up's So Very Hard To Do"

Queer theory, unlike lesbian theory or gay male theory, is not gender specific. In fact, like the term "homosexual," queer foregrounds same-sex desire without designating which sex is desiring. As a feminist, I am aware of the problems that congregate at this site. These problems are both historical and theoretical. Gay male theory is inscribed with patriarchal privilege, which it sometimes deconstructs and sometimes does not. Lesbian theory is often more narrowly lesbian feminist theory, or lesbian theory arising, historically, from various alignments with feminist theory. Through its alliance with feminism, lesbian theory often proceeds from theories inscribed with heterosexism. I will deal at length with this problem later. But for now, I would contend that both gay male and lesbian theory reinscribe sexual difference, to some extent, in their gender-specific construction. In her article "Sexual Indifference and Lesbian Representation," Teresa de Lauretis has already elucidated some of the problematic ways that sexual difference is marked within lesbian representation. For, while gender is an important site of struggle for women, the very notion reinscribes sexual difference in a way that makes it problematic for the lesbian, as de Lauretis configures it, "to be seen." This gender base also leads to problems for lesbians when a certain feminist theory defines the gaze itself, as will be illustrated later.

In contrast to the gender-based construction of the lesbian in representation, queer theory, as I will construct it here, works not at the site of gender, but at the site of ontology, to shift the ground of being itself, thus challenging the Platonic parameters of Being—the borders of life and death. Queer desire is constituted as a transgression of these boundaries and of the organicism which defines the living as the good. The Platonic construction of a life/death binary opposition at the base, with its attendant gender opposition above, is subverted by a queer desire which seeks the living dead, producing a slippage at the ontological base and seducing through a gender inversion above. Rephrasing that well-known exchange between Alice B. Toklas and Gertrude Stein at Gertrude's death bed, Alice might here ask: "Now that you're dying, tell me Gertrude, what's the answer?" And Gertrude might reply: "What's the queery?" Gertrude, the lesbian on the border of life/death, locked in language with her lover, exits through a campy inversion.

The lethal offshoot of Plato's organicism has been its association with the natural. Life/death becomes the binary of the "natural" limits of Being: the organic is the natural. In contrast, the queer has been historically constituted as unnatural. Queer desire, as unnatural, breaks with this life/death binary of Being through same-sex desire. The articulation of queer desire also breaks with the discourse that claims mimetically to represent that "natural" world, by subverting its tropes. In queer discourse, as Oscar Wilde illustrated, "the importance of being earnest" is a comedy. Employing the subversive power of the unnatural to unseat the Platonic world view, the queer, unlike the rather polite categories of gay and lesbian, revels in the discourse of the loathsome, the outcast, the idiomatically proscribed position of same-sex desire. Unlike petitions for civil rights, queer revels constitute a kind of activism that attacks the dominant notion of the natural. The queer is the taboo-breaker, the monstrous, the uncanny. Like the Phantom of the Opera, the queer dwells underground, below the operatic overtones of the dominant; frightening to look at, desiring, as it plays its own organ, producing its own music.

This un-natural sense of the queer was, of course, first constituted as a negative category by dominant social practices, which homosexuals later embraced as a form of activism. Historically, the category of the unnatural was one of an aggregate of notions aimed at securing the right to life for a small minority of the world's population. This right to life was formulated through a legal, literary, and scientistic discourse on blood, which stabilized privilege by affirming the right to life for those who could claim blood and further, pure blood, and the consequent death sentence, either metaphorically or literally, for those who could not. Against the homosexual, this right was formulated as the seeming contradiction between sterile homosexual sex and fertile heterosexual practice; that is, before recent technological "advances," heterosexuals may have babies because of their sexual practice and queers may not. From the heterosexist perspective, the sexual practice that produced babies was associated with giving life, or practicing a life-giving sexuality, and the living was established as the category of the natural. Thus, the right to life was a slogan not only for the unborn, but for those whose sexual practices could produce them. In contrast, homosexual sex was mandated as sterile—an unlive practice that was consequently unnatural, or queer, and, as that which was unlive, without the right to life.

Queer sexual practice, then, impels one out of the generational production of what has been called "life" and history, and ultimately out of the category of the living. The equation of hetero = sex = life and homo = sex = unlife
generated a queer discourse that reveled in proscribed desiring by imagining
sexual objects and sexual practices within the realm of the other-than-nat-
ural, and the consequent other-than-living. In this discourse, new forms of
being, or beings, are imagined through desire. And desire is that which
wounds—a desire that breaks through the sheath of being as it has been imagined within a heterosexist society. Striking at its very core, queer desire
punctures the life/death and generative/destructive bipolarities that enclose
the heterosexist notion of being.

"Was It the Taste of Blood? Nay . . . the Taste of Love"

Although, as a queer theorist, I eschew generational models of history, I
would like to perform the reading of certain texts, not as precursors, fathers,
or mothers of a youthful time, but as traces of she-who-would-not-be-seen,
whose movement is discernible within certain discursive equations. The
compound of wounding desire, gender inversion, and ontological shift is
early configured in mystic writings. The mystic women authors, such as
Hrotsvitha von Gandersheim, Teresa of Avila, or Hildegard von Bingen write
of reveling in the wounding, ontological desire. Yet their precision in marking the social oppression in the feminine position of such desire makes the
gendering of that desire mimetic—stable in its historical resonances. Gender
slippage, performed through the ontological break, may be found in the
writings of an early male mystic—marking both oppression in the feminine
and liberation in the adoption of it.

The works of John of the Cross, although not literally queer, begin a tradition that will be taken up later as literal by Rimbaud, Wilde, and more
recently Alexis DeVeaux. John's wounding desire is articulated in several
ways, but often as a fire, as in his treatise, the *Living Flame of Love*: "had not
God granted a favor to [the] flesh, and covered it with his right hand . . . it
would have died at each touch of this flame, and its natural being would have
been corrupted" (49); or, "the healing of love is to hurt and wound once
more that which has been hurt and wounded already, until the soul comes to
be wholly dissolved in the wound of love" (61). The flame of this desire not
only corrupts natural beings, but sears into a world where being is reconfigured. John, the mystic lover, desires a being of a different order—one who

does not live or die as we know it. In order to "know" this being, the senses and thus epistemology must be reconfigured. In his poem "The Dark Night of the Soul," John lyricizes this reconfiguring of the senses necessary for his tryst (*Poems*). Then, in "The Spiritual Canticle," where his love finds full expression in the trope of marriage, John inverts his gender, writing his desire as if he were the bride with the other being as the bridegroom. John, the bride, languishes for her lover, seeks him everywhere, finally reaching him: "Our bed: in roses laid/patrols of lions ranging all around. . . . There I gave all of me; put chariness aside: there I promised to become his bride" (*Poems* 7–9). And the bridegroom says to John: "I took you tenderly hurt virgin, made you well (13)." The wound of love liberates the lover from the boundaries of being—the living, dying envelope of the organic. Ontology shifts through gender inversion and is expressed as same-sex desire. This is queer, indeed.

Historically, John's queer break-through from "life" also signaled a break with a dominant discourse that legislated the right to life through pure blood. His works were written in Spain during the so-called Golden Age, with its literature and social practice of honor and pure blood: the dominant discourse was spattered with the blood of women and their illicit lovers, but ultimately aimed, in the subtext, against the impure blood of Jews and Moors (the figure for illicit lovers a cover for *conversos*). The Golden Age tragedies set the scene of desire in the context of the generational model, the family and the potential family, in a verse that conflates racial purity with sexual honor, and spilt blood with the protection of pure blood.[1] Writing his poems in a cramped prison cell designed to torture, John defied the generational, heterosexual mandate by a counterdiscourse that set desire in gender inversion: he countered the conflation of race/love/life in a discourse that imagined and orgiastically embraced the un-dead.[2] Blood, in the dominant discourse which was writing racial laws along with such tragedies, is genealogy, the blood right to money; and blood/money is the realm of racial purity and pure heterosexuality. Looking forward several centuries, one can see the actual tragic performance of this dominant equation in Hitler's death camps, where, among others, both Jews and homosexuals were put to death. More recently, one can see such tropes operating in the anti-AIDS discourse that conflates male homosexual desire with the contamination of blood.

I would like to read from this dominant discourse of blood, death, purity, and heterosexual generation in its most obscene form: Hitler's *Mein Kampf*. I apologize for quoting such a text, for, on the one hand, I can understand the necessity of censoring it as they do in Germany; but, on the other hand, this text sets out the compound I am here addressing in its most succinct form—the horror story of the obscene notion of the right to life for racially pure heterosexuals and death for the others.

> The Jew . . . like the pernicious bacillus, spreads over wider and wider areas. . . . Wherever he establishes himself the people who grant him hospitality are bound to be bled to death sooner or later. . . . He poisons the blood of others but preserves his own blood unadulterated. . . . The black-haired Jewish youth lies in wait for hours on end, satanically glaring and spying on the inconspicuous girl whom he plans to seduce, adulterating her blood and removing her from the bosom of her own people. . . . The Jews were responsible for bringing Negroes into the Rhineland, with the ultimate idea of bastardizing the white race. (quoted in Poliakov 1)

Such discourse invented the vampiric position—the one who waits, strikes, and soils the living, pure blood; and it is against this bloody discourse that the queer vampire strikes, with her evacuating kiss that drains the blood out, transforming it into a food for the un-dead.

The dominant image of the vampire began to appear in Western Europe in the eighteenth century through tales and reports from small villages in the East. In literature, Mario Praz observes in *The Romantic Agony*, the vampire appears in the nineteenth century as the Byronic hero who destroys not only himself but his lovers. Praz finds "the love crime" to be essential to the figure, who early in the century was a man, but in the second half—what Praz calls "the time of Decadence" (75–77)—was a woman. For the purposes of queer theory, the most important work in the dominant tradition is "Carmilla" by Sheridan Le Fanu, the first lesbian vampire story, in which the lesbian, desiring and desired by her victim, slowly brings her closer through the killing kiss of blood. In the dominant discourse, this kiss of blood is a weakening device that played into male myths of menstruation, where women's monthly loss of blood was associated with their pale, weak image.[3]

In the counterdiscourse, Rimbaud builds on the elements in John, writing those revels into a more literally queer poetry. To the gender inversion Rimbaud adds a moral and metaphysical one. The ontological break remains, but heaven becomes hell, and the saint becomes the criminal. In his *Season in Hell* such desire once again makes the male lover into the bride, but Rimbaud's lover is now the "infernal bridegroom." His wounding love is more literally painful, and this pain, this love, this ontological shift, as in John, creates a new epistemology—a reorganization of the senses. Along with these inversions, Rimbaud also revels in the mythical impurities of blood and race. One example from *A Season in Hell*: "It's very obvious to me I've always belonged to an inferior race. I can't figure out revolt. My race never rose up except to loot: like wolves after beasts they haven't killed" (3–4). His sepulchral, racially inferior, dangerous queer rises up to walk in *Illuminations*:

> Your cheeks are hollow. Your fangs gleam. Your breast is like a lyre, tinklings circulate through your pale arms. Your heart beats in that belly where sleeps the double sex. Walk through the night, gently moving that thigh, that second thigh, and that left leg. ("Antique" 25)

This is a fanged creature, who promises the wound of love that pierces the ontological/societal sac.

But it is Oscar Wilde who wrote the queer kiss in *Salome*. At the end of the play, Salome stands with the severed head of Iokanaan in her hand. Herod, who looks on in horror, commands that the moon and the stars, God's natural creation, go dark. They shall not illuminate the transgressive, unnatural kiss. Wilde has the moon and stars actually disappear, and in the vacuum, outside of natural creation, Salome says:

> Ah, I have kissed thy mouth, Iokanaan, I have kissed thy mouth. There was a bitter taste on thy lips. Was it the taste of blood? . . . Nay, but perchance it was the taste of love. . . . They say that love hath a bitter taste. . . . But what matter? What matter? I have kissed thy mouth, Iokanaan, I have kissed thy mouth. (66–67)

Wilde wrote these lines in 1892—when they were first uttered on stage, after issues of censorship, Wilde was in prison. The immorality, or the taboo status of this desire, socially expressed in Wilde's incarceration, becomes a life/death break in his writing—the wound that decapitates the natural and delivers it into the hands of the queer who desires it.

Now, in the nineteenth century, this queer compound led by inverted brides and Oscar Wilde in drag as a dancing girl, the feminized gender that shifts ontologies, was also represented as lesbian desire. Baudelaire's lesbians in "Femmes Damnées Delphine et Hippolyte" lay in their chamber:

"Reclining at her feet, elated yet calm,/Delphine stared up at her with shining eyes/the way a lioness watches her prey/once her fangs marked it for her own" (304). After their love-making, Baudelaire sends them down to hell, out of this life, desiccated by their dry desire, as he called it, the "stérilité de votre jouissance (307)." At least, in Baudelaire, *jouissance* belongs to the lesbian couple. Nevertheless, once again the fangs, the death, the other world of the living dead. But what was the metaphorical bride of inverted gender is represented here as lesbian desire—the gender trope of the double-feminized.

I read lesbian here, the two "she's" together, as a trope. The term does not mimetically refer to a gender in the world. In queer discourse, "she" is the wounding, desiring, transgressive position that weds, through sex, an unnatural being. "She" is that bride. "She" is the fanged lover who breaks the ontological sac—the pronominal Gomorrah of the queer. When two "she's" are constructed, it is a double trope—a double masquerade. To read that desire as lesbian is not to reinscribe it with dominant, heterosexist categories of gender, for lesbian, in queer theory, is a particular dynamic in the system of representation: the doubled trope of "she's," constructed in the dominant discourse as the doubly inferior, the doubly impure, and recast in the queer as Wrigley chewing gum celebrates it: "double your pleasure, double your fun."

I realize that this seems to be a move away from the material, historical condition of lesbians. Yet the entry point of this theory rests upon my entrance, as an adolescent, into the speaking and hearing, reading and writing about my sexuality. Insofar as I am queer, or lesbian, this identity is in consonance with the discursive strategies that those words represent historically: my desire and my sexual practice are inscribed in these words and, conversely, these words—the historical practice of a discourse—are inscribed in my sexual practice. Take, for instance, my years of furtive pleasure between the sheets, or my years of promiscuous tweeking and twaddling. Both eras were performances of the double trope of the "she," either as the doubly inferior, marked by oppression, or as double pleasure, reveling in transgression. To ask "will the real lesbian please stand up," when she is embedded in the dominant discursive mandate to disappear, or in the subcultural subversion to flaunt her distance from the "real," is like asking the vampire to appear in the mirror. (She made me write that. For now is the time of her entrance on screen.) The double "she," in combination with the queer fanged creature, produces the vampire. The vampire is the queer in its lesbian mode.

The En-tranced Take: The Lesbian and the Vampire

So finally, now, the vampire can make her appearance. But how does she appear? How can she appear, when the visible is not in the domain of the queer, when the apparatus of representation still belongs to the un-queer? Thus far, we've had the fun, fun, fun of imagining the liberating, creative powers of the queer in representation. Unfortunately, daddy always takes the T-Bird away and the vampire, those two "she's" in the driver's seat, is left standing at the cross-roads of queer theory and dominant discourse. Although the "she" is not mimetic of gender, "she" is shaped, in part, by her pronominal history—that is, how "she" is constructed elsewhere and previously in language. Along the metaphorical axis, "she" is somehow the queer relative of the other girls. What this "she" vampire flaunts is the cross—the crossing out of her seductive pleasure, the plenitude of proximity and the break. Thus, the dominant gaze constructs a vampire that serves only as a proscription—is perceived only as a transgression: interpolated between the viewer and the vampire is the cross—the crossing out of her image. Dominant representation has made of the vampire a horror story.

But this site/sight of proscription lingers in the theoretical construction of the gaze in feminist theory as well—specifically in theories of the gaze proceeding from psychoanalytic presumptions. There, the vampire is subjected to the familiar mode of "seduced and abandoned," or "the recreational use of the lesbian," for while such heterosexist feminist discourse flirts with her, it ultimately double-crosses her with the hegemonic notion of "woman," reinscribing "her" in the generational model and making horrible what must not be seductive. The vampire as the site or sight of the undead leads such feminist discourse back to the mother's right to life, where fruition becomes the counterdiscourse of exclusion. For example, taking Kristeva's cue that the birthing mother is transgressive, flowing with the milk of semiosis, the cover photo on Jane Gallop's *Thinking Through the Body* fixes the gaze at the birthing vaginal canal of the author, suggesting that her head may be found inside the book.[4] In other words, Mother Gallop's site of fruition counters discursive exclusion. But does not the feminist political privileging of this sight, designed to empower "women," re-enliven, as the shadowy "other" of this fertile, feminist mother, the earlier categories of the "unnatural" and "sterile" queer, transposed here from dominant discourse to feminist troping on the body?[5] Further, the melding of mother and desire into the hegemonic category of "woman's" plenitude also masks the transgression at the very site of fruition by both the "racially inferior" and the "sexually sterile." Because my desire is for the vampire to appear/disappear, guided by the pain of exclusion, I must now critically read the feminist theory of the gaze and of "woman" in order to reclaim her (the vampire's) role in representation.

Popular lore tells us that if we look at the vampire without the proscriptions that expel her, our gaze will be hypnotically locked into hers and we will become her victims. The feminist theorists, aware of the seductive quality of the vampire's look, excavate the proscription to discover the desire below. For example, Linda Williams's ground-breaking article "When the Woman Looks" constructs a certain dynamic of women looking at monsters. Williams notes that when the woman sees the monster, she falls into a trance-like fascination that "fails to maintain the distance between observer and observed so essential to the 'pleasure' of the voyeur." As the woman looks at the monster, her "look of horror paralyzes her in such a way that distance is overcome (86)." Hers is an en-tranced look, and the fascination in it could be read as a response to lesbian desire.

However, Williams's notion of proximity in the look proceeds from the hegemonic notion of "woman." As Mary Ann Doane phrases it, woman is "[t]oo close to herself, entangled in her own enigma, she could not step back, could not achieve the necessary distance of a second look (75–76). Thus, Williams's reading of woman's trance-like lock into the gaze with the monster is an extension of "woman's" condition in the gaze. How this "woman" is locked in the gaze, or what constitutes her pleasurable proximity, figures Williams, is her identification with the monster—a shared identification between monster and woman in representation: since they both share the status of object, they have a special empathy between them. In other words, this entranced seeing and proximity in the vision, consonant with psychoanalytic theory, rests upon the special status of "woman" as object of the viewer's scopophilia—and hence the shared identification of woman and monster. I want to come back to this premise later, but let us continue for a moment to see how Williams situates sexuality within this monstrous looking.

Within the horror genre, she observes, it is in the monster's body that the sexual interest resides, and not in the bland hero's. The monster's power is one of sexual difference from the normal male; thus, the monster functions like woman in representing the threat of castration. So, as Williams would have it, when the woman looks at the monster and when the cross is removed from before her gaze, they are totally proximate and contiguous, alike in sexual difference from the male and transfixed, outside of scopophilia, in the pleasures of shared sexual transgression. Desire is aroused in this gaze, but

Williams quickly defers it to identification. In relegating the proximity and desire in the trance between woman and monster to (female) identification, Williams has securely locked any promise of lesbian sexuality into an Oedipal, heterosexual context.

This "woman," then, in Doane, Williams, and others, is really heterosexual woman. Though her desire is aroused vis-à-vis another woman (a monstrous occasion), and they are totally proximate, they identify with rather than desire one another. Their desire is still locked in the phallocratic order, and the same-sex taboo is still safely in place. What melds monster to woman is not lesbian desire—trance is not entranced—but finally daughter emulating mother in the Oedipal triangle with the absent male still at the apex. By inscribing in this configuration of looking a sexuality that is shared and not male, Williams both raises the possibility of the site of lesbian looking and simultaneously cancels it out. Like the image of the vampire in the currency of dominant discourse, this heterosexist configuration of the gaze seems to derive some power for its formulation by careening dangerously close to the abyss of same-sex desire, both invoking and revoking it. The critical pleasure resides in configuring the look by what it refuses to see. Thus, the revels of transgression enjoyed by the queer remain outside the boundaries of heterosexist proscription. You can hear the music, but you can't go to the party. Nevertheless, the site/sight of the monstrous is invoked and, though horrible, is sometimes negatively accurate and often quite seductive.

The hegemonic spread of the psychoanalytic does not allow for an imaginary of the queer. It simply reconfigures queer desire back into the heterosexual by deploying sexual difference through metaphors. For example, Kaja Silverman's "Fassbinder and Lacan: A Reconsideration of Gaze, Look, and Image" reconstructs the Lacanian "gaze/look" formation through the homosexual films of Fassbinder. For some of us queers, Fassbinder has pioneered a same-sex desiring cinematic apparatus—not only in his narratives, but in his camera. The queer spectator's pleasure in the films is constructed partially through the subcultural signs upon which the camera lovingly lingers (and/or ironizes), partially through the sense of camp and its distance from the real, which he employs for his political critique, and partially through the way he situates homosexual desire within national narratives. In fact, it is the dense overlay of these techniques that makes the films so homosexual in their signification.

For example, in *Querelle* (1982), the remake of Genet's novel, Fassbinder uses painted backdrops for the outdoor scenery. The two-dimensional, highly-saturated-color, painterly drops of the seaport mark the distance of this sexual site from "real" water and "real" boats. Fassbinder visually refers to the camp discourse of sailors, rather than to the reality of the sea. In the foreground, the camera lovingly follows the ass of the muscular seaman, who will later be seen, pants down, bent over the table. The relation of the camera to the ass certainly refigures forms of desire untouched by the Lacanian preoccupation with the penis. The anus is not itself a signifier of lack, and only comes to represent lack when tropes of sexual difference are reinserted into the discourse, feminizing it, while the penis is retained as signifier of the "masculine."[6] This is the move Silverman makes in deploying the heterosexist psychoanalytic model to read a homosexual text:

> Whereas classic cinema equates the exemplary male subject with the gaze, and locates the male eye on the side of authority and the law even when it is also a carrier of desire, *Beware a Holy Whore*[1970] not only extends desire and the look which expresses it to the female subject, but makes the male desiring look synonymous with loss of control. . . . It might be said doubly to "feminize" erotic spectatorship. *(62)*

Even though Silverman has placed "feminize" within quotation marks, she must retain the category and the bipolar stability of the phallic male to configure the gaze. At worst, this is the kind of thinking that, in street discourse, produces the male homosexual as effeminate.

This model, if one can read the subcultural signs, is also disrupted by Fassbinder's Petra von Kant, a truly queer creature who flickers somewhere between haute couture butch lesbian and male drag queen, making sexual difference a double drag. In amazonian strength (camped up through her gown with metal Walkyrie-like breastplates) and bondage before the young femme (camped up by the roped fall of the same gown, which forces her to walk, on the make, with bounded steps), Petra performs melodramatic tirades before yet another painted backdrop. The drag show, so emphatically marked, and the lesbian designs of Petra, in sex and fashion, delight the homosexual with codes that seem incongruous with the Lacanian conclusions Silverman draws: "Fassbinder's films refuse simply to resituate the terms of phallic reference. Instead, [they] seek to induce in the viewer a recognition of him or herself as 'annihilated in the form . . . of castration' "[79]. It seems to me, instead, that Petra's embellished, elegant discourse, flowing before volumetrically rendered, corpulent, half-clothed bodies on the backdrop, suggests a surfeit of subcultural signs of queer desire, glimmering with the ghetto and distanced from both the real and the law of the traditional phallic world.

My point here is not to disallow the heterosexual feminist perspective in theories of representation, but to point out that, when it creates the unmarked category of "woman" as a general one that includes queers, or when it displaces queer desire by retaining, in the gaze/look compound, sexual difference and its phallus/lack polarity, that perspective remains caught in a heterosexist reading of queer discourse. Moreover, I suggest, the pleasure in theorizing the look that such a perspective affords appears dependent on disavowing or displacing what should not be seen.[7]

But now I must once again register the vampire's perturbations in this discourse. She is perturbed by this lengthy encounter with heterosexism and is agitating for her return to the discourse. As far as she is concerned, the heterosexual overlay of the queer is just another version of *Guess Who's Coming to Dinner*. So allow me to return to the site where the vampire appears/disappears, that is, in the configuration of proximity. In vampire lore, proximity is a central organizing principle—not only in the look, but also in the mise en scène.

In his work on the supernatural, Tzvetan Todorov maintains that the central diegetic force in these tales is their atmosphere—an atmosphere of proximity. Settings in fog and gloom connect the disparate elements of the structure through a palpable, atmospheric "touching." Judith Mayne, writing on *Nosferatu* (1922), agrees, describing the twilight as a "dangerous territory where opposing terms are not so easily distinguishable" (27). From the entranced look, through the mise en scène, to the narrative structure, proximity pervades the vampire lore. But why is this proximate potential represented as horror by the dominant culture? There is a supernatural tale that unlocks the code of the prohibition against this proximity—Freud's paper on the Uncanny. Freud's entry, so to speak, into the uncanny is through the notion of the double and of doubling processes, such as the feeling that we have been somewhere before. Thus, the uncanny for Freud is a kind of haunting proximity. In fact, Freud's endpoint is in a haunted house.

> To many people the idea of being buried alive while appearing to be dead is the most uncanny thing of all. And yet psycho-analysis has taught us that this terrifying fantasy originally had nothing terrifying about it at all, but was filled with a certain lustful pleasure—the fantasy, I mean, of intra-uterine existence. (397)

For in German *unheimlich* (uncanny) implies, on one level, un-homely. So, Freud continues, "this *unheimlich* place, however, is the entrance to the former *Heim* [home] of all human beings [and] the prefix '*un*' is the token of repression" (399).

So this proscribed proximity, the very world of vampires and of the "entranced" women who view them, is the desire for what Freud calls intrauterine existence. More than the fog, the gloom, the cobwebs, and the twilight, Freud's article serves as an exact description of the vampire's sleep in her coffin: toward the end of every night, she races back there, to her native soil, and enjoys the lustful pleasure of being buried alive and dead— her intrauterine recreation. However, while Freud unlocks one repressive code to liberate a certain pleasure, his notion of intrauterine pleasure further defers the actual pleasure proscribed here. And the feminist psychoanalytic theorists carry on his tradition: his intrauterine pleasure, this *jouissance*, can only be enjoyed as a pre-Oedipal *jouissance* with the mother.

If, for Lacan, sexuality is dominated by the phallus in a trench coat, for Kristeva and her ilk, it is the masked mother. The feminist allocation of this lascivious pleasure of proximity with the mother is simply a bad hangover from too much Freud—it shares his anxieties and proclivities. When Freud imagined this lustful recreation, he imagined the mise en scène as dirty and musty, with the sense of an old vampire who's about to exhibit her true wrinkled self. That's Freud's sexist anxiety about the wrinkled, musty vagina displaced onto an ageist fantasy of the old mother. Moreover, the idea of this pre-Oedipal *jouissance* with the mother reinscribes Freud's patriarchal obsession with genealogy and sexuality as generative—part of the nineteenth-century proscription against homosexuality. Locating *jouissance* in a mother keeps heterosexuality at the center of the picture—the son can insert himself into the site of *jouissance*. As Hamlet gleefully puts it in Müller's "Hamletmaschine," "the mother's womb is not a one-way street."[8]

Yet the history of anti-Semitism is also marked in Freud's preoccupation with "home" here; the founder of what the Nazis termed the "Jewish science" locates a so-called primal desire in returning to the home—a desire that became painfully identificatory for the Jews in the following years, forced into exile, as even Freud himself.[9] Similarly, the vampires, often from Eastern Europe as well, who sought their lustful sleep in dirt from their *Heimat* are marked as the wandering tribe and the despised. Thus, Freud's is both a dominant discourse and a counterdiscourse: while interpolating the heterosexual into the lesbian vampiric, it is also haunted by the outsider position of a myth of "race" that violently denied the pleasure of "home." This intersection of racism and notions of *Heim* or more dangerously *Heimat* seems crucial once again, as the term and the danger reappear in this time of Germany's reunification.

On the brighter (or the darker) side of things, in tracking the vampire, we can here re-imagine her various strengths: celebrating the fact that she cannot see herself in the mirror and remains outside that door into the symbolic, her proximate vanishing appears as a political strategy; her bite pierces platonic metaphysics and subject/object positions; and her fanged kiss brings her the chosen one, trembling with ontological, orgasmic shifts, into the state of the undead. What the dominant discourse represents as an emptying out, a draining away, in contrast to the impregnating kiss of the heterosexual, becomes an activism in representation.

Now, if you watch some recent vampire films, it may seem that things are getting better. Surely, you offer, the confining nineteenth-century codes are liberalized in the late twentieth century. For example, if you watch some recent vampire films, you may note that the vampire is actually portrayed as a lesbian. But this move only reflects a kind of post-Watergate strategy of representation; that is, don't keep any secrets because they can be revealed, just reveal the repression and that will serve to confirm it. So the vampire is portrayed as lesbian, but costumed in all the same conventions, simply making the proscription literal. The strategic shift here is in revelation, not representation. Whether she is the upper-class, decadent, cruel Baroness in *Daughters of Darkness* (1971; played by the late Delphine Seyrig, who was marked in the subculture as a lesbian actor), whose coercive lesbian sex act is practiced behind closed doors and whose languorous body proscribes the lesbian as an oozing, French dessert cheese; or whether she is the rough-trade, breast-biting Austrian lesbian vampire in *Vampire Lovers* (1970), or even the late-capitalist, media-assimilated lesbian vampire in the independent film *Because the Dawn* (1988), her attraction is (in) her proscription. Only the proscription of the lesbian is literally portrayed—the occult becomes cult in the repression.

While the lesbian has become literalized in contemporary vampire films, the proscription against same-sex desire has also been reconfigured in a trope more consonant with late-twentieth century conditions. For one thing, nature isn't what it used to be, and likewise, the undead have altered with it. In the nineteenth century, the stable notion of nature as natural and of the natural as good made it possible to configure same-sex desire as unnatural—thus monster—thus vampire. Beginning with horror films in the fifties, the binarism of natural/unnatural gives way. Nature is contaminated—it is a site of the unnatural. Metaphors of Romantic organicism fail where technology has transformed. The agrarian dream gives way to the nuclear nightmare. The representation of nature, contaminated by nuclear testing in the desert, is a site for the production of monsters that transgress what was considered natural.

Hollywood produced *Them* (1954), *Tarantula* (1955), *Crab Monsters* (1956), *Giant Grasshoppers* (1957), and *Killer Shrews* (1959). The urban replaces the agrarian as a haven. The humanist scientist, such as van Helsing, warring against the perverse isolated vampire gives way to the military-industrial complex warring against its own creations. The giant tarantula created by nuclear reaction is destroyed by napalm; another monster is killed by a shift in the ozone layer.

After the 50s, the lone vampire, or the family of vampires that threatened the human community, is replaced by a proliferation of the undead. Romero's trilogy illustrates the progression: in *Night of the Living Dead* (1968), a score of the undead threatens a family-unit-type group in a house; in the second film, *Dawn of the Dead* (1977), thousands of undead threaten a smaller, less-affiliated group in a shopping mall, one of the few places remaining; and in *Day of the Dead* (1985), the undead have successfully taken over the continent, finally threatening what dwindles down to the basic heterosexual-couple-unit in a military-industrial complex.[10] Successively, the undead have eliminated the family unit, claimed commodity reification for their own in the shopping mall, and defeated the military-industrial complex. One hope remains in a kind of Adam and Eve ending of the final film, although it seems unlikely. The undead overrun things, proliferate wildly, are like contamination, pollution, a virus, disease—AIDS. Not AIDS as just any disease, but AIDS as it is used socially as a metaphor for same-sex desire among men, AIDS as a construction that signifies the plague of their sexuality. But why is the taboo now lodged in proliferation? This is Freud's double gone wild, the square root of proximity. The continual displacements in the system have become like a cancer, spreading, devouring, and reproducing themselves. The oppressive politics of representation have cathected to displacement, settling their sites/sights there again and again and again. The taboo against same sex becomes like the Stepford wives when they break down, pouring coffee over and over and over again.

These neo-undead doubly configure away the lesbian position, since same-sex desire appears as gay male. The lesbian position is only the motor for multiple displacements. Where does this all leave the lesbian vampire, then? Outside of the mirror, collapsing subject/object relations into the proximate, double occupancy of the sign, abandoning the category of woman as heterosexist, and entering representation only in a guise that proscribes her. You still can only see her, in horror and fear, when you don't.

Finally, in tracking the vampire in representation in order to perceive how she counters blood myths of race and proper sexuality, I would like to turn to a text through which she moves—a lesbian choreopoem. This form particularly suits the vampire for several reasons, but specifically in its performance structures. The choreopoem is a theatrical form created by Chicanas and black women. These are performance pieces composed of loosely related poems and performed by ensembles. In this collection of poems, the performer is not a character, though she may, for a short time, suggest one. As the lyric voice moves among the several performers in the ensemble, they collectively enact the agency, or the lyric dynamic. Sometimes the performer inhabits the subjective "I" of the poet, sometimes she is the story itself, sometimes the storyteller.

In the choreopoem "No" by Alexis DeVeaux, the subject position is that of the desiring lesbian who is also active in black revolutionary politics. The title "No" itself functions to proscribe what the dominant discourse can articulate, while at the same time tracing a counterdiscourse. "No" consists of thirty poems: several are lesbian love poems to other black women, one is about a revolutionary woman who breaks away from the sexism of her male partner in the black movement, one is about the murder of children in Selma. The ground, then, the mise en scène is the historical, social, economic, and emotional field of the black lesbian revolutionary subject. The agency, or subject position, is the itineration of that field through a collective of women, with its possibilities and impossibilities made dynamic by the lyric. In other words, the lesbian subject position is composed of this movement among performers and through the lyric "I" of the poet herself, whose desire flows through their mouths and their gestures and whose playing space is the historical and social borders of the possible and impossible for such a subject. She is both visible and invisible—visible in her lyric, collective movement and in the proximity of her politics and homosexual desire, and invisible as character or content. The poem celebrates the ethnic fashion of dreadlocks (the vampire's dread-lock) as seductive while also specifically coded as revolutionary, in proximity to a celebration of clitoral love-making between two women within their antiracist struggle; proximity/distance is marked as one. DeVeaux closes the space between women's economic and political struggles and lesbian desire. Finally, here, the vampire can enter.

And do you love me, in
this flight of poems
between
one train station &
another

do you: going home
after dinner
separate ways: love me
like this:
spilled
in your hand
an underground movement
of sentences
a calypso of rivers
the marrow of fear
And if the Russians do it
and the Cubans
and the Americans do it
if the Chinese do it too
if the women go baby
how do we name the war
And
this love
I need you: I say
trade in these train tracks
for a howl at the moon
this poem is not progressive
but long distance
and close
between the archives
of your dreams
between the hip of Montego Bay
your shameless stcp
I measure: how you do these things: and
each dread
is the revolution of another. [11]

NOTES

1. I am indebted to Yvonne Yarbro-Bejarano for this analysis of sexual/racial honor, which appears in *Feminism and the Honor Plays of Lope de Vega* (West Lafayette, Ind.: Purdue University Press, 1994).

2. For a fuller discussion of this point, see the chapter on Spain in *Aryan* by Poliakov and the chapter on "Mystic Speech" in *Heterologies* by de Certeau, especially pp. 81–86.

3. The prejudice was so convincing that a fashion arose among middle-class women to visit the slaughterhouse and drink the blood of an ox to strengthen themselves. See Dijkstra, "Metamorphoses of the Vampire: Dracula and His Daughters," in *Idols*, particularly pp. 337–38.

4. Gallop suggested this in a discussion of the cover photo at the University of California, Riverside, on January 18, 1991.

5. Gallop, however, is one of the few authors to articulate issues between lesbians and heterosexual feminists within this kind of debate (107–108). Her discussion here, clearly written in solidarity with lesbians, is important and could be pursued at length.

6. I am indebted for this point to the work in progress of my colleagues George Haggerty and Gregory Bredbeck; to Bredbeck for his work on sodomy and the anus, and to Haggerty for his reconfiguration of the effeminate in the eighteenth century. See also Miller's reading of Hitchcock in "Anal *Rope*."

7. Both Silverman's and my positions are too complex to work out in this reduced form. A more complete development of them will appear in my book, *The Domain-Matrix: Performing Lesbian at the End of Print Culture* (Bloomington: Indiana University Press, 1996), of which this essay is a fragment.

8. "Der Mutterschoss ist keine Einbahn-strasse" (Müller 91); translation mine.

9. Marjorie Garber suggested this in conversation at the 1990 Queer Theory conference in Santa Cruz, California.

10. I am indebted to Steve Shaviro for our discussions of the trilogy.

11. From an unpublished manuscript of the choreopoem "No," provided to me by Glenda Dickerson—the only director to bring this piece onto the stage. This paper should have ended with a discussion of Gomez's *Gilda Stories*, which has just appeared in print as my manuscript goes to press. But I discuss it in the longer version of this paper, included in my *Domain-Matrix*.

WORKS CITED

Baudelaire, Charles. "Femmes Damnées Delphine et Hippolyte." *Les Fleurs du Mal*. Trans. Richard Howard. Boston: Godine, 1983.

de Certeau, Michel. *Heterologies: Discourse on the Other*. Trans. Brian Massumi. Minneapolis: University of Minnesota Press, 1986.

de Lauretis, Teresa. "Sexual Indifference and Lesbian Representation." *Performing*

Feminisms: Feminist Critical Theory and Theatre. Ed. Sue-Ellen Case. Baltimore: Johns Hopkins University Press, 1990. 17–39.

DeVeaux, Alexis. "No." Unpublished ms.

Dijkstra, Bram. *Idols of Perversity: Fantasies of Feminine Evil in Fin-de-siècle Culture*. Oxford: Oxford University Press, 1986.

Doane, Mary Ann. "Film and the Masquerade: Theorising the Female Spectator." *Screen* 23, no. 3–4 (1982): 74–87.

Freud, Sigmund. "The 'Uncanny.'" 1919. *Collected Papers*. Ed. Ernest Jones. Vol. 4. New York: Basic, 1959.

Gallop, Jane. *Thinking Through the Body*. New York: Columbia University Press, 1988.

Gomez, Jewelle. *The Gilda Stories*. Ithaca: Firebrand, 1991.

St. John of the Cross. *Living Flame of Love*. Trans. and ed. E. Allison Peers. Garden City, N.Y.: Image, 1962.

———. *The Poems of St. John of the Cross*. Trans. John Frederick Nims. New York: Grove, 1959.

Le Fanu, J., Sheridan. "Carmilla." 1872. *Vampires*. Ed. Alan Ryan. Garden City, NY: Doubleday, 1987. 71–138.

Mayne, Judith. "Dracula in the Twilight: Murnau's *Nosferatu* (1922)." *German Film and Literature: Adaptations and Transformations*. Ed. Eric Rentschler. New York: Methuen, 1986. 25–39.

Miller, D. A. "Anal *Rope*." *Representations* 32 (1990): 114–33.

Müller, Heiner. "Die Hamletmaschine." *Mauser*. Berlin: Rotbuch, 1978. 89–97.

Poliakov, Leon. *The Aryan Myth*. Trans. Edmund Howard. New York: Basic, 1974.

Praz, Mario. *The Romantic Agony*. Trans. Angus Davidson. London: Oxford University Press, 1954.

Rimbaud, Arthur. "Antique." *Illuminations*. Trans. Louise Varèse. New York: New Directions, 1957.

———. *A Season in Hell*. Trans. Bertrand Mathieu. Pref. Anaïs Nin. Cambridge: Pomegranate, 1976.

Silverman, Kaja. "Fassbinder and Lacan: A Reconsideration of Gaze, Look, and Image." *Camera Obscura* 19 (1989): 54–85.

Todorov, Tzvetan. *The Fantastic: A Structural Approach to a Literary Genre*. Trans. Richard Howard. Ithaca: Cornell University Press, 1975.

Wilde, Oscar. *Salome*. Trans. Lord Alfred Douglas. Illus. Aubrey Beardsley. New York: Dover, 1967.

Williams, Linda. "When the Woman Looks." *Re-vision: Essays in Feminist Film Criticism*. Ed. Mary Ann Doane, Patricia Mellencamp, and Linda Williams. Frederick, Md.: University Publications of America, 1984. 83–99.

24

Performative Acts and
Gender Constitution

AN ESSAY IN PHENOMENOLOGY
AND FEMINIST THEORY

Judith Butler

Philosophers rarely think about acting in the theatrical sense, but they do have a discourse of "acts" that maintains associative semantic meanings with theories of performance and acting. For example, John Searle's "speech acts," those verbal assurances and promises which seem not only to refer to a speaking relationship, but to constitute a moral bond between speakers, illustrate one of the illocutionary gestures that constitutes the stage of the analytic philosophy of language. Further, "action theory," a domain of moral philosophy, seeks to understand what it is "to do" prior to any claim of what one *ought* to do. Finally, the phenomenological theory of "acts," espoused by Edmund Husserl, Maurice Merleau-Ponty, and George Herbert Mead, among others, seeks to explain the mundane way in which social agents *constitute* social reality through

Judith Butler, "Performance Acts and Gender Constitution: An Essay in Phenomenology and Feminist Theory." First appeared in *Theater Journal*. Reprinted with permission from the author.

language, gesture, and all manner of symbolic social sign. Though phenomenology sometimes appears to assume the existence of a choosing and constituting agent prior to language (who poses as the sole source of its constituting acts), there is also a more radical use of the doctrine of constitution that takes the social agent as an *object* rather than the subject of constitutive acts.

When Simone de Beauvoir claims, "one is not born, but, rather, *becomes a woman*," she is appropriating and reinterpreting this doctrine of constituting acts from the phenomenological tradition.[1] In this sense, gender is in no way a stable identity of locus of agency from which various acts proceede; rather, it is an identity tenuously constituted in time—an identity instituted through a *stylized repetition of acts*. Further, gender is instituted through the stylization of the body and, hence, must be understood as the mundane way in which bodily gestures, movements, and enactments of various kinds constitute the illusion of an abiding gendered self. This formulation moves the conception of gender off the ground of a substantial model of identity to one that requires a conception of a constituted *social temporality*. Significantly, if gender is instituted through acts which are internally discontinuous, then the *appearance of substance* is precisely that, a constructed identity, a performative accomplishment which the mundane social audience, including the actors themselves, come to believe and to perform in the mode of belief. If the ground of gender identity is the stylized repetition of acts through time, and not a seemingly seamless identity, then the possibilities of gender transformation are to be found in the arbitrary relation between such acts, in the possibility of a different sort of repeating, in the breaking or subversive repetition of that style.

Through the conception of gender acts sketched above, I will try to show some ways in which reified and naturalized conceptions of gender might be understood as constituted and, hence, capable of being constituted differently. In opposition to theatrical or phenomenological models which take the gendered self to be prior to its acts, I will understand constituting acts not only as constituting the identity of the actor, but as constituting that identity as a compelling illusion, an object of *belief*. In the course of making my argument, I will draw from theatrical, anthropological, and philosophical discourses, but mainly phenomenology, to show that what is called gender identity is a performative accomplishment compelled by social sanction and taboo. In its very character as performative resides the possibility of contesting its reified status.

I. Sex/Gender: Feminist and Phenomenological Views

Feminist theory has often been critical of naturalistic explanations of sex and sexuality that assume that the meaning of women's social existence can be derived from some fact of their physiology. In distinguishing sex from gender, feminist theorists have disputed causal explanations that assume that sex dictates or necessitates certain social meanings for women's experience. Phenomenological theories of human embodiment have also been concerned to distinguish between the various physiological and biological causalities that structure bodily existence and the *meanings* that embodied existence assumes in the context of lived experience. In Merleau-Ponty's reflections in *The Phenomenology of Perception* on "the body in its sexual being," he takes issue with such accounts of bodily experience and claims that the body is "an historical idea" rather than "a natural species."[2] Significantly, it is this claim that Simone de Beauvoir cites in *The Second Sex* when she sets the stage for her claim that "woman," and by extension, any gender, is an historical situation rather than a natural fact.[3]

In both contexts, the existence and facticity of the material or natural dimensions of the body are not denied, but reconceived as distinct from the process by which the body comes to bear cultural meanings. For both Beauvoir and Merleau-Ponty, the body is understood to be an active process of embodying certain cultural and historical possibilities, a complicated process of appropriation which any phenomenological theory of constitution needs to describe. In order to describe the gendered body, a phenomenological theory of constitution requires an expansion of the conventional view of acts to mean both that which constitutes meaning and that through which meaning is performed or enacted. In other words, the acts by which gender is constituted bear similarities to performative acts within theatrical contexts. My task, then, is to examine in what ways gender is constructed through specific corporeal acts, and what possibilities exist for the cultural transformation of gender through such acts.

Merleau-Ponty maintains not only that the body is an historical idea but a set of possibilities to be continually realized. In claiming that the body is an historical idea, Merleau-Ponty means that it gains its meaning through a concrete and historically mediated expression in the world. That the body is a set of possibilities signifies (a) that its appearance in the world, for perception, is not predetermined by some manner of interior essence, and (b) that its concrete expression in the world must be understood as the taking up and rendering specific of a set of historical possibilities. Hence, there is an agency which is understood as the process of rendering such possibilities determinate. These possibilities are necessarily constrained by available historical conventions. The body is not a self-identical or merely factic materiality; it is a materiality that bears meaning, if nothing else, and the manner of this bearing is fundamentally dramatic. By dramatic I mean only that the body is not merely matter but a continual and incessant *materializing* of possibilities. One is not simply a body, but, in some very key sense, one does one's body and, indeed, one does one's body differently from one's contemporaries and from one's embodied predecessors and successors as well.

It is, however, clearly unfortunate grammar to claim that there is a "we" or an "I" that does its body, as if a disembodied agency preceded and directed an embodied exterior. More appropriate, I suggest, would be a vocabulary that resists the substance metaphysics of subject-verb formations and relies instead on an ontology of present participles. The "I" that is its body is, of necessity, a mode of embodying, and the "what" that it embodies is possibilities. But here again the grammar of the formulation misleads, for the possibilities that are embodied are not fundamentally exterior or antecedent to the process of embodying itself. As an intentionally organized materiality, the body is always an embodying *of* possibilities both conditioned and circumscribed by historical convention. In other words, the body *is* a historical situation, as Beauvoir has claimed, and is a manner of doing, dramatizing, and *reproducing* a historical situation.

To do, to dramatize, to reproduce, these seem to be some of the elementary structures of embodiment. This doing of gender is not merely a way in which embodied agents are exterior, surfaced, open to the perception of others. Embodiment clearly manifests a set of strategies or what Sartre would perhaps have called a style of being or Foucault, "a stylistics of existence." This style is never fully self-styled, for living styles have a history, and that history conditions and limits possibilities. Consider gender, for instance, as *a corporeal style*, an "act," as it were, which is both intentional and performative, where "performative" itself carries the double-meaning of "dramatic" and "non-referential." speech-acts dif.

When Beauvoir claims that "woman" is a historical idea and not a natural fact, she clearly underscores the distinction between sex, as biological facticity, and gender, as the cultural interpretation or signification of that facticity. To be female is, according to that distinction, a facticity which has no meaning, but to be a woman is to have *become* a woman, to compel the body to conform to an historical idea of "woman," to induce the body to become a cultural sign, to materialize oneself in obedience to an historically delimited possibility, and to do this as a sustained and repeated corporeal project. The notion of a "project," however, suggests the originating force of a radical will, and because gender is a project which has cultural survival as its end, the term "*strategy*" better suggests the situation of duress under which gender performance always and variously occurs. Hence, as a strategy of survival, gender is a performance with clearly punitive consequences. Discrete genders are part of what "humanizes" individuals within contemporary culture; indeed, those who fail to do their gender right are regularly punished. Because there is neither an "essence" that gender expresses or externalizes nor an objective ideal to which gender aspires; because gender is not a fact, the various acts of gender creates the idea of gender, and without those acts, there would be no gender at all. Gender is, thus, a construction that regularly conceals its genesis. The tacit collective agreement to perform, produce, and sustain discrete and polar genders as cultural fictions is obscured by the credibility of its own production. The authors of gender become entranced by their own fictions whereby the construction compels one's belief in its necessity and naturalness. The historical possibilities materialized through various corporeal styles are nothing other than those punitively regulated cultural fictions that are alternately embodied and disguised under duress.

How useful is a phenomenological point of departure for a feminist description of gender? On the surface it appears that phenomenology shares with feminist analysis a commitment to grounding theory in lived experience, and in revealing the way in which the world is produced through the constituting acts of subjective experience. Clearly, not all feminist theory would privilege the point of view of the subject, (Kristeva once objected to feminist theory as "too existentialist")[4] and yet the feminist claim that the personal is political suggests, in part, that subjective experience is not only structured by existing political arrangements, but effects and structures those arrangements in turn. Feminist theory has sought to understand the way in which systemic or pervasive political and cultural structures are enacted and reproduced through individual acts and practices, and how the analysis of ostensibly personal situations is clarified through situating the issues in a broader and shared cultural context. Indeed, the feminist impulse, and I am sure there is more than one, has often emerged in the recognition that my pain or my silence or my anger or my perception is finally not mine alone, and that it delimits me in a shared cultural situation which in turn enables and empowers me in certain unanticipated ways. The personal is thus implicitly political inasmuch as it is conditioned by shared social structures, but the personal has also been immunized against political challenge to the extent that public/private distinctions endure. For feminist theory, then, the personal becomes an expansive category, one which accommodates, if only implicitly, political structures usually viewed as public. Indeed, the very meaning of the political expands as well. At its best, feminist theory involves a dialectical expansion of both of these categories. My situation does not cease to be mine just because it is the situation of someone else, and my acts, individual as they are, nevertheless reproduce the situation of my gender, and do that in various ways. In other words, there is, latent in the personal is political formulation of feminist theory, a supposition that the life-world of gender relations is constituted, at least partially, through the concrete and historically mediated *acts* of individuals. Considering that "the" body is invariably transformed into his body or her body, the body is only known through its gendered appearance. It would seem imperative to consider the way in which this gendering of the body occurs. My suggestion is that the body becomes its gender through a series of acts which are renewed, revised, and consolidated through time. From a feminist point of view, one might try to reconceive the gendered body as the legacy of sedimented acts rather than a predetermined or foreclosed structure, essence or fact, whether natural, cultural, or linguistic.

The feminist appropriation of the phenomenological theory of constitution might employ the notion of an *act* in a richly ambiguous sense. If the personal is a category which expands to include the wider political and social structures, then the *acts* of the gendered subject would be similarly expansive. Clearly, there are political acts which are deliberate and instrumental actions of political organizing, resistance, and collective intervention with the broad aim of instating a more just set of social and political relations. There are thus acts which are done in the name of women, and then there are acts in and of themselves, apart from any instrumental consequence, that challenge the category of women itself. Indeed, one ought to consider the futility of a political program which seeks radically to transform the social situation of women without first determining whether the category of woman is socially constructed in such a way that to be a woman is, by definition, to be in an oppressed situation. In an understandable desire to forge bonds of solidarity, feminist discourse has often relied upon the category of woman as a universal presupposition of cultural experience which, in its universal status, provides a false ontological promise of eventual political solidarity. In a culture in which the false universal of "man" has for the most part been presupposed as coextensive with humanness itself, feminist theory has sought with success to bring female specificity into visibility and to rewrite the history of culture in terms which acknowledge the presence, the influence, and the oppression of women. Yet, in this effort to combat the invisibility of women as a category feminists run the risk of rendering visible a category which may or may not be representative of the concrete lives of women. As feminists, we have been less eager, I think, to consider the status of the category itself and, indeed, to discern the conditions of oppression which issue from an unexamined reproduction of gender identities which sustain discrete and binary categories of man and woman.

When Beauvoir claims that woman is an "historical situation," she emphasizes that the body suffers a certain cultural construction, not only through conventions that sanction and proscribe how one acts one's body, the "act" or performance that one's body is, but also in the tacit conventions that structure the way the body is culturally perceived. Indeed, if gender is the cultural significance that the sexed body assumes, and if that significance is codetermined through various acts and their cultural perception, then it would appear that from within the terms of culture it is not possible to know sex as distinct from gender. The reproduction of the category of gender is enacted on a large political scale, as when women first enter a profession or gain certain rights, or are reconceived in legal or political discourse in significantly new ways. But the more mundane reproduction of gendered identity takes place through the various ways in which bodies are acted in relationship to the deeply entrenched or sedimented expectations of gendered existence. Consider that there is a sedimentation of gender norms that produces the peculiar phenomenon of a natural sex, or a real woman, or any number of prevalent and compelling social fictions, and that this is a sedimentation that over time has produced a set of corporeal styles which, in reified form, appear as the natural configuration of bodies into sexes which exist in a binary relation to one another.

II. Binary Genders and the Heterosexual Contract

To guarantee the reproduction of a given culture, various requirements, well-established in the anthropological literature of kinship, have instated sexual reproduction within the confines of a heterosexually-based system of marriage which requires the reproduction of human beings in certain gendered modes which, in effect, guarantee the eventual reproduction of that kinship system. As Foucault and others have pointed out, the association of a natural sex with a discrete gender and with an ostensibly natural "attraction" to the opposing sex/gender is an unnatural conjunction of cultural constructs in the service of reproductive interests.[5] Feminist cultural anthropology and kinship studies have shown how cultures are governed by conventions that not only regulate and guarantee the production, exchange, and consumption of material goods, but also reproduce the bonds of kinship itself, which require taboos and a punitive regulation of reproduction to effect that end. Levì-Strauss has shown how the incest taboo works to guarantee the channeling of sexuality into various modes of heterosexual marriage,[6] Gayle Rubin has argued convincingly that the incest taboo produces certain kinds of discrete gendered identities and sexualities.[7] My point is simply that one way in which this system of compulsory heterosexuality is reproduced and concealed is through the cultivation of bodies into discrete sexes with "natural" appearances and "natural" heterosexual dispositions. Although the enthnocentric conceit suggests a progression beyond the mandatory structures of kinship relations as described by Levì-Strauss, I would suggest, along with Rubin, that contemporary gender identities are so many marks or "traces" of residual kinship. The contention that sex, gender, and heterosexuality are historical products which have become conjoined and reified as natural over time has received a good deal of critical attention not only from Michel Foucault, but Monique Wittig, gay historians, and various cultural anthropologists and social psychologists in recent years.[8] These theories, however, still lack the critical resources for thinking radically about the historical sedimentation of sexuality and sex-related constructs if they do not delimit and describe the mundane manner in which these constructs are produced, reproduced, and maintained within the field of bodies.

Can phenomenology assist a feminist reconstruction of the sedimented character of sex, gender, and sexuality at the level of the body? In the first place, the phenomenological focus on the various acts by which cultural identity is constituted and assumed provides a felicitous starting point for the feminist effort to understand the mundane manner in which bodies get crafted into genders. The formulation of the body as a mode of dramatizing or enacting possibilities offers a way to understand how a cultural convention is embodied and enacted. But it seems difficult, if not impossible, to imagine a way to conceptualize the scale and systemic character of women's oppression from a theoretical position which takes constituting acts to be its point of departure. Although individual acts do work to maintain and reproduce systems of oppression, and, indeed, any theory of personal political responsibility presupposes such a view, it doesn't follow that oppression is a sole consequence of such acts. One might argue that without human beings whose various acts, largely construed, produce and maintain oppressive conditions, those conditions would fall away, but note that the relation between acts and conditions is neither unilateral nor unmediated. There are social contexts and conventions within which certain acts not only become possible but become conceivable as acts at all. The transformation of social relations becomes a matter, then, of transforming hegemonic social conditions rather than the individual acts that are spawned by those conditions. Indeed, one runs the risk of addressing the merely indirect, if not epiphenomenal, reflection of those conditions if one remains restricted to a politics of acts.

But the theatrical sense of an "act" forces a revision of the individualist assumptions underlying the more restricted view of constituting acts within phenomenological discourse. As a given temporal duration within the entire performance, "acts" are a shared experience and "collective action." Just as within feminist theory the very category of the personal is expanded to include political structures, so is there a theatrically-based and, indeed, less individually-oriented view of acts that goes some of the way in defusing the criticism of act theory as "too existentialist." The act that gender is, the act that embodied agents *are* inasmuch as they dramatically and actively embody and, indeed, *wear* certain cultural significations, is clearly not one's act alone. Surely, there are nuanced and individual ways of *doing* one's gender, but that one does it, and that one does it *in accord with* certain sanctions and proscriptions, is clearly not a fully individual matter. Here again, I don't mean to minimize the effect of certain gender norms which originate within the family and are enforced through certain familial modes of punishment and reward and which, as a consequence, might be construed as highly individual, for even there family relations recapitulate, individualize, and specify preexisting cultural relations; they are rarely, if ever, radically original. The act that one does, the act that one performs, is, in a sense, an act that has been going on before one arrived on the scene. Hence, gender is an act which has been rehearsed, much as a script survives the particular actors who make use of it, but which requires individual actors in order to be actualized and reproduced as reality once again. The complex components that go into an act must be distinguished in order to understand the kind of acting in concert and acting in accord which acting one's gender invariably is.

In what senses, then, is gender an act? As anthropologist Victor Turner suggests in his studies of ritual social drama, social action requires a performance which is *repeated*. This repetition is at once a reenactment and reexperiencing of a set of meanings already socially established; it is the mundane and ritualized form of their legitimation.[9] When this conception of social performance is applied to gender, it is clear that although there are individual bodies that enact these significations by becoming stylized into gendered modes, this "action" is immediately public as well. There are temporal and collective dimensions to these actions, and their public nature is not inconsequential; indeed, the performance is effected with the strategic aim of maintaining gender within its binary frame. Understood in pedagogical terms, the performance renders social laws explicit.

As a public action and performative act, gender is not a radical choice or project that reflects a merely individual choice, but neither is it imposed or inscribed upon the individual, as some post-structuralist displacements of the subject would contend. The body is not passively scripted with cultural codes, as if it were a lifeless recipient of wholly pregiven cultural relations. But neither do embodied selves preexist the cultural conventions which essentially signify bodies. Actors are always already on the stage, within the terms of the performance. Just as a script may be enacted in various ways, and just as the play requires both text and interpretation, so the gendered body acts its part in a culturally restricted corporeal space and enacts interpretations within the confines of already existing directives.

Although the links between a theatrical and a social role are complex and the distinctions not easily drawn (Bruce Wilshire points out the limits of the comparison in *Role-Playing and Identity: The Limits of Theatre as Metaphor*),[10] it seems clear that, although theatrical performances can meet with political censorship and scathing criticism, gender performances in nontheatrical contexts are governed by more clearly punitive and regulatory social conventions. Indeed, the sight of a transvestite onstage can compel pleasure and applause while the sight of the same transvestite on the seat next to us on the bus can compel fear, rage, even violence. The conventions which mediate proximity and identification in these two instances are clearly quite different. I want to make two different kinds of claims regarding this tentative distinction. In the theatre, one can say, "this is just an act," and de-realize the act, make acting into something quite distinct from what is real. Because of this distinction, one can maintain one's sense of reality in the face of this temporary challenge to our existing ontological assumptions about gender arrangements; the various conventions which announce that "this is only a play" allows strict lines to be drawn between the performance and life. On the street or in the bus, the act becomes dangerous, if it does, precisely because there are no theatrical conventions to delimit the purely imaginary character of the act, indeed, on the street or in the bus, there is no presumption that the act is distinct from a reality; the disquieting effect of the act is that there are no conventions that facilitate making this separation. Clearly, there is theatre which attempts to contest or, indeed, break down those conventions that demarcate the imaginary from the real (Richard Schechner brings this out quite clearly in *Between Theatre and Anthropology*).[11] Yet in those cases one confronts the same phenomenon, namely, that the act is not contrasted with the real, but *constitutes* a reality that is in some sense new, a modality of gender that cannot readily be assimilated into the preexisting categories that regulate gender reality. From the point of view of those established categories, one may want to claim, but oh, this is *really* a girl or a woman, or this is *really* a boy or a man, and further that the *appearance* contradicts the *reality* of the gender, that the discrete and familiar reality must be there, nascent, temporarily unrealized, perhaps realized at other times or other places. The transvestite, however, can do more than simply express the distinction between sex and gender, but challenges, at least implicitly, the distinction between appearance and reality that structures a good deal of popular thinking about gender identity. If the "reality" of gender is constituted by the performance itself, then there is no recourse to an essential and unrealized "sex" or "gender" which gender performances ostensibly express. Indeed, the transvestite's gender is as fully real as anyone whose performance complies with social expectations.

Gender reality is performative which means, quite simply, that it is real only to the extent that it is performed. It seems fair to say that certain kinds of acts are usually interpreted as expressive of a gender core or identity, and that these acts either conform to an expected gender identity or contest that expectation in some way. That expectation, in turn, is based upon the perception of sex, where sex is understood to be the discrete and factic datum of primary sexual characteristics. This implicit and popular theory of acts and gestures as *expressive* of gender suggests that gender itself is something prior to the various acts, postures, and gestures by which it is dramatized and known; indeed, gender appears to the popular imagination as a substantial core which might well be understood as the spiritual or psychological correlate of biological sex.[12] If gender attributes, however, are not expressive but performative, then these attributes effectively constitute the identity they are said to express or reveal. The distinction between expression and performativeness is quite crucial, for if gender attributes and acts, the various ways in which a body shows or produces its cultural signification, are performative, then there is no preexisting identity by which an act or attribute might be measured; there would be no true or false, real or distorted acts of gender, and the postulation of a true gender identity would be revealed as a regulatory fiction. That gender reality is created through sustained social performances means that the very notions of an essential sex, a true or abiding masculinity or femininity, are also constituted as part of the strategy by which the performative aspect of gender is concealed.

As a consequence, gender cannot be understood as a *role* which either expresses or disguises an interior "self," whether that "self" is conceived as sexed or not. As performance which is performative, gender is an "act," broadly construed, which constructs the social fiction of its own psychological interiority. As opposed to a view such as Erving Goffman's which posits a self which assumes and exchanges various "roles" within the complex social expectations of the "game" of modern life,[13] I am suggesting that this self is not only irretrievably "outside," constituted in social discourse, but that the ascription of interiority is itself a publicly regulated and sanctioned form of essence fabrication. Genders, then, can be neither true nor false, neither real nor apparent. And yet, one is compelled to live in a world in which genders constitute univocal signifiers, in which gender is stabilized, polarized, rendered discrete and intractable. In effect, gender is made to comply with a model of truth and falsity which not only contradicts its own performative fluidity, but serves a social policy of gender regulation and control. Performing one's gender wrong initiates a set of punishments both obvious and indirect, and performing it well provides the reassurance that there is an essentialism of gender identity after all. That this reassurance is so easily displaced by anxiety, that culture so readily punishes or marginalizes those who fail to perform the illusion of gender essentialism should be sign enough that on some level there is social knowledge that the truth or falsity of gender is only socially compelled and in no sense ontologically necessitated.[14]

III. Feminist Theory: Beyond an Expressive Model of Gender

This view of gender does not pose as a comprehensive theory about what gender is or the manner of its construction, and neither does it prescribe an explicit feminist political program. Indeed, I can imagine this view of gender being used for a number of discrepant political strategies. Some of my friends may fault me for this and insist that any theory of gender constitution has political presuppositions and implications, and that it is impossible to separate a theory of gender from a political philosophy of feminism. In fact, I would agree, and argue that it is primarily political interests which create the social phenomena of gender itself, and that without a radical critique of gender constitution feminist theory fails to take stock of the way in which oppression structures the ontological categories through which gender is conceived. Gayatri Spivak has argued that feminists need to rely on an operational essentialism, a false ontology of women as a universal in order to advance a feminist political program.[15] She knows that the category of "women" is not fully expressive, that the multiplicity and discontinuity of the referent mocks and rebels against the univocity of the sign, but suggests it could be used for strategic purposes. Kristeva suggests something similar, I think, when she prescribes that feminists use the category of women as a political tool without attributing ontological integrity to the term, and adds that, strictly speaking, women cannot be said to exist.[16] Feminists might well worry about the political implications of claiming that women do not exist, especially in light of the persuasive arguments advanced by Mary Anne Warren in her book, *Gendercide*.[17] She argues that social policies regarding population control and reproductive technology are designed to limit and, at times, eradicate the existence of women altogether. In light of such a claim, what good does it do to quarrel about the metaphysical status of the term, and perhaps, for clearly political reasons, feminists ought to silence the quarrel altogether.

But it is one thing to use the term and know its ontological insufficiency and quite another to articulate a normative vision for feminist theory which celebrates or emancipates an essence, a nature, or a shared cultural reality which cannot be found. The option I am defending is not to redescribe the world from the point of view of women. I don't know what that point of view is, but whatever it is, it is not singular, and not mine to espouse. It would only be half-right to claim that I am interested in how the phenomenon of a men's or women's point of view gets constituted, for while I do think that those points of views are, indeed, socially constituted, and that a reflexive genealogy of those points of view is important to do, it is not primarily the gender episteme that I am interested in exposing, deconstructing, or reconstructing. Indeed, it is the presupposition of the category of "woman" itself that requires a critical genealogy of the complex institutional and discursive means by which it is constituted. Although some feminist literary critics suggest that the presupposition of sexual difference is necessary for all discourse, that position reifies sexual difference as the founding moment of culture and precludes an analysis not only of how sexual difference is constituted to begin with but how it is continuously constituted, both by the masculine tradition that preempts the universal point of view, and by those feminist positions that construct the univocal category of "women" in the name of expressing or, indeed, liberating a subjected class. As Foucault claimed about those humanist efforts to liberate the criminalized subject, the subject that is freed is even more deeply shackled than originally thought.[18]

Clearly, though, I envision the critical genealogy of gender to rely on a phenomenological set of presuppositions, most important among them the expanded conception of an "act" which is both socially shared and historically constituted, and which is performative in the sense I previously described. But a critical genealogy needs to be supplemented by a politics of performative gender acts, one which both redescribes existing gender identities and offers a prescriptive view about the kind of gender reality there ought to be. The redescription needs to expose the reifications that tacitly serve as substantial gender cores or identities, and to elucidate both the act and the strategy of disavowal which at once constitute and conceal gender as we live it. The prescription is invariably more difficult, if only because we need to think a world in which acts, gestures, the visual body, the clothed body, the various physical attributes usually associated with gender, *express nothing*. In a sense, the prescription is not utopian, but consists in an imperative to acknowledge the existing complexity of gender which our vocabulary invariably disguises and to bring that complexity into a dramatic cultural interplay without punitive consequences. How?

Certainly, it remains politically important to represent women, but to do that in a way that does not distort and reify the very collectivity the theory is supposed to emancipate. Feminist theory which presupposes sexual difference as the necessary and invariant theoretical point of departure clearly improves upon those humanist discourses which conflate the universal with the masculine and appropriate all of culture as masculine property. Clearly, it is necessary to reread the texts of western philosophy from the various points of view that have been excluded, not only to reveal the particular perspective and set of interests informing those ostensibly transparent descriptions of the real, but to offer alternative descriptions and prescriptions; indeed, to establish philosophy as a cultural practice, and to criticize its tenets from marginalized cultural locations. I have no quarrel with this procedure, and have clearly benefited from those analyses. My only concern is that sexual difference not become a reification which unwittingly preserves a binary restriction on gender identity and an implicitly heterosexual framework for the description of gender, gender identity, and sexuality. There is, in my view, nothing about femaleness that is waiting to be expressed; there is, on the other hand, a good deal about the diverse experiences of women that is being expressed and still needs to be expressed, but caution is needed with respect to that theoretical language, for it does not simply report a pre-linguistic experience, but constructs that experience as well as the limits of its analysis. Regardless of the pervasive character of patriarchy and the prevalence of sexual difference as an operative cultural distinction, there is nothing about a binary gender system that is given. As a corporeal field of cultural play, gender is a basically innovative affair, although it is quite clear that there are strict punishments for contesting the script by performing out of turn or through unwarranted improvisations. Gender is not passively scripted on the body, and neither is it determined by nature, language, the symbolic, or the overwhelming history of patriarchy. Gender is what is put on, invariably, under constraint, daily and incessantly, with anxiety and pleasure, but if this continuous act is mistaken for a natural or linguistic given, power is relinquished to expand the cultural field bodily through subversive performances of various kinds.

NOTES

1. For a further discussion of Beauvoir's feminist contribution to phenomenological theory, see my "Variations on Sex and Gender: Beauvoir's *The Second Sex*," *Yale French Studies* 172 (1986).

2. Maurice Merleau-Ponty, "The Body in its Sexual Being," in *The Phenomenology of Perception*, trans. Colin Smith (Boston: Routledge and Kegan Paul, 1962).

3. Simone de Beauvoir, *The Second Sex*, trans. H. M. Parshley (New York: Vintage, 1974), p. 38.

4. Julia Kristeva, *Histoire d'amour* (Paris: Editions Denoel, 1983), p. 242.

5. See Michel Foucault, *The History of Sexuality: An Introduction*, trans. Robert Hurley (New York: Random House, 1980), p. 154: "the notion of 'sex' made it possible to group together, in an artificial unity, anatomical elements, biological functions, conducts, sensations, and pleasures, and it enabled one to make use of this fictitious unity as a causal principle."

6. See Claude Levi-Strauss, *The Elementary Structures of Kinship* (Boston: Beacon, 1965).

7. Gayle Rubin, "The Traffic in Women: Notes on the "Political Economy" of Sex," in *Toward an Anthropology of Women*, ed. Rayna R. Reiter (New York: Monthly Review Press, 1975), 178–85.

8. See my "Variations on Sex and Gender: Beauvoir, Wittig, and Foucault," in *Feminism as Critique*, ed. Seyla Benhabib and Drucila Cornell (London: Basil Blackwell, 1987 [distributed by the University of Minnesota Press]).

9. See Victor Turner, *Dramas, Fields, and Metaphors* (Ithaca: Cornell University Press, 1974). Clifford Geertz suggests in "Blurred Genres: The Refiguration of Thought," in *Local Knowledge: Further Essays in Interpretive Anthropology* (New York: Basic, 1983), that the theatrical metaphor is used by recent social theory in two, often opposing, ways. Ritual theorists like Victor Turner focus on a notion of social drama of various kinds as a means for settling internal conflicts within a culture and regenerating social cohesion. On the other hand, symbolic action approaches, influenced by figures as diverse as Emile Durkheim, Kenneth Burke, and Michel Foucault, focus on the way in which political authority and questions of legitimation are thematized and settled within the terms of performed meaning. Geertz himself suggests that the tension might be viewed dialectically; his study of political organization in Bali as a "theatre-state" is a case in point. In terms of an explicitly feminist account of gender as performative, it seems clear to me that an account of gender as ritualized, public performance must be combined with an analysis of the political sanctions and taboos under which that performance may and may not occur within the public sphere free of punitive consequence.

10. Bruce Wilshire, *Role-Playing and Identity: The Limits of Theatre as Metaphor* (Boston: Routledge and Kegan Paul, 1981).

11. Richard Schechner, *Between Theatre and Anthropology* (Philadelphia: University of Pennsylvania Press, 1985). See especially, "News, Sex, and Performance," pp. 295–324.

12. In *Mother Camp: Female Impersonators in America* (Englewood Cliffs, N.J.: Prentice-Hall, 1972), Anthropologist Esther Newton gives an urban ethnography of drag queens in which she suggests that all gender might be understood on the model of drag. In *Gender: An Ethnomethodological Approach* (Chicago: University of Chicago Press, 1978), Suzanne J. Kessler and Wendy McKenna argue that gender is an "accomplishment" which requires the skills of constructing the body into a socially legitimate artifice.

13. See Erving Goffmann, *The Presentation of Self in Everyday Life* (Garden City, N.Y.: Doubleday, 1959).

14. See Michel Foucault's edition of *Herculine Barbin: The Journals of a Nineteenth Century French Hermaphrodite*, trans. Richard McDougall (New York: Pantheon, 1984), for an interesting display of the horror evoked by intersexed bodies. Foucault's introduction makes clear that the medical delimitation of univocal sex is yet another wayward application of the discourse on truth-as-identity. See also the

work of Robert Edgerton in *American Anthropologist* on the cross-cultural variations of response to hermaphroditic bodies.

15. Remarks at the Center for Humanities, Wesleyan University, Spring, 1985.

16. Julia Kristeva, "Woman Can Never Be Defined," trans. Marilyn A. August, in *New French Feminisms*, ed. Elaine Marks and Isabelle de Courtivron (New York: Schocken, 1981).

17. Mary Anne Warren, *Gendercide: The Implications of Sex Selection* (New Jersey: Rowman and Allanheld, 1985).

18. Ibid.; Michel Foucault, *Discipline and Punish: The Birth of the Prison* trans. Alan Sheridan (New York: Vintage, 1978).

Suggestions for Further Reading

Bartkowski, Frances and Martha Satz. "Speculations on the Flesh: Foucault and the French Feminists." In Judith Genova, ed., *Power, Gender, Values*. Edmonton: Academic Printing and Publishing, 1987.

Bartky, Sandra Lee. *Femininity and Domination: Studies in the Phenomenology of Oppression*. New York: Routledge, 1990.

Bell, Shannon. *Reading, Writing, and Rewriting the Prostitute Body*. Bloomington: Indiana University Press, 1994.

Berger, John. *Ways of Seeing*. Harmondsworth: Penguin, 1972.

Body / Masquerade. Special Issue of *Discourse* 11, no. 1 (1988–89).

Bordo, Susan. *Unbearable Weight: Feminism, Western Culture, and the Body*. Berkeley: University of California Press, 1993.

Bornstein, Kate. *Gender Outlaw: On Men, Women, and the Rest of Us*. New York: Routledge, 1994.

Braidotti, Rosi. *Nomadic Subjects: Embodiment and Sexual Difference in Contemporary Feminist Theory*. New York: Columbia University Press, 1994.

Bronfen, Elisabeth. *Over Her Dead Body: Death, Femininity, and the Aesthetic*. New York: Routledge, 1992.

Butler, Judith. *Bodies That Matter: On the Discursive Limits of "Sex."* New York: Routledge, 1993.

——. *Gender Trouble: Feminism and the Subversion of Identity*. New York: Routledge, 1990.

Bynum, Caroline Walker. *Fragmentation and Redemption: Essays on Gender and the Human Body in Medieval Religion*. New York: Zone, 1991.

Castillo, Ana. "La Macha: Toward an Erotic Whole Self." In *Massacre of the Dreamers: Essays on Xicanisme*. New York: Plume, Penguin, 1994.

Cixous, Hélène. "The Laugh of the Medusa." In Elaine Marks and Isabelle de Courtivron, eds., *New French Feminisms: An Anthology*, pp. 99–106. New York: Schocken Books, 1981.

Cooey, Paula M. *Religious Imagination and the Body: A Feminist Analysis*. Oxford: Oxford University Press, 1994.

Davis, Angela. "Outcast Mothers and Surrogates: Racism and Reproductive Rights in the Nineties." In Linda S. Kauffman, ed., *American Feminist Thought at Century's End: A Reader*, pp. 355–66. Cambridge, Mass.: Blackwell, 1993.

Davis, Kathy. *Reshaping the Female Body: The Dilemma of Cosmetic Surgery*. New York: Routledge, 1995.

Davis, Natalie Zemon. "The Reasons of Misrule." *Society and Culture in Early Modern France: Eight Essays*. Stanford: Stanford University Press, 1975.

De Beauvoir, Simone. *The Second Sex*. Ed. and trans. H. M. Parshley. New York: Knopf, 1953.

de Lauretis, Teresa. *Alice Doesn't: Feminism, Semiotics, Cinema*. Bloomington: Indiana University Press, 1984.

——. *Practice of Love: Lesbian Sexuality and Perverse Desire*. Bloomington: Indiana University Press, 1994.

——. *Technologies of Gender: Essays on Theory, Film, and Fiction*. Bloomington: Indiana University Press, 1987.

Dempster, Elizabeth. "Women Writing the Body: Let's Watch a Little How She Dances." In Susan Sheridan, ed., *Grafts: Feminist Cultural Criticism*, pp. 35–54. London: Verso, 1988.

Dinnerstein, Dorothy. *The Mermaid and the Minotaur: Sexual Arrangements and Human Malaise*. New York: Harper and Row, 1976.

Disprose, Rosalyn. *The Bodies of Women: Ethics, Embodiment, and Sexual Difference*. New York: Routledge, 1994.

Doane, Mary Ann. "Woman's Stake: Filming the Female Body." In Constance Penley, ed., *Feminism and Film Theory*. New York: Routledge, 1988.

Douglas, Mary. *Purity and Danger: An Analysis of Concepts of Pollution and Taboo*. New York: Praeger, 1966.

du Bois, Page. *Sowing the Body: Psychoanalysis and Ancient Representations of Women*. Chicago: University of Chicago Press, 1988.

Ehrenreich, Barbara and Deirdre English. *Complaints and Disorders: The Sexual Politics of Sickness*. Old Westbury, N.Y.: Feminist Press, 1973.

Eisenstein, Zilla R. *The Female Body and the Law*. Berkeley: University of California Press, 1988.

Epstein, Julia and Kristina Straub, eds., *Body Guards: The Cultural Politics of Gender Ambiguity*. New York: Routledge, 1991.

Feminism and the Body. Judith Allen and Elizabeth Grosz, eds. Special Issue of *Australian Feminist Studies* 5 (Summer 1987).

Feminism and the Body. Special Issue of *Hypatia* 6, no. 3 (Fall 1991).

Flax, Jane. *Thinking Fragments: Psychoanalysis, Feminism, and Postmodernism in the Contemporary West*. Berkeley: University of California Press, 1990.

Foucault, Michel. *A History of Sexuality*, vol. 1. Trans. Robert Hurley. New York: Vintage, 1978.

———. *Discipline and Punish: The Birth of the Prison*. New York: Vintage, 1979.

Fox-Keller, Evelyn. *Reflections on Gender and Science*. New Haven: Yale University Press, 1985.

Friedman, Susan Stanford. "Creativity and the Childbirth Metaphor." *Feminist Studies* 13, no. 1 (1987): 49–82.

Fuss, Diana. *Essentially Speaking: Feminism, Nature, and Difference*. London: Routledge, 1989.

Gallop, Jane. *The Daughter's Seduction: Feminism and Psychoanalysis*. Ithaca: Cornell University Press, 1982.

———. *Thinking Through the Body*. New York: Columbia University Press, 1988.

Garber, Marjorie B. *Vested Interests: Cross-Dressing and Cultural Anxiety*. New York: Routledge, 1992.

Gatens, Moira. *Imaginary Bodies: Ethics, Power, and Corporeality*. New York: Routledge, 1996.

Gilman, Sander. "Black Bodies, White Bodies: Toward an Iconography of Female Sexuality in Late Nineteenth-Century Art, Medicine, and Literature." In Henry Louis Gates, ed., *"Race," Writing, and Difference*. Chicago: University of Chicago Press, 1985.

———. *Picturing Health and Illness: Images of Identity and Difference*. Baltimore: Johns Hopkins University Press, 1995.

Goldstein, Laurence, Jr., ed. *The Female Body: Figures, Styles, Speculations*. Ann Arbor: University of Michigan Press, 1991.

Grosz, Elizabeth. *Space, Time, and Perversion: Essays on the Politics of Bodies*. New York: Routledge, 1995.

———. *Volatile Bodies: Toward a Corporeal Feminism*. Bloomington: Indiana University Press, 1994.

hooks, bell. *Black Looks: Race and Representation*. Boston: South End Press, 1992.

Haraway, Donna. *Primate Visions: Gender, Race, and Nature in the World of Modern Science*. New York: Routledge, 1989.

———. *Simians, Cyborgs, and Women: the Reinvention of Nature*. New York: Routledge, 1991.

Humphries, Jefferson. "Troping the Body: Literature and Feminism." *Diacritics* 18 (1988): 18–28.

Hunt, Lynn, ed. *Eroticism and the Body Politic*. Baltimore: Johns Hopkins University Press, 1991.

Irigaray, Luce. *Speculum of the Other Woman*. Trans. Gillian C. Gill. Ithaca: Cornell University Press, 1985.

———. *This Sex Which Is Not One*. Trans. Catherine Porter. Ithaca: Cornell University Press, 1985.

Jaggar, Alison and Susan Bordo, eds. *Gender/Body/Knowledge: Feminist Reconstructions of Being and Knowing*. New Brunswick: Rutgers University Press, 1989.

Jardine, Alice. *Gynesis: Configurations of Women and Modernity*. Ithaca: Cornell University Press, 1985.

Jones, Ann Rosalind. "Writing the Body: Toward an Understanding of L'Ecriture Feminine." *Feminist Studies* 7 (1981): 247–63.

Kahane, Claire. "The Gothic Mirror." In Shirley Nelson Garner, Claire Kahane, and Madelon Sprengnether, eds., *The (M)other Tongue: Essays in Feminist Psychoanalytic Interpretation*, pp. 334–51. Ithaca: Cornell University Press, 1985.

Komesaroff, Paul A. *Troubled Bodies: Critical Perspectives on Postmodernism, Medical Ethics, and the Body*. Durham: Duke Univesity Press, 1995.

Kristeva, Julia. *Powers of Horror: An Essay on Abjection*. Trans. Leon S. Roudiez. New York: Columbia University Press, 1982.

———. "Stabat Mater" and "Women's Time." In Toril Moi, ed., *The Kristeva Reader*. New York: Columbia University Press, 1986.

Keller, Evelyn Fox. *Reflections on Gender and Science*. New Haven: Yale University Press, 1985.

Kroker, Arthur and Marilouise, eds. *The Last Sex: Feminism and Outlaw Bodies*. New York: St. Martin's Press, 1993.

Laqueur, Thomas. *Making Sex: Body and Gender from the Greeks to Freud*. Cambridge: Harvard University Press, 1990.

Lomperis, Linda and Sarah Stanbury. *Feminist Approaches to the Body in Medieval Literature*. Philadelphia: University of Pennsylvania Press, 1993.

Mairs, Nancy. *Carnal Acts: Essays*. New York: Harper and Row, 1990.

Martin, Emily. *The Woman in the Body: A Cultural Analysis of Reproduction*. Boston: Beacon Press, 1987.

Michie, Helena. *The Flesh Made Word: Female Figures and Women's Bodies*. New York: Oxford University Press, 1987.

Miles, Margaret R. *Carnal Knowing: Female Nakedness and Religious Meaning in the Christian West*. Boston: Beacon Press, 1989.

Miller, Nancy. "Rereading as a Woman: The Body in Practice." *Poetics Today* 6, no. 1–2 (1985): 291–99.

Mitchell, Juliet and Jacqueline Rose, eds. *Feminine Sexuality: Jacques Lacan and the Ecole Freudienne*. Trans. Jacqueline Rose. London: Macmillan, 1982.

Modleski, Tania. *Feminism Without Women: Culture and Criticism in a "Postfeminist" Age*. New York: Routledge, 1991.

Moi, Toril. "Existentialism and Feminism: The Rhetoric of Biology in *The Second Sex*." *Oxford Literary Review* 8 (1986): 88–95.

———. *Sexual / Texual Politics: Feminist Literary Theory*. London / New York: Methuen, 1985.

Morrison, Toni, ed. *Race-Ing Justice, En-Gendering Power: Essays on Anita Hill, Clarence Thomas, and the Construction of Social Reality*. New York: Pantheon, 1992.

Mulvey, Laura. *Visual and Other Pleasures*. Bloomington: Indiana University Press, 1989.

Nead, Lynda. *The Female Nude: Art, Obscenity, and Sexuality*. New York: Routledge, 1992.

Ortner, Sherry B. and Harriet Whitehead, eds. *Sexual Meanings: The Cultural Construction of Gender and Sexuality*. New York: Cambridge University Press, 1981.

Oudshorn, Nelly. *Beyond the Natural Body: An Archaeology of Sex Hormones*. New York: Routledge, 1994.

Poovey, Mary. "Scenes of an Indelicate Character: The Medical Treatment of Victorian Women." In *Uneven Developments: The Ideological Work of Gender in Mid-Victorian England*, pp. 14–50. Chicago: University of Chicago Press, 1988.

Raymond, Janice G. *The Transsexual Empire: The Making of the She-Male*. New York: Teacher's College Press, 1994.

Rich, Adrienne. *Of Woman Born: Motherhood as Experience and Institution*. New York: Norton, 1976.

Riley, Denise. *"Am I That Name?" Feminism and the Category of "Women" in History*. Minneapolis: University of Minnesota Press, 1988.

Rubin, Gayle. "The Traffic in Women: Notes on the 'Political Economy' of Sex." In

Rayna R. Reiter, ed., *Toward an Anthropology of Women*. New York: Monthly Review Press, 1975.

Russo, Mary. *Female Grotesques: Risk, Excess, and Modernity*. New York: Routledge, 1994.

Sawicki, Jana. *Disciplining Foucault: Feminism, Power, and the Body*. New York: Routledge, 1991.

Scarry, Elaine. *The Body in Pain: The Making and Unmaking of the World*. New York: Oxford, 1985.

Schor, Naomi. "This Essentialism Which Is Not One." *Differences* 1, no. 2 (Summer 1989): 38–58.

Sheets-Johnstone, Maxine. *The Roots of Power: Animate Form and Gendered Bodies*. Chicago: Open Court, 1994.

Shiebinger, Londa. *The Mind Has No Sex? Women in the Origins of Modern Science*. Cambridge: Harvard University Press, 1989.

Silverman, Kaja. *The Acoustic Mirror: The Female Voice in Psychoanalysis and Cinema*. Bloomington: Indiana University Press, 1988.

Smith, Sidonie. *Subjectivity, Identity, and the Body: Women's Autobiographical Practices in the Twentieth Century*. Bloomington: Indiana University Press, 1993.

Snitow, Ann, Christine Stansell, and Sharon Thompson, eds. *The Powers of Desire: The Politics of Sexuality*. New York: Monthly Review Press, 1976.

Spelman, Elizabeth. "Woman as Body: Ancient and Contemporary Views." *Feminist Studies* 8, no. 1 (1982): 109–31.

Stallybrass, Peter. "Patriarchal Territories: the Body Enclosed." In Margaret Ferguson, Maureen Quilligan, and Nancy Vickers, eds., *Rewriting the Renaissance: The Discourses of Sexual Difference in Early Modern Europe*, pp. 123–142. Chicago: University of Chicago Press, 1986.

———— and Allon White. *The Politics and Poetics of Transgression*. Ithaca: Cornell University Press, 1986.

Suleiman, Susan Rubin, ed. *The Female Body in Western Culture: Contemporary Perspectives*. Cambridge: Harvard University Press, 1986.

Traub, Valerie. "The Psychomorphology of the Clitoris." *GLQ* 2 (1995): 81–113.

Walker, Alice and Pratibha Parmar. *Warrior Marks: Female Genital Mutilation and the Sexual Blinding of Women*. New York: Harcourt Brace, 1993.

Waugh, Patricia. *Feminine Fictions: Revisiting the Postmodern*. New York: Routledge, 1989.

Whitford, Margaret. "Rereading Irigaray." In Teresa Brennan, ed., *Between Feminism and Psychoanalysis*, pp. 106–26. New York: Routledge, 1989.

Williams, Linda. *Hard Core: Power, Pleasure, and the "Frenzy of the Visible."* Berkeley: University of California Press, 1989.

———. "When the Woman Looks." In Mary Ann Doane, Patricia Mellencamp, and Linda Williams, eds., *Re-Vision: Essays in Feminist Film Criticism*, pp. 83–99. Frederick, Md.: University Publications of America, 1984.

Williams, Patricia J. *The Rooster's Egg.* Cambridge: Harvard University Press, 1995.

Williamson, Judith. "Woman is an Island: Femininity and Colonization." In Tania Modleski, ed., *Studies in Entertainment: Critical Approaches to Mass Culture*, pp. 99–118. Bloomington: Indiana University Press, 1986.

Woodward, Kathleen. "Youthfulness as a Masquerade." *Discourse* 11, no. 1 (1988–89): 119–42.

Wolff, Janet. "Reinstating Corporeality: Feminism and Body Politics." In *Feminine Sentences: Essays on Women and Culture*, pp. 120–41. Berkeley: University of California Press, 1990.

Yeager, Patricia. "The Father's Breasts." In Patricia Yeager and Beth Kowaleski-Wallace, eds., *Refiguring the Father: New Feminist Readings of Patriarchy*, pp. 3–21. With an afterword by Nancy Miller. Carbondale: Southern Illinois University Press, 1989.

Young, Iris Marion. *Throwing Like a Girl and Other Essays in Feminist Philosophy and Social Theory.* Bloomington: Indiana University Press, 1990.

About the Contributors

Gloria E. Anzaldua is a Chicana tejana queer pat-lache poet and dyke-feminist from the Rio Grande Valley of south Texas. Her books include *Borderlands/La Frontera:The New Mestiza*, which combines Spanish and English, poetry, memoir, and historical analysis, and *Friends from the Other Side/Amigos del Otro Lado*, a bilingual children's picture book. She edited *Making Face, Making Soul/Haciendo Caras: Creative and Critical Perspectives by Feminists of Color* , and coedited *This Bridge Called My Back:Writings by RadicalWomen of Color* and "Theorizing Lesbian Experience," a special issue of *SIGNS: Journal ofWomen in Culture and Society* (Summer 1993).

Sandra Lee Bartky is professor of philosophy at the University of Illinois at Chicago. President of the Radical Philosophy Association (Central Division), a founding member of the Society for Women in Philosophy, and an associate editor of *Hypatia*, she is the author of *Femininity and Domination: Studies in the Phenomenology of Oppression*.

Susan Bordo is Otis A. Singletary Chair in the Humanities and professor of philosophy at the

University of Kentucky. She is the author of *Unbearable Weight: Feminism, Western Culture, and the Body* , *The Flight to Objectivity: Essays on Cartesianism and Culture*, and numerous other writings on gender, culture, philosophy, and the body. She is currently working on *My Father's Body and Other Unexplored Regions of Sex, Masculinity, and the Male Body*.

Rosi Braidotti has been since 1988 Foundation Chair and professor of women's studies in the Arts Faculty of Utrecht University. In 1995 she was appointed scientific director of the Netherlands Research School of Women's Studies. She is the author of *Nomadic Subjects* (Columbia, 1994), which was translated into Italian and German, *Women, the Environment, and Sustainable Development*, and *Patterns of Dissonance*.

Judith Butler is professor of rhetoric and comparative literature at the University California, Berkeley. She is author of *Gender Trouble: Feminism and the Subversion of Identity* and *Bodies That Matter: On the Discursive Limits of Sex*. She has two forthcoming books: *The Psychic Life of Power: Theories in Subjection* and *Excitable Speech: A Politics of the Speech Act*.

Sue-Ellen Case is professor of English at the University of California, Riverside. "Tracking the Vampire" is among a series of her articles on lesbian theory, including "Toward a Butch-Femme Aesthetic" and "Toward a Butch-Femme Retro-Future," appearing in *Cross-Purposes*, edited by Dana Heller. Her latest book is *The Domain-Matrix: Performing Lesbian at the End of Print Culture*.

Mary Ann Doane is Harrison S. Kravis University Professor of Modern Culture and Media at Brown University. She is the author of *The Desire to Desire: The Woman's Film of the 1940s* and *Femmes Fatales: Feminism, Film Theory, Psychoanalysis*, and is currently working on a book entitled *Technologies of Temporality in Modernity*.

Moira Gatens is senior lecturer in philosophy at the University of Sydney. She is the author of *Feminism and Philosophy: Perspectives on Difference and Equality* and *Imaginary Bodies: Ethics, Power, and Corporeality*. She is currently working on a book on Spinoza and the imaginary.

Donna Haraway is a professor on the History of Consciousness Board at the University of California at Santa Cruz. She is the author of *Crystals, Fabrics, and Fields: Metaphors of Organicism in Twentieth-Century Developmental Biology*, *Primate Visions: Gender, Race, and Nature in the World of Modern Science*, *Simians, Cyborgs, and Women: The*

Reinvention of Nature, and *Modest Witness@Second Millennium.FemaleMan_ Meets OncoMouse_*.

bell hooks is Distinguished Professor of English at City College in New York. She is the author of several books, including *Ain't I a Woman?*, *Talking Back*, *Black Looks*, *Outlaw Culture*, *Art on My Mind*, and *Killing Rage*.

Dianne Hunter, professor of English at Trinity College in Hartford, Connecticut, edited *Seduction and Theory*. She has published studies of psychoanalysis and literature in *The Practice of Psychoanalytic Criticism*, *American Imago*, *SIGNS*, *The Psychoanalytic Review*, and *Theatre Journal*.

Luce Irigaray, French psychoanalyst, philosopher, and feminist, is best known for *This Sex Which Is Not One* and *Speculum of the Other Woman*.

Annette Kuhn is reader in film and television studies at the University of Glasgow and an editor of *Screen*. Her publications include *Women's Pictures: Feminism and Cinema*, *The Power of the Image: Essays on Representation and Sexuality*, and *Family Secrets, Acts of Memory, and Imagination*.

Audre Lorde, the late poet, novelist, and essayist, was born in the United States of Grenadian parents. Her many publications include *From a Land Where Other People Live*, *Zami: A New Spelling of My Name*, and *Sister Outsider*.

Catharine A. MacKinnon, professor of law at the University of Michigan, is an activist and expert on sex equality. She is author of *Sexual Harassment of Working Women*, *Feminism Unmodified*, *Toward a Feminist Theory of the State*, *Pornography and Civil Rights: A New Day for Women's Equality* (with Andrea Dworkin), and *Only Words*, as well as numerous articles.

Nancy Mairs is author of five books of prose, including *Carnal Acts*, *Ordinary Time*, and *Plaintext*. She has taught writing and English at the University of Arizona. Her newest book, *Waist High in the World* (about her life with multiple sclerosis) will be published in 1997.

Emily Martin is professor of anthropology at Princeton University. Her work on ideology and power in Chinese society was published in *The Cult of the Dead in a Chinese Village* and *Chinese Ritual and Politics*. Beginning with *The Woman in the Body: A*

Cultural Analysis of Reproduction, she has been working on the anthropology of science and reproduction in the United States. Her latest research is described in *Flexible Bodies: Tracking Immunity in America from the Days of Polio to the Age of AIDS*.

Tania Modleski is Florence R. Scott Professor of English at the University of Southern California. She is the author of *Loving with a Vengeance: Mass-Produced Fantasies for Women*, *The Women Who Knew Too Much: Hitchcock and Feminist Theory*, and *Feminism Without Women: Culture and Criticism in a "Postfeminist" Age*, and editor of *Studies in Entertainment*.

Mary Russo is professor of literature and critical theory at Hampshire College. She is the author of *Female Grotesques: Risk, Excess, and Modernity*, and coeditor of *Nationalisms and Sexualities* and *Designing Italy: Italy in Europe, Africa, Asia, and the Americas*.

Sandy Stone is assistant professor in the Department of Radio, TV, and Film at the University of Texas, Austin. She has published extensively on cyberspace and bodies, and as Allucquere Roseanne Stone she published *The War of Desire and Technology at the Close of the Mechanical Age*.

Sojourner Truth, 1797–1883, was an abolitionist, lecturer, and activist for the rights of women and African Americans, especially freed and fugitive slaves. Born into slavery and emancipated at thirty, Sojourner Truth was known through her autobiography, *Narrative of Sojourner Truth* (1850), and through Harriet Beecher Stowe's "Sojourner Truth: The Libyan Sibyl," published in the *Atlantic Monthly* (1863).

Patricia J. Williams is professor of law at Columbia University. She is the author of *The Alchemy of Race and Rights* and *The Rooster's Egg*.

Linda Williams is professor of film and women's studies at the University of California, Irvine, where she is director of the Program in Film Studies. Her books include a psychoanalytic study of surrealist cinema, *Figures of Desire: A Theory and Analysis of Surrealist Film*, and *Hard Core: Power, Pleasure, and the "Frenzy" of the Visible*. She recently edited *Viewing Positions: Ways of Seeing Film*, a collection of essays on film spectatorship.

Monique Wittig, French novelist, playwright, and essayist, is the author of *The Opoponax*, *Les Guérillères,*, *The Lesbian Body*, and *Across the Acheron*.